Prisoners
of Prester John

Prisoners of Prester John

The Portuguese Mission to Ethiopia in Search of the Mythical King, 1520–1526

CATES BALDRIDGE

McFarland & Company, Inc., Publishers
Jefferson, North Carolina, and London

LIBRARY OF CONGRESS CATALOGUING-IN-PUBLICATION DATA

Baldridge, Cates.
　　Prisoners of Prester John : the Portuguese mission to Ethiopia in search of the mythical king, 1520–1526 / Cates Baldridge.
　　　　p.　　cm.
　　Includes bibliographical references and index.

　　ISBN 978-0-7864-6800-3
　　softcover : acid free paper ∞

　　1. Portuguese — Ethiopia — History — 16 century.　2. Ethiopia — History — 1490–1889.　3. Pester John (Legendary character)　4. Alvares, Francisco. Preste Ioam das Indias.　I. Title.
DT384.B228　2012
916.304'3 — dc23
　　　　　　　　　　　　　　　　　　　　　　　　2012000550

BRITISH LIBRARY CATALOGUING DATA ARE AVAILABLE

© 2012 Cates Baldridge. All rights reserved

No part of this book may be reproduced or transmitted in any form or by any means, electronic or mechanical, including photocopying or recording, or by any information storage and retrieval system, without permission in writing from the publisher.

Front cover: Depiction of the Kerait ruler Wang Khan as "Prester John" in *Le Livre des Merveilles*, 15th century; background © 2012 Shutterstock

Manufactured in the United States of America

McFarland & Company, Inc., Publishers
　Box 611, Jefferson, North Carolina 28640
　　www.mcfarlandpub.com

To Susan,
for sharing the journey

Contents

Acknowledgments ix
Preface 1
A Note on the Text 5

ONE. News from Nowhere 7
TWO. Stalking a Phantom 25
THREE. The Lake of Fire 47
FOUR. Strangers in a Strange Land 68
FIVE. The Far Pavilions 89
SIX. The King and I 110
SEVEN. After Strange Gods 134
EIGHT. Divided We Fall 156
NINE. The Magic Mountain 178
TEN. The Last Crusade 201
ELEVEN. Sermons in Stone 232
TWELVE. Duty's Prisoner 259

Chapter Notes 283
Bibliography 289
Index 293

Acknowledgments

This book has undergone an unusually long gestation, having been conceived of many years ago, only to languish in drawers as other projects were taken up, labored upon, and completed. However, even in its ungainly infancy it was looked upon with favor by my Middlebury College colleagues David Bain and Jay Parini, whose early and continuing support for this enterprise has buoyed and sustained me over the decades. Whenever my confidence flagged, their aid — both practical and intangible — was always generously on offer, for which I am profoundly grateful. I must also render belated thanks for the indulgence of several of my department chairs from that era, including Sandy Martin, John Elder, and David Price.

As time passed, others assisted me in wrestling the manuscript into its current (and I hope, much improved) form. It was Tricia Welsch, for instance, who first suggested that a complete rethinking of the project might prove fruitful. Once embarked on a new course, I greatly benefited from the counsel of several talented historians whom I am happy to count as friends, including especially Paul Monod, Jan Albers, and Don Wyatt. And when, in due course, it became necessary for me to visit Ethiopia, I simultaneously became indebted to Claudia Cooper and Rob Cohen, whose advice about coming to grips with that country has been as useful as their love of its people is inspiring. On the brink of my departure for Africa, Jim Ralph was instrumental in allowing my sojourn there to last long enough to get the job thoroughly done. Once on the ground in Abyssinia, I found myself in the unfailingly competent hands of Ephrem Gezahegn, the best guide anyone could have asked for, and of his friend Taddie, Ethiopia's bravest driver. *Amase genallo* to both. Upon my return, I was the beneficiary of much ardent belief and professional effort on the part of Geri Thoma and Eleanor Jackson. When it at last came time to prepare the maps and charts for this volume, I received expert assistance from Benjamin Meader and Bill Hegman.

Any scholar who seeks to understand Portugal and Ethiopia's first significant encounter must gratefully acknowledge the labors of C. F. Beckingham and G. B. W. Huntingford, the exacting and indefatigable editors of Francisco Álvares' chronicle of that episode, *A True Relation of the Lands of the Prester John*. They clarified much that was murky, and if I have managed to see various events and people in a fresh light, it is only by benefit of standing on their broad shoulders.

Finally, I owe my greatest debt of gratitude to my wife, Susan Campbell Baldridge. For some time now, she has each and every day offered me more constant support, wise counsel, and patient understanding than anyone has a right to expect. It is a fine thing to be believed in by someone whom you look up to, and her faith in me and in this book has been, and continues to be, one of the greatest gifts I ever hope to receive. This is not so much my work, as ours.

Preface

This book's subject is the sixteenth-century journey of a small band of Portuguese into the kingdom of Ethiopia, their six years of captivity in that land, their eventual escape, and the large implications of their strange odyssey for both nations. In attempting to tell this story, however, I immediately confronted a difficulty concerning what to call the high-minded yet misbegotten enterprise the Iberians believed they were undertaking as they waded ashore in Abyssinia that spring of 1520. Given the minuscule number of Portuguese who had previously set foot in that quarter of Africa, the term "expedition" seems entirely justified, especially since the Europeans' inward tramp featured all the hardships and dangers usually associated with pursuits meriting that name. On the other hand, expeditions are not usually headed by someone calling himself (and recognized by his government as being) an ambassador, and do not often intend to exchange formal letters of understanding with whatever indigenous leaders they encounter. Because the company of Portuguese who arrived on the Abyssinian coast were led by just such a person who intended to do just that, I have decided that "embassy" is probably the more correct label to employ. And yet, the yawning chasm between what they wishfully expected to find and what actually awaited them in the Ethiopian interior made them reel again and again from the brute shock of discovery. There is simply no ready-made term to describe their errand into the unknown.

Certainly their mission's larger outlines bear little resemblance to our current master-narrative concerning first encounters between Europeans and Africans elsewhere during the early-modern period. Indeed, it differs quite markedly from that familiar tragedy wherein white men's racialist assumptions about black Africans are formed before anchor is weighed, quickly self-confirmed once landfall is attained, and then violently enacted soon after stockades are erected. Because Ethiopia was the last nation on earth that might still plausibly house the legendary kingdom of Prester John — its status as a militantly Christian country lying beyond the Islamic heartland making it superficially resemble that apocryphal realm — the Portuguese who eagerly risked their lives to reach it were half-expecting to encounter a civilization in some respects superior to their own, and were thus willing to count the Abyssinians as honorary Caucasians. And while this rare and fragile inter-racial *entente* was quickly strained and degraded once the exoticism of the Ethiopian Empire was discovered to be quite peculiarly its own rather than that specified in long-standing European fantasies, it never reverted to the exploitative and dehumanizing assumptions that prevailed elsewhere on that colonized continent. Even when, decades later, the tragedy finally arrived, it resembled the variety that Europeans tended to inflict upon one another rather than on peoples they considered their racial inferiors. While every collision between African and European cultures possesses its own unique aspects, Ethiopia and Portugal's romance of genuine idealism and stubborn misprision nevertheless remains unmistakably *sui generis*.

At the center of this exceptional story resides the equally exceptional person who left us an account of it all — Francisco Álvares, the sole priest assigned to the Portuguese mission — and it is one of my intentions to rescue him from a disservice he has suffered at the hands of previous historians. Though nearly everyone who has written on the subject of Portugal's final attempt to track down Prester John has confessed to finding Álvares attractive for his curiosity, level-headedness, and accuracy, still none has quite granted him his intellectual, imaginative, and emotional due. Pointing to the notable lack in his account of any admission that the Ethiopians practiced a monophysite version of Christianity that his superiors in Rome would (and eventually did) denounce as damnably heretical, commentators have blithely concluded that the finer points of Christology were simply beyond him. In my view, however, this is not a plausible explanation for our priest's silence on the issue. Given who he was, the office entrusted to him, where he had traveled previously, and who he befriended in Ethiopia, he surely must have come soon enough — if reluctantly and fearfully — to a full knowledge of his hosts' religious opinions. Rather than see him as oblivious to the situation, I am convinced that, in an act motivated by his oft-professed admiration for the Ethiopians and a newfound tolerance for variant Christianities engendered by his encounter with their exuberant spirituality, he deliberately withheld his knowledge of the Abyssinians' true beliefs from his ecclesiastical superiors. Furthermore, I believe he committed this act of creative dereliction precisely in order to spare the Ethiopians the onslaught of "corrective" evangelization that was in fact imposed upon them in the century after he left. Needless to say, such a reading of monophysitism's absence from his chronicle makes Álvares into a much more assertive, canny, and transgressive figure than he has hitherto been recognized as being. He still emerges from the pages of his chronicle as an attractive man — indeed, if I am correct, there are more reasons for modern readers to think him so than have yet been acknowledged.

I suppose that when one has what Joseph Conrad calls "a ripping good yarn" to relate, it is a temptation to overestimate the influence of individual personalities upon the currents of history. And yet, after giving due weight to geo-political trends of *longue durée* and the deep assumptions of incommensurate ideologies, the palpable effects of Álvares' character remain unmistakable. While his fellow Portuguese were managing first to offend and then spectacularly scandalize the Ethiopian elites, our priest succeeded in the face of obstacles that were cultural, religious, generational, and logistical to forge a genuine friendship with Lebna Dengel, the Ethiopian king, or *Negus*. And when, some time later, that king asked his new friend to gratify a fleeting royal whim, the great gears of national destiny were suddenly set to spinning with consequences visible unto the present day. As I hope to demonstrate, had Francisco Álvares been a different kind of man, Christian Ethiopia would have ceased to exist within a quarter-century of the Portuguese arrival. The happy fact of the matter is, the more scrupulously one attends to Álvares' narrative, the more his story acquires the energies and contours of popular literary genres. After all, his chronicle is, in a manner of speaking, a love story — though one involving *caritas* rather than *eros*, since Álvares managed to lose his heart not to an individual, but to an entire people. Subsequently, when he came to the agonizing realization that he must decide between either protecting the culture he had come to love or fulfilling his sworn duty, he chose the former, which makes his story one of intrigue and deception as well. And finally, for all involved it was a drama of suspense, since their homeward journey took a decade of struggle to complete, and often threatened to become a lifelong exile.

While this book's primary focus is the six years that Álvares and his companions spent within Ethiopia — as ambassadors, explorers, and prisoners — I could only tell the full story by occasionally broadening the scope of my narrative to times and places beyond the Abyssinia of 1520–26. Consequently, my first three chapters attempt briefly to sketch the history of the Prester John myth and the many endeavors it spawned, as well as to recall why, among European nations, it was Portugal that found itself poised to investigate the last, best geographical candidate for that elusive monarch's homeland. In these early pages I also attempt to outline Ethiopia's fitful but long-standing efforts to reach out to her European co-religionists. Then, as the book nears its end, I twice digress from the main story (in parts of chapters ten and eleven) to survey the consequences engendered by the embassy's release from captivity, an emancipation for which Álvares was mainly responsible. The first of these concerns the dramatic rescue mission mounted by the Portuguese in the 1540s as Abyssinia teetered on the brink of destruction at the hands of Muslim jihadists. The second covers the subsequent invasion of that land by the equally determined footsoldiers of the Jesuit order, a fate that Álvares in some measure foresaw and feared, but which his principled silence was ultimately unable to prevent.

In recounting the main trunk of the story I rely heavily on Álvares' surviving chronicle of his experiences, though not, I hope, in an uncritical spirit. Previous commentators have pronounced him to be largely reliable about the facts, and I have found no reason to disagree with them. Still, in attempting to parse his account as closely as I was obliged to, I unsurprisingly found many instances when his observations were shaped by either tactical concerns of the day or strategic designs entertained for the future. He is the best window we have on what happened, but he is fallible, and by the time he left Ethiopia he possessed a daring agenda, all of which colors his writings. One thing Álvares was not particularly good at was describing with clarity and accuracy the natural and architectural wonders of Abyssinia, and so it is on such occasions that I have found myself obliged to supplement his observations most heavily with my own. Luckily, I was able to retrace the steps of the Portuguese company during a trip to Ethiopia in 2008, where I found a remarkable amount of what Álvares described persisting essentially intact. If I am able to convey to my readers even a partial sense of what an exquisite storehouse of cultural wonders Ethiopia remains today, then another aim of this book will have been fulfilled.

In representing Portugal and Ethiopia's critical first encounter with each other and the central role that Álvares played in that tragicomic affair, I have had — as anyone must — to occasionally speculate about certain historical actors' states of mind. And there is no sidestepping the fact that my largest claim about Álvares involves just such an extrapolation, though one that I believe is more than justified by the textual evidence at hand. As I hope will become clear, some of the new facts I unearth from Álvares' account are hiding in plain sight, while others lurk discreetly between the lines. Furthermore, I fully realize that my insistence on reading a puzzling absence as the marker of a desperately purposeful intention will need to clear a higher hurdle of skepticism than many another assertion. I can only say that what convinced me was the mental and emotional caliber of Álvares' voice as expressed on nearly every page of his chronicle — a voice my readers must weigh and decide about for themselves. If in what follows I succeed in raising his testimony even a little way above the cloud of obscurity and misunderstanding in which it has too long languished, that will be enough for me.

A Note on the Text

Amharic employs a script as different from Roman orthography as Hebrew or Arabic, and thus the rendering of any particular Amharic term into a phonetic English equivalent is at best an inexact art, though the regularization of this process has steadily advanced in recent years. In general, my procedure has been as follows. When a term appears in the Hakluyt translation of Álvares whose phonetic expression is so close to that of the spelling preferred by modern scholars that readers are likely to instantly match one with the other, I have kept the original spelling within direct quotations from the translated edition while giving the modern equivalent in my own discussions of the same person, place or thing. Thus, for instance, when the subject is the Ethiopian Governor of the Seacoast, his title appears as the "Barnagais" when Álvares refers to him and as the "*Bahr-nagas*" when I do. I have followed this practice because to my mind it renders vividly the texture both of the Europeans' incomplete understanding of what they were encountering, and of Álvares' anxious attempt to get things down as accurately as he could. When a term in Álvares' translation roams too far from this standard, I have had recourse to bracketing; well-known places from the Bible or European and African geography I have rendered in their familiar forms.

ONE

News from Nowhere

The first report that there might be a powerful Christian king reigning far to the east, beyond the lands of the Muslim enemy, came to the ears of medieval Europe in the winter of 1145. It was welcome news, for the Christian possessions in the Holy Land, won a half-century before during the First Crusade, were now under threat. The city of Edessa had just fallen to an Islamic re-conquest, and fear was rife that the rest of the small and vulnerable Crusader states — Antioch, Tripoli, and especially Jerusalem — would be the next to have its churches looted and converted into mosques. The menaced Christian kings of the near east had accordingly sent Hugh, Bishop of the Syrian city of Jabala, to Italy in order to beg Pope Eugene III for aid. His appeal was urgent, and the pontiff would soon respond by calling on the European heartland to mount a Second Crusade, but amid his alarming account Hugh also managed to convey the hopeful story of a Christian victory, though one that took place far away in lands whose geography and inhabitants were almost entirely unknown to Europeans. As a witness described it, the bishop "related also that not many years before a certain John, a king and priest who dwells beyond Persia and Armenia in the uttermost East and, with all his people, is a Christian but a Nestorian [heretic], made war on the brother-kings of Persians and Medes, … and stormed Exbatana, the seat of their kingdom." From this battle, which lasted three full days since "both parties were willing to die rather than turn in flight," the monarch named "Prester John, for so they are accustomed to call him, pu[t] the Persians to flight with dreadful carnage" and "finally emerged victorious."[1] This is the first written document in which the name Prester John — literally, John the Presbyter, or Priest — appears, though it would soon become a powerful charm that would both evoke outsized hopes and instigate many doomed endeavors. Indeed, over the next four centuries Europeans would write so many words, spend so much money, and dedicate so many of their lives to finding him, that they would transform him into the most important imaginary figure in Western history.

It is probable that Bishop Hugh's narrative was a distorted account of an actual battle in which his Muslim foes fared badly, for we know that on September 9, 1141, the army of the Seljuk Turks was dealt a thoroughgoing defeat near the central Asian city of Samarqand. The Seljuk Empire, which was Muslim in religion and Persian in culture, was a vast realm that sprawled from the Dardanelles to the Aral Sea, so while on their western frontier they battled European crusaders with names such as Robert of Normandy and Baldwin of Boulogne, on their eastern flank they faced a much different opponent. Their vanquisher there in 1141 was the so-called Black Cathay empire, a culture with Chinese roots centered north of Afghanistan's Hindu Kush mountains. Of course what mattered most immediately to Hugh or to any European who heard tell of this distant rout was the setback incurred by the Mohammedan Seljuks, who were then within striking distance not only of the Crusader states but of Constantinople as well. From such distant tidings, a combination of ignorance and wishful thinking quickly painted these eastern victors as followers of Christ rather than, as in fact they were, disciples of the Buddha.

After relating his fractured version of the battle, Hugh went on to reveal details of Prester John's supposed intentions toward his western co-religionists: "After this victory the aforesaid John moved his army to the aid of the Church in Jerusalem, but ... when he had reached the river Tigris ... [he] was unable to transport his army across ... by any device." Undaunted, "he turned towards the north, where, he had learned, this stream was frozen over on account of the winter's cold. When he had tarried there for several years without, however, seeing his heart's desire realized (the continued mild weather prevented it), and lost many of his soldiers because of the unfamiliar climate[,] he was forced to return home."[2] Since in all probability Bishop Hugh was merely passing on a story that had somehow arisen out of, and gained currency by feeding upon, the collective anxiety of the threatened Crusaders, it is worth noting how well crafted it is to accomplish their strategic ends. By positing the existence of a sympathetic Christian monarch aching to come to the rescue of his fellow Christians in the Holy Land, the Crusader cause is prevented from appearing hopeless. On the other hand, by telling of his frustrating inability to cross the Tigris, no room is left for complacency — his arrival is not imminent, and thus Jerusalem and the rest of the Latin Kingdoms must be re-supplied and their garrisons reinforced if they are to hold out until he undertakes another rescue mission.[3] Of course this last is accomplished only at the cost of making him appear a bit feckless, but the choice of the Tigris as John's unlikely hindrance seems devised by an unconsciously canny calibration: every educated European knew that it was a real river, that it was at most 30 hard days march east of Jerusalem, and that Alexander the Great had crossed it and pressed on to realms more distant still. Thus if the Prester was not within Europe's grasp today, he nevertheless resided within tomorrow's imagined reach; with courage and luck

ONE. *News from Nowhere* 9

and the right map, one might be able to find him and show him the way west. In the coming decades he would maintain just such a tantalizing position vis-à-vis an ever-widening set of European aspirations: close enough to inspire visions of decisive victory, yet apparently just too far away to arrive at the hour of need.

In addition to these military dispatches, Bishop Hugh delivered another tantalizing piece of news about this king. In medieval times, a ruler's bloodline was as important a credential for leadership as any claim to strength or cunning, and the Prester apparently possessed an exalted one, for "it is said that he is a lineal descendant of the Magi."[4] Since their original appearance in the New Testament's various accounts of Jesus' birth, the Magi had subsequently undergone an imaginative transformation. In Matthew and Luke, the three wise men appear to be no more than Persian astrologers, but because the Old Testament books of Isaiah and the Psalms speak of foreign kings paying homage to the Messiah, by as early as the sixth century both popular and learned Christian traditions had promoted the Magi to the status of kings.[5] If the trio had therefore, by Hugh's time, become an amalgam of political power, arcane wisdom, religious devotion, and mysterious eastern provenance, then insisting that the Prester sprang from such loins not only began to explain his current whereabouts, but associated him at one swoop with Christianity, kingship, and magic. Thus those elements that often mixed uneasily in a feudal Europe still struggling to determine the proper relationship between secular and churchly authority, and straining to reconcile ingrained folkways with official religious doctrine, were benignly blended in this ruler from beyond the heathens' deserts. For if he was simultaneously warrior, priest, and wizard, and if, in being such, he united rather than divided his subjects and made them into a mighty nation that caused the infidels to tremble, then he was ready-made to function as a collective fantasy of cultural harmony. The fourth-century Roman emperor Constantine had seemed to promise the reconciliation of crown and cross when he harkened to his vision of *"in hoc signo vinces"* and led his legions to victory under the banner of Christ. Since then, however, king and pope had struggled fiercely with each other over the keys to power. Hugh and his contemporaries lived in a world shaped and still shaken by an ongoing Investiture Crisis, where the contest over whether the Papacy or the Crown would appoint bishops had led to, among other disasters, the excommunication of the Holy Roman Emperor and the sacking of Rome. If Prester John was both a holy priest and a secular monarch, then he was the kind of leader that many in Europe would long to meet face-to-face.

Just how deeply this figure resonated with Christendom's growing anxieties and utopian yearnings became evident two decades later when Prester John wrote Europe a letter. The original missive apparently surfaced sometime in the mid 1160s, though no twelfth-century copy of it survives and all we now possess are later versions. This elaborate hoax began by imitating the diction of ordinary diplomatic correspondence, and was addressed, logically enough, to the Byzantine Emperor, whose domains abutted the Muslim territory from whose far side this fellow Christian purported to write: "John the Presbyter, by the grace of God and the strength of our Lord Jesus Christ, king of kings and lord of lords, to his friend Manuel, Governor of the Byzantines, greetings, wishing him health and the continued enjoyment of divine blessing."[6] This by-the-book preamble is followed by a piece of one-upmanship also quite common in diplomatic discourse, establishing who admired whom first. "Our Majesty has been informed that you hold our Excellency in esteem, and that knowledge of our greatness has reached you. Furthermore we have heard from our secretary that it was your wish to send us some objects of art and interest, for our pleasure. Since we are but human we take this in good part, and through our secretary we forward to you some of our articles." His priority thus established, the Prester continues in the same vein, declaring that it is he who must be assured of the Byzantine's orthodoxy, not the other way around. "Now it is our desire to know whether you hold the true faith, and adhere in all things to our lord Jesus Christ; for while we know that we are mortal, your little Greeks regard you as a god; still we know that you are mortal, and subject to human weaknesses." This phrase is a strong clue that the letter's actual writer was himself a Latin Christian rather than a Byzantine,[7] and various suppositions about our author's identity will be aired in due course. For now, what is striking is that the imposter has taken pains to establish a clear sense of genre — this is a document of state from a sovereign who is quite comfortable with the forms through which foreign relations are conducted — a move that constructs a frame of plausibility and normality around the many wondrous accounts that are to follow.

Soon after this preamble comes the central message of hope, which can be boiled down to this: I am powerful; I am Christian; I am coming. "If indeed you wish to know wherein consists our great power, then believe without doubting that I, Prester John, who reign supreme, exceed in riches, virtue, and power all creatures who dwell under heaven. Seventy-two kings pay tribute to me. I am a devout Christian and everywhere protect the Christians of our empire, nourishing them with alms. We have made a vow to visit the sepulchre of our Lord with a very great army, as befits the glory of our Majesty, to wage war against and chastise the enemies of the cross of Christ, and to exalt his sacred name." Here the author has taken care that his fabrication will not be exposed as such if its promised hero fails to arrive anytime soon, for though the Prester has taken an oath to liberate the Holy Land, he makes no mention of when he intends to begin that campaign. However, this somewhat hazy promise is quickly followed by geographical information designed to assure one and all that the distances involved shall be no obstacle to his westward progress. "Our magnificence dominates the Three Indias, and extends to Farther India, where the body of St. Thomas the Apostle rests. It reaches through the desert toward the place of the rising of the sun, and continues through the valley of deserted Babylon close by the Tower of Babel. Seventy-two provinces obey us, a few of which are Christian provinces, and each has its own king. And all their kings are our tributaries." To a monarch holding sway over such vast swaths of territory, a thrust toward Jerusalem should be no taxing feat. It could be that this savior on horseback was even now just over the horizon.

At this point in the letter a jumbled and occasionally breathless list commences, recounting the natural wonders, moral accomplishments, and military powers of Prester John's kingdom. Some of these items are, by modern standards, just barely plausible, while others are completely outlandish, though many of the latter would not be out of place in other medieval accounts of distant lands. Running through all off them, however, is an implication that such wondrous places, animals, and events are simply the outward manifestation of, and the rightful reward for, the sinless condition of the Prester's subjects. In essence, a happy circularity reigns wherein deserving souls enjoy a second Eden lacking only the original's dirty secret of boredom. Thus "in our territories are found elephants, dromedaries, and camels, and almost every kind of beast that is under heaven. Honey flows in our land, and milk everywhere abounds. In one of our territories no poison can do harm and no noisy frog croaks, no scorpions are there, and no serpents creep through the grass. No venomous reptiles can exist there or use their deadly power." Strolling amidst this benign landscape are citizens entirely deserving of such safety and abundance, since "flattery finds no place in our land; there is no strife among us"; neither are there "liars ... nor does anyone dare to tell an untruth, for he who speaks a lie dies forthwith, or is regarded by us as dead." As it happens, though, this virtuous republic can do without the virtue of frugality, for "our people have an abundance of wealth" and thus "there are no poor among us; we receive all strangers and pilgrims; thieves and robbers are not found in our land, nor do we have adultery or avarice." If this is a kind of regained Eden then it also resembles Biblical prophesies of Christ's post-apocalyptic reign on earth, with Prester John in the role of the Savior who returns not as a despised outcast but as a figure whose sanctity is now to be accompanied by unlimited temporal power. In other words, the fact that the Prester rules such a glorious land is not at all a matter of luck; rather, he is depicted as the holy font from which his subjects' moral and material riches flow.

In Prester John's kingdom, minerals often possess a kind of spiritual charge, emitting waves of beneficial energy. His dining table, for instance, is composed of "precious emerald, with four columns of amethyst supporting it," but the expense is the least of it, for "the virtue of this stone is that no one sitting at the table can fall into drunkenness." In like manner, the gates of the royal palace "are of sardonyx inlaid with the horn of the serpent called *cerastes*, so that none may enter with poison," while the jousting yard is "paved with onyx, in order that the courage of the fighters may be increased by the virtue of the stone." Even the Prester's bed is sanctified by its materials — in this case, "sapphire, because of its virtue of chastity." As a result, though the king can boast that "we possess the most beautiful women, ... they approach us only four times in the year and then solely for the procreation of sons." While the notion that certain substances can promote specific virtues did not originate with the Prester's letter, its writer is at pains to make one understand that here this occurs with an efficacy unmatched in other locales. To the pious mind, however, an even more attractive quality of this kingdom's natural curiosities is that they operate selectively according to the spiritual desserts of he who seeks them out. This is evidenced by "a stone of incredible medical virtue, which cures Christians or would-be Christians of whatever ailment afflicts them," but only if their answers to the wardens' enquiries are "satisfactory," and only "if their faith is sincere." Thus the entire country operates as does a pilgrimage site, where it is understood that only the worthy shall enjoy miraculous healing.

As the letter nears its end, it momentarily appears as though the catalogue of spiritual wonders has degenerated into a mere recitation of imperial statistics, for the reader suddenly finds herself in the midst of one of those tedious iterations of inflated numbers that, to modern ears, all too often mar the pages of medieval literature. "We feed daily at our table 30,000 men, besides casual guests; and all of these receive daily sums from our treasury, to nourish their horses and for other expenses." This startling boast is merely a preamble, for "during each month we are served at our table by seven kings, [and] each in his turn, by sixty two dukes, and by three hundred and sixty-five counts." These blue-blooded waiters see to the needs of a regular stable of diners that include "on our right hand, twelve archbishops, and on our left, twenty bishops," with the addition of such notables as "the Patriarch of St. Thomas, the Protopapas of Samarkand, and the Archprotopapas of Susa." And, if the Prester's secular feasting is celebrated on a grand scale, so too is the more spiritual repast of holy communion, for "abbots, in the same number as the number of days in the year, minister to us in our chapel." Even here, though, amidst such unimaginative bragging, the author returns to the subject that lifts his supposed letter above the average run of such fables and allows it to appeal to something in its audience more complicated than an infatuation with things costly and huge. For, just as he reaches his finale, he uses one more seemingly boastful catalog to illuminate the humility that sets this "Priest John" apart from all other earthly potentates.

> If you ask us how it is that the Creator of all things, having made us the most supreme and the most glorious over all mortals, does not give us a higher title

than that of *presbyter*, let not your wisdom be surprised on this account, for here is the reason. At our court we have many ministers who are of higher dignity than ourselves in the Church, and of greater standing in divine office. For our household steward is a patriarch and a king, our butler is an archbishop and a king, our chamberlain is a bishop and a king, our marshal is a king and an archbishop, our chief cook is a king and an abbot. And therefore it does not seem proper to our Majesty to assume those names, or to be distinguished by those titles with which our palace overflows. Therefore to show our great humility, we choose to be called by a lesser name and to assume an inferior rank. If you can count the stars of the sky and the sands of the sea, you will be able to judge thereby the vastness of our realm and our power.

Granted, there is something incongruous about so pointedly emphasizing one's "great humility," but it was precisely this uneasy yet ideal balance of secular power and Christian virtue that granted our forgery its remarkable ability to inspire and recruit. If the document had not so exactly inhabited the point of unstable equilibrium between pomp and piety, aggression and godliness, it would never have become the vehicle for so many different varieties of utopian aspiration. This same precarious mixture of contraries is most tellingly evident some paragraphs earlier, when the Prester describes the emblems of office that precede him on all excursions away from his wondrous palace. "When we go out on horseback on ordinary occasions, there is borne before us a wooden cross, without decoration or gold or jewels, so that we may be reminded of the passion of our Lord Jesus Christ, and also a single golden vase full of earth to remind us that our flesh must one day return to its original substance, the earth. But in addition there is also carried before us a silver bowl full of gold, that all may know that we are lord of lords."[8] A simple wooden cross, an ordinary handful of earth, and yet precious metals in plenty — here, then, are the imperial standards that together announce the advent of a truly Christ-like monarch who nevertheless possesses the temporal wealth and power to win a Caesar's triumph against the barbarians. Who could be blamed for wanting to believe in him, or for risking everything to find him?

During the remainder of the twelfth century the Letter circulated widely and influentially throughout Europe. As early as 1177 Pope Alexander III officially wrote back "to his dearest son in Christ, John, illustrious and magnificent King of the Indians," stating his eagerness for contact but also warning him not to brag so extensively about his wealth and power. By the early thirteenth century we find surviving copies of the Prester's original missive translated into Anglo-Norman, French, and Italian, and no doubt many other early versions have been lost to us. Simultaneously with its rapid proliferation, the Letter accumulated much additional material as the "original" forgery — not quite an oxymoron in this case — was recopied and handed on to various parties. The dreams these usually anonymous grafters entertained of an exotic eastern savior differed in some particulars, though not at all in their penchant for the extravagant and the wish-fulfilling. One of the first inserted additions grew out of Europeans' chronic speculations about the origin of the various oriental spices that they coveted so dearly and for which they paid such exorbitant prices. It described the Prester's people harvesting pepper by setting fire to a forest of the precious seasoning guarded by two-headed serpents. When the conflagration was over, the charred trees surrendered their black and biting spice, while the incinerated reptiles were ground down into a medicinal powder.[9] Further additions sought to enlarge the field-book of animals harbored within the Prester's realm by recounting multicolored lions, horned horses, talon-wielding griffins, gold-digging ants, as well as more familiar fictional species such as the unicorn and the Phoenix.[10] To this bestiary was also added a census of human curiosities including the cannibal race of Gog and Magog, supposedly walled into an eternal captivity by Alexander the Great (though a still later version has *them* bricking up Alexander), the lost tribes of Israel, and the alluringly dangerous Amazons. One startling addition speaks of pigmies "as small as seven-year old children" who are nevertheless "good Christians and willing workers," though sadly prone to being suddenly carried away by swooping cranes. Nor is the Fountain of Youth neglected, and indeed one version of the Letter has the Prester boasting that he has bathed in it six times, a salubrious habit which accounted for his then-current age of five hundred sixty-two.[11]

Most such contributions originated from within the general circulating library of the medieval imagination, but other insertions are of a more this-worldly and topical nature, speaking to the passing political concerns of the day. When, to take one example, the Knights Hospitalers found themselves out of favor at a particular European court, a disparaging reference was inserted as if issuing from the Prester's pen: "We were told of your true and loyal courage" he writes in a French version of the document, "but there are other Frenchmen among you of your lineage and from your retinue who hold with the Saracens. You confide to them and trust them that they should and will help you, but they are the false and treacherous Hospitalers. Know that we have killed them in our country as it should be done with those who turn against our faith."[12] What all these additions demonstrate is that the Letter's promise of rescue and deliverance loomed so large in Christendom's imagination that, like a massive object in space, it captured smaller fantasies in its orbit and allowed them to glow all the brighter from its own reflected light. And thus, though completely fraudulent, it was paradoxically able to act as a kind of seal of authenticity: if the Prester claimed some strange animal existed, then the world must indeed teem with wonders; if he happened to denounce your enemy, then without doubt your cause was holy and just.

Before the Letter became a collective enterprise, however, it started somewhere as a solitary one, which leads us to the question of who the original writer might have been and what his motives were for putting pen to paper in such a way. The question of his identity has long been the subject of debate amongst historians. One scholar concludes from internal evidence that the author was a western European cleric who had spent at least part of his life in the Near East, perhaps in one of the Crusader states, and who was well versed in literatures both sacred and profane.[13] When it comes to pinning down the intentions of this well-traveled priest, however, all the scholarship in the world can still only produce a series of educated guesses. Basically, professorial opinion differs over whether the writer's motives were narrow and strategic or wider and more philosophic. As suggested above, he might have been attempting to pluck up the morale of the beleaguered Crusaders and to convince those back in the European homeland to mount another crusade.[14] A competing theory holds that he had a larger and longer-range goal, and that what he actually constructed was a utopian political tract promoting a commonwealth in which crown and cross were integral allies rather than jealous competitors.[15] Yet a third surmise is that our hoaxer was simply one more in a long line of imaginative medievals whose minds were infatuated by the supposed wonders of the mysterious East, and who concocted various fictional travelers' tales and apocryphal gospels exotic and fanciful enough to frame them to good effect. The frustrating truth of the matter is that we will never know who concocted the original Letter of Prester John, or just what cause he thought himself to be helping or harming by doing so.

In vivid contrast to its murky origins, the loud and cascading effects of the Letter are everywhere apparent in the historical record of Europe's age of exploration, and eventually culminate in the quietly remarkable figure whose words and actions lie at the center of the story to be related here. His name is Francisco Álvares, and he was a real priest, not an imaginary one, though he was every bit as humble as the fictional king was touted to be. He arrives on the scene only at the very end of Prester John's long mythical trajectory — indeed, one way to understand Álvares is as the man who sought out that myth in its last plausible redoubt and finally exposed it for the fable it was, though such was far from his original intention. And though what he encountered there did not satisfactorily accord with the legend of that fabulous clergyman-emperor, he did come face-to-face with a man who embodied his closest living approximation, and a country that was, though undeniably Christian, exotic beyond all European imagining. Furthermore, though Álvares' writings thus constitute an epic of adventure and discovery, they also narrate a romance, for the good Father fell in love along the way — not with a particular person, but with a nation and a people. This makes his love story one driven not, as most are, by *eros*, or romantic love, but rather by *caritas*, that equally heartfelt concern for the welfare and happiness of one's fellow human beings writ large. And finally, when he discovered that the people he loved harbored a dark — literally, a damnable — secret, he took counsel with his deepest inclinations and chose their welfare over his sworn duty, which renders his book a kind of legal exhibit as well, though each reader will have reach his or her own conclusion as to whether he therefore deserves to be condemned or commended for his choice.

Father Álvares was Portuguese, and in the spring of 1520 he found himself aboard a ship of his nation preparing to disembark upon a beach in Ethiopia, a kingdom where he, and many other Europeans, believed that Prester John would at last be found alive. These facts raise several questions that must be answered before we can follow our priest ashore and witness his part in the climax of this long and strange historical drama. First of all, how did we get from Hugh of Jabala's initial report of a mysterious Christian king battling Muslims somewhere on the central Asian steppes to Ethiopia, which is 2,500 miles away on the Red Sea coast of East Africa? That is to say, what manner of evidence, accurate or fanciful, led the wise men of what was now Renaissance Europe to believe that they had finally identified with certainty the homeland of the quarry for whom they had been fruitlessly hunting for fully four hundred years? Secondly, how came it to be that the Portuguese, a tiny, geographically marginal, and chronically indigent nation compared with many others in Christendom, were the first Europeans to reach Ethiopian shores in force? Was their presence there a matter of shrewd policy or just dumb luck, and had they been doggedly searching for Prester John all this time, or were they driven so far from home by another purpose altogether? The remainder of this chapter will answer the first set of questions while the next one will deal with the second.

As to where exactly — or even inexactly — Prester John's kingdom actually lay, both Hugh's report and the original Letter seemed to point to a swath of territory beginning somewhere between the Tigris and the Indus Rivers and stretching eastward from there for a vast but unspecified quantity of leagues into oriental lands unknown. This surmise was bolstered in 1219 when events unfolded that seemed a repeat of those that had originally conjured the Christian chimera nearly eighty years before. The Moslem rulers of Persia were now a people known as Khwarizmians [quar-IZ-me-ans], and they, like the Seljuk Turks before them, suddenly succumbed to an invader from central Asia, though their defeat was far more thoroughgoing and signaled a much larger shift in the balance of Eurasian political power than did the Seljuks' earlier reversal. It wasn't long before Europeans participating in the Fifth Crusade, far to the west in their stronghold at Damietta, Egypt, heard rumors of this second great Muslim humiliation and once again prematurely rejoiced. One of them, Jacques of Vitry, the Bishop of Acre, went so far as to recklessly inform Pope Honorius, King Henry III of England, Duke Leopold of Austria and the University of Pairs faculty that "a new and mighty protector of Christianity ha[d] arisen." This savior, he continued, was either Prester John himself or perhaps his son or grandson, King David, and after he finished off the Khwarizmians he intended to bring the Caliph of Baghdad into submission and then continue westward to complete the liberation of the Holy Land.[16] In point of fact, this new invader was none other than Genghis Khan, who was leading his Mongol hoards on a vast campaign of terror and subjugation that, though it would bypass Jerusalem, would eventually reach Europe itself. But not immediately. Genghis Khan soon withdrew from his Middle Eastern conquests to attend to matters back in Mongolia, and so it was not until Genghis's grandson Batu began conquering Russia, Poland, and Hungary with bewildering rapidity in 1237 that all hope died of the Mongols being synonymous with the forces of Prester John.

Luckily for the rest of Europe, Batu was also called home by internal affairs, whereupon a resulting political realignment within the Mongol Empire made further westward conquests too risky. Indeed, the resulting peace actually opened the door for several Catholic envoys to travel to the Mongol capital at Karakorum, near modern Ulan Bator, where most of them met with a hospitable reception and where all of them inquired of their hosts about the presence of a great Christian king somewhere in the east. William of Rubruck, who was at Karakorum in 1253–4, heard answers that turned his attention toward a Christian people called the Keraits, since absorbed by the Mongols, and one of their last leaders, known as Torghil. These Keraits were indeed Christians, though of the Nestorian rite. Very briefly, Nestorians believe that Christ was composed of two separate persons within a single body, one divine and one human, as opposed to the Catholic view that he constitutes a single person who is simultaneously wholly human and wholly divine. Nestorianism was declared a heresy at the Council of Ephesus in 431, but its die-hard followers found refuge under successive leaders of a Persian Empire always willing to undermine the orthodox Byzantines, and from Persia the faith had spread farther eastward to India, central Asia, and even parts of China. By the time the Prester John legend arose, what isolated Christian groups existed at all east of the Tigris were almost invariably Nestorian.

Torghil, this King of the Nestorian Keraits, had at one time been an ally of Genghis Khan but eventually came into conflict with him and was killed after a defeat in battle in 1203. When Marco Polo came to write up his own travels in the Mongol east at the very end of the thirteenth century, he calls Toghrul by a different name but repeats the story of conflict between this figure and Genghis and insists that Toghrul was "the same that we call Prester John ... about whose great dominion all the world talks." One can hear a slightly dismissive note here, and yet Polo was only following William of Rubruck's earlier lead, who himself possessed little inclination to praise dead heretics: "The Nestorians called him King John, and only a tenth of what they said about him was true. For this is the way with the Nestorians who come from these parts: they create big rumors out of nothing." This decline in the reputation of a wholly Asian Prester reached its nadir with Friar Odoric of

Pordenone, one of the last European travelers to locate him in the far east, who sniffed in the 1320s that "not one hundredth part is true of what is told of him as if it were undeniable."[17] Cultural myths that run as deep as the Prester John story do not die easily, however. If all the likely candidates for a Christian hero roaming the steppes proved to be either heretical or deceased or both, it did not mean that he never existed — it meant that he had to be somewhere else.

In his Letter, Prester John had claimed that his kingdom covered, in whole or in part, "the Three Indias," but to what actual lands did this confusing phrase refer? Medieval European geographers, dependent upon a hodgepodge of often-conflicting Classical and early Christian sources, made very free with the term "India," at one time or another referring to just about every region beyond the Saracen lands by that name. However, most of them held to a finer distinction: what we today would see as the northern half of the Indian subcontinent they named the "Nearer" or "Lesser" India; the southern half, including the Malabar and Coromandel coasts along its tapering point, they considered to be "Further" or "Greater" India, and finally, by the title of "Middle" India they meant the Horn of Africa, including Ethiopia. This last designation may seem especially wrongheaded to modern readers, but Christians of the Middle Ages conceived of Asia as beginning at the Nile and possessed a most imperfect idea of the true extent of the Indian Ocean, so that from their perspective all three of these Indias were located on the same continent and were assumed to closely abut one another.[18] Well, if Prester John was nowhere to be found in the Lesser India menaced by the Mongols, what about the Greater India that lay to its south?

It was a common Western belief of the time that the Gospel had been preached in all countries of the earth soon after Jesus' resurrection, and that thus there were likely to be Christians everywhere, though they might well be isolated and oppressed by idolaters. More specifically, the apocryphal but well-known *Acts of Thomas* insisted that the doubting apostle had converted many in Greater India to the true religion before suffering martyrdom there. And in point of fact there were a number of Nestorian communities — though certainly no Christian kingdoms or even city-states — on both the Malabar and Coromandel coasts, loosely administered by a patriarch of that rite in far-away Baghdad. Moreover, in 1122 a man calling himself John and claiming to be archbishop of the Malabar Christians had presented himself before Pope Calixtus II in Rome. This person told many extravagant tales of miracles associated with the remains of St. Thomas, which the Pope was disinclined to believe, but he did succeed in convincing the learned of Italy that there were many more Christians in southern India than was actually the case. Thus, when Europeans began to despair of their efforts to locate Prester John's holy and potent realm in the "Lesser" India abutting central Asia, it made perfect sense for them to turn their eyes to the "Greater" India below it. And, by the end of the thirteenth century they could do more than merely speculate about the matter, for the *pax Mongoliana* had now made it easier for Westerners to reach southern India than at any time since the rise of Islam. One of the first to do so was Marco Polo, returning home from China by sea, who claimed that he had there visited the actual tomb of St. Thomas, which the Prester had asserted was the most venerated religious site within his wide and various kingdom. Surveying this sepulchre and its environs with a commercial eye, however, the Venetian came away unimpressed, finding it "solitary and much out of the way" and productive of "no merchandise." Catholic missionaries who arrived not long after and likewise discovered only small pockets of heretical Nestorians were also quick to douse hopes that either the Malabar or the Coromandel coast might be the seat of the great Christian monarch so many had hoped to find.[19] This left only the third India, the "Middle" India—the one that was no actual part of India at all, but a place in Africa.

What kind of things did Europeans believe about this remaining land, and when and by what means had they come to acquire those beliefs? The literate among them could have opened their Homer or Herodotus and found a handful of Classical notions about Abyssinia—for the former its people are the "blameless Ethiopians, most distant of men," while the latter credits them with being the tallest, handsomest and longest-lived of human beings, bedecked in "the skins of leopards and lions." A more copious source of information, however, would have been the Bible, in which that nation and its people are mentioned upwards of forty times, though in a rather scattered and haphazard fashion. The New Testament seemed to indicate that the country had been Christianized at an early date, for in Acts 8:27–39 there is a brief account of St. Phillip converting and baptizing the Eunuch of the Ethiopian Queen Candace as that official returned home from Jerusalem. This was confirmed in the early Middle Ages when Byzantine contacts with Abyssinia became almost routine and indicated that a robust and expanding Christian culture had taken firm root there. By the time of the Crusades, however, the question to be answered was whether the faithful of Ethiopia had survived the astonishingly rapid and expansive rise of Islam beginning in the seventh century, which had severed almost all communications between Abyssinia and the main body of Christendom. After all, large swaths of North Africa and Syria had once been home to teeming Christian communities that had either been converted or exterminated at the hands of the Saracens, and surely the same fate imperiled this even more precariously situated country. As a monk from the monastery of Cluny complained sometime in the 1170s:

> We so seldom receive even scanty news about the Kings of Morocco ... Numidia, Libya, Cyrene and Ethiopia, that we are virtually in complete ignorance about what is happening there. The reason for this is that Christianity has been driven

from those lands by the false teaching of Mahomet, and ... those people have cut themselves off from the Roman Empire and from the Christian faith.

These fears notwithstanding, Europeans who undertook pilgrimages to the Holy Land occasionally met Ethiopians who were there pursuing the same spiritual business. Eventually the Abyssinians even received permission to occupy a chapel connected with the Church of the Holy Sepulchre at Jerusalem, though interestingly, not until the tolerant Saladin had re-conquered that city from the Crusaders in 1187. Thirty years after that date, by the time of the Fifth Crusade, Europeans had been in the Middle East long enough to begin focusing their attention southward along the Red Sea in their search for possible Christian allies who might help make some future invasion of the Holy Land into the decisive success that had so far eluded them. Such is at any rate the theme of a German pilgrim who purports to gaze in that direction atop a mountain in Sinai:

> I saw a certain land beyond Egypt whose inhabitants are called Yssini [i.e., Abyssinians]. It is completely Christian.... It is their belief that they could reach Cairo in a short time and in such numbers that if each of them carried away one stone not a single stone of Cairo would remain. And these Christians always fight the Egyptians and the Saracens whenever they can.

This optimistic report was seconded by a participant in the Fifth Crusade, whose history of that doomed endeavor includes the heartening assertion that "Ethiopia holds very broad lands and has an innumerable Christian population." Apparently such a view quickly became commonplace among the Crusaders, for Jaques of Vitry — the same who mistook Genghis Khan for Prester John — also tells of Christians residing "in a great part of Ethiopia and all the regions as far as India." Given this rising level of confidence that the Christian religion had survived intact in Abyssinia, it was only a matter of time before some European connected the dots and proclaimed that Prester John must reign not over an Asian kingdom, but one located in that part of Africa that still adhered to the true faith. The first to do so was one Jordan Catalani of Sévérac, who had journeyed eastward to take up the Catholic bishopric of Quilon on the Malabar Coast. His 1324 *Book of Marvels* has chapters dedicated to each of the Three Indias, and when he comes to describe the "middle" one which comprised the Horn of Africa, he places Prester John there alongside the kind of miraculous beings recounted in that monarch's original Letter:

> There be dragons in the greatest abundance, which carry on their heads the lustrous stones which be called carbuncles.... But all the regions round about watch for the time of the dragons and when they see that one has fallen, they wait for seventy days and then go down and find the bare bones of the dragon, and take the carbuncle which is rooted in the top of his head, and carry it to the emperor of the Aethiopians, whom you call Prester John.

Clearly, Europe's hopes for a Christian savior from beyond the land of the Moors was beginning to turn toward a different theater of expectation.

Of course the Islamic Mamluk Sultanate, which ruled Egypt from 1250 until the eve of the Portuguese arrival in the Red Sea, understood how important it was to keep Europeans as ignorant as possible about the stubborn but isolated Christian kingdom for which the latter were beginning to search in earnest. As one fourteenth-century westerner resident in Egypt lamented, "the Christians of Ethiopia would willingly have communicated with us Latins, but the Sultan of Cairo never lets a single Latin pass into their country, lest they should enter into a treaty to make war against him."[20] Nor was this the only reason prompting the Muslim blockade, for the Mamluks also had every incentive to keep European traders in pepper, cinnamon, and nutmeg from discovering for themselves how essential a highway to the spice-lands of the orient the Red Sea actually was.[21] These facts of geography could not remain hidden for long, however, especially from the merchants of the Italian trading cites, whose commercial passions drove them to be persistently inquisitive about any promising pathway by which they might outflank the trade's Mohammedan middlemen. By the thirteenth century, for instance, we find reports of Genoese boatswains building galleys at Baghdad at the invitation of the Persian Ilkhan, so that they might blockade the Gulf of Aden (where the Red Sea spills out into the Indian Ocean) and thereby strangle the commerce of the Mamluks, with whom that potentate was briefly quarrelling. The plan apparently came to nothing when the Genoese fell to brawling among themselves,[22] but their desire for access to eastern waters and the immense mercantile riches that such would bring within their grasp continued unabated. Indeed, neither Genoa nor Venice was over-scrupulous about acquiring Asian or African footholds even if it meant entwining themselves with their supposed spiritual enemy, and by the early fourteenth century both cities possessed, in defiance of several Papal warnings, well-established warehouses and even semi-official consulates at Alexandria.[23] Thus did the Venetian and Genoese merchants harbor a double incentive for pursuing contacts with Ethiopia, since it would have been both religiously more acceptable as well as potentially more lucrative to obtain their cargoes without enriching Egyptians and other infidels in the process.[24] It is probable that such interlocking considerations of piety and greed propelled the little-known expedition of the Vivaldi brothers, a pair of Genoese siblings who sailed westward through the Straits of Gibraltar in two galleys during the spring of 1291 with the hope of reaching India by sea. Despite the fact that they had level-headedly estimated that such a journey would take them a full ten years to accomplish, after a few sightings along the coast of what is now Morocco they were never heard from again. Perhaps not surprisingly, though, a legend grew up to the effect that the intrepid brothers had circumnavigated Africa and been received by that most elusive yet alluring figure of European desire, Prester John. For if he was truly an Ethiopian rather than a central Asian, then it meant that in the imagination of the West he now held the keys not only to holy wars, but to unholy profits as well.

The imaginative relocation of Prester John to the Horn of Africa was aided by the fact that from time to time a reciprocal interest could be detected emerging from that region. Throughout this era Ethiopia fitfully sent forth ambassadors toward the European stronghold of the religion it practiced in zealous isolation, sometimes begging material aid, but at other times, it seems, seeking little more than recognition and remembrance. In 1306, for instance, a group of about thirty Abyssinians who had been sent to Rome and Avignon and perhaps also to "the Spains" by their emperor Wedem Ar'ad, were delayed long enough in Genoa by contrary winds for the cartographer Giovanni da Carignano to record their answers to some questions concerning their native country. During this hold-up the visitors were apparently able to make the European mapmaker understand that Ethiopia was located more or less athwart the upper Nile, and to disabuse him of the notion that it was in any manner a province of India.[25] Furthermore, since his interlocutors were clearly Christians of some description, Carignano's resulting map and commentary mark the moment when learned Europeans began to mentally shift the homeland of Prester John from Asia to Ethiopia, an association that by the late 1400s had become the conventional wisdom.[26] Still, some of what got written down at that interview was apparently the result of faulty translation, since Carignano was also credited as declaring that the Prester's people were perfectly orthodox Christians "with this one exception, that they sing the Paternoster before the elevation of the Sacrament"[27] — an assertion that does not even remotely describe the actual tenets of Abyssinian worship.

One sort of event that could apparently spur an Ethiopian expedition to Europe was the arrival before the Emperor — or, to use his proper title, the *"Negus"* — of a Westerner, no matter whether the traveler in question was heroically persistent or profoundly lost. Sometime in the 1390s, for instance, the Florentine merchant Antonio Bartoli managed by unknown means to reach Abyssinia, and by 1402 or 1404 he was back in Italy in the company of several envoys from that nation's sovereign.[28] This was actually a pretty quick turnaround, given the propensity of the Ethiopian rulers to keep their European guests in extended, if comfortable captivity. More typical is the case of Pietro Rombulo, who arrived in 1407 and did not leave the country attended by his own brace of African ambassadors until sometime around 1444, having married an Ethiopian woman in the meantime.[29] In fact, sometime during Rombulo's lengthy stay the *Negus* Yeshak sent out envoys unaccompanied by any white man to Afonso of Aragon, asking that skilled European craftsmen be sent to him and improbably offering one of his princesses in marriage to Afonso's son. The Aragonian duly dispatched the requested artisans, though they all unluckily perished in transit, putting a halt to talk of uniting Iberia and Ethiopia in marriage.[30] When Rombulo finally was allowed to return to Italy, however, the Abyssinians who did accompany him were charged with renewing the request for a brace of carpenters and masons[31]— troubling evidence of a chronic need for assistance that the Prester John of the Letter and subsequent legend should not have required. Indeed, it seems a bit odd that none of these admittedly sporadic contacts with living and breathing Ethiopians did much to clarify for Europeans who the ruler of Abyssinia actually was, but they did not. And one would give much to hear more concerning how Latin observers squared the obvious black skins of these Ethiopians (which would have been no surprise, since Classical literature insisted on this trait) with the Prester's signal failure to mention this fact about his subjects (and himself) in his Letter, but there is scant commentary on the subject. (So little, indeed, that one wonders whether the modern concept of "denial" might have been at work.) At any rate, we know that during the Council of Florence — a conclave summoned by the Pope in 1441 to attempt to realign the eastern Christian churches with the doctrines of Rome — the Ethiopian delegates who had traveled there from their chapels in Jerusalem were at first puzzled and then annoyed that the Europeans in attendance kept saddling their beloved *Negus* with the moniker of some imposter by the name of "Prester John."[32] Complain as they might, though, this would prove the most durable of delusions.

Thus as Father Francisco Álvares was packing his trunk in preparation for finally setting foot in Ethiopia that April morning of 1520, he had good reason to believe that he would be alighting upon the soil of Prester John's long-sought kingdom. He was not the kind of man to remain stubbornly convinced of the rightness of his own opinions, but in this case stubbornness was hardly required, for the rest of literate Europe — including men much more extensively educated than himself— also believed that Abyssinia must in fact be the pious and powerful realm that had been the object of such profound fascination for so many. After all, it fit the one vital criteria: it was a Christian kingdom on the other side of the Moors — or at least the only one of any potential consequence. Every other possibility had been searched out — if Prester John was not here, then he did not exist, and that was too dispiriting a notion to seriously entertain, given that in 1520 there were Ottoman Turks encamped on the very banks of the Danube. And yet even amid such strained hopes, Father Álvares understood that he would find no actual, living person, aged as Methuselah by now, bearing the proper name of Prester John — he was not that credulous. Surely, he reasoned, it was a title of office, a mantle of kingship passed down the generations through the bloodline or by some other, perhaps superior, method of inheritance. Then too, he must have found it troubling that a nation reputed to be so powerful seemed so isolated, and gave so little evidence of might or grandeur even upon its own seacoast, but there were many possible explanations for this.

Most likely the Prester's people truly were as innumerable as the sands, and valiant and aching for battle against the infidel, and yet only lacked some one skill or stratagem or engine of war that would allow them to come fully into their rightful power — something only he and his countrymen could provide. Perhaps indeed that was why God had providentially ordained that it be the Portuguese who would first see the Prester face-to-face and be the first to offer him a European hand in holy alliance. For had not the Portuguese journeyed so much farther by means of ingenuity, daring, and guile than larger nations who had trusted to hoarded wealth and old pedigrees to fill their sails? He and his countrymen had certainly endured a long and taxing pilgrimage to stand at this threshold. They had been almost exactly a century in getting around the vast southward extension of the African continent and then sailing beyond that treacherous extremity to India and Ethiopia. And though the wondrous realm of Prester John had not been the only thing they had sought along the way, finding it had always been a central part of their purpose, an exalted hope that justified much that was unexalted, even cruel and un–Christian. In truth, Father Álvares was poised at the culminating point of a vast collective enterprise. If what lay immediately ahead of him remained yet unknown, that was nothing novel, for he and his fellow Portuguese had made breasting the unknown their nation's trademark business. Looking back from 1520, it was reasonable to believe that choosing to do so had propelled his people from poverty to riches, and from obscurity to a place at the very fulcrum of Europe's dawning imperial future.

Two

Stalking a Phantom

Hemmed in by hostile Iberian kingdoms and possessing little land suitable for farming, Father Álvares' smallish nation had long looked to the sea to feed its belly, and thus when it assumed its modern boundaries in the late Middle Ages, it naturally looked to the same element to satisfy as well its spiritual imagination and its worldly ambitions. While recent scholarship has revealed Prince Henry the Navigator's honorific title to be as much cannily manufactured as strenuously earned, it was nevertheless during his lifetime (1394–1460) and at least partly under his direction that Portuguese ships began their long reconnaissance of the West African coast. Henry, who was far-sighted enough to imagine the benefits that might accrue to Portugal if his nation could establish trading bases beyond the Muslim-dominated Sahara, was also genuinely curious about geographical matters, and consistently rewarded mariners who returned home with newly drawn maps of hitherto unknown islands and headlands. Not that his interests were entirely patriotic and philosophical; he collected a fifth of all profits from captains who plied those Atlantic waters granted to him by the crown as a fiefdom. Still, Henry can certainly be credited with turning Portuguese exploration of the African coast from a matter of lucky accidents into an enterprise that Portuguese elites came to regard as central to their national destiny; by doing so, the Prince can take credit for launching his people on a great outward journey that fundamentally changed their conception of themselves.

In the more than half century of exploration that culminated in Bartolomeu Dias rounding the Cape of Good Hope in 1488, Portuguese sailing ships progressed southward at the average rate of a little better than one degree of latitude per year,[1] their captains and crews overcoming both the imagined dangers of boiling-hot seas and giant whirlpools as well as the actual perils of contrary winds and hidden shoals. This pace was all the more impressive given that the enterprise was frequently put on hold by civil strife back home, by botched military escapades in other theaters, by Spanish and Venetian competition, and by unfavorable Papal bulls. Indeed, there were frequently years when no new coastline at all was mapped by Portuguese hands. But, as decade followed decade, the sinuous outline of Africa's shoreline — arid, then tropical, then arid once again — was marked down in the logbooks of Iberian mariners. The process was driven at every moment by numerous individuals' intersecting motivations: profit, conquest, evangelism, and unvarnished curiosity — but interwoven through all of these from the very beginning was the alluring figure of Prester John.

Because of an interlocking set of geographical beliefs that he had taken to heart, Prince Henry made it official policy for his outward-bound mariners to always interrogate the native populations about the proximity of that fabled potentate. First of all, he accepted the notion that Prester John ruled Ethiopia and not some Asian kingdom farther to the east, and that Ethiopia was itself an African land lying somewhere on or about the upper Nile. Secondly, he followed the best cartographers of his day in vastly overestimating the size — especially the southward and westward extension — of Ethiopia. Contemporary maps show a kind of continental superpower stretching from the shores of the Red Sea and metastasizing throughout the center of the African continent, bringing the borderlands of that Christian empire to within a few days march of the Atlantic seaboard. Thirdly, Henry subscribed to the existence — as attested to in the pages of the anonymous but reassuringly titled *Book of the Knowledge of all the Kingdoms, Lands, and Lordships that are in the World* — of the Sinus Aethiopicus, a great pie-shaped gulf with its narrow end to the east situated at about the same location as the actual Congo river. This supposed inland sea effectively cut the continent in half, placing, say, the east-African city of Zanzibar upon a narrow isthmus and making it possible to sail eastward at the equator to within striking distance of the Prester's vast country without the onerous necessity of rounding the tapering southern half of the landmass.[2] One can thus imagine the aged Henry's excitement when, in the late 1450s, his returning captains from south of Cape Verde presented him with their latest charts showing the African coastline turning inexorably to the east. And even when, in the 1470s, the Portuguese were forced to admit that beyond the Gulf of Guinea the edge of Africa returned to its north-south orientation with no end in sight, Henry's ghost need not have suffered posthumous despair, again because of the reputed vastness of Prester John's realm. If the Congo were merely a river and not the Sinus Aethiopicus, so be it, for here too Classical geography came to one's rescue. According to ancient authorities one could still simply row upstream until, before long, one reached a great lake nestled in what Herodotus named the Mountains of the Moon — a lake which constituted the headwaters of *both* the Congo *and* the Nile. From there, it was just an easy drift downriver to the realms of one's great Christian ally. So, given the Prester's reputed proximity to the same west-African shores where

Portuguese subjects were busily gathering slaves, gold, and civet-cats, it seemed only prudent to ask about him at every opportunity.

And they got some tantalizing replies. In 1455, two Italian captains, one a Venetian and one a Genoese, who had license from Henry to explore beyond Cape Verde, sailed their pair of caravels a short way up the Gambia River, encountering organized resistance most of the way. After a couple of close-run battles with Mandinka warriors who fought skillfully from canoes, and a subsequent parlay in which the Africans accused the Europeans of looking for black men to capture and eat (Portugal's reputation as a slave-seeking nation had preceded the pair, if in a pithily symbolic form), they made their escape to sea and turned their prows northward. When the Genoese mariner reached home he wrote an account of the voyage wherein he claimed to have penetrated the river to within a few days journey of the encampment of the King of Mali, who, he had been informed, was even then entertaining five Christian envoys from Prester John, the border of whose kingdom lay only three hundred leagues to the east. Granted the man was writing all this to his creditors, and thus had a motive to exaggerate (indeed, he also claims to have met a descendant of the Vivaldi brothers living in the bush), but the excitement this report generated and the currency it attained points up how willing Europeans were to believe that one could start out on the Atlantic coast of Africa and walk one's way to the Prester.[3]

When the Portuguese explorer Diogo Cão reached the mouth of the Congo River in 1483 he managed to gather from the natives that a great king held sway a considerable distance upstream and immediately began to entertain what might well be termed the Official Hope. Accordingly, he sent some of his shipmates into the interior under the protection of the locals, with whom he optimistically believed himself to be communicating clearly. He had agreed to wait a certain number of days for their return, but when twice that time had passed and they failed to show up, he captured some native hostages and reluctantly went on with his journey southward, though he was by no means done with tracking down this particular rumor concerning Europe's indispensable monarch. When he returned to the mouth of the great river on a subsequent voyage in 1485 Cão met with a much more promising reception. Releasing one of the by-now-bi-lingual hostages he had kidnapped on his first visit, it wasn't long before a member of the original Portuguese landing party was delivered to the beach in passable health. Encouraged, the captain dispatched some presents upstream toward a personage he now understood to be not the Prester himself, but rather the King of Congo, reckoning that this native prince might at least be in contact with the greater ruler he sought. Cão then made ready to sail as far up the reach as he could, hoping of course for smooth water all the way to the Mountains of the Moon, secure in the knowledge that his lithe and maneuverable caravels (able, with their triangular foresails, to make way within thirty degrees of a headwind) were well-suited for riverine exploration. The Congo is somewhat unusual among great rivers, however, in that while its upper course offers over a thousand miles of smooth navigability, its coastal segment quickly narrows between encroaching promontories, presenting the would-be ascender with a crescendo of obstacles that begins with strong currents and culminates in broad rapids and thundering waterfalls. It was at the foot of one of these last that Cão and his men, after abandoning the caravels for a stint of increasingly hard rowing in small boats, carved their names on the face of a smooth rock under an inscription whose bland statement belies its commemoration of a defeated hope: "Here reached the vessels of the distinguished King Dom João II of Portugal." In due course the King of Congo was also interviewed, but although he feigned polite interest in the Europeans' questions about a Christian power to the east, it was clear he possessed no genuine information. The Sinus Aethiopicus, once as wide as hope itself, had narrowed into a box canyon of unyielding fact.[4]

However, just as Cão was pounding fruitlessly on one door to the African interior, an intriguing tale arrived by means of another. In 1486 the ambassador to the court of João II (ruled 1481–1495) from the King of Benin, with whom the Portuguese were rapidly developing a lucrative trade in slaves on the Guinea coast, asserted that twenty moons' travel to the east of his master's capital lived a mighty ruler by the name of Ogané, whose power was both temporal and spiritual. Indeed, the successive Kings of Benin could not consider themselves rightly installed upon their throne until they had sent presents to Ogané and received from him in return a kind of Pope's blessing, accompanied by a ceremonial headdress, a staff of office, and — of most interest to the Portuguese — a cross to be worn around the sovereign's neck. This was no mere hearsay, insisted the Beninian ambassador, since one of his own earlier postings had been to Ogané's capital, where he himself had received a miniature version of the official cross, a talisman that marked him out as a man of high privilege when he returned to his own land. He also related that during all the time he had spent in that eastern seat he had never actually seen Ogané himself, since the monarch was perpetually concealed behind curtains — although at a final audience he had been granted the extraordinary compliment of a viewing of the monarch's foot, obligingly thrust out into plain sight from amid the intervening draperies. This last remains an intriguing detail, since Álvares was eventually to discover that the Abyssinian *Negus* was similarly concealed from subjects and suitors alike. The resemblance, however, must have been purely coincidental, since whoever this Ogané was, no Ethiopian emperor ever held sway within the two-hundred and fifty leagues (about 650 miles) of Benin that a twenty moons' march was thought to signify. Nevertheless, and by now perhaps unsurprisingly, King João's cartographers compared the ambassador's reports with Ptolemy and other Classical authorities' pronouncements about

African geography and concluded that Ogané was none other than Prester John. João in turn decided that it was high time to get a ship around the southern tip of the continent that stubbornly blocked access to his Christian brother — and to the source of all that costly pepper and cinnamon as well — even if doing so meant dodging icebergs and running before frigid gales.[5] And to do so even if such persistence flew in the face of the revered Ptolemy himself, who insisted that the Indian Ocean was but a landlocked sea, and that southward from the equator Africa only widened and widened, eventually covering all the world's southern latitudes with a solid cap of uninhabitable land.

The man who accomplished this feat for King João was Bartolomeu Dias, who departed Lisbon's Tagus River in late summer of 1487 with two caravels and a supply ship, determined to push beyond Cão's farthest point of navigation at 22 degrees south and to finally confirm or deny the presence of an eastward sea-passage to Ethiopia and the spice ports of India. Besides the usual complement of crewmen, Dias' ships carried half a dozen Africans who had been rounded up from various locations between the Guinea coast and what is now Angola. The idea was to set them ashore at various promising points with samples of precious metals and various spices so that they might inquire from what quarter the local natives got their supply of such goods, since in that direction must lie Prester John. Simultaneously, they were to talk up the power and riches of King João and explain that he would be very grateful indeed to those who could put his countrymen in contact with anyone hailing from any interior nation where the people wore crosses, or anyone who even vaguely knew the way thither. Apparently some of these conscripted ambassadors were women, for the Portuguese were hopeful that their sex might prevent them from simply being dispatched before they could deliver their message.

Also brought along for distribution — and standing a decidedly better chance of long-term survival — were a set of stone pillars referred to as *padrões*. These obelisks were usually carved into the shape of a cross at the top, or at least had a cross inscribed prominently upon one or more of their upper faces, with some sort of proclamation chiseled below, sometimes in Portuguese alone, sometimes in other languages as well. It was reported, for instance, that the *padrão* left by Cão at the mouth of the Congo carried messages in Portuguese, Latin, and Arabic, the idea being that should a subject of Prester John's happen to come across it, there would be a higher chance of his being able to translate King João's greeting. On the one hand, these pillars were a new colonial power's declaration of ownership, a heavy and durable announcement that the Portuguese had gotten to this cape or that estuary before any other European nation, and thus claimed dominion over everything animal, vegetable, mineral, and aboriginal residing thereabouts. But given European hopes about the nearness of the Prester's realm, they also represented so many poignantly hopeful letters of introduction appealing for a friendly response from out of the vast wilderness. The things must have been hell to unload from a ship, row to shore, and haul up a promontory — considering the immense consequences if the longed-for answer ever arrived, however, few who understood the purpose of such labors likely complained.

Dias' outward voyage was a steady and dogged affair, for after leaving the supply ship anchored somewhere off the southwest African coast as planned, his pair of more speedy caravels ticked off headland and bay, headland and bay, all the while nervously watching the Southern Cross rise higher and higher into the night sky. Finally, either because they were pushed by a storm or because they tired of fighting the coastal breezes that seemed always to blow against them from the south, they tacked a sweeping curve westward into the open ocean. After some days on this course the water suddenly grew cold, the winds changed direction, and when they swung back to their original line of travel, they discovered — no continent at all, just a blank horizon above an empty sea. Half in fear and half in exaltation they hurriedly made to the north and before long regained the African shoreline — but a shoreline that now ran gratifyingly west to east. As soon as they found a suitable landing place, boats were rowed upon the beach to gather fresh water and to trade for meat with the local inhabitants, whom the Portuguese were pleasantly surprised to see tending herds of cattle and sheep upon green, rolling hills. However, in a replay of so many European collisions with Africans, the initial frisson of exotic bartering soon led to some sort of cultural misunderstanding. After a variety of trinkets had been exchanged for livestock, a group of Hottentots became offended and began hurling stones, whereupon Dias himself impulsively picked up his crossbow and slew one of the natives, initiating a quick Portuguese retreat to the safety of their ships.

If commerce was off to a bad start, however, geography did not disappoint, for the caravels now followed a coast that unfurled so steadily to the eastward that the crew soon came to believe that they should claim victory and return the way they had come.

> As all the people were very weary and frightened from the great seas they had passed through, all with one voice began to complain and to demand that they should go no farther; they said that as the provisions were almost exhausted they should turn and search for the storeship which they had left behind and which was already so distant that when they reached her they would all be dead from hunger. How then could they sail any farther?

Dias, apparently of a more democratic temperament than his more famous successor Da Gama, called a general parlay to discuss the situation. He concurred that they should soon head for home, but in a gesture that prefigures the Columbus legend, he asked for three more days, a plea to which his officers and men reluctantly agreed.[6] Dias wanted to be sure that they had indeed rounded the bottom of Africa, and to this end his three days were productive of much confidence, for at the point where they dragged their last *padrão* ashore the coastline was running consistently east-north-east, tending ever more to the northward in a long, smooth ark, so that one had to stand out to sea in order to behold the beaches and headlands in the farthest distance. Ptolemy's assertion of a landlocked Indian Ocean had proved wrong and Prince Henry's gamble prescient: Africa could be circumnavigated. A water route to the material wealth of India and the equally potent imaginative riches of Ethiopia was now open before the Portuguese.

Oddly, though, they appeared to hesitate. Between December of 1488, when Dias returned with news of a sea passage to the East around the southern tip of Africa, and July of 1497, when Vasco da Gama departed to successfully follow just that route to the spice-lands of India, lies a decade of seeming inactivity that cries out for explanation. Why were the discoveries of the former navigator not immediately exploited? If the long-sought path to the source of all that exorbitant oriental merchandise was now known, what was the advantage to be gained by delay? A probable answer credits King João II with more patience and prudence than might normally be expected of an ambitious Renaissance monarch poised on the brink of such a potentially lucrative opportunity. After all, what did the Portuguese really know about India and its surrounding waters besides how, in the most general sense, to get there? It was reportedly a large place dotted with many cities — but which ones were central to the spice trade, and which mere satellites? Given the rabid hostility that the first sight of a caravel was bound to incite in the hearts of that precious traffic's Indian and Muslim middlemen (to say nothing of its Venetian retailers), it would pay to know in some detail what one was getting into before one leapt. And then there was the question of the great ally upon whom the Portuguese were counting to assist them in the cornering of markets and the subjugating of infidels. Where exactly, vis-à-vis India, was the Prester's kingdom of Ethiopia, and what were the pertinent physical characteristics of his realm? Since the Portuguese were planning to arrive by sea, it was vital to know whether that Christian potentate was wholly landlocked, or whether, as they fervently hoped, he possessed a reasonable extent of coastline that included a well-sheltered harbor or two. So, before the main force was deployed, João felt it necessary to await the return of various spies whom he had already sent on ahead.[7]

Sometime in the mid 1480s the Portuguese king had dispatched a pair of men to Jerusalem with instructions to link up there with Ethiopian pilgrims returning to their homeland and, after reconnoitering Abyssinia, to report back on the true location and extent of the Prester's realm. This gambit had come to nothing, however, for the pair chosen for the task wrote home from the Holy Land claiming that they could push on no farther because Arabic, a language necessary to their further progress, was just too difficult to learn — an excuse of breathtaking feebleness that must have infuriated João. At any rate, he was more careful in his next choice of scouts, lighting upon Pêro da Covilhã and Afonso de Paiva, the former of whom had already acquired the exacting tongue of the infidel while successfully carrying out various secret missions for the crown in North Africa. Da Covilhã and his partner were supplied with the best chart of the Middle East then available in Iberia, four hundred *cruzados* in coin, and a generous letter of credit, whereupon they set out toward the east. When they reached Rhodes they began their professional masquerade as Levantine traders, buying a shipment of honey and pressing on to Alexandria, from which, after a bout of sickness that nearly killed them both, they were able to travel by caravan to the head of the Red Sea and then take ship for Aden. At this point the duo split up, with Da Covilhã assuming responsibility for the reconnaissance of the spice ports of India while Paiva was to head directly for Ethiopia, which lay upon the western shore of the sea they had just traversed from north to south. Despite this division of labor, however, it is Da Covilhã whom we must follow, for Paiva died before he could reach the Prester's coast, leaving that task to be completed by his weary companion years later, after he had already gleaned an impressive hoard of information about where the spices came from and how they were traded.

Utilizing a remarkable combination of intelligence, endurance, and luck, Pêro da Covilhã made his way under deep disguise to the Malabar (i.e., southwestern) coast of India and soon discerned that Calicut was the busiest and most important of the spice-trading cities, its hinterlands blessed with orchards of pepper and ginger, its harbor jammed with Arab dhows and Chinese junks full of cloves and cinnamon from farther east. (Certainly when Da Gama arrived a decade later, he knew exactly which metropolis to make for, ignorant as he was of so much else.) From there Da Covilhã moved north past Goa to the island fortress of Ormuz at the throat of the Persian Gulf, learning there of an overland trade route to the Mediterranean by way of Basra which rivaled the Red Sea as a highway for costly eastern commodities. From thence he journeyed by water to the East African coast, touching at the ports of Mogadishu, Mombasa, Zanzibar, and eventually reaching Mozambique, the southern limit of Arab trading. This grand piece of espionage completed, Da Covilhã managed to return safely to Cairo and to inquire there about his erstwhile companion Paiva. He not only learned of his partner's demise, but was there accosted by two Portuguese Jews bearing new instructions from King João, the gist of which was that if both India and Ethiopia had been scrutinized, he was free to return to Portugal with honor — but that if even half the job remained to be done, he was to see to its completion himself. With emotions that we can readily imagine, the King's good servant, after writing up a full report of all that he had already seen and learned, complied with his sovereign's instructions.

The second phase of Da Covilhã's travels were even more romantically evocative than the first. His initial assignment was to escort one of the Jewish messengers on to Ormuz, where he too could take up spying for Portugal's king. That accomplished, Da Covilhã turned his sights back to the Red Sea and any possible approach to the nation of Ethiopia. Naturally enough, though, Arab vessels tended to call at ports on the eastern, Muslim side of that nearly landlocked body of water. Thus finding himself at Jiddah, he apparently followed the promptings of both opportunity and curiosity by using his acquired mastery of disguise to join a party of pilgrims headed for Mecca, becoming the first known European to visit that city at the heart of Islam. This fascinating excursion completed, he managed by a circuitous route to land at a spot in what is now Somalia and then gamely set out to walk overland into the mountain fastness of Prester John. In a feat as consistent with his previous record of accomplishment as it is nevertheless surprising, he reached his goal, becoming the honored guest of the Ethiopian *Negus* Eskender (i.e., Alexander). This monarch was in turn on the verge of facilitating Da Covilhã's return home to what would certainly have been a grateful Portuguese Court when he — Eskender — died and was succeeded by a series of emperors who exhibited that more custodial view of hospitality that was to so closely embrace Álvares and his embassy a score of years later. Indeed, our priest was to get to know Pêro da Covilhã quite well, and to wonder whether, in the wrinkled face of this rich and respected prisoner-for-life, he was beholding an image of his own fate.[8]

For his part, King João did not wait idly for his spy's dispatches to arrive, for if he was not yet ready to risk an armada round the bottom of Africa, he was nevertheless willing to send a column of men directly through its heart with orders similar to Da Covilhã's. His chance to do so arrived when one of the African hostages taken to Lisbon by Diogo Cão and later returned home to the mouth of the Congo by another Iberian captain fulfilled his captors' hopes by informing his native superiors about the power and wealth of Portugal. This in turn prompted the King of Congo to send the traveler back north once again with the next passing convoy of white men's ships, but this time as the head of an official embassy to King João bearing gifts of ivory and asking in return for carpenters, bakers, farmers, and — perhaps most promisingly — priests. Some months later the Portuguese king and queen acted as godparents when this Congolese ambassador requested Christian baptism along with his entire retinue, after which João assembled the requested clerics and craftsmen, appointed an envoy of his own to the great river's monarch, and watched with satisfaction as the whole lot pushed off for a return trip to the equator. Once there, things went exceedingly well, and before long a church was being erected at the indigenous capital, caravels were lobbing cannonballs at the King of Congo's enemies, and the headman himself was accepting baptism, abandoning the name of Nzinga a Nkuwu for that of his new ally and benefactor, João (while his principal wife became Leonor in honor of Portugal's queen). If, however, making new converts was rewarding — and in this case easy — work, it did not mean that the Portuguese were neglecting their perennial obsession with finding the more established Christians who were said to populate the lands of Prester John. As a contemporary account relates, "the [Portuguese] cosmographers," trusting in the Ptolemaic portrait of the African interior, "think that this river [i.e., the Congo] rises in the Mountains of the Moon, where the Nile has it source." Thus, when most of the Portuguese mariners boarded ship for home, there remained behind "other persons of distinction ordered to go by land and discover other distant countries, with India and Prester John as their objectives." This expedition, seeking a mere legend and with only an ancient surmise as its roadmap, unsurprisingly vanished up-river without a trace.[9] It is worth remembering, though, that in 1492, a year we automatically associate with a different feat of exploration, João's scouts were simultaneously stepping onto the Somali coast and hacking their way up the Congo, two columns of reconnaissance encompassing a continent, and both hopeful of stealing a preliminary look at their Abyssinian goal.

Whatever the virtues of João II's policy (if deliberate policy it was) of halting seaborne explorations while attempting to get a better idea of the lay of the Prester's realm, by the end of 1495 there was a new king on the Portuguese throne — Manoel I — and just a year and a half later Vasco da Gama's fleet departed for India by way of the route pioneered by Dias.

Da Gama's initial voyage of discovery must be discussed in some detail, both because of its intrinsic importance to the opening of Portugal's eastern empire, and because of the stark contrast it offers to Father Álvares' subsequent embassy to the court of Prester John. Whereas the former enterprise was shot through with hubris and racial contempt from start to finish, and ended much worse than it needed to, the latter was at least originally conceived of as an encounter between equals, and eventually managed to narrowly avoid the catastrophes that menaced it. Of course much of the difference between the pair of endeavors can be attributed to Christianity, in both a cultural and a personal sense: the Portuguese understood that the Ethiopians, unlike most other inhabitants of the East, were Christians, and Father Álvares was a conscientious priest of that religion, not an avaricious bully like Da Gama. But the truth is that the expedition into Abyssinia profited from more than just Álvares' piety. Composed as it was of men who were constantly under pressure from strange sights and customs, possessed of sublime expectations that they were forced to modify if not abandon, and uncertain as to whether they were temporary guests or permanent inmates of the country through which they rambled, the temptation to feel and act in the style of Da Gama was ever-present. That these people took up bloody-minded attitudes and committed needless acts of violence no more often than they actually did was due in large measure to Francisco Álvares' quiet powers of persuasion and example. The embassy to Prester John could so easily have become another familiar example of the tragedy of European arrival: that it became instead a fascinating alternative to such is largely the result of the presence at its heart of a man as different in temperament from Vasco Da Gama — his countrymen's public hero — as could well be imagined.

After a stop for repairs and re-victualling at the Cape Verde Islands, Da Gama's four ships — two merchants' naus (i.e. Portuguese galleons), one caravel, and one supply vessel that would be cannibalized en route — swung widely out into the open Atlantic in order to avoid contrary winds near the African coast, spending a record-breaking three months beyond sight of land and regaining the shore quite near the Cape of Good Hope. As the southern hemisphere summer of 1497 approached its height they battled unfavorable gales and currents around the continent's southern extremity, amusing themselves by occasionally opening fire on herds of seals and penguins with their canons, and going ashore for several tense bargaining sessions with the local herdsmen. By December 16th they had passed the last *padrão* left by Dias, and at first their progress into what was for Europeans uncharted territory was fairly smooth, featuring plentiful sources of fresh water, friendly natives, and fair winds. Indeed, it was not until the expedition began touching at the large commercial towns of the East African coast — first Mozambique, then Mombasa, and finally Malindi — that the Portuguese began their descent into a state of hair-trigger suspicion concerning the motives of nearly everyone they met. Of course there were genuine dangers enough attending a group of Christians unexpectedly penetrating a Muslim sphere of influence; nevertheless, much of the blame for this darkening mood must be laid to the character of Da Gama himself. The Admiral, whose bravery and determination no one can question, was also a competent and rational enough man — until, that is, he felt himself crossed, whereupon he became capable of any impulsive enormity. To make matters worse, he was all too capable of believing himself "betrayed" or the victim of "treachery" whenever a native official failed to instantly and cheerfully execute his every command.

Arriving at Mozambique in March, the Portuguese soon discerned that they were dealing with Arabic-speaking "black Moors" who had trading relations with "white Moors" further up the coast involving both precious metals and spices. Even more exciting was the news that once they pushed farther north they would find that "Prester John resided not far from [that] place" though "deep in the interior" where one could only reach him "on the back[s] of camels," a mixed report that nevertheless caused some of the Europeans to weep with joy. While thus amiably parlaying, however, Da Gama insisted that his men must at all costs mask their religious allegiance from the residents of the city. Accordingly, the Portuguese were obliged to withdraw their ships to an offshore island in order to celebrate mass, to finger some proffered Moslem prayer beads with approbation, and to equivocate unconvincingly when they were asked point blank if they weren't some sort of Turks. Da Gama managed

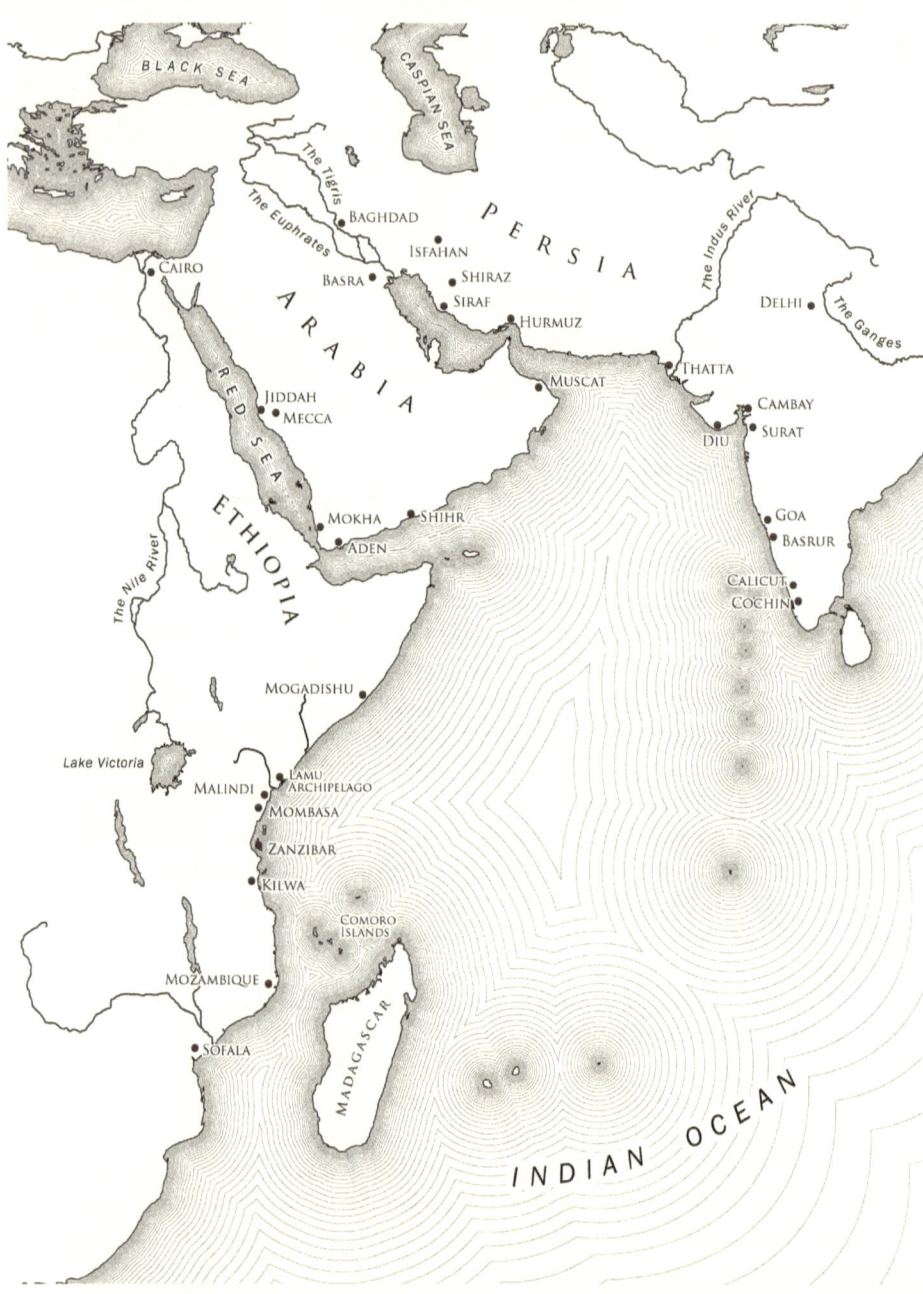

The Western Indian Ocean at the time of Vasco Da Gama's First Voyage to India. Knowing roughly where he wanted to end up, but ignorant of much that lay between himself and his goal, Da Gama's success in reaching Calicut was due to a combination of good luck and utter ruthlessness.

to coax a pair of pilots from the Sultan, but soon thereafter he began to suspect that their ruse had been seen though, and that consequently the Mozambiqueans were determined to "seize and kill [them] by treachery." Acting precipitously upon this notion, the Admiral began cannonading the town to show its inhabitants "that we were able to do them harm if we desired it." This much accomplished, the fleet departed northward at the directions of the Muslim pilots, whom Da Gama personally flogged every time they mistook an island for a headland, or failed to warn of an approaching shoal.[10]

At Mombasa in early April, trade in cloves and pepper seemed to get off to a promising start until the two captive pilots, perceiving a boat full of Muslims pass close under the prow of the Portuguese flagship, hurled themselves into the sea and were handily scooped up by their fellow infidels. Incensed at this defiance, Da Gama "questioned two Moors whom we [still] had on board, by dropping boiling oil upon their skin, so that they might confess any treachery against us." Like most victims of torture, these unfortunates told the Portuguese exactly what they wanted or expected to hear, with the result that the fleet soon weighed anchor, fed up with "these and other wicked tricks practiced upon [them] by these dogs." But this sudden departure posed a problem. Thanks perhaps to Da Covilhā's scouting reports, Da Gama was aware enough of the outlines of the Indian Ocean to realize that he would soon have to turn eastward again across open water if he was to reach his goal of Calicut in a timely manner. That meant that he had to have another pilot, not only to warn him about winds and currents — he was utterly ignorant of the rhythms of the Indian monsoon — but to guide him in the proper direction once he gained the Malabar coast. Malindi, seventy miles north of Mombasa, was probably his last chance in this regard, but by the time he arrived there he was so thoroughly suspicious that he refused to set any of his men ashore until prominent hostages from the city had been placed aboard his ships. Despite this haughty rudeness, the local King appeared well disposed toward the Portuguese and once again commerce made a tentative beginning. It was not long, however, before Da Gama hearkened to the whispers of supposed Indian "Christians" (they were almost certainly Hindus) round about the harbor insinuating that the Malindians' friendly overtures "neither came from their hearts nor from their good will." Instantly enraged, the Admiral kidnapped one of the King's counselors and simply demanded that he be given the pilot he needed. Apparently concluding that acquiescence would rid him of these mistrustful strangers faster than remonstrance, Malindi's ruler provided such, and on April 24 enjoyed the happy sight of Da Gama's fleet headed out to sea.

Inadvertent beneficiaries of the monsoon, Da Gama's sailors now beheld their sails billow tautly from the masts as their trio of bows (the supply ship having been long since emptied and burned) cut a rapid north-easterly course toward the Malabar coast. As if to give further encouragement to men so far from home, they were soon treated to the sight of the north star rising above the horizon for the first time in months, though they were now putting yet more miles between themselves and Portugal at a prodigious rate. Less than three uneventful weeks later, the Ghat mountains of western India loomed ahead through thunderstorms and squalls, and after a short run down the coast to check landmarks, their pilot informed them that they were even now approaching the fragrant city they had been so anxiously seeking. Anchoring a cautious distance from the coast, Da Gama now made use of a *degredado* to test the local reception. The term refers to prisoners who had been convicted of crimes that warranted the death penalty or permanent exile from Portugal, and who were given a chance to have their sentences voided if they agreed to act as expendable scouts — or, more accurately, as guinea pigs — on voyages of exploration. Accordingly they would be sent ashore wholly alone in order to determine with their lives whether the waiting natives were friendly or hostile, pagan or Muslim, vegetarian or cannibalistic. It is difficult to imagine a more perilous career, and the very circumstances of their employment explain why so few testaments from these figures survive. On this occasion, the *degredado* Da Gama sent ashore was taken immediately before a pair of Tunisian Moors who could speak both Castilian and Genoese, and who were thus unlikely to mistake a Frank for a Turk. Indeed, their famous first question to this convict-scout indicates that they immediately suspected that their world was about to change, and not necessarily for the better: "May the Devil take thee! What brought you hither?" The *degredado's* reply — "we came in search of Christians and spices" — might appear dangerously candid, but it pointed up a fundamental misconception that Da Gama and his men were to blithely carry about with them through the whole of their three month stay at Calicut and indeed were to haul back intact with them again to Portugal. They believed, quite correctly, that there were groups of Nestorian Christians living in India. Where the Portuguese erred was in wishfully assuming that these unorthodox co-religionists of theirs constituted the majority of the population in the great cities of India, when in fact they were but a tiny minority. Thus the *degredado*, like his commander, was tramping about on much thinner ice than he realized.

It was this same misperception that led Da Gama into an act of unwitting idolatry. When, after almost a week of parlaying, he finally came ashore himself on May 28th accompanied by thirteen of his men and all the pomp the Portuguese could display, he found himself conveyed toward the King of Calicut's residence in a palanquin surrounded by an Indian honor guard and immense throngs of gaping onlookers. Progress was slow through this "countless multitude anxious to see us," and at one point the procession hove up in front of a temple which Da Gama immediately decided was a Christian church. What better place than this to say a prayer of thanksgiving for his safe arrival and so-far cordial reception? Of course some things about this "church" looked a bit odd — instead of a cross, its entrance was dominated by "a pillar of bronze as high as a mast, on the top of which was perched a bird, apparently a cock." And the murals inside, which "they said represented Our Lady" and various saints, were, notes our chronicler uneasily, "painted variously, with teeth protruding an inch from the mouth, and four or five arms." The truth was, of course, that they were in a Hindu temple gazing at an image not of the Madonna and Child, but of Devaki nursing Krishna. Heedless of his mistake, however, and thinking that Nestorians were bound to have their own odd ways of depicting the Holy Family, Da Gama was already dropping to his knees and motioning for his comrades to do the same, a directive that prompted one nervous *fidalgo* to declare in a loud whisper that "if these be devils, I worship the true God!" — a lack of worldly sophistication that caused his ever-confident Admiral to smirk in derision.[11] And here we can pause and admire a small but pointed historical irony: because it was in part their belief in the great power, enormous extent, and vast population of the Prester's Ethiopian kingdom that led the Portuguese to grossly overestimate the number of Christians in the East generally and to take everything that wasn't obviously a mosque to be a church, it is no exaggeration to credit the Prester John legend with literally driving Vasco Da Gama to his knees before the very heathen gods whose idols he was already plotting to smash and overturn.

Once he and his men were granted an audience at the palace of Calicut's monarch — the Samudri Raja, or King of the Sea — the explorer's more secular *faux pas* were put on display. For example, it turned out that he had brought the wrong kind of gifts altogether, since the samples of cloth, hats, foodstuffs, and wash-basins that he offered up were more appropriate tributes for a primitive hunter-gatherer than the ruler of a sophisticated mercantile nation. Thus when "the Samorim" and his courtiers "saw the present they laughed at it, saying that it was not a thing to offer to a king, that the poorest merchant from Mecca, or any other part of India, gave more, and that if he wanted to make a present it should be in gold, as the king would not accept such things." At this rebuff our chronicler relates that Da Gama "grew sad," which is surely a euphemism for his usual boiling anger at any check. Eventually the navigator explained away his paltry basket of trinkets by claiming that he was merely his great nation's reconnoitering lookout, and that respectable trade goods would arrive later with another fleet, but the bad feelings that had been established on both sides never wholly dissipated.

When Da Gama attempted to get back to his ships, things only deteriorated further, for the Samudri's functionaries made difficulties about finding rowboats with which he could reach them, and furthermore kept urging him to order his vessels closer into shore, all of which convinced the Admiral that "they harbored some evil design" against him. In truth, the Calicut officials were worried that the Portuguese would sail off in a huff without paying the customary duty for use of the harbor, but Da Gama obviously could not conceive that so niggling a complaint could be the real reason that people were interfering with someone as important as he believed himself to be — surely there must be a larger, and darker, design afoot. Of course all this was made worse for the Portuguese by the fact that "fellow Christians" were acting in such a manner, a complaint that must have either mystified or further annoyed the Indian bureaucrats. At any rate, once Da Gama had regained his own decks and an understanding that would allow some actual trade to occur had been hammered out, Portuguese fears began to focus on a more plausible enemy — the many Muslim merchants who had long been doing business in Calicut. Da Gama's men initially worried that the Moors around the Samudri were purposefully mistranslating King Manoel's letters of greeting. Then, after they succeeded in landing some European merchandise, they started complaining that "the Moors only came to deprecate it," and were soon avowing that their very persons were in danger from the infidel, for "when one of us landed they spat on the ground, saying: 'Portugal, Portugal.' Indeed from the very first they had sought means to take and kill us." In effect, the Portuguese came to believe that the minds of the Samudri and his followers were being poisoned against them by a whispering campaign, and thus when, at the beginning of August, the monarch appeared to be delaying the departure of the fleet, Da Gama's men

> did not hold him as culpable as he seemed to be, for we [i.e., the Portuguese] were well aware that the Moors of the place, who were merchants from Mecca and elsewhere, and who knew us, could ill digest us. They had told the king that we were thieves, and that if once we navigated to his country, no more ships from Mecca, ... nor from any other part, would visit him.

What is refreshing about this fear is that it was almost certainly justified, since the last thing the Muslim merchants wanted to see was the repeated return to a spice port of a cultural foe who was now apparently to become a commercial competitor as well, fearing that every ounce of profit they lost would fatten the coffers of misbelievers against whom their brothers had long been waging holy war. But if the Portuguese had good reason to be wary of Moorish designs against them, the accusation that the Muslim traders were making was in turn perfectly true, for the Portuguese had no intention of sharing the spice trade with enemies of Christ, and — as they would demonstrate within a very few years — every intention of monopolizing the entirety of Indian Ocean shipping into their own hands. In the shorter term, though, Da Gama's historic visit to Calicut ended in much the same way as had his encounters in East Africa. Accusations were leveled at the Samudri, hostages were kidnapped and taken aboard the European ships, cannons were fired in anger at approaching boats deemed to be hostile, supposed spies were tortured until they "confessed" that "treasons" were afoot, the commander became increasingly incensed. It was all quite dismally familiar, with Da Gama issuing the following threat as he made ready to leave:

> He warned them at the same time to be careful, as he hoped shortly to be back in Calicut, when they would know whether we [Portuguese] were thieves, as had been told them by the Moors.
> On Wednesday, the 29th [of August, 1498], the captain-major [i.e., Da Gama] and the other captains agreed that, inasmuch that we had discovered the country we had come in search of, [and] also spices and precious stones, and [since] it appeared impossible to establish cordial relations with the people, it would be as well to take our departure.[12]

The excitement stirred by Da Gama's reappearance off Portugal in July of 1499 was intense and headily optimistic, for his ships had returned bearing not only a fortune in spices (though the cargo by later standards was puny) but also the completely erroneous information that India teemed with Christians eager to bow their knees to King Manoel. Thus by March of the next year a second and much more massive fleet had set out from Lisbon under the command of Pedro Cabral, whose mission was to continue opening up the ports of the Malabar coast to trade — by coercion, if necessary — and to violently rid the Indian Ocean of Muslim competition for that commerce. At Calicut things at first went well for Cabral, for he had brought more suitable gifts for the Samudri (son and successor of the one Da Gama had offended), and the letters he delivered from King Manoel gushing about a grand alliance between two Christian peoples seemed merely to puzzle rather than offend that Hindu ruler. Hostages were duly exchanged as per the Da Gaman manner, the Samudri authorized Cabral's men to begin trading, and a Portuguese "factory" — as colonial trading posts were then known — was established next to the harbor. For about two months the hulls of the naus and caravels settled deeper into the water as pepper and other aromatics were loaded on board, but then, in mid-December, Cabral received news that a Muslim ship currently in port was about to set sail for Jiddah with a cargo of spices. The Portuguese claimed that this departure violated a technicality of their agreement with the Samudri about getting first crack at such precious cargos, but their real distress was at the mere thought of Mohammedans realizing a profit that might otherwise go into Christian coffers. Cabral's seizure of the vessel, however, triggered a riot by the already hostile Muslim merchants in the city during which fifty-four Portuguese were killed and their factory was torched along with a good deal of purchased merchandise. In return, Cabral began burning foreign ships and bombarding the dockyards, reportedly slaying five hundred Indians. Eventually, he worked his way down and then up the coast to the cities of Cochin and Cannanur where, largely due to commercial rivalries among the Malabrian ports, he was allowed to set up new factories and do some further business before sailing home to Lisbon.

Da Gama himself was back in 1502, making his name infamous to Muslims and Hindus alike by perpetrating gratuitous acts of flamboyant cruelty. Intercepting a ship bound for Calicut from Mecca that carried rich pilgrims of that city returning home from the Hadj, he ordered it to be plundered of its considerable wealth and, when that was thoroughly accomplished, declared that he wanted it burned along with its entire complement of passengers and crew, which included many women and children. Upon hearing of this, the Muslim captain urgently asked for an interview with Da Gama and suggested that he take them all to Calicut and offer them up for ransom, which, given their high status in that city, would fetch the Admiral a vast fortune. No, answered Da Gama, recalling the incidents of Cabral's voyage, "alive you shall be burned, because you counseled the King of Cal[i]cut to kill and plunder the factor[y] and the Portuguese," and thus "for nothing in this world would [he] desist from giving [the Muslims] a hundred deaths, if [he] could give [them] so many." At this point, Da Gama's own captains attempted to deter him, "saying that he ought not to choose to lose so great wealth as the Moor offered." This undignified appeal to avarice the explorer dismissed with the neatly inverted Christian notion that "he who spares his enemies dies at his hands" and demanded that his incendiary wish be carried out. This adherence to principle almost undid him, however, since once the Muslim passengers saw that no mercy was to be shown, they pulled out a stash of weapons that had been overlooked by Da Gama's sailors in their original sacking, cut the ropes that imprisoned their vessel, rammed one of the Portuguese ships, and proceeded to engage her crew in hand-to-hand combat with the ferocity of the doomed, "not hesitating to give up their lives to the sword, sooner than to the tortures of fire." It was hours before the Portuguese regained the upper hand and the last Muslims who had hurled themselves into the sea were speared to death from small boats. And yet Da Gama was just getting started. Later in the voyage, while engaged with hostilities against the offending city of Calicut itself, and finding himself in possession of some captured vessels, he ordered his men "to cut off the hands and ears and noses of all the crews," and then had them thrown into a small boat with their feet tied together. Lest these already mutilated prisoners attempt to gnaw their way to freedom, he also directed his sailors "to strike upon their teeth with staves" until "they knocked them down their throats." With his writhing victims now "heaped up upon the top of each other, mixed up with the blood that streamed from them," Da Gama loaded the boat with combustibles, set its sails for shore, and pushed it off bearing a message to the Samudri written upon a palm leaf recommending that "he have a curry made" of the roasted contents.[13]

But however much Da Gama enjoyed such sanguinary witticisms, his day was already passing, for accumulating accounts of his arrogance and nepotism would soon culminate in a decisive fall from grace back home that would prevent him from returning to the Malabar coast for another twenty years. And in any case, King Manoel, who harbored messianic visions of a wholly Christianized East, was anxious to see Da Gama's era of hit-and-run extortion superceded by one featuring a more systematic subjection of the region. Thus the outward-bound fleet from Lisbon in 1505 carried the first Viceroy of what Manoel was now styling the "*Estado da Índia,*" an enterprise that would require bureaucrats as well as warriors. This *Estado*, envisioned as a vast if thinly-stretched network of colonies, dock-works, and factories that would eventually encircle the Indian Ocean, was intended to facilitate two endeavors. It would serve as a beachhead from which the Portuguese could begin driving all Saracens away from the spice trade while they simultaneously reached out to their mysterious but formidable Christian ally, Prester John. And, in at least the first of these efforts the *Estado* proved rapidly successful. Patrolling outward from a makeshift headquarters at the relatively friendly city of Cochin, squadrons of Manoel's caravels now on permanent station in the east employed their superior artillery to sink enough Muslim shipping and intimidate enough Indian princes to create at least a rough and temporary Portuguese monopoly in pepper, cinnamon, and other precious articles. Indeed, Portuguese progress in this regard could be accurately gauged by noting the rising levels of apoplexy the situation caused in Venice.

The Venetians, who had hitherto largely controlled the importation of spices into Europe, were quick to resent and attempt to reverse Manoel's pretensions to this lucrative commerce. As early as 1501, one of their ambassadors who witnessed the return of Cabral's fleet to Lisbon wrote home to warn his city's merchants that they would soon become "like a baby without its milk." He then took it upon himself to approach the Indian envoys whom Cabral had carried back with him and to whisper that Portugal was in fact a rude and marginal sort of place, whereas the real money could only be got by dealing with the more experienced and better-located Serene Republic. What headway he made is unclear, though it is interesting to note that two of these three envoys managed to die on Da Gama's next voyage before reaching home. At any rate, by 1502 Venetian traders in the Levant found to their dismay that there was almost no pepper to be had at either Beirut or Alexandria, a development which panicked not only merchants on the Rialto but also the Mamluk Sultan of Egypt, who that same year audaciously petitioned the Pope to beg that the Portuguese be made to stand down. However, His Holiness, who had already enthusiastically confirmed Manoel's self-proclaimed title of "Lord of the Conquest, Navigation and Commerce of Ethiopia, Arabia, Persia and India," was not about to interfere, forcing the Venetians and the Egyptians to overlook their warring faiths in order to make common cause against the upstart competitor. And so by 1508 the *Estado* was under attack by a combined Egyptian and Indian fleet substantially bankrolled by Venetian ducats,[14] and a solid victory that year temporarily lifted the pall of gloom that had settled over the Grand Canal. In early 1509, however, ships commanded by the *Estado's* Viceroy effectively destroyed this multi-national flotilla, ending any mortal threat to Portugal's eastern empire until the arrival of the Dutch and English in the following century.

Their economic fortunes secured, the Portuguese could now prosecute their other cherished purpose of seeking out Prester John in his Ethiopian stronghold, a project to which the *Estado's* next Governor — the remarkably successful Afonso de Albuquerque — had already turned his hand. (Albuquerque and his immediate successors were styled "Governors" — there was not to be another Viceroy until 1524, though the difference between the two offices was largely nominal). In 1506, while still a mere squadron commander, he had supervised the landing of a trio of scouts at Malindi, in what is now southern Kenya, with orders to make their way overland to Abyssinia. Leaving nothing to chance, he saw to it that one of the Portuguese among the party underwent circumcision so as to pass without suspicion through the intervening Muslim territory. Indeed, we can read his final orders to this expedition as a projection of his own can-do spirit upon less able men, for he ordered that after scrutinizing the Prester's realm they were simply to make their way back to Portugal by way of Timbuktu and the Senegal River, as if the intervening Sahara would prove a mere inconvenience. Not willing to accept defeat, when these travelers reappeared in Malindi two years later with no success to report, he promptly hauled them northward to the more promising Somali plains and sent them marching inland once again.

Albuquerque soon became the chief magistrate an *Estado* that, thanks largely to his own martial daring and tactical brilliance, eventually arced up from Sofala in south-east Africa, eastward through Ormuz on the Persian Gulf and down to the very tip of the Indian subcontinent. Albuquerque's attacks were so audacious that he occasionally could not long hold a city that he had captured with the aid of surprise, but in most cases, as with Ormuz and then Goa — which became the *Estado's* permanent capital — he soon came back and finished the job. Known as "the Terrible Afonso" by enemies from Africa to Malaysia, he was as capable of committing an atrocity as Da Gama, though one gets the distinct impression that he did not enjoy it and saw cruelty as a tool that a wise commander uses sparingly rather than as the first retort to any small frustration. Returning to Goa in 1512 from a fresh conquest that had extended the Portuguese writ as far east as Malacca, he found waiting for him a man accompanied by a small family retinue and a very large claim. The fellow called himself Matthew, and insisted he was an envoy from no less a personage than Queen Eleni (or Helena), dowager regent of Ethiopia and guardian of the twelve-year-old *Negus*, Lebna Dengel. True, this Matthew's features were much more middle-eastern than African — a fact that fueled enduring suspicions among some that he was a Muslim spy — but he had in his possession a letter addressed from Eleni to King Manoel that made reference to the Governor's twice-dispatched emissaries of half-a-decade before, who apparently had found their way to Abyssinia after all. Its authenticity thus established, the remainder of the missive could not help but ignite Albuquerque's own millenarian imagination, a cast of mind he shared with the sovereign whom he had hitherto served so spectacularly well. The Queen regent continued: "We are therefore sending Matthew, our ambassador, with orders to reach one of your Indian ports and tell you that we can supply you with mountains of provisions, and men like unto the sands of the sea!" The purpose for which this aid was offered chimed in perfectly with Albuquerque's own most cherished ambitions, for here was Eleni reporting that though "the Lord of Cairo is building ships to fight your fleet," she would contribute to the Portuguese cause "so many men ... as to wipe the Moors from the face of the earth! We by land, and you, brothers, on the sea!" Finally, as if privy to King Manoel's exalted sense of his own cosmic destiny, she insisted that "now is the moment come for the fulfillment of the promise made by Christ and Holy Mary, His Mother, that in the last time there would arise a king among the Franks who would make an end of all the Moors!" Accompanying this electrifying parchment was a small black crucifix that Eleni declared had been fashioned from the wood of the True Cross, as if to place a seal of unimpeachable divinity upon her call to Christian alliance and holy war.

It was not long before Albuquerque was writing his own excited letter to Manoel, telling him that "if Your Highness could but see what is going on in India since it became known that this was an ambassador from Prester John, it would seem to you as the portent of some great change, so dismayed are the [Muslims] of India. May it please Our Lord that this should be the beginning of the ruin of the house of Mecca." Accordingly, the Governor sent Matthew and his entourage off to Lisbon by the next homebound fleet. And though Albuquerque's jealous enemies would make that voyage to Europe a living hell for Matthew and his entourage, once there King Manoel would receive Eleni's cross from his hands on bended knee with tears of joy flooding his eyes.[15] A year later Matthew would find himself on a vessel returning to India, accompanied by a hoard of splendid gifts for Prester John, a prestigious ambassador to his court, and a hand-picked group of supporting experts and artisans, including a mild-mannered, open-minded priest by the name of Francisco Álvares. It seemed as if the first official embassy from Portugal to Ethiopia was going to be a grand affair, lacking nothing that befitted the first contact between two great Christian monarchs who intended to launch a new Crusade together as allies and brothers.

Back at Goa, however, apocalyptic fantasies had already lured Afonso de Albuquerque into precipitous action. Once he read Queen Eleni's letter, he was consumed by the desire to immediately accomplish what had long been a Portuguese priority — to invade that Muslim redoubt, the Red Sea, and to make at least preliminary contact with the subjects of Prester John. It was a sobering fact, of course, that no European hull had ever breached that narrow, nearly land-locked ocean, and that its winds were known to be desiccatingly hot and perilously fickle. The Governor, however, had every reason to be confident of his own abilities and to trust to his remarkable luck — if indeed he attributed his charmed tenure in the East to no grander force mysteriously at work. Had he not, after all, made a career of subduing Muslims and other heathens across three thousand miles of largely uncharted ocean and alien shore? And here was Queen Eleni's letter, offering allegiance, beseeching aid, and warning of looming dangers to both their nations. The Bible itself had prophesied that one day Ethiopia would "stretch out her hands unto God" — did not the arrival of Matthew indicate that the appointed hour had now arrived? Surely, given such signs, the only sin would be hesitation, the only apostasy caution. Accordingly, with the Prester's ambassador still en route to Lisbon, he gave orders for his fleet to make ready.

Three

The Lake of Fire

When Afonso de Albuquerque put out to sea from Goa on February 7, 1513, he was a man who had just received new incentives to complete a difficult and thus long-delayed chore. The twin aims of making contact with Prester John and finishing off the last vestiges of the Muslim seaborne spice trade had been at the heart of Portuguese strategy in the East from the beginning, but if these projects had languished while the Terrible Afonso had been distracted elsewhere, he could rightly claim that what had diverted his attention were golden opportunities from which he had consistently forged impressive victories. But now that the Portuguese flag flew at both the eastern and western extremities of the Indian Ocean, and now that Ethiopia had sent the Governor an eloquent written appeal for aid and alliance, it was the Red Sea alone that filled the horizon of Albuquerque's ambitions. That body of water was crucial to both the search for religious allies and the monopolizing of commerce for straightforward reasons of geography. As to the first enterprise, Prester John's Christian Ethiopia was said to occupy the southern half of its western shore, though oddly that great monarch apparently controlled no part of it with a navy of his own despite his many other reputed powers. As to the second, while the Red Sea functioned as highway for spice shipping emerging from or approaching Egypt, at its southern end it was connected to the wider Arabian Sea only by the narrow Bab-el-Mandeb, or "Gate of Tears," a strait barely 20 miles wide with an island obstructing the middle of it. Once through it, Muslim captains bound for the orient could evade Portuguese patrols by trusting themselves to the broad emptiness of the Indian Ocean or by hugging literally thousands of miles of involuted coastline. But if Albuquerque could, as he put it to his king, "lock the gate of the Straits," then the sea lanes would be closed to any traffic which the Portuguese chose not to allow. With Mohammedan coffers thus emptied, and European armies marching alongside newfound Ethiopian allies, Islam could at last be crushed.

The Gate of Tears was guarded by the city of Aden, located at the southern

THE RED SEA IN THE EARLY SIXTEENTH CENTURY. The Portuguese hoped that, with the aid of the Christian monarch they knew as "Prester John," they could gain control of it and subsequently strike at the heart of Islam.

tip of the Arabian peninsula in modern-day Yemen, one hundred miles to the east of the Straits. The exquisite perfection of Aden as a defensive position cannot be exaggerated. It is separated from the mainland by a narrow isthmus of land which, three miles from shore, widens to encompass the caldera of an extinct volcano. The western semicircle of this caldera is intact; the eastern half has collapsed and been replaced by a beach. In the sixteenth century the city itself sat wholly inside the half-ruined cone, its back thus protected by a curving ring of jutting peaks, while its beachfront was spanned by a defensive wall that connected on either end with the last ramparts of the surrounding crater, forming a perfect half-moon of impregnability. A siege of Aden was impossible, for though located in an extremely arid climate, an ancient and sophisticated network of cisterns kept it plentifully supplied with water. Furthermore, there were watchtowers erected on each of the highest crags of the sheltering caldera, so surprise attacks upon this natural fortress were also out of the question. The political position of the city mirrored its physical situation, for while its Governor owed some notional fealty to the Sultan at Cairo, he was practically independent, his considerable wealth guaranteed by the vessels that either transshipped their cargoes in his harbor or put in for food, water, and other necessities. Those seeking respite at Aden must have comprised a diverse group, for they included both the hardened crews of mercantile ships involved in the spice trade and diligent pilgrims performing the Hadj, or ritual journey to Mecca that able-bodied Muslims were expected to undertake at least once in their lives. The *Estado's* Governor was equally anxious to put an end to both kinds of voyages, but one could not construct a more discouraging sight for the eyes of any would-be attacker than the interlocking natural and man-made defenses of Aden.

Albuquerque dropped anchor in the city's harbor on Good Friday, March 25th at the head of an armada that carried 1700 Portuguese and 1000 native Indian fighting men within its twenty-four hulls. He was immediately able to see that the citadel's beachfront wall was in fine repair and crowded with soldiers, its battlements well supplied with artillery. Still, with more hope than expectation, he opened negotiations with the Sheik, asking him if he was inclined to simply surrender — he was not. Thus, the next morning at sunrise, Albuquerque's men began to make their way toward the beach in small boats. Right from the beginning, things began to go wrong for the Portuguese. The harbor proved shallower and rockier than expected, forcing men to wade ashore, whereupon many of those who were carrying matchlock rifles discovered that their powder had become too wet to use. Nevertheless, under steady assault from the top of the wall, the invaders made their way forward carrying scaling ladders that had been specially constructed to carry four to six men abreast. Breaking into three parties, one under the direction of Albuquerque himself, the other two headed by trusted lieutenants, the Portuguese pushed this scaffolding against the defensive rampart and began their perilous ascent.

Ironically, it was an initial success that led directly to the Portuguese defeat. Groups of soldiers from both of the lieutenants' groups managed to gain the top of the wall in surprisingly short order, whereupon some of them sent up a cry of "Victory, victory! Portugal! Portugal!" Meanwhile, the Governor's squadron, finding to their chagrin that their ladders were too short for the section of the bulwark they were attempting to scale, abandoned their own position and rushed over to join their fellows upon those latticeworks that had already carried some to the top. One cannot underestimate how important it was to a *fidalgo's* chivalric prestige to be among the first to scale an enemy's battlements — there was no renown to be had by being the last man over. As a result, the pair of effective ladders quickly became overcrowded with too many men attempting to beat their comrades to the top and before long they snapped and folded under the combined weight of flesh and steel. Albuquerque, remaining cool under fire and misfortune, now gave an order that sounded reasonable but which had dire consequences, ordering men to get between the broken ladders and the wall and to prop up the former with their halberds. A halberd is a sharpened pike with double axe-heads sprouting from either side of the shaft just before the point, making it a weapon with which one could both stab and chop. Sticking the business end of these into the interstices of the scaling ladders worked for a while, but when they ultimately failed to carry the weight of those rushing once again to martial glory the result was both wall-scalers impaled on halberds and halberdiers crushed by falling men in armor. The Portuguese means of ascent having now utterly collapsed, those of the attackers who had attained the rampart's top were either quickly overwhelmed by the city's many defenders or forced to jump for their lives.[1] Albuquerque's men splashed back in disorder to their boats, reddening the shallow waters of the harbor as they retreated.

The Governor did not attempt a second assault on Aden, which was inconsistent with his usual iron-hard determination to best his foes no matter how unpromising the battlefield, but explainable when one considers his hopes concerning Prester John. Aden was indeed a strategic lynchpin, but there was a chance that the Ethiopians might be able to furnish the Portuguese with a naval base that was actually *inside* the Red Sea. If this were the case, then suddenly the importance of the fortified city he had just failed to conquer became significantly lessened. It was thus the two-fold nature of Albuquerque's mission — war against Muslims, diplomacy with the Prester's people — that in all likelihood convinced him to push on toward the Gate of Tears after merely burning a few Saracen ships in Aden's harbor. Once arrived at the Bab-el-Mandeb, he saw no reason to disguise Portugal's first incursion into the Red Sea, and passed through the Straits with pennants flying and cannons firing. His reasoning was that no matter whether the Sultan of Cairo — hearing reports of the infidel's brash entrance upon his home waters — would be intimidated into

THREE. *The Lake of Fire*

keeping his fleet in port or provoked into sending it out, either decision would eventually translate into Portuguese domination of the waterway.

Albuquerque had always been a lucky commander as well as a bold and brilliant one, but once he ventured within the Gate of Tears, his close bond with the goddess Fortuna seemed to dissolve. The winds of the monsoon, which he was counting on to blow him northward toward the enemy ports of Jiddah and Suez, failed unexpectedly early, leaving him no choice but to pull up at the Kamaran Islands, barely a sixth of the distance toward the ocean's northern end. To find oneself becalmed during a Red Sea summer is to slowly roast to death. The desert sun, directly overhead, shines with its full brilliance nearly every day, while the flat, placid water reflects back an equally brutal and inescapable glare. The Red Sea, because its connection with the Indian Ocean is so restricted, because no rivers of any size empty into it, and because the sun's work of evaporation proceeds without obstructing cloud cover, is one of the hottest and most saline stretches of ocean water in the world. The average summer surface temperature of the sea at the Kamaran Islands is 86° (30° C)—there was no relief to be found in that briny soup. Albuquerque attempted to keep his men busy by having them beach and careen some of their ships, but such labor in those conditions was often a fatal undertaking. Luckily the largest of the Kamarans offered some fresh-water springs, but the available food was almost entirely in the form of shellfish, and never of a sufficient quantity for such a large company. Before long the men were toppling palm trees to gnaw desperately at their roots. Marooned from mid-May to mid-July, over 500 of the Portuguese and nearly all the Indian troops perished (a differential that says much about the hierarchy of hunger under the fleet's Iberian captains). By the time the southward monsoon began to make an escape possible, the Governor had gathered a bit of intelligence from local sheiks, but such was his only accomplishment. By far the most exciting event during their captivity had arrived in the form of a vision that had appeared to the west, above the Ethiopian coastline:

> While we were all there lying at anchor waiting for the favor of Our Lord, there appeared over against the land of the Prester John a cross in the heavens, very clear and resplendent.... And when a cloud passed over it, the cloud was rent in several parts without touching the cross or covering its clearness. This cross was beheld by everyone in the fleet, and all with many tears fell down on their knees and worshipped it.[2]

Was this a sign from on high informing the Portuguese that victory against the Saracens would only be theirs once they sought out their Christian brothers awaiting them in Abyssinia? Undoubtedly some interpreted it as such, but that did not change the fact that by then the armada's survivors were simply too reduced and exhausted to attempt anything more ambitious than an escape from that lake of fire at their first opportunity.

Just how profoundly Albuquerque felt he had failed, and what a stain he considered his Red Sea invasion to be upon his otherwise sterling record, can be gained from the fact that once he returned home, he did something quite uncharacteristic. When writing his reports to King Manoel, the usually plain-speaking Governor became evasive, mealy-mouthed, and mendacious. Instead of admitting that the whole affair was a cursed fiasco, he wrote in a way that seemed to deny that he had intended to attack Jiddah and Suez even had he been granted the opportunity to do so. Also, he made no mention at all of the harrowing losses among his men to hunger and dysentery on the Kamarans. Instead, his report is filled with, as one scholar puts it, "minute descriptions of everything that grew, crept, crawled, or walked along the Red Sea shores," as if his whole purpose had been taxonomic and anthropological rather than martial. Finally, he asserted that the mere presence of a Portuguese fleet in the Red Sea, no matter its helpless state and feckless wandering, must be remembered as "the greatest blow [against] the house of Mohammed for a century."[3] All of this bluffing and circumlocution was to no avail, however, since Albuquerque's enemies back at Manoel's court briefed their sovereign fully on how futile and embarrassing the whole affair had been. Ironically, it was likely the combination of such transparent evasions with the Governor's usual blunt manner of addressing his king that finally did him in. In his more characteristic vein, for instance, he was fully capable of complaining pointedly to his royal master: "But do not require of me every year an account of what I am doing as if I were a tax-gatherer, because four ill-mannered fellows, who sit at home like idols in their pagodas, have borne false witness against me, but [rather] honor me, and thank me." And, if it was just within the margin of safety to blame the King's advisors for bad decisions emanating from the throne, at times the Terrible Afonso wrote from outside that rhetorical shelter: "I must say to you, sire, that you must be careful of the orders and directions you send, for each year ones arrive which contradict the others, and each year you change your mind and [send me] new counsel. India is not ... something you can play around with."[4] Albuquerque's enemies at court were always warning Manoel that the preternaturally successful Governor, having conquered so much territory, meant to crown himself emperor of his own eastern empire. Such fears, though utterly without merit, weighed upon Manoel. He managed to contain them as long as Albuquerque kept winning, but a dangerous and insubordinate rival whose luck had run out was someone whom the King allowed himself to believe he could well do without. Soon after hearing of the Red Sea debacle, Manoel appointed the favorite of Albuquerque's detractors as the new Governor of India.

As the question will have a very direct bearing on how and when Father Álvares finally got to Ethiopia, it is worth asking why Albuquerque possessed such vehement enemies in the first place. The answer involves the fact that there were two warring factions at Portugal's court, each espousing a diametrically opposed ensemble of ideas about how the nation's new eastern realms should be administered and about what, ultimately, they were good for. On one side stood what might be called the Millenarians, who included Albuquerque and, most of the time, King Manoel himself. These men believed that Portugal had been allowed to discover the sea road to India and beyond in order to fulfill a grand Christian destiny. Their overall goals were both wide and lofty, encompassing an Eastern world that, under the influence of Iberian religion, law, custom, and commerce, would eventually emerge from its barbaric self-imprisonment and turn its face toward truth and light. In the orient of their humanitarian imagining, false religions such as Islam and Hinduism would be gradually eradicated by both arms and example until, perhaps after a generation or two of brutal conquest and patient evangelization, the world might be adequately prepared for the second coming of the Savior. On the ground and in the near term, this view favored the steady acquisition of new territory for the crown, the building of military forts and other infrastructure, the pursuit of exploration, the support of Christian missions, and — most gallingly to some — the curbing of private ventures promising immediate monetary gain for the sake of a coordinated and far-flung project of gradual empire-building. Arrayed against these high-minded dreamers were the Exploitationists, who saw the *Estado da Índia* as a rich orchard of heathen wealth ripe for immediate picking. They envisioned independent captains of strong mettle braving hazards for the sake of quick enrichment, and thus viewed the bureaucratization of the *Estado* as a wrong-headed policy that would lessen profits in the name of a self-important delusion. What was the point of spending money on building fortresses, time on negotiating with infidels, or deck space on hauling priests about when the surest way to riches was a fast caravel, loaded cannons, and a nose for targets of opportunity? To these advocates for a regime of what amounted to soft piracy, Albuquerque was their great enemy, for as we have seen he fully bought into the eschatological version of Portugal's future, and thus tolerated no freebooting among the captains who plied the waters of, as he viewed it, his and God's *Estado*.

It is this ideological battle which explains why Ethiopia's ambassador to Portugal, the man known only as Matthew, suffered a journey from India to Lisbon and back again that was profoundly schizophrenic. At Goa, Albuquerque treated Matthew as if he were in his own person the royalty he only represented, feasting him and decking him out with finery and luxuries. However, when he was sent on to Portugal by the Governor in company with effusive letters to King Manoel, the ships that carried him were commanded by captains who had long chafed at the Terrible Afonso's strict control over their itch to raid and plunder independently. Accordingly, Matthew immediately found himself at the mercy of persecutors who accused him of being a Muslim spy, deprived and humiliated him at every turn, and sexually assaulted the women in his entourage. Once docked at Lisbon, though, his world inverted itself once again, for as we have seen, Manoel was as elated as Albuquerque to behold an ambassador from the fabled Prester John standing before him in the flesh. Furthermore, when it came time to choose a Portuguese ambassador to accompany Matthew back to Ethiopia, the King picked Duarte Galvão, a *fidalgo* best described as the Grand Old Man of the Millenarian faction, and one whose interest in Matthew would therefore have been both keen and sympathetic. By the spring of 1515, however, when a fleet was readied upon which the pair of envoys could journey East, the Exploitationist cabal had succeeded in poisoning Manoel's pliable mind against Albuquerque, and hence that armada was commanded by his confirmed enemy, the spectacularly incompetent Lopo Soares de Albergaria, who also carried orders declaring him the *Estado's* new Governor. The presence on board of the venerable Galvão probably prevented Matthew from again being physically abused as he had been on the westward journey, but it was clear that Lopo Soares had nothing but contempt for everyone and everything connected with Prester John. To the new Governor and his circle, the whole idea of reaching out to Ethiopia was another impractical scheme of that daydreaming despot, Albuquerque. Any money spent on sending ships into the Red Sea to chase down the world's shyest Christian meant less money to spend on projects that stood at least a chance of paying off, and thus anyone connected to the enterprise was as good as a thief. Accordingly, toward the end of the voyage when the fleet was sailing down the Indian coast, Lopo Soares flatly refused Matthew's entreaties that they put into shore so that his suddenly ailing nephew might be seen by a physician.[5] The boy's subsequent death certainly instilled a hatred of the *Estado's* new leader in Matthew, and possibly contributed to the envoy's gradual mental unhingement, which would later manifest itself in ways that would put Portuguese lives in danger. In all justice, though, Matthew had by this time little reason to love the people among whom his Queen had sent him on a mission of hope and fellowship.

One of the reasons that Matthew was suspected of being an agent of Islam had to do with the fact that while it was generally understood that Ethiopians were black people, Matthew himself was several shades whiter. His exact ethnic heritage remained obscure, but there is some evidence that he might have been an Armenian by birth. How he found himself living in Abyssinia and how he became the trusted agent of Queen Eleni are equally unclear, though the Dowager in her letter to Albuquerque took pains to explain that while he was not originally a man of her country, he unquestionably spoke for her nation's interests. Still, the truth was he looked more like a Saracen than an Ethiopian. To the Millenarians, on the other hand, Matthew's whiteness was a genuine comfort. Almost all the literature and iconography concerning Prester John, even that which insisted that he ruled Ethiopia, painted him as an unambiguously white man. Thus to find that the only sanctioned ambassador from that

Three. *The Lake of Fire* 55

monarch's supposedly advanced and enlightened land was a Caucasian chimed in comfortingly with the racial assumptions of the time. It kept alive the hope that though the mighty Prester John might include black Africans among his subjects, he himself and perhaps his court and maybe even his most important citizens might be as fair-complexioned as any European. Matthew's skin was thus a text that opposed Portuguese political factions read in radically divergent ways.

Albuquerque received the news of his dismissal as he was sailing home to India from the site of his latest triumph, for in the preceding months he had somewhat erased the bitter taste of Aden by managing to re-plant the Portuguese flag at the town of Ormuz, which was strategically placed at the throat of the Persian Gulf. Moreover, though he had arrived in that harbor accompanied by many ships and men, he had won permission to construct a fortress there by sharp diplomacy and a single targeted assassination rather than through a general slaughter. Because Ormuz constituted one end of the caravan route to Allepo on the Mediterranean, it was crucial to Portugal's fortunes in the East, for even if she succeeded in blockading the Red Sea with the Prester's aid, much of the spice trade could still have been kept in Muslim hands by means of this overland alternative. Even his detractors were compelled to admit that Albuquerque always saw the big picture with unwavering clarity. Now, already in the grips of the dysentery that would soon kill him, he read the dispatches ordering him to step down in favor of Lopo Soares with bitter resignation. As his son tells it, "He lifted up his hands and gave thanks unto Our Lord and cried: 'In bad repute with men because of the King, and in bad repute with the King because of the men, it were well that I were gone.'" Fervently wishing for a last glimpse of the Indian city he had transformed into Manoel's eastern capital, he hung onto life until his ship had cleared the bar at Goa. After being assisted to the doorway of his cabin, he gazed a final time on the centerpiece of his earthly works and then quietly surrendered to death.[6] Given what Lopo Soares was soon to make of the grand *Estado* that Albuquerque had almost single-handedly constructed, his end was mercifully timed.

Also arriving in India with the new Governor's fleet was Father Francisco Álvares, concerning whose life up until that December of 1515 only scant records exist. We think he may have been born in the provincial capital of Coimbra, and we know that before he embarked for the East he served as chaplain and almoner to King Manoel I, which meant he conducted masses at court and oversaw at least some of the King's charitable distributions. Either Manoel himself or some other courtier must have admired the man, for the office of sole priest on the embassy to Prester John would, even before the fact, have been recognized as a potentially crucial one. At any rate, it proved an inspired choice. The subsequent life of this quietly remarkable cleric has become known to us through his own written account of the Abyssinian expedition, though the section recounting his voyage to India upon Lopo Soares' flagship alongside Matthew and Galvão has apparently been lost. But at this point he does join the larger story of Portugal's first bewildering collision with Ethiopia, and we begin to see his name mentioned alongside others whom need, desire, or chance had cast into the same star-crossed enterprise. For instance, we know that besides Álvares and the pair of ambassadors (i.e., Matthew and Galvão), two other members of the embassy arrived in Goa that winter: Lopo de Vilalobos, the mission's secretary, and Lourenço de Cosmo, who was to oversee the gifts being sent to Prester John by King Manoel. Perhaps not surprisingly, more is known about these gaudy material objects than about some of the men who accompanied them, for they constituted a treasure trove that would not be out of place in a fairy-tale or some legend of piratical adventure:

> There were suits of armor inlaid with gold and silver, costly shields, swords of the most supple steel. For Prester John's repose Manoel sent a magnificent canopied bed, with four fine linen sheets nearly five yards in length, six bulky mattresses stuffed with merino wool, bolsters and pillows embroidered in gold, a woolen blanket embellished with Manoel's armorial bearings. A splendid dining table, a tablecloth of silk and gold, a gleaming dinner service, a brocaded chair [studded] with silver nails, Flemish draperies of silk and gold.... Nor were the spiritual needs of Ethiopia neglected: the ambassadors were to bring altarpieces, organs, bells, devotional pictures, illuminated missals, thirty books of catechism, a thousand volumes of pious works suitable for the young, candles, vestments, and other religious items. And there was much more, to a total value of some 30,000 *cruzados* of gold.[7]

Surely this was a hoard sufficient to prove to Prester John that he was dealing with a kingdom that could well boast of its own wealth and power. The problem, of course, was that it was now under the control of a man who cared very little about its intended recipient, and very much about acquiring wealth for himself. At any rate, the cargo now had to gather dust and the men bide their time for the space of an entire year, since Lopo Soares was in no hurry to complete what he considered the fool's errand begun by his predecessor. Thus Father Álvares, along with Duarte Galvão, Lopo de Vilalobos, and Lourenço de Cosmo scoured the docksides for whatever knowledge they could gain about Ethiopia while attempting to learn something of the Abyssinian language from the increasingly embittered Matthew.

The new Governor's Red Sea armada, when it finally left Goa in February of 1517, seemed almost big enough to render it invincible no matter how unfit its commander might be, for it boasted thirty-seven ships and 5400 men — indeed, its bloated size may have been dictated by Lopo Soares' inward knowledge of his own incapacity as a military leader. He would likely have found reasons to further delay his putting to sea had he not received dispatches via Rome and Lisbon warning that the Egyptian Mamluks had launched a fleet in hopes of repeating their victory of 1507 against the *Estado*, intent this time on a knockout blow. He had been ordered to intercept this force, but as it turned out Soares would twice invoke the exact wording of his instructions as an excuse for laziness and outright cowardice. Meanwhile, the unwise orders given to the Mamluk commander insured that Portuguese India would be under no real threat from these Muslim squadrons. Instead of proceeding directly against Goa and the other Portuguese strong points on the Malabar Coast, the Saracen admiral had been directed to first attack and subdue Aden, whose obnoxious independence Cairo's Sultan was no longer willing to brook. As Albuquerque could have foretold him, this was not something one casually undertook while on the way to doing something else. The result was a bloody and wearying combat in which the rock-ringed city was badly shaken but remained unvanquished, while the decimated Egyptian fleet was forced to retreat back into the Red Sea to Jiddah in order to lick its wounds. And so when Lopo Soares' outsized armada suddenly showed up in Aden harbor a few weeks later its Sheik, knowing that he could not repulse a new attack so soon after the last one, offered to surrender immediately if only the Portuguese would defend him from the expected return of the Mamluks. Incredibly, Soares declined this offer over the collective howls of his captains (many of whom were veterans of Albuquerque's assault), claiming that he only had orders to fight an Egyptian fleet at sea, and that if the city was truly anxious to become a Portuguese possession he would be glad to accept its surrender on his way back to India. Having thus blithely disdained to accept as a gift the prize that Albuquerque had fruitlessly expended precious blood to seize, he sailed his fleet on toward the Gate of Tears. The Sheik, meanwhile, sent prayers to Allah for the miracle of Lopo Soares de Albergaria and quickly began rebuilding his defenses.

Once through the Bab-el-Mandeb, a combination of storms and the Governor's reckless disdain for expert advice began to strip vessels and men from the Portuguese armada. The Red Sea is in places an especially shallow and reef-infested body of water, though limiting oneself to daylight running with a good lookout posted usually sufficed to keep one's ships off the rocks. Soares, however, perhaps in his eagerness to quickly be done with an enterprise for which he had no stomach, gave orders for full sails to be put on throughout the night and ignored the entreaties of the local pilots to keep well clear of shore. Before long, four ships were at the bottom of the ocean with most of their officers and crewmen, including Duarte Galvão's son and some of the fabulous merchandise meant for Prester John. In addition, the vessel carrying Father Álvares and Matthew got separated from the main fleet and found themselves bewildered among the Dahlak Islands, an archipelago tantalizingly close to the Ethiopian shore, where its anxious captain kept it anchored for three weeks. Thus did the priest and the ambassador miss out on the lame and frustrating climax of the main fleet's operations. Pulling up before Jiddah, the harbor city that served Mecca, Lopo Soares seemed to be within inches of a stunning victory, if only he had possessed the nerve to see it through. The town then possessed both an inner and an outer harbor, and while it was true that the navigable channels between the two were few, narrow, and within range of the defender's artillery, the near certainty that the fleet's massive firepower would prevail once the lagoon had been reached argued for risking the maneuver. After all, Mecca, the very seat of Islam, lay within fifty miles of where the Christian vessels were now poised — Albuquerque would have accepted such odds in a heartbeat. Lopo Soares, however, dithered for eleven days, only to finally announce that his orders directed him only to engage in deep-water fights with enemy fleets, not to storm costal cities. After withdrawing, the dispirited and near-mutinous armada managed to make it as far back as the Kamaran Islands before the winds died, inaugurating a repeat of their predecessors' purgatory of heat, thirst, and death.

Eventually, a caravel carrying Lourenço de Cosmo, the embassy's giftkeeper, managed to find the errant ship that held Álvares and Matthew. This latter vessel hauled anchor and proceeded to rejoin the rest of the fleet by means of whatever brief puffs of wind might inch it across the narrow sea, but De Cosmo's caution was apparently overmastered by the proximity of the Dahlak Islands to the Prester's reputed coastline. His plan was to hire a native pilot to take him to any Ethiopian port where he could at least make initial contact with the people whose monarch he had been deputed to shower with riches, but such dutifulness was to be his undoing. Matthew warned him that the Dahlak Islanders were fanatical Muslims, but Laurenço ignored his advice to wait until the mainland could be attempted directly. Stepping boldly ashore, neither his sense of mission nor his proffered gold availed him anything, for he was summarily killed by the natives while his shipmates barely escaped with their lives. Once all the vessels were back sweltering at the Kamarans, the embassy suffered another loss, for Father Álvares was soon obliged to extend last rites to Duarte Galvão, the elderly ambassador whose heart had already been broken by seeing his son's life thrown away. Enfeebled as he was, Galvão had repeatedly begged Lopo Soares to drop him and the rest of the envoys on the Prester's shore, whose mountainous hinterland was just visible to the west, but the Governor would have none of it. Digging the ambassador's shallow grave in the sands of the Kamarans — close beside those of the 800 other Portuguese casualties — Father Álvares must have felt as though he was burying the entire enterprise to which he had once so enthusiastically dedicated himself.

When, in mid-July, the winds allowed the fleet to escape through the Gate of Tears, Lopo Soares decided to reveal to everyone just how hollow had been his excuse for not attacking Jiddah by ordering the sacking of the defenseless town of Zeila on the Somali coast. He then returned to Aden, only to discover that the Sheik, having re-supplied his city and re-entrenched its defenses over the summer, was now strangely unenthusiastic about renewing his offer of surrender. Indeed, the Portuguese were reduced to having to purchase drinking water from this second Gibraltar they might have ruled. After this last humiliation, the fleet merely dispersed, its disgusted captains looking for something, anything to sink, loot, or pillage before they limped back to India. Álvares and Matthew returned to Goa alive, though once there they saw the only surviving officer of the embassy — the secretary, Lopo de Vilalobos — decamp for Portugal in disgust.[8] Of the gifts that had been so carefully transported ten thousand miles in order to more firmly join Manoel and his Abyssinian ally, those that were not rusting at the bottom of the Red Sea or which had not rotted in the heat of the Kamarans were taken by Lopo Soares for his own use or distributed to his cronies. All in all, it looked as if the new Governor of India had done a remarkably thorough job of insuring that the most cherished project of both his illustrious predecessor and his king would never come to fruition.

He whose career lives by the favor of an easily-persuaded monarch, however, is also likely to see it end that way, and such was the fate of Lopo Soares de Albergaria, for King Manoel soon replaced him with a *fidalgo* named Diogo Sequeira. This latest Governor was somewhat more competent than his unmourned predecessor, though perhaps the law of averages alone guaranteed that much. And though he was not a member of the Millenarian party in regards to the *Estado*, it still meant something that the chief Millenarian happened to be the king of Portugal. At any rate, it seems clear that Sequeira came east with orders both to invade the Red Sea once again, and to transport Matthew and whoever might be willing to accompany him to within wading distance of Ethiopia. One of those who remained very willing was Franscisco Álvares, for when Sequeira's flotilla left Goa in order to attack Jiddah in early 1520, he was pacing the same deck with the nervous and morose Abyssinian envoy whose travails he had now shared for five years, and who had been away from his adopted homeland for nearly a decade.

This time around, the fickle winds of the Red Sea began dying as soon as the Portuguese were clear of the Bab-el-Mandeb, convincing the Governor that dropping off the pair of holdouts might be all he would be able to accomplish on this campaign.[9] As his fleet slowly drifted toward the sea's western shore, however, the flagging morale of Sequeira's sailors was suddenly lifted by a spectacle unfolding in the heavens. As Álvares himself tells it, he was lying on his bed in his cabin "when there was a great tumult among the whole galleon's company, and they called [him] to get up and come to see a great sign which was appearing in the sky." He did his best to gain the open decks above, but in the general crush of knees and elbows at the ship's narrow ladders he was prevented from ascending in time, a personal disappointment for which he had a ready, and typically self-deprecating, explanation: "And when I went above there was nothing to be seen, and in this uproar, some giving thanks to God and others weeping for joy, everyone told me how for a good while they had seen a big red cross in the sky, which I for my sins did not see." This apparition was apparently taken by the becalmed sailors to be a heavenly benediction promising great success, for "after seeing this sign nobody slept and everyone talked of this miracle till it was morning and time to celebrate the festival of Easter with bombards and music."[10] But was this scarlet cross above the Prester's land really so straightforwardly benign? Seven years earlier Albuquerque's men had beheld much the same display, and it had presaged only disaster, defeat, humiliation, and death. There would likely have been a few veterans of that previous debacle on board Álvares' ship, but if the priest sought out anyone whose eyes were troubled and downcast that night and inquired why they shunned the general celebration, he kept such conversations to himself.

Certainly Álvares betrayed no hesitation once it became clear that a landing on the Prester's territory was actually going to prove possible. He could have easily declined to disembark, for the Governor, like most of the anti-Albuquerque faction, thoroughly mistrusted Matthew and was thus very reluctant to drop off a priest he admired on an unknown coastline with someone he suspected of being a closet Muslim. When he informed Álvares that he was considering putting Matthew ashore without a companion, however, the cleric's response was unequivocal: "I answered His Lordship that by the said Saturday it had been five years since I had left Lisbon by order of the King our lord, with the intention of making this journey and that this desire of mine had not changed, for it seemed to me that I was serving God and the King." Álvares' trust in Matthew's credentials was, of course, quite justified, though as we shall see the envoy had been away from Ethiopia for so long by this point that those who sent him forth had been replaced by others with quite different motives and priorities, to whom he was now something of an embarrassment. More interesting is the fact that Matthew, who had reason enough never to want to see a Portuguese face ever again, had pointedly asked the Governor that Álvares be landed alongside himself. The request was a testament not only to Álvares' steadfast friendship for the much-abused man, but also to the fact that Matthew's own sense of mission was not quite dead within him. He still apparently wanted to return to his king bearing with him some manner of European, if only to show that his mission unto these strange and turbulent folk had not been entirely in vain. Both men, then, fairly danced with impatience to get on dry land.

On April 9th the fleet came to anchor between two settlements, one hugging the Ethiopian mainland and the other upon an island about "two crossbow shots" from the shore. These were, respectively, the largely Christian town of

Arquiquo and the mostly Muslim city of Massawa, both of which paid annual tribute to the far-distant *Negus*. It took the Portuguese a while to puzzle out the local political situation, however, since the residents of both towns, exercising the usual prudence of costal peoples in uncertain times, had fled to the hills at the sight of the unfamiliar ships, and thus it was not until the next day that a delegation cautiously approached the vessels at anchor. This party, says Álvares, consisted of one Christian and one Moor, and given their uncertainty about who they were "welcoming," one suspects that the pair fully believed only one of them might be returning home that night. In fact, the two religions coexisted in uneasy peace upon that arid costal plain of what is now Eritrea, nominally subject to the Christian king of Ethiopia but fronting a Red Sea that was essentially a Muslim lake. As for the Prester's undisputed territory, it began only at the towering escarpment clearly visible some miles to the southwest, where the edge of the Ethiopian highlands marked a boundary both geographic and religious, level desert giving way to mountainous greenery at the same point where the veneration of Mohammad yielded to the worship of Christ. As it happened, the Governor and the rest of the Portuguese were so glad to see the Christian half of the deputation that the Moor unexpectedly received some collateral friendliness as a result. Sent back in peace and bearing an impromptu load of gifts, this vanguard was soon followed by the "Captain" (as Álvares calls him) of Arquiquo. (A few days hence the Portuguese would enter the mosque of neighboring Massawa and, with the help of its minority Christians, forcibly convert it into a church, their sudden arrival having instantly wrecked the fragile social equilibrium). This Captain reported that he in turn had already sent word to the *Bahr-nagas*, or Ruler of the Seaboard, an official appointed directly by Prester John himself, who would doubtless arrive as soon as the general prohibition upon travel during the octave (i.e., the eight-day period) following Easter had expired. One can imagine that this struck Portuguese ears as just about the most agreeable excuse for a delay they could hope to hear.

Not so scrupulously pious were a group of monks from a nearby monastery, for they began streaming into Arquiquo the next day, explaining "that as soon as they heard say that Christians were in the port, a thing they so much desired, they had begged leave of their superior to come and make this journey in the service of God." There was a joyful meeting between these anchorites and the Governor's landing party on the beach, during which the Ethiopians claimed that "for a long time they had been expecting Christians, because they had prophecies written in their books, which said that Christians were to come to this port; they would open a well in it, and when this well was opened there would be no more Moors there." Of more immediate importance, however, was the fact that several of the monks recognized Matthew and greeted him with gestures of warm respect, "kissing his hand and shoulder, because such is their custom."[11] This caused the Ambassador's immediate rehabilitation in the eyes of all the Europeans who had previously looked askance at him, and a simultaneous shift in their view of the country that lay before them. If Matthew was indeed the real thing, then somehow the whole hitherto speculative and doubtful enterprise was real as well; a life of riches, adventure, and romance now seemed to palpably dangle before anyone bold enough to grasp for it. Immediately there was a rash of desertions as sailors surmised that making their way in twos and threes to Prester John's jewel-encrusted court was immeasurably better than risking passage back through Muslim waters to Goa. It wasn't long before Sequeira realized that he needed to seize control of this giddy moment and re-constitute something resembling an official embassy on the spot. This could only be an act of improvisation, however, for besides Álvares and Matthew only the odd man here and there remained of what had been, only three years previously, a bespoke and committed cadre well-studied in all the pertinent lore concerning Ethiopia and the Prester. The question now was, who exactly to pick from among the far less suitable candidates currently to hand.

Before he could come to a decision, however, word reached the ships that the *Bahr-nagas* had arrived at Arquiquo at the head of two hundred horsemen and two thousand infantry, and thus the Governor had to go immediately ashore for a high-level parlay between, roughly speaking, equals. The Portuguese accordingly set up some tents on the beach where the conference could be held, but difficulties of diplomatic protocol immediately arose. The Ruler of the Seaboard, it seemed, was not willing to travel down the shore to a location where Sequeira would be waiting for him, since such an arrangement would imply that he was a man of inferior rank, bestirring himself for the convenience of one above him. The Governor, shrugging off any annoyance he might have felt and probably still buoyed by his general reception so far, agreed to have the tents moved halfway toward the town and then ensconced himself in the pavilions there to await his host. But it was still not on, for the *Bahr-nagas* yet again refused to bestir himself toward a stationary European, no matter how short the walk might be. Finally, after some negotiations by Matthew, it was decided that carpets and chairs were to be set up on the beach halfway between where Sequeira now was and the edge of the town, and that both men would walk toward this point of finely balanced vanities simultaneously. Now, as many of the Governor's fellow countrymen were notoriously touchy about the punctilios of rank and dignity — Vasco da Gama, for instance, had flattened heathen capitals in answer to far less presumption — it is worth speculating why he took things so calmly. It was not just because he knew his counterpart to be a Christian; rather, it must be remembered that the Prester John legend had prepared the Portuguese to expect an experience in Ethiopia completely unlike those they routinely assumed they would encounter anywhere else in

Africa or other eastern lands. The fabulous Letter and its many elaborations had set them up to believe that they would here be encountering a civilization which was at least the equal of their own, and possibly even its superior. These were to be no leaping, half-simian savages — these were the happy and dignified citizens of the Prester's mighty empire, who like all peoples who had reached such an elevated pitch of civilization, possessed a healthy sense of their own worth. The *Bahr-nagas*'s stubbornness was therefore not perceived as being offensive — on the contrary, it was reassuringly in harmony with the script.

Once the parlay was fairly underway, these good impressions were only reinforced, for the *Bahr-nagas*, a striking brown-skinned figure (i.e., not a black person) sporting, in Arab fashion, a white linen shirt and a turban of the same color and fabric, said just what his guests wanted to hear. He both listened and answered "like a prudent man," and before the interview was over took a cross into his hand and "swore on that on which Our Lord Jesus Christ suffered, in the name of the Prester John and in his own, that he would always favor and help to favor and assist the men and affairs of the King of Portugal and his Captains who came to this port, or to other lands where they might be able to give them assistance and favor, and also that he would take the Ambassador Matthew into his safe keeping, and likewise other ambassadors and people, if the Captain-Major [i.e., the Governor] should wish to send them through the kingdoms and lordships of the Prester John." Of course during all of this friendly talk the *Bahr-nagas* had not the slightest notion who this person "Prester John" might be, but each time the Portuguese pronounced this name, and each time the Abyssinian answered using his sovereign's actual title — "The *Negus*" — and his rightful name — "Lebna Dengel" — both parties no doubt considered such brow-furrowers a mere difficulty of translation and not, as it actually was, the grinding noise of a headlong fantasy just beginning to run aground upon the rocks of a wholly divergent reality. At any rate, the conference ended with a fraternal exchange of gifts and warm feelings on both sides.

Now, says Álvares, many on board the ships "clamoured and asked favour of the [Governor], each man for himself to be allowed to go with Matthew on an embassy to the Prester John, and here they all affirmed by what they saw that Matthew was a true ambassador." Quickly weighing whatever he had so far discerned about the characters of the men crowding about him, Sequeira chose his embassy. Heading it would be Dom Rodrigo de Lima, a personage about whose background little is now known, though much the same must be admitted concerning most of those who went along with him. He was definitely a *fidalgo*— that is, the son of a prominent family — and perhaps hailed from Santarém, a town on the Tagus River. Some details of his character will emerge soon enough, but it seems a reasonable choice to have made, for though overly stiff and stubborn, he was no outright fool. The Governor's choice for lieutenant fell on Jorge d'Abreu, whom subsequent events would reveal to be a more mercurial and choleric man than his commander. D'Abreu appears to have prided himself on his horsemanship, to have kept his appearance smart, and to have cut a rather dashing figure — dashing enough, at any rate, to eventually infatuate the Ethiopian King in a way that would dangerously inflame the expedition's by-then smoldering divisions. Continuing down the list, one João Escolar was to function as the embassy's secretary, while another João — Goncalves, this time — became the interpreter and factor. (As to whether this Goncalves actually knew any of the Ethiopian languages, Álvares is silent; in all probability he was merely versed in Arabic). Seeing to the troupe's health would be a kind of barber-surgeon named Joam Bermudez, whose subsequent trajectory would take him back to Portugal, then to Ethiopia a second time, and finally to Portugal yet again, during which travels he would build a remarkable career on little more than audacious prevarication and prove himself one of the most remarkable self-promoters of all time, and certainly one of the luckiest. As we shall see, before he was done he would manage to masquerade as the Papal administrator of Abyssinia, as the indigenously-appointed head of the Ethiopian church, and even as the Patriarch of Alexandria, annoying, slandering, and interfering with more sober and serious souls at every turn. As of now, though, he was no more than the embassy's bandager and bleeder. Rounding out the party were a dozen others, including a nephew of Álvares,' various servants — some free, some enslaved — belonging to Matthew and Dom Rodrigo, and, somewhat surprisingly, both "Manoel de Mares, player of organs," and "Lazaro d'Andrade, painter." These last choices were not quite as perverse as the perfumers sent sailing to Jamestown, however, for it was known that the Prester had previously — though rather troublingly out of synch with his prevailing legend — requested that western craftsmen be sent to his realm. Little did they know that the *Negus* already kept a small academy of European brush-men in genteel captivity, and that his view of artistic patronage would be found to be disturbingly proprietary. Álvares ends this manifest with himself, acknowledging with his usual modesty the presence of a lone "unworthy priest."

In hurriedly choosing the members of the embassy and assigning them their various titles, the Governor bequeathed to the travelers what can only be called a fatal ambiguity. The way Dom Rodrigo de Lima understood things, Jorge d'Abreu was merely his designated successor in the event of his own death, and held no special status within the expedition until such time as that misfortune transpired. For his part, D'Abreu had heard it differently — he was the party's second-in-command, and thus a figure who could look forward to being consulted about all major decisions, and who could expect his opinions to be taken into consideration by his chief. This confusion concerning D'Abreu's rank, exacerbated by a fundamental clash of personalities between the two men, would result in a festering resentment that would nearly doom

THREE. *The Lake of Fire* 65

the embassy, and which would mightily offend the monarch they were so anxious to impress. If Sequeira left this matter dangerously uncertain, however, he left no doubt at all as to which member of the group held the lion's share of his trust: "the [Governor] here said, in the presence of all: 'Dom Rodrigo, I do not send the father Francisco Álvares with you, but I send you with him, and do not do anything without his advice.'" It no doubt pained Álvares to have to report so self-complementary an injunction; had it been followed more rigorously, the embassy would have saved itself a hefty toll of much worse discomfort.

Men were not the only things that had to be chosen on short notice from among a sadly diminished store, for there remained the problem of what gifts to bring along with the embassy. Such cashes of presents sent from one monarch to another were no mere formality or courtier's nicety — rather, they were often intricate forms of diplomatic communication, telegraphing significant information about the two parties' expectations of each other, and especially about who would be the senior and who the junior partner in their relationship. Thanks to Lopo Soares, however, Manoel's massive gilded epistle to the Prester had been lost in transit. Now, when Rodrigo de Lima and Álvares looked frantically about them, all they could manage was "a rich sword, a rich dagger, four pieces of tapestry, some rich cuirasses, a richly gilded helmet and two *bercos* [i.e., small cannons], four gun chambers, some balls, two barrels of powder, a map of the world, [and] some organs." The repeated use of the word "rich" here seems an exercise in nervous self-persuasion, for in point of fact the embassy which had once been intended to march inland bearing the material proof of Portugal's newfound status as a world power would now leave dragging behind them the sixteenth-century equivalent of a garage sale. As it turned out, their arrival at the court of the *Negus* bearing only such paltry lumber was destined to make just as bad an impression as they feared it would. Ironically the map, which was probably one of the few items actually appropriate to the occasion, was destined to cause a different, though no less serious problem — before, that is, it became the accidental instrument through which the expedition was allowed to return home and, eventually, the entirety of Ethiopian Christianity was preserved from annihilation. Though no one yet knew it, the Europeans were themselves importing something close to a magical object into Ethiopia's supposedly magical kingdom.

Within three weeks of their Easter sighting of that flaming red cross hanging over the Prester's mountains, those Portuguese lucky enough to have been chosen by the Governor were ready to penetrate the ramparts toward which, they now felt certain, that omen had been summoning them. On Friday, April 27th, the embassy and its baggage were disembarked from the ships and lodged by the *Bahr-nagas* in quarters on the outskirts of Arquiquo. Once ensconced there, however, they were informed that nothing further was to occur until

Monday, and for a reason that must have given Álvares and most of the other Portuguese their first taste of doctrinal uneasiness. As the Father explained, "in this county they keep Saturday and Sunday, Saturday for the Old law and Sunday for the New, and therefore we remained [there] both the two days." This observing of twin Sabbaths may strike modern ears as benignly inclusive, but Catholic doctrine insisted that the New Testament had superseded the Old, not that the two were to collaborate in sculpting the weekly rhythms of Christ's people. Back in Europe, such "Judaizing" had been the supposed crime of literally thousands of the Spanish Inquisition's tortured and incinerated victims, and thus anxiety surely accompanied boredom as Álvares and his colleagues cooled their heels over the course of the weekend.

While they waited, Matthew — who, as a voyager returned home after many hard years, admittedly had much to be excited about — became strangely agitated and began urging that the embassy fundamentally change the plan of march they had so recently agreed to. The *Bahr-nagas* had contracted to supply the Portuguese with "riding horses and camels for the baggage," and apparently to accompany them part way toward the *Negus'* capital, but during the enforced wait "the Ambassador Matthew urged Dom Rodrigo and all of us that we should not go with the Barnagais although he was a great lord, and that we should do much better to go to the monastery of Bisam." This was so, he claimed, because "from that place we should get better equipment than from the Barnagais." Given that it seems a dangerously ungrateful matter to spurn aid from the constituted authorities of a country upon whose shore one has just dropped from the skies, it is a real question as to why Matthew even got a hearing, much less eventual acquiescence. Perhaps Dom Rodrigo, like Álvares, felt sorry for the man for having been so despicably treated by Westerners for so long; perhaps his newfound rehabilitation possessed an outsized momentum; or perhaps it was just that Matthew could by now argue in flawless Portuguese. Did the embassy in general — and Álvares, the European closest to him — understand that Matthew was so anxious to get to the monastery of Bizam because that was where, upon his departure from Ethiopia ten years before, he had stored all his worldly goods? Did they think they owed him that much? Whatever the real reason, come Monday, "Dom Rodrigo, doing this at [Matthew's] wish, sent to tell the Barnagais that we were not going with him, and that we were going to Bisam."

The reaction to this startling declaration was interestingly understated. We are told that "the Barnagais, not grieving on this account, went away and left us." Why did he not grieve — or for that matter, thunder mightily? It might be that he was relieved to part company with the embassy, understanding the reasons why Matthew, though a genuine ambassador, was not likely to receive a prodigal's glad reception once he got to Court with his train of "Franks" in tow. Alternatively, he might simply have felt preoccupied by other affairs and thus glad to find the strangers willing to guide themselves toward the interior, for it is a fact that he was fighting constant battles against encroaching Muslim foes all up and down the desert coastline. (And yet he seemed fully cognizant that these were not just *any* strangers). Or perhaps Dom Rodrigo's announcement had instantly convinced him that the embassy was composed entirely of fools, and that they were thus likely to come to a bad end along with anyone unwise enough to aid them. Here again, we can only speculate, but what we do know for sure is that the Portuguese themselves were uneasy about what they had done. As a practical matter, they had only managed to collect "eight horses and no more, and thirty camels for the baggage" from the grandee they had spurned. But more than that, they seem from Álvares' spare account to have understood that by taking this impulsively reckless first step in what was supposed to be a journey important enough to deserve their best-considered wisdom at every moment, they had already outrun whatever luck they might have possessed: "So we were discontented, knowing the mistake we were making in leaving [the] Barnagais to please Matthew."[12]

Hence, the last day of April 1520 saw the Portuguese embassy to the wondrous court of Prester John trudging away from the coast by means of a dry riverbed whose chalky course zigzagged toward the green-speckled slopes ahead. At their back, the fleet that had promised to stay resolutely in harbor until some encouraging word had been heard concerning their progress inland soon scattered at news of a Muslim armada in the offing. In their midst, overloaded beasts of burden brayed and kicked under piles of precious water-skins and gimcrack presents. At their head walked a man whom they had, after many misgivings, taken as their sole guide, and whose behavior, always peevish and impulsive, was becoming more frighteningly erratic with every passing hour he spent under the relentless sun of his regained homeland. As with all hopeful seekers after utopia, the odds were decidedly against them.

Four

Strangers in a Strange Land

    The flat coastal plain, ten miles wide at Arquiquo, over which the embassy first had to tramp, is as arid as any other piece of Red Sea shoreline and a true desert by anyone's definition. By contrast, the Ethiopian Highlands, whose steep eastern ramparts they could see rising before them, are generously watered. A massive geologic uplift whose floor of 5000-foot-high plateaus is punctuated by peaks reaching up to 15,000 feet, it scours enough rainfall from the yearly monsoon between June and September to support, at various elevations, savannah, thick forests, and alpine moorlands. Aptly referred to as "The Roof of Africa," there are some heights upon it lying above timberline, though it is entirely situated between only six and sixteen degrees of the equator. Grandly arcing through this sky-island of grass, farm-field and timber are swift-running rivers that have eroded chasms whose bottoms often lie a thousand feet below the tablelands that drop away precipitously at their lips. One of the grandest of these is the Blue Nile, whose source lies in the mountainsides that slope downward into the massive Lake T'ana, the Highlands' central catchment for their bounty of wind-borne precipitation. The rising of the Blue Nile in Ethiopia had long fed the Crusading fantasies of men like Afonso de Albuquerque, who dreamed of joining European engineering to Abyssinian labor in order to divert the river's early course and thus parch Muslim Egypt into submission. As Father Álvares could now testify, however, the Blue Nile is somewhat of an exception among Ethiopian torrents in that its waters actually reach an ocean. Far more numerous are watercourses that, however full, broad and roiling they appear in the canyons of the high plateau, break forth into the surrounding torrid lowlands only to waste themselves in brackish swamps and meandering arroyos before they can find an outlet to the sea. To the members of the embassy, trudging up just such a dun-colored wash toward the greener peaks beyond, the Prester's realm must have appeared as a vast, inverted vision of the castles of their European homeland — watery battlements surrounded by a forbidding moat of sand and stone.

FOUR. *Strangers in a Strange Land* 69

It was during the noontime halt on this first day of marching, as Álvares was attempting to identify some hardy trees that struggled up from the dry riverbed, that the camp was surprised by the arrival of a stranger on horseback. Our priest's initial reaction to this interloper is significant, because it again reveals to us one of his and his companions' deepest assumptions about what manner of people they expected to encounter as their journey advanced. "[T]here came to us a gentleman named Frey Mazqual," he tells us, "which in our tongue means servant of the cross." (This is close — the actual translation is "Fruit of the Cross"). "In spite of his blackness he was a gentleman, and said he was a brother-in-law of the Barnagais, a brother of his wife. Before he reached us he dismounted, because such is their custom, and they esteem it a courtesy," after which he "came up to us like a well born man, well educated, and courteous." As mentioned before, despite the fact that Ethiopians were understood to be black, Prester John was repeatedly described in print, in art, and in oral tradition as a white man. Thus Álvares' unselfconscious surprise that this person could be both black and a "gentleman" serves to remind us of two things. Firstly, that he and the others in the embassy, given their nation's pioneering role in establishing the African slave trade, instinctively associated blackness with backwardness. And secondly, that they would have expected — or at least hoped — to see the Prester's subjects getting whiter and whiter as they approached his fabled court. What they were actually about to discover, however, was that the farther they left the Red Sea and its Arabic ethnicities behind, and the deeper they penetrated into the Ethiopian Highlands, the blacker and blacker the people they encountered were actually going to become. No doubt for some in the party this would prove a visceral visual blow from which their other, related hopes concerning Prester John would receive a severe bruising. However, for all his initial shock at encountering a gentlemanly black man, Father Álvares was not to be among their number.

This brief passage also tells us something important about how Álvares went about writing his account of the expedition, for it indicates that he began keeping notes right from the beginning of his adventures — notes that preserved the emotions of the moment. When he came at last to translate those running accounts into the more finished prose of his published tome, he obviously took care to convey into the latter some of the immediate feelings captured by the former. We can be sure about this because, taken as a whole, his *True Relation of the Lands of the Prester John* leaves no doubt that he grew to think of the Ethiopians in ways that were essentially color-blind. Certainly any phrases even hinting at the implicit racism of that initial "in spite of" soon disappear, never to return — and yet here the revealing phrase remains, un-expunged despite the writer's evolving reactions toward the black faces that surrounded him. This is a boon to readers of Álvares' text, for it means that when his words convey awe, or confusion, or anger over a particular incident, we can be reasonably certain that he was experiencing those very things at the time, which makes us more intimately his traveling companions than could a wholly retrospective account thoroughly sanitized by considerations of dignity. Álvares' reliance on notes exposing his own frailties and bafflements also renders the story more dramatic, while at the same time testifying to his honesty — perhaps even more convincingly than the complete absence from his pages of any dragons, cannibals, or magical stones.[1]

One person apparently unimpressed with Frey Mazqual's gentlemanly bearing was Matthew, who, as soon as he saw him speaking with Dom Rodrigo, flew into a rage, "saying that he was a robber." Whether he challenged the stranger directly is unclear, but once the embassy's train of mules and camels had been roused and set on their way again, "Matthew, who was in front, left this road which was wide and level and went among thickets and mountains where there was no road, and made the camels go that way, and all of us with them, saying that he knew the country better than anyone else, and that we should follow him." The explanation both for Matthew's strange words and sudden actions is that he desperately wanted the embassy to undertake a side trip to the monastery of Bizam, which contained his personal property. But now Frey Mazqual's arrival had effectively provided the Portuguese with a second guide, and one who would know that the road to the Prester's court did not in any way lead through the alpine religious house that Matthew longed to visit. Unsurprisingly, when Frey Mazqual witnessed Matthew's sudden detour "he said that we were [heading] away from any road, and that he did not know why that man did this. We all began to cry out to [Matthew], because he was taking us through rough country to lose and break what we carried with us, ... traveling where the wolves went." The mounting uproar from the embassy eventually convinced Matthew that he had no choice but to return to the main trail, but the anguish of veering away from his cached valuables led to "a fainting fit during which we thought he was dead for more than an hour."[2] The confused and frustrated embassy, after a lengthy afternoon of rough going, managed to regain the high road by day's end, where they were met by a caravan traveling from the interior to the coast, confirming that they were once again in the proper path toward the country's seat of power.

Sleep brought no peace to the Prester's long-suffering envoy, however, for the next morning Matthew became even more insistent that they ascend the sheer escarpment, at whose foot they had now arrived, toward the isolated pinnacle of Bizam. Frey Mazqual warned the Europeans that "the road to the monastery was such that baggage could not go there [even] on men's backs" but Father Álvares, as he had done once already at Arquiquo, took up Matthew's cause. Whatever arguments he employed, they had the desired effect; the party reluctantly swallowed its fears and "followed the will and fancy of Matthew." Álvares soon came to rue his own powers of persuasion, however, since before many miles had been covered "there [were] great altercations about this traveling, and whether we should turn back to the high road which we had left. Seeing this, Matthew begged of me to entreat the Ambassador Dom Rodrigo and all the others to be pleased to go to the monastery of Bisam, because it was of great importance to him, and that he would not remain there more than six or seven days." To this renewed plea Álvares parenthetically adds, in a rare display of mordant wit, "he remained there forever, for he died there"—the unusual tone explainable by his retroactive dissatisfaction at himself for having acted as advocate for a man he had already ceased to trust. Still, in the moment the priest must have hoped that dubious decisions made from motives of charity would merit divine protection, for he once more spoke on Matthew's behalf and "at my request all decided to do his wish." But things only got worse quickly, fears and tempers rising with every hard-fought yard they ascended, the caravan now clawing and stumbling single-file through

> much more precipitous ground and channels than those of the day before, and larger and denser woods. Going on foot with the mules unridden in front of us, we could not advance; the camels squealed as though sin was laying hold of them. It seemed to all that Matthew was bringing us there to kill us or to have us robbed; and all turned upon me because I had done it. There was nothing for it but to call on God, for sins were going about in those woods: at midday the wild animals were innumerable and had little fear of people.

Just when it looked as if the embassy had reached a tipping point of dread and anger that would earn both Matthew and Father Álvares a trail-side lynching, the party at last gained a more level upland where the thick brush gave way to planted fields and hilly pastures, and where startled farmers and shepherds left their labors to greet them. The general relief was palpable, and Álvares barely had time to notice with a fresh variety of alarm that these approaching rustics were "almost naked, so that all they had showed" when down from the farther heights "there came to us six or seven monks of the monastery of Bisam." Needless to say, this was a variety of Ethiopian that our priest was intensely curious to behold. Several of these anchorites were "very old men" who "from their age and from their being thin and dry like wood" appeared "at first sight to be men of holy life." He also observed that one among the group was even more antiquated than the rest, to whom the others "all showed reverence, kissing his hand," whereupon the Portuguese followed suit because "Matthew told us that he was a Bishop"—though he also testily notes that "afterwards we learned that he was *not* a Bishop." This correction, which seems to partake of his new skepticism toward Matthew, is probably also laden with unspoken relief, since it is doubtful that the man, from a European perspective, looked the part of a prelate. At any rate, these monks quickly took charge of guiding the embassy and providing it with food, and after two days the Europeans were rather comfortably ensconced at a place called St. Michael, one of Bizam's subsidiary monasteries situated at the foot of the last, vertiginous footpath winding upwards toward the main establishment. At this juncture, since it appeared that the embassy was placated and willing to take Matthew at his word that they would all depart again toward the Prester's seat in about a week's time (after such a climb, they were probably thankful for the rest), the courtly Frey Mazqual took his leave of the group, carrying away what impressions of "Franks" we do not know. Little did any of them suspect how quickly they would wish him back.

The sudden respite from hard traveling seems only to have given the Portuguese leisure to vent their accumulated frustrations in proper form, for their first night under thatched roofs also saw the initial irruption of the internecine feud that would eventually come close to dooming the embassy outright. Álvares' account of the fracas is almost maddeningly vague, but again his description may be true to its lived moment in that he does not yet relate it as being part of a pattern with a well-established cast villains and victims.

> And on [that first] night ... Satan did not cease from weaving his wiles, and caused strife to arise among our people, and this on account of the Ambassador's carrying out that which he had to do, and ought to do for the service of God and the King, and for the safety of our lives and honour: [but] ... there were men in the company who were not going to do all that seemed fit to [Dom Rodrigo, and] upon this [dispute] they came to using their spears. God be praised that no one was wounded. [Eventually, though] I made them good friends, blaming them for using such words, since he was our Captain, and that which was for the service of God and the King was an advantage to us all, and that we ought not to do anything without mature deliberation.

The priest does not say who instigated this brief mutiny nor what directive of Dom Rodrigo's provoked him, but given subsequent events, this seems likely to have been Jorge d'Abreu's first outbreak of violent umbrage at the Ambassador's refusal to treat him as the embassy's second-in-command. Here Álvares clearly takes Dom Rodrigo's side, and in future — given D'Abreu's remarkable susceptibility to the sin of wrath — such would generally be the case, though our narrator would also come to deplore the Ambassador's haughty dismissiveness toward his excitable subordinate, as well as his leader's stiffly unforgiving nature.

No sooner had Álvares succeeded in cooling the embassy's heated emotions than he and his fellows received a nasty surprise from the equally feverous brain of Matthew. The envoy had promised a halt in the vicinity of Bizam lasting no longer than a week, with many sacks of food and beasts of burden folded into the bargain, but now he was reading from a different script. In a tumbling rush of lies and excuses, he claimed that he had just written a letter himself to Prester John, to Queen Eleni (the dowager who had originally dispatched him), and to the *Abuna*, or Patriarch, of the Ethiopian church, and

FOUR. *Strangers in a Strange Land*

that any mules for the party's use would only arrive with the answer to this missive, which could not be expected in less than forty days. "He did not stop at this," recounts a scandalized Álvares, but went on to assert that the Bishop of Bizam himself would be sent from Court to escort them to the Prester, and that all must await his appearance, since he would be bringing all needful supplies for overland travel himself. Besides, their guide continued, winter was coming on, and it would last three months, and no one journeyed during that season, and thus they had better buy supplies hereabouts and hunker down for the duration. By "winter" Matthew meant the Ethiopian rainy season, and Álvares admits that "in this matter of the winter" their guide "did not lie, for nobody in this country travels for three months, that is, from the middle of June, July, August, to the middle of September" — though the embassy would in fact wind up doing exactly that, exposing themselves to many weeks of waterlogged misery in their dutiful eagerness to reach the court.

There is little doubt that this latest pronouncement would have led to a final breach between the embassy and Matthew had not dire sickness chosen that very moment to descend in sudden force upon all those gathered at St. Michael, incapacitating them for weeks. Before long "many were in danger of death and often bled and purged," including the band's physician, Joam Bermudez, leaving the rest with "no other remedy." Luckily, though, in a brisk euphemism for what must have been a rather disgusting process to witness "the Lord was pleased that purging and bloodletting came to [Bermudes] of itself," so that the doctor soon "regained his health and thereafter ... worked for the rest of us with all his strength." (Given all the black mischief that Bermudez was eventually to cause on two continents, this image of him assiduously plying his healing art is welcome yet incongruous). Matthew, spared for nearly a fortnight, eventually fell ill as well, whereupon "many remedies were used for him," a regimen which apparently produced dangerously misleading symptoms of recovery. "Thinking that he was already well, and as though delighted and pleased," the impatient envoy "ordered his baggage to be got ready" and left the rest of the writhing embassy to make his way toward Bizam with all haste. Two days later, however, an urgent call for Joam Bermudez's attentions came from farther up the trail, for Matthew had fallen ill again, this time more virulently than before. Álvares, forgetting his grievances against the man when confronted with a sinner *in extremis*, accompanied the doctor on the difficult climb, though he only arrived in time to deliver the last rites: "I confessed him and gave him the sacraments, and at the end of the three days he died, on 23 May 1520." Despite the fact that Matthew's selfish obsessions had nearly wrecked the embassy before it had fairly begun, his death apparently struck the Portuguese as an event requiring whatever pomp they could muster, for "as soon as he was dead there came thither at once the Ambassador, and Jorge d'Abreu, and Joam Escolar the clerk, and a great number of the monks of

Bisam. We took him with great honor to bury him at the said monastery, and did the office for the dead after our custom, and the monks after their custom." Was this in part a propitiatory act by the Portuguese—an attempt to appease the unquiet soul of their closest link to Prester John, a man so traumatized by Europeans that his long-awaited homecoming had only triggered in him a fit of monomania? Perhaps they hoped that by seeing Matthew properly buried providence might quickly guide them to his replacement, for it was not at all clear where they would now look for someone to lead them across the vast stretch of unknown territory that still intervened between themselves and the Prester's capital. The frightening truth was that, less than a month into their journey, the embassy was as becalmed as any vessel sweltering beneath the doldrums of the Red Sea.

At first the dazed Portuguese decided to passively wait for the promised Bishop of Bizam to appear, but as week passed into week there was "no news of the arrival of the said Provincial" and "we were thus without any remedy, and had been waiting for a month ... and we did not know what to do." At last, they decided that they had no choice but to apply somehow to the *Bahrnagas*, the official whose protection and guidance they had so recklessly spurned upon the beach at Arquiquo. It was a hefty dish of crow to chew upon, but the only alternative seemed to be to "remain there and perish." When the monks of Bizam got a whiff of this plan, however, they heatedly remonstrated with Dom Rodrigo, swearing up and down that the Bishop was only ten days away and even insisting upon hearing "an oath from all of us on a crucifix that we would wait for the said ten days" before accepting anyone else's assistance in moving towards the court. It seems clear that the monks thought some great advantage would accrue to their order if their Bishop were the one to take charge of the Europeans and introduce them to the *Negus*. At this point, however, the specifics of the Abyssinians' domestic politics were beyond Álvares' grasp, and so he recounts the monks' extreme reluctance to hand over their guests to another party as a vaguely sinister mystery. At any rate, Dom Rodrigo sent several men "to the Barnagais to ask him to remember the oath which he swore and promised to the [Governor] of the King of Portugal, which was to favor and take into his keeping the affairs of the King, and to be pleased to give us equipment for our journey."[3] Ten days later, still with no sign of an approaching bishop, some sort of vaguely positive answer arrived from the Ruler of the Seacoast. As it turned out, however, the Portuguese had begged favor of a man who had in no way repented his earlier decision to wipe his hands of this ungrateful collection of strangers.

It is entirely in keeping with his self-abnegating character that, in describing the sickness that overcame the embassy, Father Álvares neglects to mention whether or not he personally became ill. If he did, he must have been one of the earliest to fall victim and subsequently to recover, for we know that when

FOUR. Strangers in a Strange Land

he was not himself tending to those in need he managed to accomplish something he had been aching to do since he first set foot in the country a month before: observing how the Ethiopians conducted a mass. There is a breathless quality to his description of the Abyssinian rites, and one can imagine the terrible anxiety that must have gripped him as he followed the monks to their monastery's chapel in order to see for himself how the clergy of this profoundly alien land presumed to conjure and confer the body and blood of Christ. He had read somewhere that they were Nestorians; he had seen already that they were Judaizers; there was no telling what he was actually going to witness.

Minor Ethiopian houses of worship typically consist of a series of concentric circular spaces that resemble an archer's bull's-eye, and though such round churches are much more common in the south of the country than in the north, the building at Bizam appears, from Álvares' description, to have been of that design.[4] The outermost wall encloses an unroofed churchyard, bounded on the inside by the wall of the church-building proper. Penetrating this latter, one discovers an outer nave fronted by yet a third curving partition that divides the outer nave from an inner one. Finally, all of these nested circles surround, in Russian-doll fashion, a central sanctuary accessible only to priests. It is this innermost holy-of-holies that contains the *tabot*, a portable altar-slab of wood or stone, and it is this *tabot* alone that is consecrated by a bishop and thereby endows whatever building happens to house it with the sanctity to function as a church. The altar, which is set up just outside this midmost sanctuary, can therefore at best be seen by only half those standing within the inner nave and by almost no one in the outer nave or in the churchyard, since the concentric walls are only punctuated by three doors located to the officiating priest's left, front, and right. Thus the most striking difference between the interior of a European and an Ethiopian church is that while the former is designed to afford maximum visibility of the Eucharist to the congregation, the latter is designed to remind them of the profound distance between things sacred and things profane. And, though our priest could not have known it at the time, this typical arrangement of brick, thatch, and mud could stand as the material embodiment of the heresy that he would eventually discover lurking at the heart of Ethiopian Christianity. In the moment, however, Álvares, nervously downplays this stark architectural statement by focusing only on those of the building's structural details that would be familiar to Westerners. Thus, according to him, St. Michael's house of worship "looks quite like a church building, constructed like ours," since it has "three entrances, like ours, one principle one, and two side ones." He does admit that these portals are covered not with doors but rather with curtains whose fringes are adorned with many small, tinkling bells, but otherwise one could get the impression that he was investigating a cathedral in Lisbon or Lyon. Continuing on, he approvingly reports that "the body of the church is built with aisles [he must mean

Plan of a Typical Ethiopian Church

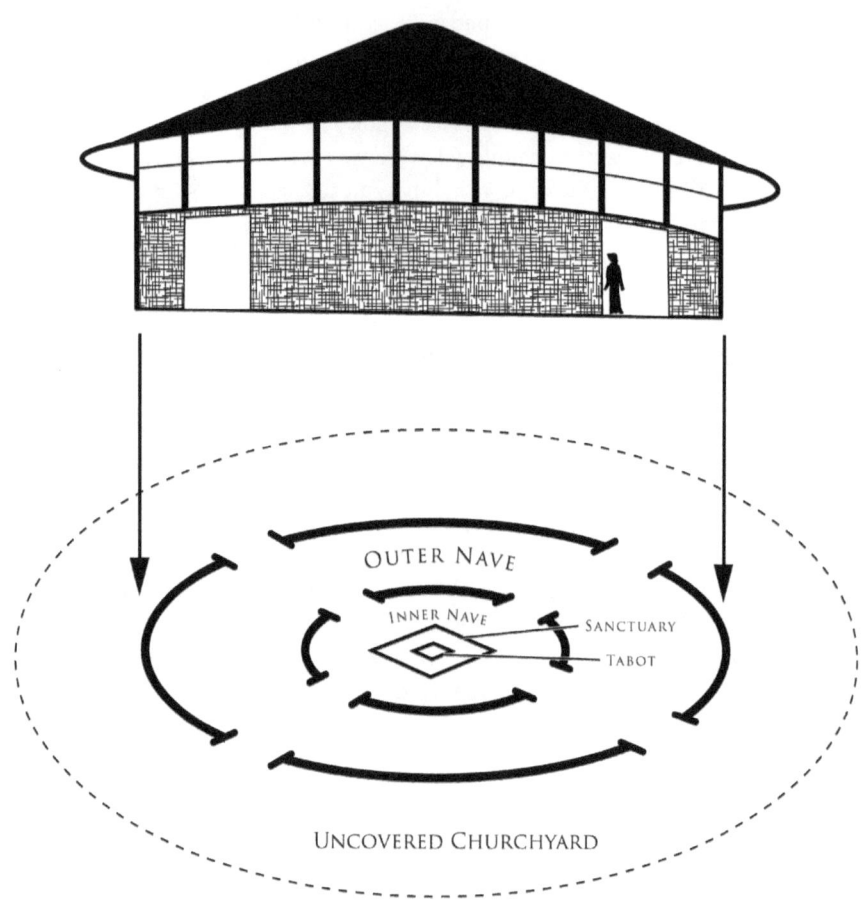

Plan of a typical Ethiopian church. So relieved was Álvares to find recognizably Christian ceremonies performed within Ethiopian churches that he played down the religiously significant physical differences between them and the churches of Renaissance Europe.

the concentric naves] very well constructed, and their arches are very well closed." The altar, furthermore, was clearly recognizable as such, featuring an altar stone and a large basin or chalice, all of which was decoratively topped by "a canopy on four columns." Because he limited his attention to the isolated details rather than to the building's fundamental conception, all could thus far be pronounced satisfactory.

FOUR. Strangers in a Strange Land

Interestingly, Álvares passed over in haste the processional crosses carried by the priests as they entered and exited the church, objects which today are the cherished holdings of many a European and American museum, perhaps because their intricate glories only reveal themselves upon close inspection, and his eyes were too busy to focus on much besides what went on at the canopied altar. The mass proper began strangely (to his mind), with a trio of priests bringing forth a portrait of the Virgin, around which the congregation began to chant and promenade hand-in-hand, "shouting and leaping as if in the *chacota*"—a Portuguese country dance having nothing to do with religion—and each time they passed the image "making a great reverence to it." One can feel our narrator's natural optimism beginning to fight with dark fears when he nervously observes of this practice that "certainly it has a good appearance and causes devotion, from being a thing done for the praise of the Lord God." Only later would he come to realize that the Ethiopians' wild gyrations were performed in pious (if invigorating) imitation of the biblical King David, who in Second Samuel is said to have "danced before the Lord with all his might" in celebration of the return of the Ark of the Covenant to Jerusalem. And only when he came to understand that his Abyssinian hosts believed that their nation had actual physical possession of that selfsame Ark would he appreciate their *chacota* for the mode of continuing religious thanksgiving that it really was.

The next phase of the ceremony involved the priests fetching the host from an outbuilding accompanied by cross, censor, and bell, and here Álvares reports with satisfaction that they returned to the church with "the bread of wheat flour, and without leaven, made at that very moment, very white and nice." Once back at the altar, wine was poured out, and the crucial acts of consecration and communion began, though it seemed this Eucharist was to involve two distinct classes of communicants. Inside the church proper stood—for there was nary a chair or bench within the tabernacle—men in holy orders, while outside in the uncovered churchyard milled the laity. It was this insistence upon a kind of spiritual segregation that accounted for a new source of unease, for the prayers and gospel were "rather shouted than intoned," and the holy word of God was promulgated "as fast and loud as the tongue can speak and the voiced be raised," though parts of the service were apparently read both from the altar and from an outer church-door. One gets the distinct impression that between all the leaping and yelling, Álvares struggled through much of the ceremony on the brink of sensory overload.

When it came to the mystical heart of the mass, though, our priest was given—or willed himself to find—just enough evidence of orthodoxy to keep his fondest hopes alive. With the noisy sermon now concluded, a hush fell over the sanctuary as the Bible was ceremoniously kissed and the altar repeatedly censed. The host, which had been covered by a black cloth, was now revealed and held in the celebrant's left hand while with his right thumb he punctured it five times in the pattern of a cross. Then, without elevating the host, "he consecrates in his language, and with our own very words." This was the vital thing, of course — that the words be the same as those spoken under the dome of St. Peter's — though it was most unlikely that Álvares in his present state could have told for certain that they *were* just the right words. Still, he must believe it, and so when it is time for the transubstantiation of the wine, he repeats the phrase again: "he does as much with the chalice ... and says over it our own very words, in his language." This point of crisis successfully passed — or at least wishfully interpreted — the denouement follows a path of consoling familiarity. The celebrating priest "administers the communion [bread] ... in very small portions from the bowl which the deacon holds[,]" while a sub-deacon follows close behind with a chalice, lifting "the blood with a spoon ... and giv[ing] a very small quantity to [each] person who has [just] received the body." So relieved is Álvares by the sight of these well-understood gestures that now even a dubious novelty is reported calmly: "there is also on one side another priest with a ewer of holy water, and the person who has received the communion" holds out "the palm of his hand and [takes]... some of that holy water, and with it he washes his mouth and swallows it." Such gargling could be overlooked because by now the really important action — the sharing of God's healing substance — was benignly spreading outwards, first to those in the covered cloister, "and thence to the laity who [were outside] the principle door." When all had been served, the officiating priest cleaned the bowl and chalice with the remaining holy water, a chanted recessional struck up from somewhere unseen, and "the communion ended, [whereupon] as many as [were] in the church, and outside of it, bow[ed] their heads, and [went] away in peace."[5] It was settled: they were recognizable Christians, and for Álvares that was everything. Their mass, for all its oddities, contained no outright blasphemies — and that, for the time being, was sufficient.

Which is not to say there were not some awkward moments when European and Ethiopian church-going practices were first observed side by side. For one thing, the Prester's monks insisted that everyone must remove their shoes before entering a tabernacle, which seemed to have a Mohammedan flavor about it, though they explained the prohibition by means of God's injunction to Moses to "take off thy shoes from off thy feet, for thou art on holy ground" (Exodus 3:5). A different Portuguese habit gave the locals even more offence, for if the anchorites were "surprised at our coming into the church with our shoes on," they were "still more [upset] at our spitting in it," a casual desecration to which the foreigners could offer only the thinnest explanation: "we excused ourselves, saying it was our custom." Similar strictures concerning purity were in force everywhere within the writ of Bizam, for while, as would have been the case in Europe, the monastery was an exclusively male abode, the Abyssinian prohibition on contact with females extended to the animal realm as well: "This monastery, and the others that are subject to it, have this rule in addition, that no females enter them, that is to say, neither women, nor she-mules, nor cows, nor hens, nor anything else that is female.... [And so] when I [arrived] there they came [out] to the distance of a cross-bow shot to [confiscate] my mule, and they took her away to their farm." Compared to the Ethiopians, the Portuguese were beginning to appear rather lax.

Perhaps the most serious clash of customs, though, was one that pointed to doctrinal as well as procedural differences. As the disease ran its course, the Portuguese had begun holding their own masses in the monastery church at St. Michael on a fairly regular basis, but when they attempted to do the same on one particular Monday, the monks "did not allow us to say it, at which we were much scandalized and aggrieved, and it seemed to us that they had some evil suspicion of us, not knowing why they acted so." The reason for this refusal turned out to be that, according to the Abyssinian reckoning, Lent began "ten days before the beginning of [Catholic] Lent," and since "these people follow[ed] the Old Testament as regards fasting," and thus only held it permissible during this period to eat after sundown, a daytime mass in which the host was to be consumed would, in their eyes, violate the Lenten vow of hunger. "This secret we did not know," explains Álvares, "and we had no one to explain it to us," and "thus we felt aggrieved without cause."[6] Well, not entirely without cause, given Rome's dim view of all such Judaizing practices, but here, as he would always strive to do throughout his captivity in this land, our priest attempted to downplay the differences and highlight the congruities between Catholic and Ethiopic doctrine. Indeed, when confronted during his first months ashore with anything that was heterodox or potentially blasphemous, Álvares was capable of penning a deftly equivocal phrase: "as we were in a new country it seemed to us very good." One wonders — are these the words of a guest who genuinely expects to find a satisfactory explanation for everything odd once he has gained more familiarity with his hosts, or of one who is only temporarily holding his tongue because it is rude for newcomers to voice their true alarm at the outrages they are beholding? With his perhaps unconsciously nimble phrasing, Álvares appears to diplomatically split the difference.

But he also got to lay his eyes upon something unexpectedly familiar, and though he narrates the episode steadily enough, it was a find that could well have unnerved him almost as much as any of the foreign customs that were now his daily fare. Apparently the monks of Bizam at one point gave Álvares a tour of their liturgical treasures, some items of which they only brought out from the sacristy to celebrate this or that particular saint's day or religious feast. Among these items he was shown "a great cloth, like a piece of tapestry, on which is the crucifix and figure of Our Lady and the apostles, and other figures of patriarchs and prophets, and each one has his Latin name written, so that no man of the country [i.e., no Ethiopian] made it."⁷ It must have given him pause. Was this woven mural brought overland from Europe by some unremembered traveler of the Dark Ages; had it been purchased from a Moor to whom it had fallen as booty in a Crusaders' battle; had it been woven here by some homesick exile with no prospect of return? Though in some measure representing a piece of home, it could not have brought much comfort to our priest, for despite the unknown specifics of its provenance it was a reminder that Franks had indeed been here before, just as Ethiopians had been to Europe — and yet, why hadn't such long-continued contacts between the two Christian civilizations amounted to more? Was there some fundamental incompatibility, some distance between them beyond that imposed by geography, which left only such meager scraps to mark their traffic with each other? After all, during the reign of Justinian the Great (527–565 C.E.) Ethiopians had walked the streets of Constantinople without drawing a stare, and yet, a full millennium later, here were Álvares and his fellows still so dangerously ignorant of so much concerning Abyssinia. He could well have wondered if the embassy's own finery would wind up in just such another storage room a century or two hence, there to be puzzled over by yet another wandering envoy.

By June 4th those Portuguese (unnamed by Álvares) who had gone to beg favor of the *Bahr-nagas* had arrived back at the monastery accompanied by a lieutenant of that governor and a wholly inadequate number of mules. There were thus more delays as this adjutant scoured the countryside for more beasts of burden while the embassy made ready to depart. The holy brothers of Bizam, however, were still apparently determined to make the Europeans tarry until their oft-evoked but as-yet-unseen bishop appeared. "Whilst our baggage was out in the road for our departure, and the men and oxen ready, the monks came and talked so much to the people" — i.e, the drovers and porters — "without our understanding them that they upset our departure, so that we again took in our baggage, and the Ambassador again sent another time to the Barnagais, and Joam Escolar the clerk went thither with the man of the Barnagais, and they remained there six days." Yet more oxen and mules returned with this party, and June 15th was re-designated as the date of embarkation, though "even then the monks were set on impeding us greatly, as though they wished us evil." The embassy managed to set off despite this continued interference, though the shortfall of animals was still such that they had to leave several small cannon and some powder behind. Then, apparently because of the monks' whispering campaign, "a rumor arose among the negroes who were carrying our baggage ... that there were robbers ... who were waiting for us in the road." Exasperated, the impatient Dom Rodrigo seemingly had recourse to coercion, though Álvares is evasive about it:

> Nevertheless we did not on that account refrain from making the baggage go on in front through the bushes, because the road was narrow. The Ambassador and

all those that were with him determined [if need be] to die upon the King's goods. The negroes were much amazed at the courage of [our] ten or twelve men, who did not fear passing such steep mountains, where it was said there were multitudes of robbers. Thus we went away, divided, with the oxen and negroes, with their burdens in front of us, going forward on our course. We traveled through very wild mountains over ascents and descents and a very bad stony road.[8]

By using the term "negroes," Álvares is attempting here to differentiate the black people who were slaves from the other black people — his hosts — who owned them. Would the fact of black-skinned slave owners driving black-skinned slaves have disturbed the Portuguese? On the one hand it should not have, for thanks to Portugal's eighty years of experience with the Atlantic slave trade, all of them would have understood that such arrangements were common on the African coast south of Cape Verde. Portuguese captains, after all, bought their negro slaves from negro slavers who raided in the interior. And yet, on the other hand, to see such a practice in the flesh might well have given them pause, for by 1520 the Portuguese were well down the path toward constructing a moral justification for slavery that was racial in nature. In historical terms, this attitude was a recent development, for in past times servile status and skin color had not been so closely aligned. For instance, during the gradual "Reconquest" of the Iberian peninsula (approx. 800–1492), the presence of olive-skinned Muslim slaves in Portugal had been a common sight as captured Mohammedan foes were put to work in fields, manor houses, and upon the decks of ships. (Matthew had been given just such a "servant" by King Manoel before he began his journey homeward, and several members of the embassy had brought along with them slaves of various hues.) Likewise, indebtedness, criminal activity, or just having been born a Slav could also have consigned one to a life of bondage in Renaissance Lisbon. However, once Prince Henry's caravels had rounded the westward bulge of Saharan Africa and crossed the mouth of the Gambia river in the 1440's, a comparative glut of black slaves became available by means of both raiding and barter, inevitably tincturing Portuguese notions of what kind of person was "naturally" suited to be a bondsman. Ironically, the first European auction of black slaves occurred in Lisbon in 1441, the same year Pope Eugene IV was welcoming Jerusalem's Ethiopians to the Council of Florence in hopes of reuniting the Roman and Eastern churches. By 1500, it is estimated that 150,000 black slaves had been forcibly transported to Portugal, there to be sold outright or shipped on to other European locations.[9] But were all of the Ethiopians' chattel black people? Many could well have been lighter-skinned Muslims captured by the Prester's subjects along the Red Sea coast or in the deserts stretching northward toward Egypt. It is interesting to reflect that such a state of affairs was likely to have made the Portuguese more uncomfortable in 1520 than it would have in 1420, when who was fit to be a slave was believed to be more a matter of the content of one's character (i.e., one's religion, one's crimes, one's insolvency) than of the color of one's skin. Still, in some ways this was a dissonant undertone within a larger harmony, for when it came to the naturalness, the inevitability, the unremarkable *rightness* of slavery as an institution, both the Portuguese and the Ethiopians were of one mind.

Once they emerged from the high-altitude prison that Matthew had sentenced them to, the embassy found the going easier, for the country was now "flat ... [with] fallows and tillage, in the fashion of Portugal." Álvares once again had leisure to turn his attention to the "very handsome and tall but unknown trees," and to the "infinite quantity of apes in herds," which were "the size of sheep, and from the middle upwards hairy like lions"—in other words, baboons. Things were looking up, for they were once again upon the high road, fast approaching the capital city of the *Bahr-nagas*. If, however, they flattered themselves that the Ruler of the Seaboard would be glad to welcome them back with an affectionate embrace, they had another thing coming. Thus, when they arrived at the substantial town of Debarwa, where the *Bahr-nagas* did in fact keep his principle "Beteneguz" (*beta Negus*) "which means house of the King," it was only to be informed that "the Barnagais [had] departed hence, before our arrival, to another place, the capital of another district." As Álvares relates, this was taken by the company to be an unsubtle hint: "It seemed to us that his departure was in order not to have to receive us." And, as if to underscore how disagreeable the sight of the Portuguese would indeed have been to the once-scorned Governor, "some told us that he had gone away with pain in his eyes."

After three days of fruitless waiting at Debarwa, five of the embassy, including Father Álvares and Dom Rodrigo, set out on mule-back to hunt down the *Bahr-nagas* and, as tactfully as possible, renew their request for animals and supplies. Although our priest had only known Dom Rodrigo a relatively short time, he must have been anxiously aware that the Ambassador did not possess a temperament suited to the asking of forgiveness, and surely worried that he would botch his required role of penitent suitor. Having arrived after a full day's ride at the town to which the Governor had reportedly removed himself, the party took time only to pray briefly at the door of a church before presenting themselves at the official residence. (This *beta Negus* was undoubtedly bigger than most Ethiopian dwellings, but probably did not differ in its physical layout from the ubiquitous pattern of a circular exterior stone wall topped by a thatched conical roof.) "Thinking that we should at once speak to him," the Portuguese were instead told one of those humiliating courtier's lies that it is equally impossible to believe or protest against: the guards "did not allow us to enter, saying that he was sleeping," and though the envoys "waited a good bit [they] had no means of speaking to him." Hoping to find the great man in better temper the next morning, they repaired to a "goat

FOUR. Strangers in a Strange Land

shed" for the night which was provided only with "two ox hides with the hair on to sleep upon," though someone apparently gave them a sheep to slaughter for their supper along with bread and wine.

Come the morrow the petitioners may have felt refreshed and optimistic, but in truth they were about to get their first taste of the Kafkaesque gate-keeping protocols that the Ethiopians could instantly erect to protect any official from the requests of favor-seekers. After waiting a long time outside their lean-to, "a message came for [them] to come." Once again assembling before the residence, they found themselves confronted with "three men like porters, each one with his hide whip in his hand" who "would not let [them] enter [the courtyard], saying that [they] should give them some pepper, and they kept us a good while at the gate." The main body of the embassy did in fact carry a number of bags of pepper with them, since the precious substance was both spice and specie at many places in the East, but it is unlikely the five would have thought to take any of it along on this side trip, and besides, the stiffly correct Dom Rodrigo would have bristled at the mention of a bribe. How the stalemate was resolved Álvares does not say, but he goes on to relate that "passing through this gate we arrived at [the building's door], at which stood three other porters who seemed more respectable persons." Better dressed though they might have been, this trio of functionaries was apparently no more accommodating than the last, for they "made us wait more than half an hour standing upon a little straw, and the heat was so great it killed us." Dom Rodrigo was now fed up, and "the Ambassador sent to say that he should bid us come in or he would return to his dwelling." This ultimatum, sent toward the inner sanctum by means of "one who seemed to be of higher position," was apparently the right approach, for before long "word came that we should enter."

The Portuguese found the *Bahr-nagas* reclining upon his *catre*, or rawhide couch amid a room darkened by "poor curtains" and attended by his wife, for apparently he still suffered from some sort of eye problem. Whether this malady was real or symbolic, however, remained unclear, since when, "having made our obeisance, the Ambassador offered him a physician to cure him," the Governor curtly "replied that he had no need of him, as though he did not thank him for it." Seeing that pleasantries were thrown away, Dom Rodrigo launched into a pro-forma declaration of what a grand favor the *Bahr-nagas* would be doing for both of their nations' respective rulers if he would only provide some beasts of burden, telling him that he would unstintingly relate His Lordship's generosity to Prester John once he got to Court — which of course could also stand as a kind of threat. This theme the Governor cut off abruptly, "asking what it was that we required," whereupon Dom Rodrigo reiterated that he "wanted oxen and asses for baggage, and mules for the Portuguese. To this the Barnagais replied that he could not give any mules, [but] that we might buy them ourselves; that he would give orders for the rest, and would send a son of his with us to the court of the Prester John, and with that he gave us our dismissal."[10] Thus the petitioners returned to Debarwa bearing only a surly promise for their pains.

During the week that followed, in which the embassy attempted to buy a sufficient number of pack animals from the local population and awaited the arrival of whatever black-sheep son or nephew the *Bahr-nagas* was willing to spare them by way of a guide, Father Álvares had time to note the customs of the country. His attention naturally gravitated anew toward religious matters, but now the tone and pace of his observations were less agitated, for having satisfied himself that the Ethiopians did not blasphemously mishandle the incarnate Christ during their masses, he could cast a calmer eye on their other spiritual practices. This can be seen in his relation of the scandalous news that regular Abyssinian priests (as opposed to monks) could and did marry. He attempts to sugar this sizable pill for his Catholic readers by pointing out that while Ethiopian laymen could have many wives, a priest was chastely confined to the possession of only one, and thus concludes that "they observe the law of matrimony better than the laity." Furthermore, extramarital sex among men of the cloth was not tolerated, for "if a priest sleeps with another woman whilst his wife is alive," he is defrocked and can neither "enter the church any more, nor ... enjoy its property." In fact, even the priests who merely become widowers cannot marry a second time without surrendering their liturgical office. In rank contrast to such strict propriety among the clergy, the sensuous layman not only marries multiply, but frequently divorces as well, a practice made all the easier by the commonness of pre-nuptial agreements among Ethiopian couples. Under such loose treaties the holy bonds of matrimony can be dissolved by allowing a pre-determined number of cattle to change hands, "and so they separate when they please, both the husbands and the wives." More troubling still, "they do not think it strange for a brother to sleep with the wife of his [deceased or merely divorced] brother." This error was due to that unfortunate Judaizing tendency that the Prester's people were so susceptible to, for in their defense they cited the Biblical story of Aaron and the fact that it "was the usage of the Old law" that a "brother raises up his [brother's] seed." But even amid this lascivious welter, observes Álvares, the sternly forbidding hand of the Abyssinian Church is seen, for no polygamous layman may enter into a church or "receive any sacrament" and in fact the clergy "hold him to be excommunicated." As a result, men who are getting on in years frequently divorce all their wives except "the one he had last, who [is] the youngest," so that he might sneak back into God's good grace before Death surprises him in the midst of all his accumulated sins.[11] Given such a general state of affairs, Álvares' implicit argument is that a married priest is not so hard to get one's mind around, and one can't help but smile at his charmingly transparent effort at damage control.

Baptism, however, he could not treat so strategically, for the thought of infant souls in jeopardy was acutely painful to him, and we several times hear his objections to the Ethiopians' practices. There is no mistaking his genuine alarm at the fact that "they [wait to] baptize males at forty days, and females at sixty days after their birth, and if they die before [attaining that age] they go without baptism." In the face of this perilous delay, the polite restraint of the newly arrived guest instantly falls from him: "I, in many times and in many places, used to tell them that they committed a great error, and went against what the Gospel says." The Abyssinians' reply, though a fit argument for a medieval scholastic debate, was not likely to banish Álvares' anxieties: "They answered me many times that the faith of their mother sufficed for them, and the communion which she received while in a state of pregnancy." But this was not the only practice that disturbed him, for if baptism came too late, first communion struck him as arriving absurdly early, since the two in fact occurred simultaneously. "Every child that receives baptism, male and female[,] receives the communion [bread], and [even though] they give it in very small quantities, and cause it to be swallowed by means of water," it still struck him as a risky business. In constant fear of the newly sanctified child being ushered directly to heaven as a result of choking to death on the host, our priest here too repeatedly insisted to the Abyssinians "that this communion was very dangerous, and in no way necessary." And there was one more practice involving children that he insisted could not be justified by even the most rigorous mining of the Old Testament for an irrelevant precedent. In the midst of remarking that the Ethiopians circumcise their male children he makes this declaration: "And let not the reader of this be amazed — they also circumcise the females as well as the males, which was not in the Old Law."[12] Álvares gives no indication of how widespread this practice was, and there is even some question whether, given his shyness about all matters of female sexuality, he fully understood what it entailed. Moreover we must recognize that his objection to it is due to its lack of doctrinal sanction, and not to the pain, injury, and lasting deprivation accruing to its female victims.

Our narrator's other observations at this time mostly concern the land lying about Debarwa, which he found to be abundantly planted with a variety of crops and thickly settled with "large villages and very good ones, all on high ground." He was discovering that most Ethiopian towns were similarly located some distance away from the roads on a piece of elevated land, with the larger silhouette of the local church crowning the apex of the hill. He was also taken with the quantity of wild game available in the area, remarking "that it is a chase [i.e., a hunting ground] that is very pleasant for the Portuguese," for "in the mountains are many pigs, stags, tapirs, gazelles, [and] deer," while down in the valleys were found "hares in great quantity, so that every day we killed twenty or thirty of a morning, and that without dogs, but [merely] with nets." He seems genuinely puzzled as to why, given such opportunities for stalking, the Ethiopians did not follow the hounds more frequently, exaggeratedly claiming that "nobody hunts or fishes, nor have they the wit nor a way, or the will to do it; on this account the game is very easy to kill, because it is not pursued by the people." He later returns to the point, asserting again that "all the game is almost tame, because it is not pursued."[13] One might think this would constitute an Eden-like prospect full of charm for religious man. However, reading such passages one gets the distinct impression that the un-priestly temptation with which Álvares struggled most sorely was a yen for the pleasures of the chase. Indeed, had he been a laxer cleric he might have resembled Chaucer's Monk, that rather-too-worldly sportsman for whom "hunting for the hare/Was al his lust." Still, given our priest's steady and scrupulous care for his fellow human beings, it seems hard-hearted to begrudge him an occasional afternoon of galloping over the countryside with a crossbow and net.

When the embassy finally pulled out of Debarwa to begin the long southerly leg of their journey on the 28th of June, Álvares says that they were "joyful and contented" to be again on the move after so long a delay, but their good spirits were soon dashed. After only half a league, the porters who had been recruited from among the locals suddenly laid down their burdens, "saying that their boundary went no further, and that [people from] another town had to take us further on," which was made worse by the fact that it was now "in the full force of winter of this country" and thus raining heavily almost all the time. The next week became an ordeal of frustrated shuttling between dispiriting sights upon the road and infuriating snubs before the Governor. "In these days the Ambassador and those of us that were with him did not rest: at one time we went to the baggage, which was a league and a half away from us, at other times to our lodging, at others to the house of the Barnagias, to require him to send men and animals." Before long an exasperated Dom Rodrigo was threatening that he would order the Prester's gifts "set on fire, and [instruct the embassy to] go [its] way unhindered." (Given the presents' paltry value, though, this was a hollow menace.) In answer to such blusterings, the *Bahr-nagas'* "speech was always favorable, but the deed never done." At one point hopes rose because the party "met with good words" from the Governor, but "on the following day a gentleman from the Court of the Prester John arrived, and the Barnagais gave him such a reception that he forgot us." Dom Rodrigo, no doubt offended at being made to understand that his errand was considered less important than some merely internal matter, applied to the gate of the residence once more, whereupon the *Bahr-nagas* "dismissed us saying that for the love of God we should leave him as he was sick." This was too much for the *fidalgo* to let pass with politeness:

> The Ambassador was angry and said that he [i.e., the Ruler of the Seaboard] remembered badly and performed worse what he had sworn and promised to the [Governor] of the King of Portugal, that is to say, to assist us and order equipment

to be given us for our journey, that he forgot all this, and also that he was not mindful of the friendship which they had established and sworn since he did so little for the affairs of the king of Portugal. Neither of this account did he make any more haste, but always excused himself on account of his guest, and of being ill."

But if being ignored in favor of someone from Court rankled Dom Rodrigo, being treated similarly on account of the next set of visitors was felt as an even more degrading slap. On July 6th a company of Moors rode into town to deliver their country's annual tribute to the *Bahr-nagas*, which consisted of a brace of magnificent horses. Comments Álvares, somewhat acidly for him, "as the arrival of the Moors redounded to [the Official's] profit, neither his guest nor his sickness hindered him. The reception and honour which the Barnagais paid to these Moors gave us great trouble." Seeing themselves trumped by infidels, paranoia began to set in, and soon a few members of the embassy had convinced themselves that the *Bahr-nagas* was actually interfering with their increasingly desperate attempts to buy oxen and mules from the local people, "telling the vendors not to sell them, and that if they sold them they would be punished, and the gold would be taken away from them." His motive for this was reputed to be the desire to sell his own beasts to the Portuguese and thereby profit from the strangers he continued daily to insult.

What it was that finally halted this dangerous slide in relations between the grudging host and his outraged guests Álvares does not clearly specify, but after a few more days the embassy had apparently managed to scrape together sufficient mules on which to mount themselves while the *Bahr-nagas* had actually delivered to them a trio of camels to assist with the baggage. Perhaps the arrival of his champion steeds had sweetened his mood. Thus, "with great fatigue we set out from this place, amid heavy rains and storms, which harassed us; for at this time it is the depth of the winter." By this date the Portuguese had not yet come to fully realize what a Quixotic thing they were doing by traveling at all during the rainy season, since "in all this time [the Ethiopians] do not travel, and yet we were hurrying on our journey, for we did not know the usage of the country, or the danger we were running into." Progress was slow and miserable, and only four leagues (a league being approximately three miles) were covered in three days "on account of the severe storms," which were also responsible for "everything that we carried with us getting spoiled." But, upon hearing from their balky and unreliable porters that they were nearing the southern border of the *Bahr-nagas's* realm, spirits rose anew and Dom Rodrigo chose to ride ahead in order to make contact with the ruler of the next territory. It was his hope that with this new man — the "Tigremahon," (*Tegre-makuannen*) or governor of Tigre province — the embassy could begin again with a clean slate and meet with the kind of welcome and practical assistance that they believed their mission deserved. On July 28th word came back to the main column from the Ambassador to continue on with all speed to the river that marked the territories' frontier, for there apparently a better reception had been arranged — or at least promised. And so, "amid heavy thunderstorms, winter weather, and rains," the travelers began to negotiate "a very rough road and a very deep descent for the distance of another league," and "went to sleep within the circuit of a church in fear of tigers, and much vexed by the storms." The next day brought "rocky mountains, and ridges with thickets of trees without fruit, but all very green and beautiful and unknown to us," until at last they debouched onto the bank of broad, swift river at which "the kingdom of the Barnagais ends, and that of the Tigremahom begins."

If they could only get across this dangerously rain-swollen flood, their prospects looked promising, for "from the other side of the river we heard kettledrums and a noise of people: we asked what it was, and they said that a Captain of [the] Tigremahom had come for us." In fact, says Álvares, "we found a fine body of people come to fetch us; they might be 500 or 600 men to carry our goods." This was a signal change to be sure, but as was becoming routine, there was a last-minute hitch. "At once there was a dispute between the people on either side of the river. Those of the country of [the] Tigrimahom said that they had not got to take the baggage except in their country; and those of the Barnagais, that they had no obligation except to place it on the shore close to the water in their country; and they engaged in great shouting and quarrelling about this matter." In the end, however, "they finished amicably, agreeing to take the baggage across together so that neither side should remain aloof, but what was fair should be done."[14]

Precisely because Álvares does not specify who brokered this compromise, it is more than likely that it was his own doing. The phrasing of the solution — that "neither side should remain aloof, and what was fair should be done" — has a ring of modest self-satisfaction about it, which is about as much as he ever allowed himself, no matter what feats of the spirit he eventually achieved. The embassy would have need of such peaceful arts in the months ahead, for though they had finally escaped from the malign neglect of the *Bahr-nagas,* they had as yet covered less than half the distance of their inward march toward the elusive monarch they were seeking. There would be, in all senses of the phrase, many rivers yet to cross. And that having been accomplished, their outward trek would then be a matter of years, not months. As the pressures exerted by sights unfamiliar, by customs and actions that appeared inexplicable, and by hopes — not betrayed exactly, but challenged and transformed — continued to mount, fraying the tempers and upending the equilibrium of nearly everyone in the embassy, Francisco Álvares would emerge as the calm center of stability and sanity. Amidst a splintering community of travelers very far from home, he would time and again muster all his moral courage and simple eloquence to insure that none "should remain aloof." If his success was destined to be merely partial, it would yet be enough to get most of them home alive.

Five

The Far Pavilions

Crossing from the territory of the *Bahr-nagas* to that of the *Tegre-makuan-nen* meant accelerating from a frequently interrupted crawl to a continuous sprint, for on the latter's side of the river the embassy's porters were numerous, accommodating, and apparently athletic, hustling the baggage southward "so vigorously that we could not keep up with them on our mules." Released from the constant rounds of delicate and frustrating negotiations over transport and supplies, Álvares could now devote his full attention to the details of the country through which they passed, commenting first upon the increasing size of the mountains that now loomed above them: "we here began to enter amongst very high and [steep] peaks, which appear to rise up to the sky, so high are they," though "the area on which they stand is not extensive, and all are separated one from another." He further observed that these vertiginous massifs, a signature of the Ethiopian Highlands known as "*ambas*," were frequently "as broad at the top as [they were] at the bottom, for it is all scarped like a wall, of sheer cliff." This was only a slight exaggeration, since the Roof of Africa's terrain consists mainly of a radically eroded high plateau, with the remnant islands of the alpine plain isolated from one another by steeply plunging gorges. And as if this did not make their ascent difficult enough, it is often the case that the final approaches to these lonely aeries are guarded by battlements of fully exposed rock over a hundred feet high whose faces are in fact nearly vertical. Still, the flat summits of these geographic holdouts often encompass a good deal of acreage, and despite their seeming inaccessibility, were seldom allowed to remain completely fallow, and thus "all those that can be ascended, even though there is danger in it, have chapels on them," though "we could not think by what way people could go to build them."[1] In time, Álvares was destined to come across an *amba* whose summit was not employed as a spiritual refuge for the unworldly, but rather as a place of imprisonment for the flower of Ethiopian royalty—an alpine nether-world where those whose blood was deemed to be dangerously indistinguishable from that of the current *Negus*

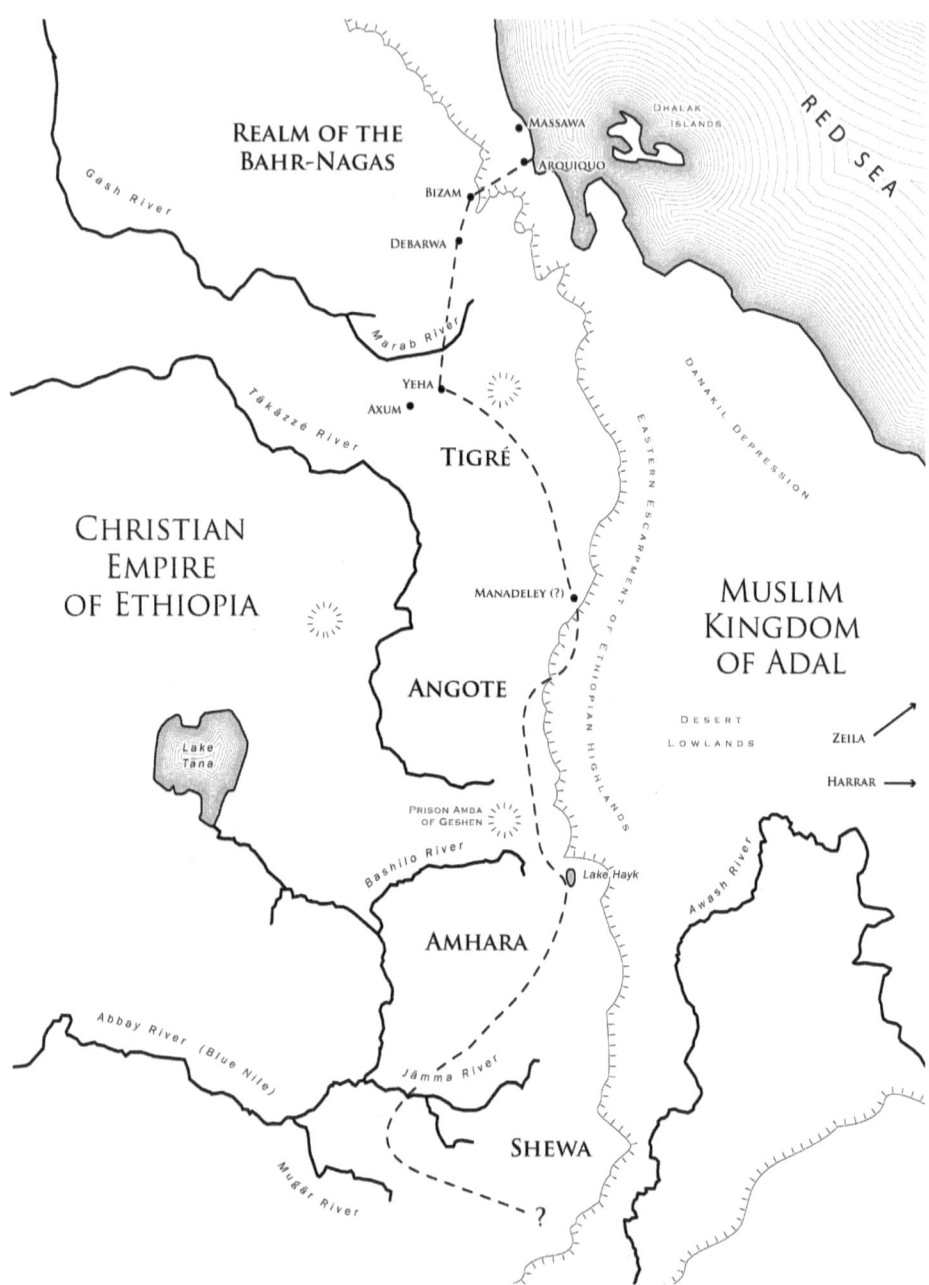

ROUTE OF ÁLVARES AND THE PORTUGUESE EMBASSY IN 1520. Leaving the Red Sea in spring, they arrived in early autumn at the Court of Lebna Dengel, *Negus* of Ethiopia, whom the Europeans persisted in calling "Prester John." Traveling at the height of the rainy season made their mountainous trek all the more harrowing.

were sentenced to live out a ghostly life in exile. However, he would also discover that this banishment could be broken at any time by a messenger from the real world below, announcing the death of the current king and bearing a summons to one chosen inmate to descend and take up the Abyssinian crown. Álvares, looking back at the brutal and chronic dynastic wars of his own continent, would be forced to admit this cruel institution's usefulness in promoting the nation's peace, and would come to view it with a painful ambivalence.

Complaints during this stretch of the journey tended to be mild and laced with self-deprecation. For instance, on fasting days (of which there are many in the Ethiopian calendar), food would only be delivered after dark and then it was sometimes not to a European's taste. At one point, this repeated deprivation prompted Álvares and his clerk to the naughty expedient of closing the doors of a church into which pigeons had flown and then slaughtering that flock of innocents in the house of God, a caper that was still remembered by the scandalized townspeople when he revisited the place "some years later." Despite such self-reliant foraging, however, our priest confesses that he and his friends often found themselves "horrified at eating meat without bread, and bread without meat, and bread without salt." He also noted that though there were fewer beggars and cripples here than in the previous province, the clothes of Tigrean womenfolk continued to violate European standards of decency, for their loose-fitting costumes were such that "at every little movement one can see from one side of the body to the other what man wishes." Álvares' objection rises above mere prudery, however, for he fears such costumes must coarsen men's criteria for choosing their wives: "In Portugal and Spain people marry for love, and because they see beautiful faces, and the things inside are hidden from them; in this country they can well marry [for other reasons] as they see everything for certain." Accommodations varied: at one halt they were put up in a snug and spacious *beta negus*, one of many scattered residences left empty but ready at all times for the use of the Prester's roving officials (a thing only the "Tigremahon" himself could have arranged). As Álvares explains, "no one meddles with [these houses] or goes in, except while the lord is there; and when he goes away nothing is left inside except the open doors, and sleeping couches ready for use, and a place for making a fire." On other nights, however, they slept outdoors in tents, which must have been mightily uncomfortable since the almost incessant rains of the Ethiopian "winter" continued to saturate the ground. On such evenings "the people who carried our baggage made a great fence of thorny bushes for us, and for the mules, which was to defend us from the wild beasts."[2] Our priest at first believed that such makeshift enclosures were a piece of timid overkill, though later on, when the embassy's pack animals regularly began succumbing to the attacks of nocturnal carnivores — which were mostly hyenas and jackals, but upon which

Álvares always conferred the frightened honorific of "tigers"—he was glad enough to be sheltered within those prickly walls.

Not long after crossing into Tigre province the embassy was lodged for a night at a town whose modern name is Yeha, and it was here that Álvares had his first close encounter with the remarkable relics of Ethiopia's ancient history, and where he began to appreciate the fact that the Abyssinians possessed a cultural inheritance every bit as fascinating as the wish-fulfilling fables generations of Europeans had projected upon them. At Yeha he noted "a very good church of Our Lady, well built, with the middle aisle['s roof] raised above the two ... edges, ... its windows very well constructed, and all the church vaulted." In other words, he was encountering a stone rectangular church featuring a raised central clerestory stretching along its main axis that was supported by interior columns, in a style resembling the European Romanesque. Its sheer familiarity must have lifted his heart, but his attention was soon drawn away from it by an equally impressive but altogether more mysterious structure. This was "a very large and handsome tower" remarkable "for its height and the good workmanship of the walls, and for its width," for though it was clearly "damaged ... yet it is plain it was a royal affair, all of well-hewn stone."[3] What in fact lay juxtaposed in this tower and sanctuary were two phases of Ethiopian civilization about which even the most learned Portuguese had only the vaguest idea. The tower, for instance, carries to this day inscriptions which link it to the Sabean culture that once flourished across the Red Sea in south Arabia, and was erected in honor of a fertility god named Ilmukah over half a millennium before Christ, when Yeha was the thriving capital of a nation known as Damot.[4] But even this monument fails to delimit the backward-stretching history of Abyssinia, for in Egypt there exist hieroglyphic descriptions of the region dating to 3000 B.C.E., when Pharaohs traded down the Red Sea with a land they called Punt, purchasing myrrh, gold, ebony, ostrich feathers, and exotic animals in exchange for finished goods like cloth, tools, and jewelry.[5] Thus even the six-hundred-year-old Prester John who appeared in some of his Letter's more fanciful variants was an upstart beside the kings who first claimed sovereignty over the land that Álvares now trod.

As for the church he admired at Yeha, it dates from the Axumite civilization, which flourished from the first century before Christ until the rise of Islam, and which represented the most robust expression of Ethiopian power before Álvares' time. We know from the Roman writer Pliny and other sources that by the first century C.E. the Axumite port of Adulis was a major transshipment point between the Roman Empire and India, as well as the center of an export trade that included tortoise-shell, rhinoceros-horn, hippopotamus hides, obsidian, ivory, apes, and slaves. The people of Axum worshipped gods that were roughly synchronized with those of Greece and Rome, and were the only indigenous African nation to coin their own money. Indeed, it is from these coins that we can quite accurately date the arrival of Christianity in Axumite lands, for the first issue of currency under the reign of King Ezana (ruled c. 321–360) bears the pagan symbols of the sun and moon, while a second series of a few years later carries the inscription of the cross. For several centuries the kings of Axum were the most powerful monarchs between Byzantium and Persia, and letters from Christian Constantinople arrived asking favors and offering advice accompanied by only minimal condescension. What brought about this Abyssinian empire's decline was the bewilderingly rapid rise and spread of militant Islam, which succeeded in closing down the Red Sea to Christian traffic as the Persians never could. After this onslaught, as Edward Gibbon memorably exaggerated in his *Decline and Fall of the Roman Empire*: "Encompassed on all sides by the enemies of their religion, the Aethiopians slept near a thousand years, forgetful of the world by whom they were forgotten."

Though Álvares could not know it at the time, the church at Yeha was intimately connected with painful facts about the Ethiopians' religion toward which his spirit of honest inquiry was even now beginning to lead him. It was founded by Abbâ Afsê, one of the "Nine Saints"—that is, one of the refugee monks from Syria who, at the end of the fifth century, fled to Abyssinia after their version of Christianity was declared heretical at the Council of Chalcedon in 451. Abbâ Afsê and his eight companions, like the Eastern Christians who had already converted King Ezana and his court almost a century before, believed that Christ, rather than being both fully divine and fully human, as Catholic doctrine insists, was rather composed of one wholly divine substance, and hence were known as "monophysites" (mono=one, physis=substance). This distinction may seem utterly abstract and academic to modern sensibilities, but it was deadly serious stuff to Álvares' superiors in the Catholic Church. To have a false conception of the nature of the Savior was a heresy, and heresy was a pernicious and damnable sin for several reasons. To begin with, under Christian teaching God and Christ were the perfect embodiments of truth, so to worship these beings with a mistaken notion of what they fundamentally *were* was to adore not them but a different deity altogether, making one akin to an idolater. Indeed, worse than one, since fully alternate religions such as paganism or Islam or Buddhism were clearly distinguishable from Catholic orthodoxy by ordinary believers, while Christian heresy was not. Thus heresy had a particularly insidious way of insulting God by both distorting His perfected image and by subverting the discipline and order of His Church. It was for this reason that, in the eyes of Rome, an Abyssinian who kept a Saturday Sabbath, or needlessly circumcised his penis, or even took to wife his brother's widow could still—*probably*—enter the gates of heaven, but one who had a faulty notion of the essential nature of his Savior decidedly could *not*. Did Álvares, listening with interest to the local priests discourse about the origins of the church building whose seemingly familiar lines he was admiring, put together the far-eastern provenance of its founders with the Chalcedonian dates and begin to genuinely worry for the souls of his hosts? He was not an especially learned man, but he would have already known that the Ethiopians had strong ties with the Patriarch of Alexandria, and that Alexandria was the very capital of Monophysite heresy. Did these ties amount to a shared apostasy? If he did entertain such fears, they would have vied with countervailing hopes, precisely because of that thousand-year sleep evoked by Gibbon. After all, the Abyssinians had been so isolated for so very long—wasn't it just possible, or even likely, that they had preserved among themselves the truest, sparest, and most unpolluted form of Christianity? If any people should have been safe from doctrinal corruption, shouldn't it have been these, so hermetically sealed off since shortly after the close of Biblical times? Back in Europe, many newly emergent Protestants, hearing word of Ethiopia's wakening, would soon entertain just such hopes. In writing his impressions of Yeha, it is this brighter prospect to which our priest tacitly inclines, mentioning only that both the tower and the church were associated with Candice, "the Queen of the Ethiopians," whose eunuch, according to Acts 8:27, was baptized by the apostle Phillip himself and who then passed on his presumably still-pristine faith to his mistress and her people.[6] More—and far more troubling—revelations would confront Álvares in the months ahead as he came into increasingly close contact with important figures in the Ethiopian Church—men who would prove zealous and articulate defenders of the unique doctrines of their national faith.

For now, though, our priest's acquaintance with Ethiopian antiquities and the richly layered history they revealed was only beginning. Four years later, for instance, Álvares would spend eight months in the former capital city of the Axumite Empire—itself called simply Axum—which was not more than thirty miles to the southwest from where he presently stood. There he would see and haltingly attempt to describe for his readers the numerous monumental stone obelisks that still testify to the ambitions and grandeur of a nation whose writ eventually extended from the Nubian deserts of the west to what is now Yemen in the east. The most impressive of these stelae are intricately carved to resemble something surprisingly akin to modern skyscrapers, with a door and even a door-handle etched on the ground floor, and above this row upon row of windows representing a Babelesque apartment tower rising toward the heavens, all of which is crowned with a decorative capital. Those still standing reach heights of seventy-five feet, while the biggest of them, which is now fallen, once stood almost a hundred feet tall and represents the largest block of free-standing stone ever worked by human hands. It is typical of Álvares' instinctive optimism that he evidenced no fear of these pre-Christian monoliths, and indeed tried to bring them into the familiar orbit of the Bible by deciding that the inscriptions upon some of them, which neither he nor his Ethiopian hosts could read, "must be Hebrew."[7] Despite the magnificence of

Axum, in the year following his residence there the priest would find himself in a place even more remarkable: the sunken city of churches named Lalibela. There he would discover that, however impressive King Ezana's fields of spires might be, Ethiopia's most exquisite treasures of hand-chiseled rock incongruously began at one's feet and extended downward into the very earth itself.

When, as July turned into August, the embassy met with the *Tegre-makuannen* himself, they at first found him in every way a pleasant contrast to the *Bahr-nagas*. Arriving at his seat and being told that he was at church, the Portuguese set off toward the chapel and met the Governor and his lady as they were coming home, finding them proceeding in "very good state, like the great lords they are," and "accompanied by many great [subsidiary] lords" in their train. Álvares reports that "this Tirgrimahom [was] an old man, of good and reverend presence," and that, thankfully, "his wife came entirely covered up with blue cotton cloths," a costume so satisfactory to morality that "we did not see her face or any part of her body, because it was all covered up." Furthermore, the couple seemed to have a sense of the import of encountering fellow Christians from so far afield, for the Governor asked our priest for his cross and after "kiss[ing] it ... ordered that it be given to his wife to kiss," which she did "through her wrapper, and gave us a warm welcome." Here, as it seemed to the flattered and relieved Portuguese, was a ruler "altogether grander than the Barnagais," and things did seem to proceed swimmingly for the space of a few days until, as the *Tegre-makuannen* prepared to go on a journey of state, Dom Rodrigo asked him "to equip us well for our journey." Perhaps the embassy's leader simply had an unappealing way of begging — or was it demanding? — favors, for suddenly things turned chillier, with the Governor replying curtly that while he would arrange to have the Prester's presents transported, the travelers must fend for themselves when it came to hiring porters for their own gear and supplies, and "with this he dismissed us and went his way." Downhearted and confused, the Europeans returned to their own quarters, but soon hit upon a fallback plan of simple directness: they would attempt to soften-up the *Tegre- makuannen* with an expensive gift. It is interesting that Álvares specifies the bearers of this flattering tribute — which included "a rich dagger and a sword furnished with a velvet scabbard and gilded hilts" — as being "Jorge D'Abreu and Mestre Joam [Bermudez]." Why the two of them, and not Dom Rodrigo? Did the proud *fidalgo* feel himself above such fawning errands? Most probably he did — and thus the gambit itself was almost certainly their idea and not his. If these surmises are correct, it underscores how the Ambassador's stiffness could at times border on the sclerotic, since the offering of such gratuities to those in power was commonplace in sixteenth-century European court culture. Still, given that D'Abreu had already quarreled with Dom Rodrigo (and would soon do so again), it must have irked the latter when in response to this polite bribe "there came a message that they would carry all our goods, and that in all his lands they would give us bread, wine, and meat to eat."[8] If D'Abreu needed anything to nourish his belief that he rather than Dom Rodrigo possessed the necessary abilities to command the embassy, this turnabout of the "Tigremahom" must have banqueted his ambitions.

Once more supplied with ample backs, both human and animal, to bear their luggage, the embassy again set out southward on August 9th. Though progress was steady, it was clear that Dom Rodrigo was increasingly anxious to reach the Prester's court as soon as possible, being no doubt mindful that their only hope of leaving the country the following year resided in a Portuguese fleet that was scheduled to drop anchor at Massawa (island sister-city to the beachfront town of Arquiquo) in the spring, but which would certainly not be inclined to linger in what were essentially Muslim waters if the embassy were tardy in arriving back at the coast. This impatience was demonstrated in his response to a curious Ethiopian grandee who sent word requesting that the party detour from their route in order to pay him a brief visit, since he himself had no permission to enter the "king's houses" in which the travelers were sporadically being lodged along their route. To this piece of indolent curiosity the ambassador replied curtly that "he had come a distance of 5000 leagues, and whoever wished to see him might come to his lodgings, for he was not going to go out of them." And so as they hurried on, comfortable nights spent in the *Negus'* snug guest-homes alternated with rough sleeping in "some very vile places," with the rain as the only constant, for the skies sluiced down torrents almost every day, turning their road into a reddish-brown quagmire and even the highest campsites into swamps. Then, at the end of a particularly soggy day, the porters provided by the *Tegre-makuannen*, who had until now given good service (sometimes even outdistancing the main party by several miles before dark), went on a mysterious strike. The Europeans ambled around a bend only to discover all their gear "set down in the middle of a plain where there was much water." After so much hard-won progress, it was a dispiriting tableau, Álvares sighing that "it grieved us to see our goods thus," and that it left the travelers dangling "at [their] wits' end." Once again and without warning, their hopes appeared every bit as waterlogged as their linens.

It was at precisely this moment that the cavalry, in a manner of speaking, rode up to their rescue, though at first blush it appeared to more closely resemble some sort of ambush. Suddenly there was a clatter of hooves as a party on mule-back with an entourage of runners beside them burst upon the milling collection of Portuguese and Ethiopians. The leader of this squadron, who sported a monk's costume, made straight for "the Tigremahom's Captain ... who had charge of our baggage," seizing him "by the head ... and [giving] him blows" until "the Captain was covered in blood." Reacting instinctively in defense of the Abyssinians whom they knew and against these strangers, the Portuguese drew their swords and closed upon the interlopers. According to

Álvares' breathless account, "the Ambassador ... laid hold of the monk by the breast, and was going to strike him," while the rest of the embassy "came up with him carr[ying] their arms ready," until a dozen of their spear-points were jostling "almost at the breast of the monk." The menaced anchorite, now realizing his danger, commenced to cry out in a language that, while not at all resembling one of the tongues of Ethiopia, still communicated nothing intelligible, and thus it is doubtful this strange outburst would have saved him had not Jorge d'Abreu, that vain and dapper man-of-the-world, managed to recognize in it a few words of broken *Italian* and hurriedly pushed his comrades' shafts to the ground. There must have been a few moments of stunned paralysis as D'Abreu explained to the thwarted rescuers what manner of speech he had just heard. Then, the battle averted, the Europeans clustered around to hear the monk "tell how he had come by order of the Prester John to cause our baggage to be carried, and that he had been amazed at [the negligence of] that Captain," asserting that "what he had done to him he did because he had made such bad arrangements" for honored guests of the *Negus*.

This might have excused the man's behavior in most eyes, but Dom Rodrigo, no doubt acutely aware that d'Abreu had now twice saved the embassy from real trouble in the course of a week, felt his dignity imperiled and "answered that it was not the time to make a disturbance, especially in his presence, for it seemed to him those blows had not been given to the Captain, but to him, since he had given them in his presence, and that he felt it deeply." Ruffled feathers having been duly displayed and "all having been restored to peace"[9] — we can guess by whom — the monk announced that he was going to continue on up the road that the embassy had just traveled and employ the powers of his office to commandeer sufficient animals to insure the travelers' uninterrupted progress, for no peasant or governor would dare resist him. Thus this violent apparition of a man parted ways with the Portuguese before he could explain how he had learned his smattering of Italian. (The fact was that he had once made a pilgrimage from Ethiopia to Rome, something only a minuscule number of the Prester's subjects had accomplished.) But he would be back soon enough, and indeed back to stay, for this was Zaga Za Ab, the irascible abbot whom the *Negus* would eventually appoint to travel back to Europe with the embassy as his ambassador to the Portuguese court, and with whom our priest would come to share an uneasy friendship during his long sojourn in the Prester's land. It would be an unlikely pairing, but then again Álvares rarely refused the hand of kindness to anyone, even to those whose own hands, like Zaga Za Ab's, were too often turned to far less Christian purposes.

Having no way of knowing whether the monk was a legitimate majordomo of Prester John or not, the embassy did not slacken their pace as he went about his confiscatory errand on their behalf. In truth, though, it was lucky that they encountered him no later than they did, for their road now led them into a district that was troubled by chronic wars with the Saracens who thereabout bordered the *Negus'* realm. Álvares speaks of the rains slackening, the temperature rising, and of broad vistas opening up through passes to the east, so it is quite possible that they were briefly emerging from the Ethiopian highlands and skirting the arid lowland plains that stretched toward what is today Djibouti and Somalia. These were the homelands the Dobas, Adelis, and other Islamic peoples who, with quite regular alternations, either paid a resentful tribute to the Abyssinian king or revolted against him. These tribes looked in turn for support to the Muslim Kingdom of Adal, whose centers of power were farther east toward the Horn of Africa, in the cities of Dakar, Harrar, and Zeila, the last of which was located on the Gulf of Aden just outside the Gate of Tears. Because one of the seventh-century Axumite kings had given shelter and succor to a group of Mohammad's first disciples fleeing persecution in Arabia, Ethiopia had long been a tolerated Christian kingdom in Muslim eyes. This designation never did much to interrupt the chronic state of war that had existed between the *Negus* and his immediate Islamic neighbors for nearly a millennium, but it did tend to mean that the latter could only count on their own limited regional manpower to carry the battle forward. During the previous decade, for instance, raids into the highlands by Mafouz, the Emir of Harrar, had become commonplace during Lent, when he could count on the scrupulously pious Ethiopians being weakened by fasting. But as destructive as such forays had sometimes proved, they had remained skirmishes of local ambition, and besides, the current *Negus*, Lebna Dengel, had routed and killed Mafouz in 1517. But if the situation on Abyssinia's eastern border therefore seemed to be nothing more than an ongoing irritant, even now Muslim emirs in Cairo and Mecca were turning worried eyes on Portuguese incursions into the Red Sea: if the *Negus* was going to make common cause with European infidels, then the days of opportunistic raiding might have to give way to a season of committed religious war under the green flag of *jihad*.[10] Though in 1520 the thunder may still have been distant, a great storm had begun to gather around Christian Ethiopia — one that the Portuguese had carried thither in their wake.

But if this borderland was increasingly the site of war it was at this season also a natural nexus for trade, and Álvares was surprised to find himself passing through a strikingly multicultural market town whose name he translated as "Manadelay," in which he found "every kind of merchandise that there is in the world, and merchants of all nations" including hawkers "from [Jiddah,] ... Morocco, Fez, Bugia [i.e., Algeria], [and] Tunis," as well as "Turks, Roumes from Greece [i.e., Byzantines], Moors of India, ... [and buyers from] Ormuz and Cairo." It was in this place that Zaga Za Ab caught up with them, proving as true as his word by "bringing mules and camels to carry us," which caused "some of [the Portuguese] ... to receive him with joy and pleasure, having [conveniently] forgotten [their] first meeting." What methods of intimidation he had used to procure these beasts remained unclear, but thanks to Álvares' encounters first with the brothers of Bizam and now with Zaga Za Ab, our priest was learning that Ethiopian monks were not adverse to employing guile and muscle to get their way. By contrast, it was near this town of Manadelay that the embassy had its first encounter with Abyssianian nuns, finding them to be of a much more obsequious disposition: "the nuns came to wash our feet, and drank of the water after they had washed them ... saying we were holy Christians from Jerusalem."[11]

Trade may have remained brisk in Manadelay, but the surrounding countryside was clearly on a war footing. The current flare-up had apparently been caused in part by the reigning *Negus'* refusal, against long-standing custom, to take as one of his wives the daughter of the local Muslim King, his reason being her "large front teeth" which he found unsightly. One wonders what the local inhabitants of these precincts thought about Lebna Dengel's subordination of the public weal to his personal standards of beauty, for his fastidiousness had forced them into battle against a motivated enemy, it being "a law amongst [the Dobas] that they cannot take a wife without a man's being able to prove that he has killed twelve Christians." Thus was sex both the *causus belli* and the battle cry together, though this somewhat comical congruence did not prevent this war from morally brutalizing its combatants, as Álvares soon discovered to his dismay.

> In this country I saw a priest with poisoned arrows; and I criticized it as being ill done, as he was a priest. He answered me: "Look that way, and you will see the church burnt by the Moors, and close to it they carried off from me fifty cows, and also they burned my beehives, which were my livelihood; for that reason I carry this poison, to kill him who has killed me." I did not know what to answer him, with the sorrow that I saw in his face and perceived in his heart.

One can imagine Father Álvares' pained expression during this interview as his devotion to principle vied, as always, with his instinctive sympathy for the sufferer before him.

And here, past the halfway point of their inward journey, this local ambivalence must have been shadowed by a more general disappointment as well — for surely this was a far cry from the peaceable kingdom bragged of in the Prester's original missive. Álvares had waded ashore knowing full well that "Prester John" was at best an exalted office rather than an ageless messiah, and that his subjects would likewise tend to bleed when pinched, but still, he had grounds to hope that at least some of the sinful propensities of men might not have taken root in this antipodean Christian stronghold. Alas, he was discovering that the Abyssinians were as thoroughly fallen as everyone else. And then too, it could no longer be denied that the Prester's Letter was also proving a false guide to the country's supposed material riches, even if this was a much less important failing in our priest's eyes. He had, for instance, already noted some weeks previously that salt "was in all the country [as] current as money," being carved for convenience into tradable blocks "a span and a half in length, four fingers thick and three across, [whereupon] it goes loaded on carts and beasts like faggots." Now, crossing yet another internal border from Tigre into a land called Angote, he discovered that in this new territory not only salt but iron too was coin of the realm, except that the metal was exchanged in the form of ugly, shovel-like slabs, such that "six or seven blocks of salt are worth one piece of iron."[12] Legends of the Prester had spoken of a citizenry whose purses hung heavy with doubloons stamped from the purest silver and gold. It must have been difficult, then, to discover that what actually passed for money in his kingdom were the most basic elements of the common earth.

As the embassy at last drew near to the Prester's capital, they came under sudden attack by both nature and man. Having just passed out of the district troubled by preparations for war, the party stopped for their midday meal by the side of a small river "in the very good shade of alder trees," for "it was very hot, and the sun and day were very bright." Álvares reports that during this respite they were "divided into two parties, on each side of the water," though still "at speaking distance," since "the river did not bring water enough to [irrigate] a garden." *Two parties*— had there been another quarrel, then, or was this an innocently random division? Either way, they were soon united in peril:

> Meanwhile thunder began a long way off, and we said that these were dry thunderstorms such as there are sometimes in India. Feeling safe, without there being here any wind or rain, and the thunder having ceased, we began collecting the baggage to set out [again].... The halt [thus] having ended ... Mestre Joam [Bermudez] went sauntering along the river up stream for the necessities of nature, and immediately came back running, and calling out with loud shouts: "Look out, look out." We all looked in the direction from which he came shouting, and we saw water coming, of the height of a lance (without any doubt), and quite straight and square: and we could not take care sufficiently to prevent its carrying away part of our goods.

This flash flood deprived our priest of his breviary and a bottle of wine he carried for the purpose of celebrating mass, though luckily he had previously wrapped up his silver chalice in a goatskin and hung it from a tree branch, thereby preserving it from the inundation. As for the rest of the party, "from one it took his cloak, form another his hat, from another his sword," and forced them into such frenzied poses of flight that "on the one hand it was a fearful thing, and on the other a matter for laughter." All in all, "it was a thing not to be believed," for "as this water came suddenly, so also it passed away in a short space of time," such that "even this day we crossed over it, [though] we did not see in it the [same] rocks which we had seen before."[13] All during this waterlogged Ethiopian "winter," it must have appeared to the Portuguese that the skies were taking their orders from Mecca.

As August gave way to September, the embassy were told they could look forward to the waning of the rainy season, but just as the heavens relented the population seemed to rise up against them. Soon after crossing the river that separated the province of Tigre from that of Angote, the column encountered villages that "would not receive us or carry our baggage," and whose inhabitants cast insults at Zaga Za Ab and occasionally attempted to rough up his men, who responded in kind. The reason for this intermittent hostility was that the *Negus*, for reasons of political expediency, would often show favor to particular towns by exempting them from certain kinds of intrusions by, or service to, royal officials. And since almost all of the sixteenth-century Ethiopian economy functioned by means of in-kind exchanges rather than coinage, these exemptions represented important benefits to the towns so honored, and such grants of immunity were thus jealously guarded and interpreted according to the letter.[14] Zaga Za Ab did not attempt to hide his royal commission as he escorted the embassy toward the Prester, and it is easy to imagine what the long line of weary Portuguese, with their strange appearance, cumbersome baggage, and line of exhausted porters looked like to the various village headmen: they looked like an immanent demand for onerous and open-ended assistance in the King's name.

This pre-emptive resistance took a particularly virulent form on September 13th, when Álvares says an unnamed village "collected together to shake the dust out of us." Rushing up some hills that bordered the road, the citizenry "threw stones so thickly that they seemed to rain upon us" such that "well did we think of our deaths." Our priest was one of the few to escape injury, for "five or six men of the monk's" and Bermudez too "came out with broken heads." Their ambush successful, the villagers then proceeded to take prisoner several of the wounded Europeans, the physician included. Álvares managed to flee the battle and rode hard to catch up with Dom Rodrigo, who had again gone on ahead of the main party. When, the next day, he breathlessly related the story of the rout to his leader, the Ambassador "hurried [his] saddling, mounting and departure, saying that he would die for the Portuguese." Arriving back at the scene of the melee, which was now marked by the strewn remnants of much of the embassy's baggage, they discovered that the governor of this province, the *Angoteraz,* was already on the scene and anxious to give assistance. In typical fashion, however, Dom Rodrigo was too incensed by the insult to his mission to acknowledge the Governor's good intentions, ordering the interpreter to "tell the Angoteraz that I do not come to see him nor that monk who is with him, but [that] I come [only] to seek the Portuguese whom I have lost in this country." It was at this point Bermudez limped in fresh from escaping his captors and "much covered in blood," though his reappearance did not solve the question of what to do next. "After much discussion between the Ambassador, Angoteraz, and the monk upon this affair," Dom Rodrigo was persuaded to decamp to the Governor's residence some league and a half distant in order to recoup. Once there, the *Angoteraz* apparently attempted to soothe the Europeans' sore bodies and resentful minds (and perhaps his own embarrassment) with a flood of alcohol, for his hospitality "all over-flowed with drink." Ethiopians brewed both a mead and a wine made from honey, as well as distilling several varieties of spirits from various local plants. Apparently it was the mead that was on offer now, poured out with a liberal hand from "four very large jars" into "goblet[s] of crystalline glass." Several strong toasts of friendship were proposed and swallowed, and yet, says a disapproving Álvares, the Governor's cronies "would not let [us] go if we did not drink more," and that even when "all the jars were finished ... he ordered more to be brought." At last, the bandaged and now inebriated Portuguese excused themselves, "saying we were going away to relieve ourselves." Such rapid alterations of cruelty and kindness must have befuddled the embassy as much or more than their host's plentiful liquor.

Shocking as the villagers' attack had been, Álvares was characteristically just as disturbed by the retribution meted out to them. Once Dom Rodrigo was moving onward again, Zaga Za Ab attempted to persuade the baggage section of the column, to which our priest was attached, to return to the offending village in order to witness him and the Angoteraz's men "do[ing] justice." As impatient of delays as their leader, the Portuguese of the second column declined to wait until the demonstration could be performed, though they saw the fruits of it soon enough. On the first or second night of their continued march, Zaga Za Ab reappeared at their fireside encumbered by "two mules, a cow, and eight pieces of cloth, which [the townspeople] gave him for the blood they had shed." Like most Ethiopian villages, the guilty settlement had been little more than a collection of round huts constructed of mud walls and thatched roofs, bearing few amenities beyond the means of basic subsistence, and thus Álvares took no satisfaction from such evidence of their further impoverishment. As he sourly noted, "this is [the monk's] justice, and no other, namely, to take away their property, which is only mules, cows, and cloth, from those who can do little." Indeed, the priest was in an almost continual state of dismay at Zaga Za Ab's heavy whip hand, for their guide roughly confiscated food and extorted labor all along the route, even "order[ing] priests and monks to be flogged" if they resisted him. At one point the Ambassador himself complained that the Portuguese had brought along enough gold and pepper to buy their own food, and that they could easily find meals enough to purchase at every village "if he, the monk, did not take them by force from those that brought them," causing the next town up the line to bring out nothing for fear of having it summarily appropriated. Finally, because the "Captain of some villages ... did not come up at once with the people who lived there" to offer assistance, Zaga ordered his men to destroy their bean fields. "It was pitiful to see such destruction," laments Álvares, and when members of the embassy criticized this gratuitous rapacity, Zaga Za Ab simply replied that "such was the justice of the country, and [thus] each day he ordered many of those who carried our baggage to be flogged, and ... took from them mules, cows, and pieces of cloth, saying that so should be treated whoever gave poor service."[15] One wonders whether our priest eventually wound up spending so much of the next decade at Zaga Za Ab's side out of some strange affection for his opposite, or in order to try to patiently turn him from his violent habits.

Up till now the embassy had been traveling down the eastern edge of the Ethiopian highlands in a consistent southerly direction. It was at this point, however, in the vicinity of Lake Hayk — about two hundred miles northeast of the country's present-day capital, Addis Ababa — that they turned to the southwest and began to penetrate into the heart of the high country. Álvares appears to have been impressed by the size of this lake, though it is hardly the largest in Ethiopia, and mentions the monastery of St. Stephen that occupies an island in its middle planted thickly with citrus groves, reachable only by a raft of bulrushes which the monks polled along. Lake islands were a common site for monastic establishments in Ethiopia, and their isolation was the visible marker of the social, spiritual, and intellectual separation between Abyssinia's anchorites and those who made up the country's regular clergy. The latter were, for the most part, minimally educated, lacking in zeal, and thoroughly imbedded in, and dependent upon, the secular communities whose religious needs they served. By contrast, it was the monasteries that were both the repositories of Ethiopia's history and culture (including many of her material treasures) and the breeding ground of religious inquiry and reform, their only rival in this regard being the royal court itself, though which many monks irregularly rotated. Though Álvares may not have grasped the fact yet, in having visited both Bizam and Lake Hayk, he had now encountered the major houses of the two competing monastic orders within the Prester's realm — respectively, that of Ewostatewos and of Takla-Haymanot — the names referring to the reformist monks who founded or at least inspired their two differing rules of cloistered life in the thirteenth and fourteenth centuries. This pair of monastic orders had been bitter antagonists in controversies surrounding both the Ethiopian Church's ties to Alexandria and the question of the Saturday Sabbath. Ewostatewos, whose influence was strongest in the north around Bizam, had been a champion of observing the Old Testament holy day, while Takla-Haymanot's followers, concentrated in the south, decried it as foreign to the Coptic (i.e., Egyptian Monophysite) Church from which Ethiopian Christianity was spiritually descended. The controversy became so heated that the Ewostatewons began refusing to recognize the authority of the Alexandrine Patriarch and all those who had been consecrated as priests under his auspices. This amounted to just about every Ethiopian in holy orders, since from the time of King Ezana's initial conversion it had always been the Egyptian Coptic Church that had sent the Abyssinians their reigning *Abuna*, or archbishop, who alone could confer the priesthood on Ethiopian acolytes. The controversy eventually infected Court politics and threatened to tear the country apart along religio-geographical lines, prompting Zara Yaqob (ruled 1434–1468), the wildly successful *Negus* who had largely shaped the Ethiopia Álvares was now encountering, to call a Church Council in 1450 to resolve the dispute. Due in part to Zara Yaqob's strong guiding hand and shrewd maneuvering, a compromise was reached wherein the double Sabbath was enshrined as an official aspect of Ethiopian religious calendar and the Ewostatewons agreed to re-submit themselves to Alexandrian authority.[16] Given that this agreement had both enshrined a Judaizing practice and cemented ties with a heretic church, in the eyes of an orthodox Catholic such a compromise could only have appeared as a compact with the Devil.

Despite all the cultural and natural curiosities scattered along Álvares' route of travel, this stretch of his journey is perhaps most remarkable for something that our priest does *not* mention, for we know from other sources that it was near lake Hayk that the Portuguese were joined by their nearly-forgotten predecessor in exploration, Pêro da Covilhã. This silence demands an explanation, for considering the minutiae of the passing scene that our priest often feels obligated to relate, surely the unexpected reappearance of a man who had vanished into Abyssinia a quarter-century before and who had long been presumed dead deserves a mention. Much later in his narrative Álvares does get around to relating Da Covilhã's remarkable career as a favorite of both Queen Eleni and Lebna Dengel (despite the later monarch's distrust of the dowager), his marriage to a high-born Ethiopian woman, and his association with the other captive Europeans, but here, at the moment of reunion, he says nothing, starkly departing from his usual habit of day-by-day reportage.

This lacuna can, however, be explained. First of all, Da Covilhã's actual arrival could not have been a surprise, for soon after his own sudden appearance the royal functionary Zaga Za Ab must have informed the embassy of the existence of a brace of captive Franks resident at the Prester's court, Da Covilhã included. Also, this news was likely to have been too disturbing to quickly digest, since a natural question to put to Zaga Za Ab would have been, "How long have they been here?" If the monk answered truthfully, he would have said, "As long as I can remember." So, when the resurrected explorer did eventually rendezvous with the embassy's column, the startling news that his very presence confirmed — i.e., that it was not the custom of Ethiopian Kings to allow their European visitors to return home — had already been turning over and over in the minds of Álvares and his fellows for some weeks. Thus our priest most likely did not commit the reunion to paper because he was as yet radically unsure of its larger implications. Indeed, the members of the embassy were now presented with some deeply disturbing prospects, the first and most visceral of which must have been a growing fear that they too would be made into perpetual exiles. But the news also threatened their sense of purpose, already sorely tried by hardship and delay. Their assignment was not merely to inform Prester John that Christians had arrived in India in force; that fact the monarch already knew, for it had been the reason behind Queen Eleni's dispatch of Matthew ten years before. Rather, they were expected to re-emerge from his land bearing crucial facts and hard promises that might decide the fate of nations: how many men could the Prester lend to a crusade across the Red Sea; how many tons of gold would he contribute to the war chest of Christendom; how many engineers would he need to complete the diversion of the Nile away from Cairo? Da Covilhã, of course, had been charged with a similar royal imperative to return and report — if his fate was now to be theirs as well, then their central place in the history of global Christian conquest would, as his had, diminish to a footnote. But surely, they must have told themselves, an official embassy duly representing his majesty King Manoel would stand immune from this caprice of the Prester's that had hitherto incarcerated lone travelers and lost wayfarers. Surely their fate would be different — wouldn't it?

The appearance of Da Covilhã certainly did nothing to sweeten the general mood of the party, for as they crossed the increasingly difficult terrain of the province of Amhara, simmering tempers flared again. After a long and sleepless night fending off, by means of lance-thrusts at their circling eyes, the hyenas that Álvares still insisted were tigers, "there were disputes between Jorge d'Abreu and the Ambassador about a very small matter." Small it may have been, but here for the first time our priest identifies the two principals in these wrangles as Dom Rodrigo and his deputy. Perhaps the Ambassador had ordered D'Abreu to stand a midnight guard over the threatened mules, an assignment that the latter felt incommensurate with his dignity. We do not know, for Álvares still appears distracted into unusual reticence, noting only that the next day after a difficult morning's ascent of "a very high mountain," the travelers took their midday rest "separated from one another, because of the quarrels which had taken place." This sounds serious, despite the priest's deadpan tone, for while the Portuguese had hitherto often separated their column for considerations of logistics and safety, this is the first record of their segregating themselves due to festering quarrels. It would not by any means be the last.

The lofty mountain that Álvares mentioned was just one of many that the embassy had to either scale or skirt as they closed in upon their ultimate goal. The section of the country through which they were now passing features peaks that rise above 13,000 feet and is bisected by numerous canyons whose narrow floors can rest as much as 9,000 feet below those summits. In the priest's relation of the journey's final weeks, fascination alternated with fear. On the one hand, the wide vistas provided a chance to see at a glance the vast extent of the Prester's country, and to muse anew about its strategic position in Portugal's global designs.

> And because from here there was a very extensive view as far as the eye could see towards the west, I asked what countries were in that direction, and if they all belonged to the Prester John. They told me that for a month's journey in that direction were the dominions of the Prester; after that, one entered mountains and deserts, and after them very vile people, very black and very bad. In his opinion, these lasted for a distance of fifteen days' journey, and when these were finished, there came white Moors of the Kingdom of Tunis.

This fancifully foreshortened view across the Ethiopian massifs, the Nile valley, and the outstretched Sahara beyond must have been invigorating, for it seemed to place Christian Abyssinia on the battlements of a high castle, enjoying a position of tactical advantage over the Muslims of North Africa who busied themselves in mischiefs below. Being told — correctly — that the rivers rushing below fed into the Blue Nile also inevitably gave rise to talk concerning the fond dream of diverting Egypt's lifeline and parching Cairo's beys and emirs into submission. Although actually seeing such relentless torrents locked so deeply within narrow runnels of rock must have brought home the fact that changing their courses by means of a ditch here or a canal there was sheer wishful thinking.

On the other hand, when the view was not inspiring, it was terrifying. Álvares relates that in the initial week of October they passed, in quick succession, first through a chasm "so narrow that a man cannot go on horseback, and the mules scrape the stirrups on both sides, and so steep that a man goes down using his hands and feet." That then, "coming out of this narrow pass one travels by a ridge which is about four spans wide," along which he "would affirm that goats could not pass ... safely." Indeed, the embassy dismounted and shooed their mules along before them "like someone sending them to perdition, and we [scrambled] after them with hands and feet down the rock." Given such precarious footing, it did not surprise Álvares to hear that this vertiginous crest-line was known as "The Destruction of Donkeys." In subsequent years, he says, "we passed these gates many times, and ... never ... without finding beasts and oxen dead," their bones whitening far below.

This trial, however, was among the last of their inward journey. Having crossed a final thundering river, the mountains suddenly gave way to plains harboring both open grassland and tilled fields, and dotted with windswept villages. The rains were over now, and the sun shone on this high and verdant plateau with a welcome constancy — it was as if the nation that for so long had seemed hemmed in by storm clouds and cliffs was now belatedly opening itself up before them, allowing them to at last stride across firm ground, to cast off their sodden hats, and breathe deeply in the dry, bright air. One can palpably feel Álvares' prose unclench its hitherto anxious grip on the passing landscape. And then, mounting a gentle rise on the afternoon of the tenth of October, they beheld at last the object of their half-a-year's trek into the unknown: "on this Wednesday we saw in the distance, to our great joy, the tents and camp of the Prester John, which seemed endless, and covered the whole countryside."[17] There is more relief than surprise in Álvares' words, and surely Zaga Za Ab and the other accompanying Ethiopians had told their guests, in a general way, what to expect — but still, it must have been to European eyes a most extraordinary sight. Covering the plain below them was a city containing, at best estimate, somewhere between 20,000 and 40,000 souls, making it the rival of all but Europe's largest capitals. But instead of being an agglomeration of brick, stone, and wood divided by twisting streets of varying widths, this metropolis was a vast, orderly array of tents, its acres of multi-colored fabric silently rippling in the afternoon heat, giving the place the appearance of some sprawling quilt designed for the likes of a giant.

Zaga, pointing here and there before the gaping Portuguese, would have first identified the white, flag-topped residence of the *Negus* himself, situated upon a slight prominence at the very center of the metropolis. Surrounding this royal palace was a curtain wall of draperies that separated his inner courtyard from a wider outer one, itself surrounded by a linen rampart nearly two miles in circumference. (The resemblance of the Court's layout to that of a standard Ethiopian church was not accidental, symbolically casting the *Negus* in the role of the sanctifying *tabot* kept hidden within the central holy-of-holies.) This enclosed outer ring held within it the dozen separate tents of the permanent members of the Court. These elites included the Queens of the Right and the Left hand, the Queen Mother (who had charge of the Prester's children), the *Abuna*, the military commanders or *Bitwaddads*, also of the Right and Left hand, and sometimes the heads of the two monastic orders. Sharing the circular enclosure with these residences were the King's two private chapels, one dedicated to St. Mary, the other to the Holy Cross, as well as the King's kitchens and the barracks of his elite royal guards. The curving outermost wall of draperies that encompassed all these various pavilions was interrupted by thirteen gates, six to the left of the main entrance and six to the right, with the principal portal ceremonially guarded by a pair of chained lions. Just beyond this final linen palisade were stretched the ropes and awnings constituting the royal treasury, the court of justice, the reception hall where the *Negus* heard his subjects' petitions, a pair of prisons (their walls of mere fabric like the others'), and his majesty's principal public church. Then, outward from this already vast imperial preserve, in a series of concentric squares, lay the compounds of the Abyssinian nobility, each a smaller version of the *Negus'* apartments, and each including tents not only for the lord himself, but for his own complement of retainers, from men-at-arms to brewers and grooms. Beyond this neighborhood could be seen a section of the city designated as a market, purposely located close by a "Church of the Market Square" in which accusations of sharp practice were adjudicated, and segregated into a Christian section for the selling of staples and a Muslim quarter where foreign items such as cloth, guns, and spices were hawked. Beyond this and sprawling out more haphazardly toward the edges of the city were the lesser erections of the millers, mechanics, artisans, and other subjects of middling status, far too small and numerous to count, until at the outer fringe the kaleidoscopic hues of the tents themselves gave way to the thatched lean-tos of the poor and the bare blankets of the beggars. Punctuating all were the wide and lofty church-tents, bearing the sign of the cross upon their gently undulating roofs.[18]

No doubt Álvares and his countrymen, once this vision had sufficiently settled into their minds, were keen to press on toward this gossamer city, but Zaga Za Ab restrained them, warning that what they saw before them might well vanish before they could arrive. He was not joking. For at least a hundred years the Abyssinian capital had been a portable metropolis, ready to fold itself onto horse-and-mule-back and reconstitute itself on a moment's notice. As one historian explains, the whim of the *Negus* was the sole determiner of where the seat of government would reside on any given day:

> Secrecy preceded the entire event; indeed, the king was known to ride out of the capital in the middle of the night while the population of the settlement slept. The word of the king's departure would flash around the camp and the task of moving ensued. The lower classes would pick up their meager belongings, such as wine pots, various household items, and the wooden poles that supported their thatch abodes. The gentry supervised the disassembly of their numerous tents and had their belongings packed on animals by servants. In a short time [only] an empty meadow remained, boasting few vestiges of the crowds who had just vacated it. The accompanying army would then divide into ... [a] vanguard, [a]rearguard, and ... two groups guarding the [long column's] flanks.... The porters required to carry a portion of the king's goods alone were estimated to number 5,000–6,000. Church paraphernalia, wine, beer, and arms all had to be carried. The move commonly involved a journey of at least 10 or 20 miles and two or three days of traveling.

This arrangement may at first appear both cumbersome and giddy, but there was a good reason for it. Ethiopia had long been a nation besieged on many fronts by a Muslim foe that could often muster impressive numbers and firepower for any given incursion into the Christian highlands. The mobile capital, however, allowed the Abyssinians to fight running battles against such an enemy without scattering their own forces, permitting them to wear down the invaders through attrition. In essence, "the roving capitals of Ethiopia were guerrilla cities," and any attempt at attack confronted the invader with an instant insurgency. As Zaga Za Ab himself was to testify many years later in

Europe, this flying metropolis had the added advantage of obliging the nobility to "exercise themselves continually in military actions, for we are surrounded on all sides with enemies of our faith with whom we have often many conflicts, always, or for the most part, with success through the goodness of God." Thus was the seat of Prester John a place whose insubstantial lightness, so reminiscent of something from a fairy-tale, was the product of a grim history of blood and steel.[19] No, Zaga Za Ab explained to Dom Rodrigo, he would find out where the capital was going next, and take them to *that* place instead — it was what the *Negus* would desire.

From our own distanced vantage point we can understand that the bright, lithe city which the weary embassy now at last beheld was both an emblem of all they were discovering about Ethiopia, and a test of their ability to surmount the psychological challenges those discoveries entailed. After all, they had at last arrived at the fabled court of Prester John — and yet, since Prester John was himself only a fable, they had also done no such thing. And though the place was undeniably beautiful, at the same time it was utterly different from what any of them had been led to expect, for in all the legends of the Prester his capital had been touted as a location of massive solidity — weighed down by profusions of precious stones, by monuments in solid marble, by endless iterations of hammered gold. In the minds of the Portuguese, disillusionment would now begin to war ferociously with an openness to re-enchantment. At stake would be their conception of their own enterprise as either a triumph or a farce, and of themselves as either Christian knights or the most pitiable of dupes. And although we are privy only to the private thoughts of Álvares himself, it appears from his account that in the months ahead our priest, almost alone among his fellows, came to accept this startlingly unforeseen place for the marvel that it was, while most of the others would fail to perceive it as anything more than second best, a jesting swindle upon their dreams. Feeling cheated of their one chance at fabulous wealth and fairytale glory, the disappointed would soon succumb to wrath and folly.

Six

The King and I

Despite Zaga Za Ab's assurances that the Prester's entire capital would soon be on the move, it is clear that Álvares and his fellow Portuguese either did not fully comprehend — or did not quite believe — what they were being told, for our priest betrayed disappointment when an official arrived from Court who confirmed the monk's assertion that the embassy must now turn their backs upon the airy metropolis. His feelings are understandable, for it must have been agonizing to veer aside on the very brink of their destination after undergoing so many varied and perilous trials to reach it. However, even as their new minders led them more than a league in what seemed to be exactly the "wrong" direction, the party was distracted from their frustrated misgivings by the odd appearance and behavior of their new escorts, which included in their number "six or seven horsemen going in front of us on very good [mounts] pretending to fight and amusing themselves, all with their faces covered." It was, however, only some days later, as the myriad of tents comprising the Prester's city began to spring up around the once-empty piece of ground where they had been told to halt, that the real purpose of these gaudy outriders became apparent. Someone, perhaps Zaga Za Ab, must have let slip the secret — that one of the mounted men had been none other than the *Negus* himself, desiring to catch a first clandestine glimpse of the Franks who had so suddenly descended upon his country and who claimed to be the bearers of such important tidings. And as we try to imagine just what the disguised king made of our priest and his road-weary companions, we should also ponder how he imagined his own role in the larger cultural collision that their presence before him heralded. After all, we already know so much about what the Europeans desired him to be — indeed, needed him to be. But if to them he was the last, best hope for a living, breathing Prester John, what was he to himself? Had he ever heard of the man for whom the strangers were searching? And if he had, would he have considered himself a fair likeness?

In the letters he would later dictate to both king and pontiff in Europe,

Six. The King and I

Lebna Dengel (which translates as "Incense of the Virgin"), the reigning *Negus* of Ethiopia in that autumn of 1520, would style himself, among other things, "a descendant of the lineage of Judah, son of David, son of Solomon." He meant this genealogical claim to be taken literally, for it was his and his countrymen's belief that the rulers of Ethiopia were descended in a direct line from these Old Testament patriarchs through the Queen of Sheba, whom they took to be an Abyssinian. Opening First Kings, one reads that Sheba's empress, having heard accounts of Solomon's vast learning, visited the Jewish monarch in Jerusalem in order to "prove him with hard questions." In the Biblical version of the story, the Queen is satisfied with Solomon's answers and departs after bestowing rich gifts upon him. According to the Ethiopians' own chronicles, however, she also received a carnal reply that impregnated her with more than just wisdom. This ravishment having been accomplished by means of a trick, Solomon's post-coital slumbers were troubled by a dream in which he beheld the sun, which up until then had shone directly upon Israel, shift its position in the sky such that its beams would now and forever favor Ethiopia. This account goes on to assert that the Queen of Sheba returned to her native land quick with child and there gave birth to a boy, Menilek, who eventually returned to Israel as a young man in order to receive his father's blessing. Solomon desired his son, whom he confirmed to be his first-born, to remain with him in Jerusalem, but Menilek insisted upon keeping a promise to his mother to return to Abyssinia. Acquiescing in sorrow, the King ordered the eldest sons of his courtiers and high priests to accompany Menilek on his homeward journey. This youthful crew, not wishing to cross the foreign deserts involved without divine protection, removed the Ark of the Covenant from its dedicated temple by stealth and carried it with them to Ethiopia, where it supposedly resides to this day within a church at Axum. It was this elaborate and fanciful piece of Old Testament addenda that undergirded Lebna Dengel's belief that the blood of Israel's Biblical patriarchs ran unpolluted through his veins.

This myth of royal origins was first written down in the *Kebra Nagast,* or "Glory of Kings," during the expansionist reign of the *Negus* Amda Seyon in the middle of the fourteenth century. It was in part motivated by a desire to paint Amda Seyon's grandfather as the "restorer" of a "Solomonic" line of kings that had supposedly been eclipsed by the usurping "Zagwe" dynasty between about 1137 and 1270. Once this self-serving narrative of overthrow and recuperation had become entrenched in the Abyssinian cultural psyche, subsequent Ethiopian *Negus*es could see themselves as the inheritors of a bloodline that not only encompassed the leaders of the glorious Axumite Empire, but which stretched backward beyond even those princes to include monarchs who had shepherded God's chosen people in centuries well before the advent of Christ.[1] And if the Ethiopian kings thus saw themselves as the proud descendants of

Judaism's Golden Age, they also claimed to be the defenders of a long and heroic Christian inheritance, for the New Testament story of St. Phillip's conversion of Queen Candice's eunuch implied that Abyssinians became followers of Christ within a generation of the Crucifixion, long before Rome knew a Pope or Constantinople a patriarch. His nation having subsequently been surrounded by zealous religious enemies since the rise of Islam, the reigning *Negus* could in fact proclaim that his forefathers had continuously kept the Christian faith alive amid their native peaks and gradually spread it by cunning and might across much of the sprawling Roof of Africa. And thus there was a kind of rough equivalence of self-regard between the European phantasm called Prester John and the Lebna Dengel who had just laid stealthy eyes upon our priest, for if the former reported himself in his Letter to be descended from one of the Magi, was it a lesser boast to count King David and Solomon among one's ancestors? And if the *Negus'* realm could not match the Prester's in terms of immense wealth and immaculate piety, it had nevertheless struggled in reality with the same enemies of Christ that were supposedly pitted against its fictional counterpart, and across the centuries it had faltered but never yet succumbed. In these respects at least Lebna Dengel resembled the very man his European guests were looking for. If, through the lens of their historical fantasies, they wished to see the Ethiopian king as a man bearing upon his shoulders a hefty mantle of destiny, it is unlikely the *Negus* would have disagreed with them.

Having stolen a look at his European visitors, Lebna Dengel wasted little time in ordering their official reception, though his own and his countrymen's idea of what such a ceremony should entail would both amaze and frustrate the embassy. Five days after he had planted his personal residence in its latest location, the *Negus'* immense city finished reassembling itself around him; by mid-morning of that fifth day a messenger had been dispatched to rouse the Portuguese. (By now the envoys were being housed in a large and sturdy pavilion that the Prester had ordered to be substituted for the tattered rags that the party had spent half a year soaking under. It must be understood, however, that this swap did not entail the visitors having to move an inch from their originally designated spot, for the new tent was erected in exactly the same place, such being the location relative to the *Negus'* dwelling where visiting dignitaries were *always* housed. If the Ethiopian capital was thus a kind of moveable feast, it was one for which the dishes and the place settings never varied no matter what quarter of the nation was currently hosting the banquet.) One can feel Álvares' giddy excitement as the summons arrived:

> On Friday, [19] October, at the hour of [nine in the morning, Zaga Za Ab] came to us in great haste, for the Prester John had sent to call us, and said that we should bring what [gifts] we had brought for him, and also all our baggage, as he wished

Six. The King and I 113

to see it. The Ambassador [however,] ordered [only] that to be loaded which the [*Estado's*] Governor] had sent for him, and no more. We dressed ourselves and arranged ourselves very well, God be praised; and many people came to accompany us on foot and on horseback. So we went in order [of rank] ... as far as a great portal, where we saw innumerable pavilions and tents pitched like a city in a great plain, that is, some white tent[s] of the Prester John ... and, in front of the white tents, one very large red tent pitched, which they say is set up for very great festivals or receptions.

Despite the presence of this crimson audience hall, the ceremony was going to be an entirely outdoor affair, centering around two long alleys of cloth-wrapped metal arches, resembling croquet wickets that a man could easily walk under. These parallel rows of trellises stretched outward from the aligned main portals of the Court compound's outer and inner linen walls, such that if one peered straight down the roofless colonnade they formed one might just discern the entrance to the *Negus'* cloistered residence in a vanishing perspective. The embassy's approach to these arbors, accomplished on horseback and directed only by the gestures and shouts of the summoners who rode or jogged alongside them, passed unnervingly near to the dusty paddocks of the four chained lions that always preceded the Prester's retinue on state occasions, each pawing the ground or roaring at the strange scents of the Europeans. Well to the right and left of the awaiting wickets, beyond a pair of intervening open spaces patrolled by men on plumed horses and by bare-chested whip-handlers who continually cracked out warnings, stood a huge crowd of spectators. The multitude stared intently at the troupe of strangers, more in curiosity than agitation, aligned in neat rows as if by prior assignment. It was not only the size of this throng that impressed our priest, but the beauty and richness of many of their costumes, which appeared far more colorful than those he had been used to seeing upon the road, and which included the pointed head-dresses of abbots and other high Church officials.

Dismounting at a signal from their escorts, and having duly received from these and retuned to them the Abyssinian courtesy of lowering their right hands to the ground, the Portuguese were suddenly confronted by the sight of a new honor-guard rapidly approaching them down the multi-colored archways. "There came to us fully sixty men like courtiers or mace-bearers ... half-running, because they are accustomed so to run with all the messages of the Prester." The appearance of this new retinue was like something out of a fevered dream, for while from the waist down each of them sported "girdles of colored silk" ending in "long fringes reaching to the ground," their shoulders were draped with "tawny, very shaggy ... lion skins" set off by "collars of gold" inlaid with "jewels and false stones." At the moment this jogging pride of leonine satyrs engulfed the embassy and shouldered them toward the trellises amidst a swelling roar from the crowd, it must have seemed to the hopeful travelers that Prester John's kingdom was at last offering up the caliber of ostentatious spectacles promised in the pages of its beguiling Letter.

This atmosphere of portentous grandeur was only increased by the arrival of the Prester's high officials, who now began stepping forward to confront the Portuguese at the entrance to the be-draped archways. First came the *Bitwaddad*, a senior minister of the government, but like so many Ethiopian officials, he was only one of a pair. The *Bitwaddad* of the Right Hand was the chief military officer, and was now on campaign in far-distant precincts against the Moorish enemies of the Prester; the man who stood before them was the Left-hand *Bitwaddad*, who defended and administered the capital in its various peregrinations across the landscape. Though an impressive figure, he discombobulated the Portuguese by making no word or gesture of greeting while several awkward minutes passed in silence — his functions on such occasions perhaps being more protective than diplomatic. All parlaying, it turned out, was to be the office of the elderly "Guardian of the Hours" or *Aqabe sa'at*, who now emerged from the red reception tent and shuffled toward the waiting and increasingly disoriented Europeans. This "Cabeata," as Álvares always rendered his title, was at once the ranking ecclesiastical figure attached to the Court, a judge of last appeal, and a privy councilor of the King — indeed, he was the only person who regularly enjoyed unrestricted access to the person of the *Negus*. It was he who, planting himself firmly before Dom Rodrigo, inquired of the Ambassador in a loud and formal voice, "what he wanted and where he came from." This was reassuring to the Portuguese, for it sounded like the preamble to a royal audience at any European court — surely they would be laying eyes on Prester John himself before the hour was out.

Dom Rodrigo replied through the translators (Portuguese to Arabic, Arabic to Amharic) in an equally public tone that "he came from India, and was bringing an embassy to the Prester John, from the Captain-Major and Governor of the Indies for the King of Portugal." The *Aqabe sa'at*, seemingly satisfied with this reply, turned about and slowly tottered up the colonnade, eventually disappearing into the Prester's residence, where presumably some equally choreographed announcement was made into an inclining royal ear. Some minutes later the Cabeata re-emerged into daylight and headed back down the lanes toward the Portuguese. If, however, the latter now expected a polite bow and an offer to "come this way," they were quickly disappointed. Again looking Dom Rodrigo square in the face, the old man demanded to know who he was and why he had come there. Caught off guard, the Ambassador could do no more than repeat his former reply word for word, whereupon the Prester's official, again betraying no hint of dissatisfaction, set off to deliver anew this information to his master. The sun climbed higher overhead and the surrounding crowd continued to murmur and stare until the *Aqabe sa'at* was seen to be making his third approach down through the wickets. Standing a third time before the strangers, he once more with an impassive countenance asked of them their origin and their business. Dom Rodrigo, utterly perplexed, blurted out a retort of honest distress: "I do not know what to say."

"Say what you want," replied the Cabeata in a kindly tone, "and I will tell it to the King." These oddly intimate words of encouragement, suggesting that the Ambassador was a penitent in a confession booth rather than the central figure in a large historical painting, convinced the touchy *fidalgo* that he was being toyed with and instantly brought to the surface his easily injured sense of dignity. "The Ambassador replied that he would not deliver his embassy to anyone except his Highness, and that he would not send to say anything except that he and his company sent to kiss his hands, and that they gave great thanks to God for having fulfilled their desires in bringing Christians together with Christians, and for their being the first." In other words, this was far too important a moment in the destiny of nations for games, and *he* knew it if the Prester's obviously senile functionary did not. As had occurred months before at the threshold of the *Bahr-nagas'* residence, however, an angry reply seemed to break through some settled fog ceremonial entropy — when next the Cabeata reappeared from within the imperial residence, "on reaching us he said that the Prester John sent to say that we should deliver to him what the Great Captain [i.e., the *Estado's* Governor] had sent him."

If any among them had not been sweating already, they must have begun now. Daily fending off the unexpected dangers of the road, they had almost been able to forget the deplorable nature of their official gifts and how badly offering up such trash would reflect upon themselves and the nation they represented. We know, however, that this idyll of denial had now suddenly come to an end because a panicked Dom Rodrigo, acting wholly against character, "asked us what he ought to do, and that each of us should say whatever he thought of it." This nervous committee could only conclude that the presents must be surrendered with a falsely brave face, but that for good measure they should toss in "four bales of pepper which were for our own expenses." This done, they undoubtedly prayed that their paltry goods would disappear into the Prester's tent and never be mentioned again by the offended monarch — but it was not to be, for the Court's etiquette required that they drink deeply from their cup of humiliation. The offering was indeed carried into the royal residence, but "afterwards it was brought back to the arches where we were. And they came and stretched the hangings [i.e., the tapestries and fabrics] which we had given on the arches, and so with the other things. Having set everything in sight of the people, they caused silence to be made, and the Chief Justice of the Court made a speech in a very loud voice, declaring, piece by piece, all the things which the [Governor] had sent to the Prester John." Father Álvares was by this time fairly well versed in Amharic, but one wonders whether his facility was keen enough to catch any accents of irony, sarcasm, and contempt as this distressingly short and unimpressive catalog was bellowed at the surrounding masses. After it was over — and it couldn't have lasted long — the Gift Crier seemed to end on an ambiguous note, instructing "that all were to give thanks to the Lord God because Christians had come together, and that if there were any whom it grieved, that they might weep, and any that rejoiced at it, that they might sing. And the great crowd of people who were near by gave a great shout as in praise of God, and it lasted a good while." Was this acclimation of the multitude sincere or merely a conventional gesture of protocol? No one among the Portuguese could tell for sure, but the embassy's worst fears seemed justified when the whole ceremony was brought to an abrupt and confusing end. As our priest starkly reports, "and with that they dismissed us."[2] They had simply assumed, of course, that all the pomp they had witnessed so far that day would issue in nothing less than a face-to-face encounter with the monarch himself. Apparently, though, the Ethiopians had other ideas. Yet they could still hold out hopes that the Prester would be — as his Crier seemed to suggest all men should be — too overjoyed by this first confluence of two Christian powers to resent the tattered state of the sorry tributes the strangers had offered up. As events were quickly to prove, however, Lebna Denel was in no way inclined to overlook the grievous insult he came to believe his guests had dealt him.

This royal anger, however, was not immediately apparent, for soon after they returned to their tent they discovered that they were the recipients of a lavish gift of delicacies from the *Negus*, including what Álvares appears to describe as an entire heifer baked into some sort of immense pastry and "stuffed with spices and fruits." Not only were there copious amounts of these foods, but the dishes were familiar enough — or by this time had become familiar enough — that they "could not have too much of it." Thus the men spent the next two days, which were the Ethiopian Saturday and Sunday sabbaths, happily gormandizing and remarking to each other about the impressive sights they had witnessed during whatever kind of ceremony — not an audience, clearly, but perhaps a reception, or even an inspection?— they had just participated in. Come Monday, however, they became aware of a rumor sweeping through the capital that the Portuguese were keeping back for themselves some of King Manoel's gifts to the *Negus*. Dom Rodrigo barely had time to become angry at being thus accused of both greed and duplicity before Zaga Za Ab arrived bearing a proposition which indicated that the slander had been believed — and perhaps even inaugurated — by the Prester himself. The monk calmly announced that if the embassy would surrender the rest of the gifts they were obviously hoarding, the King would guarantee that when it came time for the party to depart, they would be amply supplied with food at no expense to themselves all the way back to Massawa. The Ambassador took this accusatory bargain in especially bad humor because of his previous outrage at Zaga

Za Ab's campaign of whip-and-cudgel appropriation from defenseless villages during their inward trek. He replied that whatever might be the custom in this country it was not the habit of Portuguese gentlemen to rob poor people as they traveled about, and that King Manoel was not so indigent a sovereign as to send off his representatives on important missions without providing them with sufficient goods and monies to pay their own expenses along the way. This display of high dudgeon apparently elicited little more than a shrug from Zaga Za Ab, but as soon as he was gone all food deliveries to the embassy's tent ceased forthwith. Perhaps even more ominously, word came from DaCovilhã and the other resident Franks, who had been dropping in regularly, that they had been forbidden to approach or speak to the newcomers on pain of the *Negus'* severe displeasure. It was now distressingly clear that even their spontaneous addition of the pepper reserves had failed to swell the embassy's collection of odds and ends into even so much as a *believable* present, much less an adequate one.

On Tuesday morning the Europeans awakened to cries from throughout the city that the *Negus* had departed, and before they could scrape together a breakfast from the weekend's leftovers tents were coming down all around them. Zaga Za Ab was apparently loitering pointedly nearby, for when Dom Rodridgo stepped out to question him about when the embassy might expect the mules that would transport their gear to the Prester's next encampment, the monk had a ready reply. He said that since the Portuguese were so accustomed to refusing hospitality and paying their own way even in countries where they were guests of a great King, that De Lima could buy whatever mules he needed from whomever he could find to sell him such animals, but that he had better hurry up about it because soon this section of the plain would be as empty as they had found it a few days before. This provoked a haughty retort from the Ambassador to the effect that neither he nor his father nor his father's father for many generations back had soiled their hands with trade and that he had no intention of turning merchant now when he was in the midst of performing an honorable service for king, country, and the Christian religion. Despite this bluster, by Thursday no mules had arrived and Dom Rodrigo was made sufficiently nervous by the continued evacuation of everyone but the embassy that he sent Father Álvares and the interpreter, Joam Gonçalves, onward toward the departed Court in order to plead their case for beasts of burden. Impatient to be starting back for the coast, he also charged them to inquire as to just when he might be granted an actual audience with the Prester, and to state that if it wasn't going to be anytime soon that he would like to submit his official communications from King Manoel in writing. Once arrived, the pair of envoys managed to effect a brief interview with the *Bitwaddad*, but that official was politely evasive, and thus "gave us no answer, but spoke of things that were irrelevant, as for instance, whether the King of Portugal was married, and how many wives he had, and how many fortresses he had in India, with many other questions beside the purpose." As our priest had already learned, Ethiopian courtiers were masters at deflecting any question they found inconvenient.

"So," sighs Álvares, "we returned without any conclusion," though once he was back with the main party both advice and practical assistance did begin to arrive from the Prester's captive Franks. Of course their visits to the Portuguese tent now had to be accomplished by stealth, and only during those times when Zaga Za Ab was elsewhere occupied, for it was clear their erstwhile guide "was [now] attached to us as a guard." Among these fellow Europeans our priest counted, besides their unofficial leader Da Covilhã, several Genoese, two Catalans, a Greek, a Basque, and a German. (Interestingly, he states that some of them had been prisoners in Jiddah who had been so cruelly tantalized by Lopo Soares' aborted attack on that city in 1517 that they had impulsively stolen a brigantine and attempted to follow the retreating Christian fleet, washing up across the Red Sea at Massawa.) These exiles were all agreed that advisors close to the *Negus* had become convinced that Dom Rodrigo was holding back further bales of pepper originally designated as gifts, and that the Portuguese should therefore hand over some of their remaining private store "because otherwise we should not have leave to return, because this was their custom, never to allow any one to return who came to their kingdoms." With such living examples of the truth of this claim whispering before them, Dom Rodrigo reluctantly acquiesced to a tactic that would clearly be read as an admission of guilt: "we agreed to give to the Prester four out of the five bales of pepper that we still had, and to keep [only] one for our expenses." And, as long they were stooping that low they determined that they might as well take out some additional insurance. The *Negus* had initially asked to inspect their baggage as well — alright then, they would turn over some of that too. "We also decided to send him four chests covered with leather, which were among the company, in which came clothes, and this because we thought he would be pleased with them, being something not found in that country." With servants and mules provided by the resident Franks (for despite their lack of freedom, the captives seldom wanted for worldly goods), the embassy made its way across the high plateau toward the Court's latest bivouac.

Arriving at that place the Portuguese discovered that the Prester's city had re-congealed not around the usual royal tent, but rather around a substantial stone house, longer than it was wide and roofed by thatch, which was apparently substituting for it. The linen walls of the inner and outer courtyards had likewise been replaced by high hedges of thorn — much larger versions of the prickly barricades that had sheltered some of the embassy's campsites from hyenas along the road. Otherwise, though, the rigorous conformity of the Ethiopian Court was still in evidence, each grandee's tent in its one unalterable position

Six. The King and I

vis-à-vis the Prester's central domicile, their bright tops like the stars of a familiar constellation that nightly wheeled through the sky but never changed its internal arrangement. Once the Portuguese were settled into their new tents, an odd request arrived from the *Negus* by means of a page — he wanted to know whether any of them possessed a gold or silver cross, for if they did he would like to see it. They in fact had none of such metal, the last one having been thrown away upon the disdainful *Bahr-nagas,* but one of Álvares' plain wooden crucifixes was dispatched in its place. This was soon returned to them by the page with a message that the Prester "rejoiced much that we were Christians." Was this meant as some sort of rebuke, as if to say that, given their supposed attempt to hoard the gifts, that the King had begun to suspect they were Moors or pagans? Rather than puzzle out whether he had been again insulted or not, though, Dom Rodrigo used this opening to report that he had at the ready several bales of top-quality Indian pepper and some sturdy chests filled with clothes that he would be delighted to send to the royal apartments. To this the Prester replied that he had no need of anything more from the Portuguese and that in fact he had already given away to the poor most of what they had previously presented to him. (To the poor? Was this yet another dig at the dismal quality of the presents?) Besides, reported the page, the *Negus* had been informed by Matthew's slaves that most of the riches meant for him had been instead lavished on the Viceroy's favorite churches back in India. This prompted a hurried explanation from Álvares to the effect that while he had indeed occasionally hung up certain of the Prester's tapestries on feast days during the embassy's extended delay in Goa, that each and every one of them that survived the unpleasantness of 1517 had been delivered to His Highness. What occurred next was again difficult to interpret.

> When this answer had gone, another messenger arrived to say that the Prester ordered that the Ambassador should come at once with all his people and company (this might be about three hours after sunset). We all began quickly to dress ourselves in our good clothes to go whither we were summoned. When we were [fully] dressed, [however,] another message came that we were not to go: so we all remained like the peacock when he spreads his tail and is gay, [but] when he looks at his feet becomes sad: so pleased we were at going, so sad at stopping behind.[3]

Had these countermanding instructions been the evening's final calculated insult, or was there some more benign explanation? Was the embassy being cruelly teased, or had the Prester just gotten sleepy? Attempting to read the royal mind and to influence it in the absence of hard information was quickly becoming an obsession with the Portuguese, for with every day that passed without an audience, the prospect of their extended exile seemed all the more certain.

It was now the very end of October, and during the next week the embassy would twice be invited into tantalizing proximity with the *Negus,* only to be frustratingly rebuffed on the very brink of the conclusive interview that they sought. The first of these abortive approaches commenced with their being unexpectedly summoned to the royal compound "two hours after nightfall"— they were soon to discover that Lebna Dengel was an inveterate night-owl who preferred doing business by candlelight. Arriving at the outer gate, they were kept waiting by functionaries in a cold, sharp wind for over an hour, whereupon several members of the party decided to fire their muskets into the air — either to relieve the boredom or remind those within of their presence. If the latter end was intended, this shooting immediately accomplished it, for soon a message via page from the Prester arrived asking why they hadn't brought more firearms with them. To this Dom Rodrigo replied dryly that it was because they thought they were on a diplomatic journey to see friends and not raiding the land of an enemy, as if airing the possibility that he might now be reconsidering that assumption. No sooner had this answer been sent in than "five principal men" arrived at the portal and made ready to escort the Portuguese toward the *Negus'* sanctuary. Progress inward, however, turned into a halting, Mother-May-I sort of affair, for this brace of officials, forming a line in front of the Europeans and flanked by candle-bearers on each side, only advanced about five paces toward the stone building before they halted and began to sing out, each one after the other, "Here they are, whom you ordered, Lord." According to a startled Álvares, "each one said these words quite ten times" until at last "we heard a cry from within ... in a very loud voice," ordering them to proceed. Again, though, only five paces were covered before another halt was called and the whole roundelay began anew, and "of these pauses they made quite ten from the first entrance to the second." Once the inner courtyard had been reached the content of the cries changed a bit but not the pace of progress, so the embassy was thoroughly frozen by the time they reached the foot of a dais that had been raised in front of the stone building's solitary entrance. This platform was flanked on either side by eighty additional candle-bearers held in straight lines by long canes that stretched across their chests, the central isle that opened between their ranks being completely covered in thick carpets all the way up to the house's threshold. This opening itself was hung with curtains of gold brocade and silk, behind which, obscured from view and safe from the elements, presumably sat Prester John himself.

As soon as the Portuguese were assembled on the platform, a message was sent out from the *Negus* "without any other preliminary," demanding to know where the rest of his gifts were. Clearly it was time for the embassy to lance this boil by any means to hand. Therefore, "the Ambassador replied that if His Highness would hear him, he would give him an explanation of everything," and launched into a highly sanitized version of how Lopo Soares had been responsible for the destruction of most of the Prester's presents. The King was informed that back in 1517 "the presenter of the articles" (i.e., Lourenço de

Cosmo) had been killed on the Dahlak Islands, that the "winds ha[d] been contrary," and that therefore Lopo Soares' fleet had been unable to "fetch the port of [Massawa]." It was then admitted that King Manoel had sent out his next fleet from Portugal not knowing of this failure, and hence carrying no replacement gifts, and that this next fleet (which had brought the embassy) had justifiably "not [been] certain of being able to make the port of [Massawa]," and thus had been sent "to the Red Sea strait [only] to conquer Moors," and perhaps again assault Jiddah. This explained, continued Dom Rodrigo, now drifting from partial into outright lies, "why they had not brought [all] the pieces and things which the King of Portugal had sent [the Prester], which were in India all together and looked after." This answer seemed to appease the *Negus* somewhat concerning the whereabouts of his gifts, but toward the end of his misleading tale Dom Rodrigo had also mentioned Matthew's journey to India, Portugal, and back again, as well as that envoy's untimely death at Bizam. Now the Ambassador was surprised to discover that these seemingly inoffensive remarks had apparently turned the Prester's unease in a new direction, for they brought a sharp reply from within "that he had not sent Matthew to Portugal." Come to think of it, the *Bitwaddad* had muttered much the same thing among his other "irrelevancies" in the days preceding. What was this sudden distancing — or disownment — all about?

On a literal level the Prester's statement was quite true. Lebna Dengel had been born near the turn of the century, which meant that he had been only a boy when Queen Eleni, who was acting as Regent during his minority, dispatched Matthew to India with the letter that had so stirred the heart of Albuquerque and the rest of the Portuguese millenarian party. Eleni had begun life as the daughter of a Muslim chieftain who paid an annual tribute to the Ethiopian King, and only converted to Christianity when she became the junior wife of the *Negus* Zara Yaqob. It was this background, as well as her native shrewdness, that gave her a clear-eyed understanding of just how isolated the highland Christian empire was amid an encircling Islamic world. This wily survivor remained a trusted advisor to Lebna Dengel's father, the *Negus* Na'od (ruled 1494–1508), during which time she advocated friendly relations with the lowland Mohammedan kingdoms, but the increasing influence of jihadists in Harrar and Adal had rendered such appeasement ineffective, and thus after Na'od's death she shifted tactics and appealed for help to the newly-arrived Portuguese in India. This plan was obviously now on the brink of bearing fruit, but in the meantime Lebna Dengel had come of age and in 1517 the young king had routed and killed his main Muslim enemy, Mafouz. Thus, however well disposed the current *Negus* was toward a larger Christian alliance between Ethiopia and Portugal, he felt in no immediate need of rescue by anyone and resented any implication that he might.[4] Furthermore, he and his courtiers were cognizant enough of the wider world to understand that the result of Portugal's "rescue" of the Nestorian Christians in India had resulted in India becoming effectively a Portuguese possession. Thus the King and his advisors were morbidly anxious about what Eleni had told Matthew to promise the Portuguese in return for their aid a decade ago. Had she given away the store? She claimed she hadn't, but as far as Lebna Dengel was concerned there was something of the witch about the aged Eleni, and thus who could tell what the real truth was? He thus had to make these Franks understand that Matthew had never spoken for him.

At that moment, however, the deceased envoy was the last thing Dom Rodrigo wanted to talk about. He wished to see the Prester face-to-face, for he possessed — understandably for a European — a fixed idea that such would be the only circumstances under which he could adequately fulfill his charge of delivering a formal diplomatic message from King Manoel and the Governor. One also gets the feeling that Lebna Dengel had begun to understand this, and was willing to purposely frustrate the Ambassador in order to extract some candid and perhaps damning confession from him, either concerning the gifts, or Matthew's charge, or some other matter. At any rate, there was to be no satisfaction for either party this night, for "messages went and came without any conclusion, and so they dismissed us."

The very next night, however, the Portuguese were called back, encountering only minor variations in regard to the preliminaries. This time, for instance, they were requested to shoot off their muskets at the outer gate as soon as they arrived there, and Álvares now counted a full 200 candle-bearers as well as additional "resplendent people on both sides [of the dais], all in a row with drawn swords and shields in their hands, and placed as though they were about to slash one another." This time the *Negus* wanted to quiz Dom Rodrigo about firearms, asking him who possessed the better guns and artillery pieces, the Moors or the Portuguese, and which side was more afraid of the other's musketry. De Lima answered with nationalistic swagger, claiming that "since the Portuguese were valiant in the faith of Jesus Christ, they had no fear of the Moors; and if they had had fear they would not have come from such a distance, and without necessity, to [fight] them." Well enough, continued the Prester, but who taught the Moors to make muskets and cannons in the first place? One can understand his interest, for since 1517 when the Ottomans had replaced the Mamluks as the Islamic masters of the Nile and Red Sea, firearms had been making their way into the hands of Ethiopia's ever-encroaching enemies, while the Abyssinians possessed none of their own. He thus seemed to harbor a dark suspicion that the Portuguese or some other European power had shown the infidels how to manufacture such guns in order to realize a Judas-like profit. However, Dom Rodrigo's answer that "the Turks were men, and had the skill and knowledge of men, perfect in all respects excepting in faith," seemed to mollify the King on this point.

Six. The King and I

The next message to emerge from behind the curtains was a request for a demonstration of Portuguese sword-fighting, and the Ambassador, tempering his impatience, ordered two of his men to make some passes at each other. "They did it reasonably well," says Álvares, "and yet not as well as the Ambassador desired that things Portuguese should be done: and as the Prester sent to ask for others to come out, the Ambassador said to Jorge d'Abreu that they should both go out." Even given the polite fiction that swordsmanship improved with social rank, this was a perilous decision for Dom Rodrigo to make. Knowing the tensions that had already alienated the two men — knowing that they had briefly come to swords'-point in anger already — our priest must have trembled to think how easily this "demonstration" could have turned into a duel in deadly earnest. Indeed, one could easily have concluded then and there that the Ambassador possessed no self-knowledge whatsoever. One *could* have, that is, except that what came next made it appear that Dom Rodrigo's decision to spar with his rival was in fact a risky plan to advance the embassy's business. After the conclusion of the demonstration (which "the Prester could see ... very well from behind the curtains, and took great pleasure in"), Dom Rodrigo tried to capitalize on the fact that he had just humiliated himself by becoming a kind of juggler for the *Negus'* amusement, and asked his own favor in return:

> At the end of it all the Ambassador sent to tell the Prester John that he had done that to do him service, and that otherwise he would not have done it, even though they gave him 50,000 *cruzados*, for any other prince in the world, unless he were ordered to do it by the King of Portugal his lord, to whom he was bound. And he begged His Highness to hear him, and learn what the [Governor] of the King of Portugal had ordered him to say, and to dismiss him, that he might be able to join the fleet at the time of its arrival, so as not to cause expense without profit.

The *Negus'* rejoinder to this plea solidifies one's suspicions that he was now consciously attempting to exasperate his guest, for "an answer came that we had now just arrived, and had not seen even a third part of his dominions, [and] that we should rest." When the Portuguese Governor sailed again into Massawa, continued the Prester, he would no doubt send a message to Court — that would be the time to talk about the embassy leaving. Before then, he had many ideas to discuss with the Portuguese about building permanent forts at Massawa, Zeila, and other places, and about opening safer routes to the Holy Land — all this was going to take time. "The Ambassador answered that these were [also] the desires of the King of Portugal, and that he still begged of him to hear him, and if he determined not to hear him," to permit him to send his official pronouncement in writing. To this the *Negus* replied that he was not averse to seeing something in writing, but that he would prefer that any such communication first be translated into Amharic — would his honored guest mind seeing to that?—and now, if it wasn't too much trouble, he would like to witness a demonstration of some Portuguese dances. When the embassy at last returned to their tent in the wee hours of the next morning, the King's servants "came after us with 300 big loaves and twenty-four jars of wine."[5] It seemed just the kind of feast designed to anchor one to the ground.

And so a stalemate had developed, with Lebna Dengel deliberately delaying the business of the embassy out of some unsettling fear or misgiving about the Portuguese, however ill defined. The debacle of the gifts had apparently sown doubts in him about their national character; he was fearful about what "hearing" King Manoel's message might obligate him to do; he didn't seem to like Dom Rodrigo's manner. It wasn't that he was planning to walk away from an alliance with Portugal, and he probably wasn't seriously considering keeping the embassy captive as he had the other Frankish travelers, but he was clearly listening only to the voices of caution, mistrust, and delay—both those emanating from his advisors and those coming from within himself. Things might have remained at this pass for a very long time if it hadn't been for Father Álvares. As of yet the Prester did not appear to have taken much or perhaps any notice of our priest. This is not remarkable, given the peculiar circumstances of the clergy within Ethiopian culture. Because their level of education could frequently be minimal, because they were not celibate, because they often worked the ground and traded in the marketplace much as laymen did, and because there were so very many of them relative to the population of the kingdom as a whole, Ethiopian priests simply did not stand out from the background of society to the extent that they did in Renaissance Europe. In the estimation of the *Negus*, if the Franks had brought along a priest, it did not automatically mean that he was anyone special, or that he might offer a window onto Portuguese society any different from that of his secular companions. Indeed, he might not have gotten to know Álvares at all had it not been for the fact that among the random things from inside the embassy's tent that the *Negus* kept asking to be shown — swords, armor, gunpowder, silk stockings — he also requested to see the wafer-iron used to make the host for mass. It was a weary Dom Rodrigo who decided that the priest might as well haul over that particular item to the royal compound for yet another session of show-and-tell.

Something about the bearing and discourse of Álvares must have appealed to the young King as he watched from behind his curtains while the padre explained how the machine managed to turn out thin crackers imprinted with the figure of a cross. Álvares' Amharic was getting stronger by the day, and that probably aided the process, though if a translator was now occasionally superfluous, the pages were still kept busy protecting the *Negus* from the dishonor of speaking directly to commoners. At any rate, he must have got a strong inkling that further contact with this man might reveal a truth about his guests that could settle his mind about them one way or the other. Accordingly, he invited our priest to return the next evening and to bring with him as much of his priestly gear as he could carry, for he desired a complete explanation of how each separate piece of equipage contributed to performing a mass. As it turned out, he was also looking for a good debate, and Álvares did not disappoint him in either regard.

Our priest reports that he arrived at the *Negus'* compound along with "the full vestments, the chalice, corporals [i.e., altar cloths], altar stone, and cruets," and that the monarch began the proceedings by carefully examining it all, "piece by piece." His first question involved the altar stone, which while smooth on top, was underneath "[but] little squared, and of the nature and fashion of the [natural] stone." Obviously comparing it with Ethiopian *tabots*—those exquisite replications of the Mosaic tablets that served to consecrate each of his nation's churches—he asked why "if there were such good craftsmen in Portugal" they didn't finish the job. Álvares replied that it was very steady and served him well, but the *Negus* insisted that "the things of God ought to be perfect, and not imperfect." Then they turned to the vestments, whereupon the King "bade me dress myself as if to say mass; and I dressed myself in his presence." As he donned the liturgical items, the priest explained the symbolic associations of each, such as the alb's standing for the robe for which Pilate's soldier's had diced, the girdle for the chastity of priesthood, and the maniple for the cord which bound Christ's hands on the way to Golgotha. At some point in this lesson Álvares heard the Prester's own voice crying out in surprised approval, and, when he had pushed on through the stole and the chasuble, once more a clearly audible royal compliment broke through the curtains. Perhaps remembering himself, the delighted King then "again spoke to the interpreters, and they said that he ordered me to disrobe and tell him over again what each piece signified." This done, the *Negus* "declared with a very loud voice that we were Christians who had all the Passion in full." Both message and messenger seemed to be giving satisfaction so far, but the going was about to get thornier.

Pivoting without warning from matters of costume to questions of schism, the Prester demanded to know where the true head of Christ's Church resided, in Rome or in Constantinople? Álvares replied that the Pope in Rome was the Church's sole leader, citing both the familiar pun from the Gospel of Matthew wherein St. Peter (in Latin, "Petrus") is described by Jesus as the rock ("petram") upon which his earthly church will henceforth be founded, and the Nicene Creed demanding adherence to "one Catholic and Apostolic Church." The *Negus* shot back (by means of the interpreter and the page) that such was a good account of Rome's credentials, but that it had been St. Andrew who had first brought Christ's Church to Constantinople and St. Mark who had brought it to Alexandria, and that thus the Church possessed more than one coequal foundation-stone. (It was from the Alexandrian Coptic Church, recall, that the Ethiopian clergy traced their own roots, and from which they still received their sole *Abuna*, or archbishop.) "To this I replied that his reasoning assisted mine," proclaimed our priest with a Jesuitical flourish, "because St. Peter was the god-father and master of St. Mark, and he had sent him to those parts: and thus neither Mark nor [Andrew] could make churches except in the name of him who sent them, and thus their churches were [mere] members of the head which sent them." The King was willing to rest satisfied with this answer, but now wanted to know why Portuguese priests didn't marry, since the same Council of Nicaea that Álvares had already invoked had ordained that clergymen should wed. Our priest responded that the only issues he knew to have been settled at Nicaea were those involving the wording of the Creed aforementioned and the awarding to Mary of the title "Mother of God." Come now, said the *Negus*, several of the holy apostles were married, so it must be acceptable for mere priests to emulate them. This statement prompted Álvares to attempt an apostle-by-apostle refutation, during which he asserted that St. Peter had fathered his daughter before he was a follower of Christ, that St. John the Evangelist had left his marriage in order to serve Jesus, and that after the crucifixion all the apostles so zealously preached the Gospel that they had neither the time nor inclination to pursue pleasures of the flesh. And, in a not-so-veiled criticism of what he deemed the disturbingly secular lives of the Ethiopian clergy, he added that the Church demanded celibacy from priests so that they might be "more pure in their consciences, and not take up their time with wives and children, herds, farming, and property." The *Negus* gave no ground, however, for "they replied to this that their books ordered that they should marry, and that so Paul had spoken." This was apparently an allusion to that patriarch's well-known adage in First Corinthians that it is better to marry than to burn, and by this point one wonders whether Father Álvares wasn't feeling rather heated himself. So far the debate had been cordial, but he must have had a growing sense that his answers to these delicate questions might carry large implications for the embassy's future.

At one point in the evening The *Negus* denounced Pope Leo the Great (papacy 440–461), claiming that he had "broken" many things that were "ordained and sworn" at Nicaea. This was because the Ethiopians, being monphysites, recognized no Council after Nicaea and especially not Chalcedon (451), which had denounced monophysitism as heretical and which had occurred during Leo's term of office. That this — by far the most explosive point separating the Abyssinian king and the Portuguese priest — was successfully negotiated must have been partially due to some disarming aspect of Álvares' manner, for he claims to have defended the ancient Pope rather stoutly. "I answered that I did not know of them"— i.e., of Leo's supposed violations of Nicene doctrine—

but it seemed to me that if he had broken any of them, they would be such as touched the heresy which was great at that time, and that he would approve those which were necessary and profitable to the faith, and that otherwise he would not have been confirmed and canonized as a saint, as he is.

It is pretty clear from the above response that Álvares did not yet fully grasp what the Ethiopians' specific problems with Leo and the Council of Chalcedon actually were, and that thus this rather general defense did not enrage the King or any of his assembled courtiers, even though it contained the fatal word "heresy." He hadn't, after all, specified *which* belief he was labeling a heresy. But still, this encounter must have pushed him a bit farther toward the conclusion about his hosts which, eventually, he would reluctantly and painfully reach. He must therefore have been unspeakably relieved when the *Negus* next asked him to sing a Latin hymn or two.

By the time the performance was finally brought to an end, Lebna Dengel was showing, through the medium of Álvares, an enthusiasm for the Portuguese presence that he had not yet evidenced when Dom Rodrigo stood before him, exclaiming several times "that we were [indeed] Christians, as though still he had doubted it." When, in reply to a query as to why the Europeans hadn't yet said a mass of their own while at Court, our priest responded that he had not got a suitable tent for it, the *Negus* promised that he would instantly supply one. He wanted to witness a Catholic mass, and he wanted his people to witness it too, speaking like someone who had decided that he had little to fear from any differences that might there be revealed for all to see. It was clear that the long night's grilling of our priest on religious issues had begun to re-focus the King's eyes upon the larger picture — upon the prospect of a Christian alliance, a liberated Holy Land, and the potential destruction of Islam. That it had also taken the earnest and unassuming good nature of Álvares to accomplish this — that the progress of affairs of state had had to await the advent of the proper human touch — is not so surprising. Lebna Dengel was still only twenty-four, and his minority had been in many ways the lonely one often reserved in various kingdoms for the throne's appointed heir. When he instinctively liked someone, and felt sympathy and sincerity flow his way in return, it made an impression that carried much before it. For our priest, meanwhile, it had been a long and taxing examination for a man no longer young: "it must have been past midnight when we went away," he says, and "all the evening was spent in what has been related, without an idle moment."

Not that the Prester came around immediately. This first interrogation of Álvares had occurred on the night of November 5th. On the 8th the embassy was summoned only as far as the outer gate and peppered with questions by a runner from the royal apartments, asking why they had landed at Massawa instead of somewhere else on the coast, why they didn't display religious tattoos as the Ethiopians did, and other seemingly disconnected queries. Dom Rodrigo "replied to each of the questions as was fitting; and, moreover, he requested [the King] to give him leave and dispatch us on our journey." However, "upon this there came [only] a reply that we were not to fear, that we should soon go." On the 9th the *Negus* sent to the embassy's tent asking to see swords and breeches, and eventually asked so many questions that Álvares uncharacteristically informs us that they "are not written down to avoid prolixity." Then, the night of the 12th, the Prester delivered "five very beautiful horses" to the Portuguese pavilion, "desiring the Ambassador and four others to ... come and pretend to fight before his tent." Dom Rodrigo apparently complied with this new request for him to turn entertainer, though our priest understatedly relates that he "was not much pleased, because it was not his way." The next day the King sent the embassy a fine silver chalice for their trouble, and yet more inquiries, this time about how fresh water was carried at sea. The day after that, His Majesty was asking for a list of all their names and what the allegorical meaning of each might be. On the 15th, an armored horse was paraded before the Europeans and they were asked whether "there were any such arms in Portugal." And so it went for two full weeks: plenty of communication at a cool distance, but no hint of just when the formal audience for which Dom Rodrigo burned might take place.

During this same interval, however, Father Álvares had been holding his Catholic masses, and doing so in a very public way. The tent in which he accomplished this had been, as promised, promptly delivered. As it happened, this pavilion, which was constructed of brocade and velvet, had an interesting provenance, for "they said that four years ago the Prester had taken it in the field from the King of Adel, who is the Moorish King, lord of Zeila and Barbora"—i.e., the defeated and deceased Mafouz of Harrar. "And so the Prester sent to say that we should bless the tent before saying mass in it, lest some Moor should have committed sin in it." Wasting no time, our priest performed his first service the next morning to a congregation that was mostly, though not exclusively European, for "there came to it as many Franks as had been at the Court these forty years, and also some men of the country." Those few Ethiopians in attendance must have reported to their master that nothing in a Roman mass appeared immediately destructive of faith and morality, for by Saturday the 17th "the Prester John [had] ordered all the lords and grandees of his Court to come and hear our mass, and likewise on the following Sunday, when there were many more than on the Saturday." If our priest had scruples about encouraging the Judaizing double Sabbath of his hosts in this way, their response drowned out such doubts: "according to what appeared to us from their behavior, and [from] what was told to us by the Franks that we found in the country, and also [by] the interpreters who went about with us, they were astonished by and very much praised our services." Indeed, the courtiers appeared sufficiently impressed that Álvares even claimed to have made some headway with them afterwards in denouncing their insistence on stuffing first-communion crusts down the throats of newborn babes.

So successful were the proffered masses that by Monday night our priest was back in front of the Prester's curtained dais, again answering theological questions. This time around he clearly understood what was at stake, for he nervously reports that the King prodded him on a number of issues, "and I answered him as God helped me, to some of them, 'I do not know,' and to some of them, 'It is so.'" Most of the queries seemed designed to reveal whether the Bible that Westerners read was the same as that perused by Abyssinians. It was not, in several important respects, for there were a number of scriptural writings held to be sacred by the Ethiopian Church — most notably the books of Enoch and Jubilees, but others as well — that had been rejected as apocryphal by Rome. Still, the Prester's questions, as well as Álvares' answers, were at first constructed in such a way as to inadvertently blur this discrepancy. When, for instance, the priest was quizzed as to "how many Prophets prophesied the coming of Christ," or "how many books each prophet had made," or "how many books St. Paul wrote," Father Álvares made a number of observations but worked round to saying that he supposed it was often a matter of how one divided up the holy word of God into chapters convenient for reading and teaching, and that some Christians might do this differently than others. This worked for a while, but before the night was out the *Negus* put forth a query that was not so amenable to equivocation. "Then there came another question asking me to say all the books of the prophets, Apostles, and Evangelists of the Old and New Testaments, [and] how many books there were there in all." The correct answer, from a Catholic perspective, would have been sixty-six. And yet at this point Father Álvares did something surprising — something which indicates both that he knew the embassy's success might be riding on his answers, and that sometimes God's greater purposes require even a priest to tell a fib. "I had already heard among them that there would be eighty-one books, and because of what I had heard, I answered that there were eighty one." Such a surrender of principle to expediency, however, instantly drove a guilty qualification from his lips to the effect that he really could "not affirm anything positively, because for six years [he] had been sailing about, and had no books with [him], and [his] memory would break down." But our priest's lie had already performed its work, for "the answer came that I had a good memory, and that my replies were the truth, although I had given them as opinions."[6] Álvares was probably even more grateful to see the end of this grilling than he had been of the one before.

However uneasy our priest may have felt about his actions, his strategic prevarication did the trick; the very next night the embassy was ordered to present themselves in full dress at the royal compound, and this time it was to be for the real thing. After another three hour wait at the outer gate, which was apparently just as customary at Court as a polite bow, their progress inward was surprisingly swift. A special reception tent had been set up within the inner courtyard, close by the house the *Negus* had lately been using, before which they now beheld "many more people assembled than on any of the other times, and many with arms, and many more [with] lighted candles." All told there were over a thousand guards present, some dressed in coats of mail, others displaying metal plates and studs upon their silk and velvet clothing, and all possessed of shields, spears, battle-axes, and swords. Fanning out from the tent's entrance between these martial columns were a multitude of rich carpets that wholly covered the intervening ground, on some of which ceremonial garments had been carefully laid out. No sooner had the Portuguese begun to take in this spectacle than the *Aqabe sa'at* emerged from a wall of curtains that hung just behind the tent's opening and spoke some words to Dom Rodrigdo, which Da Covilhã, standing just behind him, translated. Apparently the men of the embassy were to deck themselves out in the provided robes and capes before they proceeded further, which the Ambassador ordered his people to do. All seemed to be going well until it became clear to Jorge d'Abreu, who had quickly grabbed the richest cloak for himself, that Dom Rodrigo considered himself to be exempt from this ceremonial masquerade. Perhaps he thought it part of his official office to appear before the *Negus* only in authentic Portuguese finery — but whether it was his idea or the *Aqabe sa'at's*, this implied distinction between De Lima and D'Abreu was soon compounded by the "Cabeata" taking the Ambassador by the arm and leading him alone through the intervening curtains, leaving the rest of the now doubly-dressed envoys behind. D'Abreu visibly fumed at this perceived slight, and apparently determined then and there to make both Dom Rodrigo and Prester John understand that he was in every way the Ambassador's equal.

After a few minutes delay Álvares and the others were bidden by the returning *Aqabe sa'at* to enter the tent themselves, passing through at least two sets of draperies before finding themselves in an inner chamber dominated by "a large and rich dais with very splendid carpets," its apex shielded by yet one more line of curtains. Here they discovered Dom Rodrigo, down on one knee and now dressed in what are described as "some of the King's own clothes." Exactly what these garments consisted of is not clear, but what is plain is that they again clearly communicated to D'Abreu that a firm distinction was being made between himself and the Ambassador. Dom Rodrigo, speaking over his shoulder, ordered his men to kneel likewise in a row some steps behind him. His lieutenant, however, smarting from this new insult to his dignity, boldly broke ranks, strode forward, and knelt at the Ambassador's very shoulder. De Lima's outrage at this presumption can well be imagined, but now was not the time to castigate a rebellious subordinate, for they were on the very brink of peering into Ethiopia's political equivalent of the Holy-of-Holies. They were at last going to see the long-sought Prester John face-to face, whom innumerable men in ages before them had only imagined as through a glass darkly.

Somewhere a stone bell was struck, producing a low and melancholy note, and slowly, before the upturned faces of the kneeling Portuguese the last set of curtains were drawn aside by unseen hands, revealing Ethiopia's King of Kings atop his four-stepped dais, seated upon his throne of state. Or rather, *nearly* revealing him, for suspended upon cords too thin to perceive there hung still "a piece of blue taffeta before his face which covered his mouth and beard." But the ceremony of unveiling was not yet completed: as the Europeans looked on in silence another bell would sound from time to time, "and from time to time they lowered [the blue cloth] and the whole of his face appeared, and again they raised it." Álvares describes the man he so briefly beheld:

> He had on his head a high crown of gold and silver, that is to say, one piece of gold and another of silver from the top downwards, and a silver cross in his hand.... The Prester was dressed in a rich mantle of gold brocade, and silk shirts of wide sleeves.... From his knees downwards he had a rich cloth of silk and gold well spread out like a Bishop's apron, and he was sitting in majesty as they paint God the Father on the wall.... In age, complexion, and stature, he is a young man, not very black. His complexion might be chestnut or bay, not very dark in colour; he is very much a man of breeding, of middling stature; they said that he was twenty-three years of age, and he looks like that, his face is round, the eyes large, the nose high in the middle, and his beard is beginning to grow. In presence and state he fully looks like the great lord that he is.

Let us first address the racial aspect of Father Álvares' account. When he tells us that Lebna Dengel was "not very black" and in fact possessed skin that was "chestnut or bay" in hue, what are we to make of it? Can we assume that his racist habits of mind were causing him to see what he (and so many other Europeans) wanted to see? Or can we put it down to the combined effects of candlelight, fluttering draperies, and an ageing man's failing eyesight? There is an explanation, however, which absolves our priest from all delusions, psychological or somatic. Since it had long been the custom for the *Negus*es of Ethiopia to marry the daughters of Muslim potentates on the fringes of their empire, it may well have been the case that the successive Lions of Judah had cumulatively inherited more of the distinctly Semitic characteristics of Arabian peoples than the average Abyssinian commoner: ages of matrimonial statecraft may in fact have served to lighten his skin. Since Álvares never mentions the subject again, such speculations must mark the limit of our knowledge, for no reliable image of the man has come down to us.

As for the rest of the description, what is striking is its lack of either elation or disappointment. Our priest had apparently fully reconciled himself to discovering that "the Prester John"—and there is a world of hard-won realism in that simple preceding article — was not going to resemble in appearance and accoutrements the figure of hope and legend. And yet no whiff of disappointment is detectable either — the young monarch is rendered as dignified, alert, vigorous, and winning. In Álvares' portrait he appears as what he was: a Christian king ruling a realm beyond the territory of the Moors, and thus to our priest and all his fellow believers a person whose existence was providential without being miraculous, hope-giving despite his unmistakably ordinary humanity. Álvares does not say if Lebna Dengel's eyes sought out anyone in particular during his fleeting appearance before the embassy, but if our priest was indeed so favored on that night he was not the man to mention it. We can make our own guesses, for it is clear that the King and the priest had already traveled — given the formality and cultural distance that would always color their mutual relations — remarkably far down the road to genuine friendship.

When the curtains closed and the *Negus* told Dom Rodrigo that he again might stand, D'Abreu also rose to his feet. Again, though, there was barely time for a dagger-like stare before the *Aqabe sa'at* was standing before the Ambassador holding up a silver bowl, into which he indicated that the letters from King Manoel were to be placed. De Lima kissed the missives he had been so anxious to part with and lifted them along with their Amharic translations into the receptacle, whereupon they were delivered up the steep steps of the dais to the *Negus*, "who read them very speedily and said as he read them: 'If these letters are from the [Governor], how do they speak for the King of Portugal?" Dom Rodrigo explained that the King spoke through his Indian Governor without dilution or alteration, as the latter was the faithful servant of the former. The Ambassador then undoubtedly braced himself, from sheer force of habit, for more peevish interrogations — but unexpectedly "here the questions ceased." Instead, the King simply declared that he gave "many thanks to God for this favor which had been granted to him in seeing those [Christians] whom his predecessors had not seen, and [whom] he had not thought he [himself] would see." From then on the talk was all turkey and brass tacks: the *Negus* wanted Portuguese help in building forts at Massawa and Zeila, and to support such new installations "he would give all the stores and men ... and gold and provisions that might be necessary." From those citadels, he continued, the two nations' combined forces would be able to choke off the food and ammunition supply to Aden, Jiddah, and Mecca. This done, Cairo itself would be sufficiently weakened that they might attack it together. Were the Portuguese prepared to attack Zeila soon? Dom Rodrigo replied, in what was no mere brag, that "where the power of the King of Portugal reached, the towns became unpeopled, and they did not wait even for the shadow of the ships."

The change in the royal demeanor was startlingly complete, for "in this conversation about capturing and building these fortresses we spent a great deal of time, to the Prester's extreme pleasure; he showed there was nothing he wanted more than this." Dom Rodrigo, feeing oppressive weights lifted from his shoulders and nearly drunk with relief, spontaneously volunteered to stay on as Captain of any fort erected at Massawa or Zeila. For his part, the Prester capped the interview by declaring that the day of Ethiopia's isolation from the rest of Christendom had come to an end, "and that he would not spare anything he had in the world in order to find a way of opening some road by which he could join up with the Christian princes" of Europe. Oh, and one more thing—Dom Rodrigo and the Viceroy and King Manoel and everyone else must understand that he had never sent that notorious liar Matthew as ambassador to anyone. With that, the *Negus* declared that he would immediately begin dictating his reply to the Portuguese throne, and that the embassy should begin its preparations for returning to the coast. "And so," concludes Álvares, "we took leave with good words, and we went away pleased, chiefly with having seen and spoken to him." One wonders—did anyone else among the travelers understand who had authored this timely reversal of fortune?

And so the embassy had reached, so to speak, its furthest point of inward navigation: they had followed the great river of dream and aspiration to its long-disputed and well-hidden source. Like many real headwaters, it had been found in the isolated high country, and gave little hint of the mighty torrent it became downstream. Still, Dom Rodrigo could properly congratulate himself on having successfully sought out his man and delivered to him the vital words of his own sovereign. One imagines him emerging from the *Negus'* tent into the torch-lit night buoyed by a sense of genuine satisfaction at the results of his labors—until, that is, he recalled the disrespectful antics perpetrated by D'Abreu at the very moment of success, under the very eyes of the monarch they had come to honor and beseech. There must have been many angry words exchanged within the hearing of the assembled courtiers and guards, though Álvares records none, and it is almost certain that the Portuguese returned to their tent in two separate, murmuring columns headed by two proudly irreconcilable men. What is beyond doubt is that the embassy's homeward journey, which they should rightly have undertaken in the fellowship of mutual achievement, would instead become a long and wasting ordeal under the shadow of internecine hatreds they were seemingly powerless to overcome.

Seven

After Strange Gods

If Father Álvares was inclined to congratulate himself on moving the embassy's business forward, he was granted little leisure in which to do so. While it was clear that the *Negus* liked him, it was also apparent that the priest's answers to the King's questions had exposed differences between the Catholic and Ethiopian churches that both Lebna Dengel and his advisors wanted to better understand. So far the exchanges on potentially explosive topics had been cordial, but this was in part due to the fact that both the Abyssinian sovereign and Álvares himself had pulled punches, held fire, and mouthed diplomatic niceties in response to disturbing news. As the monarch and the priest became more comfortable with each other, it was almost inevitable that a new frankness should begin to enter their exchanges, highlighting the significant divergences between their respective faiths. Ethiopia had been cut off from the main current of Christendom for eight hundred years — and yet the Prester's people were justly proud of defending their faith against the forces of Islam with no help from their European co-religionists. If they differed from Catholic teaching on certain points of doctrine, those beliefs and practices had been forged in the crucible of continuous and successful holy war. For his part, Father Álvares was reluctantly finding himself cast as the lone representative of a Catholic hierarchy that insisted on its right to parse the heretical from the orthodox for all who called themselves Christians. Thus, his newly-minted bond with the young king was about to be tested. On the night of November 21st, not twenty-four hours after Dom Rodrigo's successful audience with the *Negus*, Álvares was summoned once more to the royal apartments to explain further the pretensions of Rome.

The first thing troubling Lebna Dengel was that the letter to him from the Portuguese Governor had made mention of certain saints of whom he had never heard, such as St. Jerome, St. Dominic, and St. Francis. Furthermore, Sequeira had boasted that King Manoel had set up monastic houses dedicated to these worthies in Benin, in the Congo, and in India. The *Negus* was of course familiar with monastic orders, since few places on earth could boast a higher per-capita population of monks than Ethiopia, but of the Dominican and Franciscan orders he was wholly ignorant. Álvares did his best that night to sketch out the biographies of these religious men and of the mendicant rule of life that had sprung up from their example and inspiration, saying "much to him of the great houses of these blessed saints which there are in France; and [how] from them had proceeded many other saints on account of the holy lives they led." However, as his *Flos Santorum* [Book of Saints' Lives] was back at the Portuguese tent, he admits that his account was somewhat garbled and "not consecutive." His Majesty requested that the priest bring this book next time, but it soon became clear that what was really agitating him was a more fundamental issue than which miracles might be attributable to which Western saint. What the Prester most wanted to know was why there seemed to be so many *more* saints in Europe than in Ethiopia. They had a sprinkling of their own, of course, such as Takla Haymanot and Ewostatewos, the founders of Abyssinia's two main monastic institutions, but apparently this was a paltry number compared with the host of the blessed currently venerated among the Franks. Why, the King asked Father Álvares, did *he* think such a disparity existed?

It was a perilous moment, for a crude equation of the number of martyrs with the religious zeal of a people is a tempting, if lazy, mental shortcut, but our priest handled it deftly. The difference, he replied, was due to the fact that Europe had long been ruled by "many pagan Emperors and their lieutenants who were cruel men" and who had tried to force the populace to "worship idols and follow the bad religion." Under such conditions, the power of God's truth as revealed by Scripture and the testament of evangelists could not help but inspire many to undergo the ordeal of the stake or the arena in witness to their faith. Ethiopia, however, having been so long ruled by virtuous Christian kings, naturally produced fewer such sacrifices. It was all, at base, a function of good government long enjoyed. (So much so that in fact martyrdom was not, and had never been, a requirement for sainthood in the Ethiopian Church.) Lebna Dengel greeted this reply with enthusiasm, asking if the priest could calculate the exact date at which the country's leaders had been Christianized. Álvares said "it seemed to [him] that it [c]ould not [have been] a long time after the death of Christ, because this country was converted by the eunuch of Queen Candace, who was baptized and instructed in the faith by the Apostle St. Phillip." *Ten A.D.!* shot back the Prester, pointing out that "since that time until now Ethiopia had always been ruled and governed by Christians, and therefore there had not been martyrs here, [for] it had not been necessary." Álvares had sidestepped yet another man-trap.

If he was still dexterous in avoiding new trouble, however, revisiting already-trodden ground betrayed him into impolitic candor. When asked again why the Roman Pope should be considered the head of all Christians, our priest repeated his arguments of the previous evening, only to find that "they then came to another matter, namely, whether we [i.e., the Portuguese] did all that the Pope commanded." He replied that yes, they did, since as God's representative on earth, invested with the power to bind and loose both here and in heaven, he deserved complete obedience. "Upon this they answered me that if the Pope ordered anything which the Apostles had not written, that they would break it; and if [even] their [*Abuna*] were to order it, that they would burn it, that is, the order." Although there was no official doctrine of Papal infallibility in the sixteenth century, Álvares argued in response that between the Pope's own sanctified state, the guidance he received from the Holy Spirit, and the accumulated weight of centuries of learned commentary available to him in the Vatican's libraries, that the Pontiff would never—*could* never—order anything irreligious or heretical. Rightly anticipating that the third leg of this triad would be the one his hosts would be most skeptical about, he immediately went on the offensive concerning the extra-Biblical apologetics of various renowned theologians, but in the process blurted out something more besides: "Like the Holy Father," he insisted, "so also Cardinals, Archbishops, Bishops, Patriarchs, and other rectors of the Church are preachers and proclaimers of their holy faith, *of which the country of the Prester was in great need* [italics mine], for if there were any learned men in his country, they [were] so for themselves only and not in order to proclaim, declare, and teach others."

This was Álvares' first direct, public criticism of the Ethiopian Church as a whole, revealing his belief that it signally lacked evangelical zeal. He had observed that while the Abyssinian clergy were punctilious about seeing that all rituals were correctly performed, all holy days strictly observed, all homage cheerfully offered up, and all fees promptly paid, that they were little concerned with explicating the Bible to their parishioners or in exhorting them to perfect their lives through imitations of Christ or in proselytizing the heathen. If there was some justice to his complaint, there were several historical reasons for the state of affairs he deplored. First of all, since Ethiopian priests were not celibate and commonly engaged in trade, it was difficult for them to vigorously promote by example or even oratory an un-worldly ideal to their flocks. Perhaps too, the deep and still-vital Jewish undercurrents of Abyssinian Christianity had cast it as the faith of a people chosen and apart, more concerned with keeping the flame of truth burning safely and steadily amidst a surrounding world of hostile unbelievers than with spreading that fire to neighboring lands. Indeed, the physical structure of Ethiopian churches testified to a defensive and protective ethos at work—the sanctifying *tabot* hidden safely away within the Holy-of-Holies, surrounded by concentric spaces reserved for the spiritually elect, while most laymen heard the word of God preached only from the church's outer door. If, though, the Ethiopian Church appeared inward-looking and reified compared with its expansive European cousins, we should also not forget that in the West religious zeal did not exclusively manifest itself as so many Sermons on the Mount. To be a resident of the Iberian peninsula at the beginning of the sixteenth century was to live in a culture where acts of Christian enthusiasm regularly included both the official expulsion and the "spontaneous" massacre of large numbers of Jews; where, in the aftermath of a long Reconquest, supposed "secret Moors" were daily led to the executioner and "insincere" converts were made the targets of constant and tireless inquisitors; where many sniffed brimstone in the successes of their rivals or in the innocent customs of native peoples. Religious feeling took many dark forms in Renaissance Portugal, and even the mild and steady Father Álvares, when assaulted during a distraught mood by the sight of Ethiopian religious practices he found viscerally objectionable, would soon urge his hosts to employ in their stead the blood-soaked measures that were commonplace in his homeland.

For their part, the Prester and his advisors ignored the priest's criticisms and curtly answered his championing of his Pontiff by asserting that they "were not bound to observe what the Pope ordered, but only the Council of [Nicaea, whose doctrine] was wholly from the Apostles." Nicaea again — that was *their* Petram, the rock wall beyond which they would not follow any Saint or Pope, especially, as Álvares would eventually learn, in matters concerning the essential nature of the Savior. This audience thus ended on a less genial note than had the last one. Tomorrow send along your Book of Saints' Lives, our priest was told, for the *Negus* was inclined to read about these holy men Jerome and Francis and Dominic. And he was especially eager to know what the Franks had written about Pope Leo and his heretical council of Chalcedon.

By now Father Álvares was saying a public mass each Saturday and Sunday, as well as on feast days. On the 25th of November — St. Catherine's Day — he officiated at a service to which "the Prester John sent some canons and priests of the principal clergy of his house." This performance, like the previous ones, met with a generally favorable response, some reporting that "they had heard a mass not of men but of angels," and "never expected to see such another." However, what made this service principally memorable was the attendance of Nicolo Brancaleone, "a Venetian painter ... who had been for more than forty years in this country." Like many of the other captive Franks, "he was a much respected person, very rich, and a great lord of a big [estate] with many vassals." In other words, he had fared much as had that other wayfaring Westerner, Pêro da Covilhã. But because Brancaleone was a painter, it was possible to see his cross-cultural experience — his adaptation to a condition of permanent exile — projected upon Abyssinian church walls in vivid color. Today, for instance, in the Museum of the Institute for Ethiopian Studies in Addis Ababa, one can view one of his surviving depictions on wood of St. George slaying the dragon. The choice of subject itself already conforms to Ethiopian preoccupations, since George is Abyssinia's most venerated male saint, but still there is much that is unmistakably Italian about his execution — the clothing of his figures, their gestures, the perspective within which they are juxtaposed. Indeed, it is not until one focuses upon the eyes of St. George that the hybrid nature of the picture leaps out at one, for there staring back at you are the large and rolling almond orbs that are the hallmark of the Abyssinian school of religious painting. Father Álvares was soon to see some of Brancaleone's work face to face — portraits that were later destroyed in a Muslim invasion — and could not but have taken note of how they vividly illuminated an imagination half European and half Ethiopian. In the years the followed, when his own escape from the Prester's realm was very much in question, he no doubt recalled them from time to time, finding in them a prophecy of how his own thoughts must eventually take coloring from the land he could not leave, and slowly lose the original habits and qualities imbued by his far-away home. With what unease or acceptance he digested such musings, we cannot fully know.

That November, however, it looked as though Brancaleone would not get to enjoy the presence of his fellow Europeans for long, for the Prester now seemed in a mood to grant Dom Rodrigo's request for "dismissal." Late that very night — "at such a time that we were already asleep" — the insomniac King summoned the embassy's leaders, who were ushered into the royal compound "with the same formalities as [at] other times." From behind the customary curtains, the Prester announced that "the Franks might go away in peace." This release, however, was accompanied by the admission that he had not yet even begun to draft his replies to the *Estado's* Governor and King Manoel. But never mind, he said, that job would take a while, given that "he had to write with letters of gold, and ... [therefore] could not write immediately." Thus, the Ambassador was to "go on slowly at his own pace," and when the official letters were done, he would send a runner after the embassy to deliver them into Dom Rodrigo's hands. This was actually a rather accommodating offer, since it showed that Lebna Dengel had heard and understood the Ambassador's warning that the Portuguese fleet would appear at Massawa no later than the spring and would subsequently not have leisure to linger there for long. It was also practical, for it recognized that the cumbersome troupe of Europeans would take far longer to retrace their steps northward than would a small party of Abyssinians charged with overtaking them on the King's business. Dom Rodrigo, however, was having none of it: "the Ambassador replied that he would not go away without an answer, because thus he could not give a good account of himself." The subtext here was that De Lima had seen enough of the *Negus'* peevish and mercurial behavior to fear that he might not write at all, a failure which would consign the *fidalgo* to the prospect of returning to India with absolutely nothing to show from the Land of Prester John but bizarre travelers' tales that would, in the absence of evidence, likely be disbelieved. No, he would wait until the King was finished writing, no matter how long it took, though he still "entreated His Highness to dismiss him in time for him to find the fleet of the [Governor]" at Massawa. It was a risky decision, but the Ambassador no doubt felt he had little choice. At any rate, this recalcitrance did not offend his host, for "the Prester answered with his own mouth that he was pleased."

If Dom Rodrigo was staying put, however, Lebna Dengel was immediately on the move, lighting out for (literally) new pastures with that unannounced suddenness that was his royal prerogative:

> On Monday, the 2[6]th of the said month, in the morning, they told us that the Prester John was going away to another place (as in fact he did go), and it was like this. He mounted a horse and set out with two pages, and no other people; he passed in sight of our tent maneuvering his horse. There was a great tumult in our quarter, and cries of: "The Neguz is gone, the Neguz in gone," and this throughout all the camp: everybody started off after him as hurriedly as he could.

The night before, however, the King had left the embassy something of a poisoned gift — though this was surely not his intention — for shortly after the audience he had "sent a very good horse to the Ambassador, at which some of our company murmured, as though it grieved them." Just who was doing the loudest murmuring is not much in doubt, for there is no mention of D'Abreu getting so much as a pony. But any grumbling over this mount was merely a prologue, for the *Negus'* subsequent delivery of additional beasts of burden set the embassy's smoldering internal tensions to flaring once again. Apparently still in a generous and attentive mood, the King did not neglect to send the Portuguese approximately fifty mules and a brace of slaves to assist them in following him to his new campsite. Dom Rodrigo, understandably flustered by the sovereign's abrupt departure just as needful business seemed on the brink of getting accomplished, and characteristically convinced that it was vital for he himself to remain as close to the *Negus* as possible, requisitioned the best mules for his own use, including several more than he actually needed in order to shadow his host in good order. In this manner De Lima and a few picked favorites managed to spring smartly away after their royal quarry, leaving most of his underlings to struggle with an inadequate number of broken-winded beasts. It was some time later, when the bulk of the Portuguese were just struggling into the Prester's re-forming capital, that the *Negus' Ba'ala mashaf,* or Master of Books, stopped by the guest tent to inquire if the Franks had been provided with everything they had needed to smoothly accomplish the move.

> The Ambassador answered that he kissed His Highness' hands for this visit, and that we had come very well, and that they had given him all the things which His Highness had ordered. Upon this Jorge d'Abreu said that he should not say that, for they had not given all the mules, and those that they had given were one-eyed

or blind, and the slaves were old and worth nothing, and that such as it all was, the Ambassador had taken [the best of] it without giving anything to any one. The Ambassador answered that he should not say so, that all the mules and slaves and other things were perfect. Jorge d'Abreu answered: "If they gave perfect mules and slaves and other things, you have got them, and to you they give mules and horses, and to the others they give nothing, henceforward it must not be so."

This shouting match quickly escalated into a physical confrontation, with De Lima and his adversary taking "to swords and lances" and delivering "a good number of blows and thrusts" that resulted in "one small wound, which was given to Jorge d'Abreu." And where was Father Álvares during this sanguinary brawl? As he matter-of-factly states: "I with my crozier [was] in the midst making peace, for these acts seemed to me evil." It is almost an allegorical tableau, our priest gamely plunging once more into a perilous breach opened by the folly of others. However, despite his muscular attempts at peacemaking (one hopes his cozier met a cranium or two), the embassy in the immediate aftermath once again split into two separate camps, with D'Abreu and several cronies leaving the official tent to find what shelter they could enjoy as far as possible from what they considered the insufferable airs of their chief. More seriously for all their fortunes, the altercation had transpired under the bewildered eyes of the Master of Books, who wasted no time in informing his sovereign. Unforeseen by the embassy, the Prester and his courtiers would soon begin viewing the internecine hatreds of the Portuguese through the lens of their own anxieties about their status vis-à-vis European Christendom. After all, what would those in Lisbon or Rome think if the Portuguese returned home in a state of civil war? No matter what favorable reports of Ethiopia one faction promulgated, these were sure to be angrily refuted by the other. And wouldn't an expedition disembarking at dagger's-point be bound to reflect badly on Abyssinian hospitality, customs, and character? Given their constant in-fighting, it might be better to keep them here than to allow them to return home to either spread or inspire angry tales.

Still, Lebna Dengel's first impulse was to try to defuse the quarrel by acting as an honest broker between the two parties. As an initial measure, he announced that henceforth the animals and slaves assigned to move the Portuguese about would be assigned and driven by one of his own captains, thus removing their contentious distribution from De Lima's hands. The King's announcement of this was tipped with a barb aimed at Dom Rodrigo, for the *Negus* mocked the Envoy's earlier prideful complaint by saying that "he well knew that neither the Ambassador nor those that came with him were merchants to undertake to convey baggage or goods, or to load it or carry it." He then ordered the two parties in the dispute to sit down some distance apart from each other in a field of high grass close by the Imperial residence. The two men and their respective backers were thus close enough for pages to swiftly carry messages between the Prester and both factions, though the contending parties could not clearly see each other or hear what the other group was saying. The logistics of this conference established, "the first message that came from within was to say: 'Why do you quarrel' and ... begg[ing] us to be friends." De Lima's anger at his subordinate, however, had apparently crossed some fatal threshold, for he refused the request, replying that this was not the first time D'Abreu and his followers had committed offenses "against him and against the service of the King of Portugal." Given these facts, he sent his own request back to the *Negus*: "he begged His Highness to order them to keep apart from his tent and company." That is to say, he was now sufficiently offended to wish that the hitherto intermittent fracturing of the embassy should become permanent, a bifurcation that he was proposing be enforced by the Prester himself. "Whilst this answer was going, there came another message to beg him that they would be friends," but "the Ambassador sent word that he was not going to be his friend, nor should he [from now on] go in his company." Dom Rodrigo had donned his helmet and pulled up his drawbridge.

The *Negus*, however, was equally determined, for his reiterated requests for explanations and unrequited pleas for amity stretched on from ten in the morning until well into the night — indeed, he seems to have been trying to wear down the two parties by keeping them squatting uncomfortably in the weeds until they saw things his way. As Álvares reports, the men had long since become "very cold as we were without food" when Dom Rodrigo finally lost patience and "sent word to the Prester to give us leave, for it was not usual to keep such persons day and night without need, [and] without food in the cold fields." The King, no doubt wearied himself by De Lima's intransigence, released the Portuguese and sent a messenger after the Ambassador "asking him not to take his being kept waiting amiss, [since] he had done it in order to hear both sides." Then, apparently in a final attempt to sweeten Dom Rodrigo's mood, the *Negus* sent along to De Lima's tent "large presents of bread and wine and meat." As it turned out he also complied with the letter of the Ambassador's request by providing D'Abreu and his friends with separate housing. The nature of this new dwelling, however, made it difficult to see the King's acquiescence as anything but an unsubtle slap at De Lima, for instead of granting D'Abreu a tent that was inferior to the official guest residence, he put him up in the pavilion of the absent *Bitwaddad* of the Right Hand, who was still away at the wars. This impressive silken edifice, grander and considerably closer to the royal apartments than the tent Dom Rodrigo sulkily returned to, may not yet have signaled any special liking on the *Negus'* part for the volatile D'Abreu, but it clearly communicated royal displeasure with the attitude of the embassy's leader.

In the wake of his unsuccessful peace conference, the Prester seems to have hit upon an odd and indirect way of putting pressure on Dom Rodrigo to relent, though its results were harrowing enough. Even as the shivering De Lima was leaving the field of high grass, a messenger caught up to ask him "if we had [with us] any good wrestlers," a question he brusquely "excused himself" from answering, "as it was night." A day or so later, however, Lazaro d'Andrade, whom Álvares describes as the embassy's painter (he probably means something like an illustrator) "was standing near the King's tent, and was invited to wrestle." His opponent was to be the Court champion, one Gabra Maryam (Servant of Mary), a convert from Islam and a "strong, broad-shouldered man ... who [was] clever with his hands." Andrade, apparently acting on impulse, accepted the challenge and began to grapple, though before long Gabra Maryam managed to break one of his legs, after which the on-looking Prester had him carried to the Portuguese tent on the shoulders of four men, his writhing form covered with "a dress of rich brocade" as a kind of consolation prize. The next day the *Negus* sent an inquiry as to whether Dom Rodrigo had anyone else in his tent who might like to take on his fighter, "and as the Ambassador saw that there were others there who were ready to go and avenge the painter, he sent two picked wrestlers." These were Estevam Palharte and Ayras Diz, the former a servant (perhaps a slave) of the Ambassador's, while the latter assisted the embassy's clerk. Diz was the first to enter the ring with Gabra Maryam, but soon found himself hurled outside it accompanied by a broken arm, whereupon Palharte declined to fill his place because, says Álvares, "he found himself alone and was afraid." As no more volunteers from the Portuguese tent were willing to step up, the bouts now ceased, but one wonders about the point of it all. Was the *Negus* enacting a kind of violence by proxy upon Dom Rodrigo, using a sporting venue to crush the limbs of the men of his faction whom diplomatic etiquette otherwise prevented him from chastising? If so, it suggests that the Ambassador had angered his moody host more thoroughly than he understood.

By contrast, Álvares continued to notch his belt with incremental successes, again demonstrating his tact when dealing with a potentially divisive issue. "Whilst we were in this plain and camp of the Prester," he explains, the Portuguese were steadily meeting more of the captive Franks, both those who followed the Court and those who, hearing of the visitors from Europe, rode in from their far-flung estates. It was about this time that "the black wife of one of them named Mestre Pedro Coriero, a native of Genoa, happened to be delivered, and when the child was eight days old, he asked me to baptize it." When we recall Álvares' distress at the Ethiopian custom of not baptizing infant males until the fortieth day or females until the sixtieth, it becomes clear that this was not a request that he was going to refuse. Contemplating the fate of babies who died unbaptized was unbearable to him, and he saw administering the rite as his clear duty as a Catholic priest. Firm in his decision, however, he decided to take a gamble and ask the *Negus'* permission first. He might have figured that the news of what he had done would get out regardless, but of course it would have been much more dangerous to afterwards defy a royal refusal than to just act immediately without the King's prior agreement. He therefore must have felt that his previous demonstrations of Roman ritual had been received well enough to make the Prester and his high churchmen more curious to see a Catholic baptism than apprehensive about (in their eyes) its precipitous nature. Accordingly, "I went to the tent of the Prester and sent to tell him how they asked me for baptism according to our custom, and that His Highness should give his orders what I was to do. A message came at once that I was to baptize it and give it all the sacraments as is done in France [i.e., the land of the Franks], and in the Roman church, and to allow to come to the baptism and sacraments as many of the people of the country as wished to be present." His hunch had been right — in fact the *Negus* even volunteered to supply the oil for the ceremony.

This ritual was conducted on December 10th — as before, "there came to it many of the most honorable and principal people at Court," and as before, the reviews were good. In part this was due to our priest's willingness both to think ecumenically and to act the part of a showman. For instance, "at this baptism we held a cross uplifted, because such is *their* custom" [italics mine], and furthermore he "officiated as slowly as [he] was able." Because of this, he reports with evident satisfaction, "the people who were present were astonished, according to their gestures and what was said by the Franks and our interpreters who understood them[, for] the Court people said that this office was ordained by God, and they went away as much comforted as if they had eaten good food."[1] Were the Abyssinian nobles and ecclesiastics really as impressed with Roman practices as Álvares claimed? No doubt some of their praise was diplomatic politeness, and even today Ethiopians can muster very indirect ways of articulating disapproval. But surely some of it was relief—relief akin to the kind that Álvares had felt after viewing his first Ethiopian mass. What they saw was obviously a recognizable version of their own sacrament, a cousin to their own procedures — and given their knowledge that the main body of Christians lived in Europe, and that they themselves inhabited the furthest and most isolated outpost of their own religion, they were thankful to see anything that looked familiar from this black-robed priest. Ultimately, however, it was not so much ortho*praxy* (correct action) that would lead the Roman and Ethiopian churches into tragic contention, but rather ortho*doxy* (correct believing). Such differences on points of faith were, of course, difficult to discern at first blush.

No sooner had our priest attained this small victory than the Prester, again without any warning whatsoever, was once more on the move. During this sojourn Álvares had the opportunity to describe the details of the King's usual entourage, for at times the Portuguese were allowed to travel in relatively close proximity to the royal person. The *Negus* was carried to his new campsite (or more accurately, city-site) upon a common mule, but that is where anything common about the trip began and ended. To protect him from the eyes of the unwashed, he was surrounded on four sides by mounted pages who held up four curtains by means of poles, creating a kind of mobile throne-room which completely contained His Highness as he crossed plain, hill, and stream. Jogging along inside this enclosure were six other pages, two having hold of ornamental tassels that hung from the royal mule's bridle, two with their hands continually upon the animal's neck, and two keeping pace with his haunches. More pages still, to the number of twenty, preceded the Prester's enclosure on foot, while out ahead of them cantered his personal stable of six "very handsome and richly caparisoned horses" and "six mules saddled and very well furnished," each with their own brace of attendants to keep them strictly in formation. Nor was the aristocracy absent from the procession, for taking the very foremost position were twenty of the chief men of the kingdom dressed in their Court finery. Meanwhile, scouring the country for possible dangers to the left and right "at the distance of at least a musket shot" rode the two *Bitwaddads*, accompanied by as many as six thousand soldiers as well as the four chained lions that were the living symbols of the *Negus'* majesty and power. These officers would sometimes scout as far afield as a league from the main party, but, says Álvares, "if the road is rocky and shut in by cliffs, so that it is not possible to pass except all by the same road, one of the Betudetes goes forward half a league, and the other stays as far behind." And here, as always, there was a precise precedence at work, for "the one that goes forward is he of the right hand, and he of the rear [is] of the left hand." Just behind the Prester followed a phalanx of porters who carried on their heads one hundred jars of mead and one hundred brightly colored baskets filled with bread, all of which was distributed to the various attendants at the King's discretion once the journey was completed.[2]

So much for the immediate royal party, but of course such functionaries amounted to only a small portion of the peregrinating city that followed the *Negus* wherever his whim directed him. Álvares remarked that "it is unbelievable how many people always travel with the Court; for certainly for a distance of three or four leagues from each place at which they break camp the people are so numerous and so close together that they look like a procession of Corpus Domini in a great city." This intermittent pilgrimage included all levels of Ethiopian society, from "the great lords and great gentlemen," each of whom "moves a city or a good town of tents, and loads, and people on mules," down to the swarming commoners, who "carry with them their poor dwellings," including the thatch and poles, while upon their heads swayed rude pots and pitchers. Cruelly burdened as these last obviously were, they still had to scamper off the road when other aspects of the Prester's capital came trundling by, especially the sanctifying *tabots* that could render any building that housed them, whether of stone or canvas, into a church:

> The altar ... stones of all the churches are treated with much reverence on the way, and are carried only by mass priests, and always four priests go with each stone.... [T]hey carry these stones as if on a stretcher raised on their shoulders, and covered with rich cloths of brocade and silk. In front of each altar or stone ... walk two *zagonaes* [roughly deacons], with thurible [i.e., censer] and cross, and another with a bell ringing it. And every man or woman who is going on the road, as soon as he hears the bell goes off the road, and makes room for the church; and if he is riding a mule he dismounts and lets the church go by.

The great bulk of this multitude had no exact idea where they were going, and could only scan the landscape ahead until they saw the sparkling white residence tent of the Prester newly-pitched in the distance. Coming at last upon it, the people "settled down each one in his place, as it had been arranged already, that is to say, on the right hand or the left, far or near." It sometimes happened that the *Negus* did not actually employ this tent as his home, preferring to sleep at a monastery or large church complex somewhere in the vicinity, but this did not change the tent's status as the central and orienting structure of the re-constituted capital. Still, says Álvares, it was not difficult to tell when the Prester was absent from it, since "in the tent which is thus pitched they do not fail to make solemn instrumental music and singing, yet not so perfectly as when the lord is there." Although our priest was equally in the dark about where the end of this particular removal would place them, or whether he would find the *Negus* there in person or not, he noted, no doubt with relief, that the capital was moving north, "turning back along the road by which [the embassy] had come."[3] It was perhaps another indication that the Prester sympathized with the Portuguese desire to reach Massawa in time to catch the fleet, for if His Majesty kept moving in this direction then even his tardy progress on the answering letters might not prevent them from making the rendezvous after all.

By the time the *Negus'* capital was stationary once again, Christmas Day was approaching. This holiday was always heralded by the construction of a special platform just outside the royal compound, which the Portuguese could see arising as they settled into their two mutually hostile pavilions. The purpose of this erection, which would eventually be surrounded by curtains that could be briefly lifted away by means of pulleys, was to give the *Negus'* people a fleeting view of their sovereign without obstruction. Such unmaskings occurred thrice yearly, at Christmas, Easter, and on Holy Cross Day in September, and though they coincided with high points of the ecclesiastical calendar, their origin was not ancient and religious, but recent and political. One of the serious weaknesses of the Ethiopian institution of kingship was that it had no codified procedure for succession. The recently deceased King's eldest son was always a viable candidate, but in point of fact the choice of the next *Negus* fell to the group of ministers who occupied the most powerful positions at Court at the time—figures such as the *Bitwaddad*, the *Aqabe sa'at*, the *Abuna*, and the Queen Mother. Oft-times in the past these grandees had skipped over an heir apparent whom they considered unqualified or uncongenial to their plans and chosen another candidate—either a younger son, or some nephew or cousin long imprisoned atop the vertiginous *Amba* Geshen. Such had been the case with the great Zara Yaqob who had spent the twenty years of his youth and young adulthood in comfortable captivity amid his fifty-acre aerie until his Court backers had plucked him down and pitched him headlong into the maelstrom of royal cares and responsibilities. His reign had turned out to be very successful politically, but there were those who blamed the increasing despotism and paranoia of his final years on his early isolation from any semblance of a normal human community. Then too, there was every reason to believe that a coterie of de-facto regents would be likely to prefer a weak candidate for the throne above a strong one.[4] Indeed, Lebna Dengel himself had not been the eldest son of his father but rather the chosen candidate of the *Abuna* Marcos and the dowager Queen Eleni. According to Álvares, though, the actual provocation for the current thrice-yearly viewings had been the gambit of a courtly cabal who, late in the last century, had kept the death of Lebna Dengel's uncle, King Eskender (ruled 1478–94), a secret from the populace for the space of some years, the better to see their own designs to fruition. Thus the current *Negus* exposed himself not so that his people could adore him all the better, but so that he could convince them that he was still drawing breath. Given the strict and minute regimentation of so much Court procedure—the careful parsing out of one set of specific duties to an official of the left-hand and another to an official of the right—this ambiguity shadowing every royal succession was an odd and frequently dangerous anomaly.

Father Álvares' Christmas mass was to stand as his last and most successful command performance, the high water mark in his public campaign to at once reassure his hosts that Catholic ritual was roughly similar to their own and, where it differed, to make them instinctively feel its (as he would have it) superiority. He had not arrived in Ethiopia expecting to undertake such a labor, for all his highest hopes concerning the Realm of Prester John implied his not *having* to do it—but he had come to see the necessity of such demonstrations, and was by now quite visibly warming to his task. That he had at least partially won over the most important member of his audience is underscored by the playful, almost teasing tone in which the *Negus* asked him what his plans were for the coming holiday. "On Christmas Eve, already midday or more, the Prester John sent to call me, and asked me what festival we held next day. I told him how we celebrated the birth of Christ, and he asked me what rites we observed, [so] I told him what we did about that." Unsurprisingly, the King wanted to see the entire spectacle with nothing omitted, and also predictably, our priest was glad to comply. The *Negus*, in order to insure his unimpeded view without compromising his need to remain cloistered, ordered that several tents near to his apartments be removed and that the Portuguese church tent — that same which had been taken as booty from the hated Mafouz — "be pitched at the principle door of his [own] tent, so that there would not be more than two fathoms between the church" and the royal residence. Thus the King and his party sat curtained at the entrance to his own pavilion, looking across a small open space and through the opening of the consecrated tent to the altar our priest had set up at the latter's far end. For his part, Álvares showed that by now he knew his likely audience well and was willing to cater to their tastes, rounding up "six of us who understood church matters and could sing well" into a makeshift choir. Furthermore, he introduced some props to produce a particular effect: "I took as many books as I had got, although they were nothing to do with the feast, but only to make up a number, because they [i.e., the Ethiopians] are much given to asking for books; and I opened them all upon the altar." The musical pieces these half-dozen Franks began to recite were likewise chosen more for esthetic impact than religious requirement, for Álvares confesses that "we prolonged these matins [i.e., morning prayers] a good deal with proses, hymns and canticles which we introduced, for we could not do anything else, as we had nothing marked out, and we were looking for what could be best sung or intoned." And, when pages from the Prester began arriving one after another asking details about what the lyrics meant, our priest is equally blunt about his invented replies: "I pretended what I did not know, and told them they were [from] books of Jeremiah, which spoke of the birth of Christ; and so of the Psalms of David, and other prophets." As a result, the *Negus* "was pleased and praised the books." One could be forgiven for fearing that our priest's guiding motto was shifting from "God's purposes must be served" into something akin to "the show must go on" or even "the customer is always right."

After this musical program was over the Prester's personal chaplain emerged from the royal tent and exclaimed that "he would have rejoiced if the service had lasted till next morning, [for] it had seemed to him that he had been in Paradise with the angels." This sounds like high praise, and it might sincerely have been intended as such, but then again it might have been mere boilerplate, since those very words were central to an extremely familiar story concerning Ethiopian sacred music. On many a church mural Yared the Deacon, a real personage and the inventor of a system of musical notation that first brought hymns into Abyssinian churches, is depicted as singing in front of King Gabra Maskel (ruled 550–564). The King, utterly enraptured with the melodies, is unaware that he is leaning upon a spear that has punctured Yared's foot. Yared himself, immersed in his own compositions, is equally unaware of his injury. Where did Yared learn such hypnotic art? The legend has it that he was briefly carried to Paradise by angels, where he heard and learned to transcribe "the plain song of Heaven," and hence he is often painted surrounded by doves, to remind viewers of his celestial sojourn.[5] Nevertheless gratified at this possibly rote response, Álvares announced that it was now time for him to hear confessions, which of course the *Negus* was found to be anxious to observe as well. Before long our priest was seated upon a kettledrum, with hooded penitents from the embassy or from among the captive Franks (it had been a long time since some of *their* last confessions) kneeling one after the other in front of him. To aid the King's observations, a great torch was placed in the ground close to Álvares, while the chaplain curled up next to him on the ground — "with his elbow on my knees" — the better to hear this sacrament that was enacted very differently within Ethiopian Christianity. When all was done, again "this honorable priest" gushed with praise: "May God permit the Naguz give me leave to remain with you all my life, for you are holy men and do things completely." But now we must again ask: was the chaplain — and were his ecclesiastical colleagues looking on from behind the *Negus'* curtains — really as happy with Álvares' demonstration as their King seemed to be? After all, back in Europe many of Henry VIII's churchmen would soon be applauding in public the theological enthusiasms of the all-powerful sovereign whom they were anathematizing in private. And as we shall see, if in fact Lebna Dengel was significantly more infatuated with Catholicism than his ecclesiastical bigwigs, he was only marking out a trail that, within the lifetimes of his grandsons, would lead his country into catastrophic civil war. Whatever the truth of their feelings now, the Ethiopian prelates would soon be revealing to Álvares a churchly practice or two indigenous to their own brand of Christianity — practices he would not respond to with anything resembling approbation.

It was now time for the mass proper, and both priest and Prester contributed to make it into a memorable spectacle. It being Christmas, Álvares wanted to start the ceremony with a candlelight procession around the interior of the church tent, and accordingly got his Portuguese lined up and marching, his few candles dispersed equally among them, a large cross and a picture of the Virgin swaying at their front. Almost immediately a message came from the *Negus* saying that while this chain of worshipers was impressive, they really ought to march outside the curtained wall — not the wall of the church tent, but the great circular wall of draperies surrounding his entire royal compound — "so that all the people might see it." To this end he ordered "fully 400 candles of white wax from his tents for us to carry lighted in our hands." Clearly so much illumination would require more celebrants in the procession, and these he also provided, until Álvares found himself at the end of an immense human rope "beginning with the Portuguese and white men, and going on with his people as far as the candles went." This doubly-expanded procession was accomplished, says our priest, with "as much decorum as we were able," though by the time they were all back inside the church it was "very late on account of the great circuit we made." Now, as he returned to the altar, he discovered that "inside our church tent were all the great men of the Court that there was room for, [while] those [who] could not find room stood outside, because from the altar as far as the Prester's tent all was clear down the middle in order that His Highness might see the office of the mass." Turning to face this massive throng, it was Álvares who now decided to add something special and striking to the ceremony. When it came time to "asperse" the altar and perhaps some of the nearest among the congregation with holy water, he boldly marched down the empty central corridor, stepped out into the open space between the two tents, and cast several handfuls of the sanctifying droplets over the intervening curtains and onto the heads of the royal party concealed behind it. It was a bravura move — simultaneously a public act of obeisance and a private recognition of personal connection. One could almost see Prester John beaming through the dampened silks.

The *Negus*, however, was not the only one to feel Álvares' cleansing shower, for that day he shared the reviewing bench not only with the *Aqabe sa'at* and other Church officials, but with his principal wife, with the Queen Mother, and, most intriguingly, with the aged Queen Eleni. One would give much to know the reaction of that aged lady to the religious performance that was unfolding in front of her, for recall that in a direct way it was all her doing. It was she who had first reached out to the Portuguese, and now here they were before her, offering assistance to be sure, but also bringing strange rituals and implied disparagements, even in the gestures of this gentle priest. As William Blake would one day ponder about God and the tiger he created, did she smile her work to see? One thing was certain: this was as close as she was going to get to any member of the embassy, for as the dispatcher of Matthew she was eyed with chronic unease by Lebna Dengel. He worried that were any of the Portuguese to speak with her, they might well use the opportunity to demand the fulfillment of some outrageous promise made to them by her unstable emissary. And again one wonders — did *she* wish to speak with *them*? She was a repository of over half a century of Court experience, and yet also an outsider who could view her country objectively; she was a long-term strategic thinker, and yet old enough to have few personal agendas left to pursue. Could she only have made contact with one of these ambassadors from beyond the seas, she might have been able to pass along some vital piece of advice, some key to her countrymen's hearts that might have prevented the Portuguese from making fatal errors. The *Negus*, however, was not about to let that to happen.

When the Christmas mass was at last concluded, Father Álvares may have felt that his sustained and elaborate efforts had earned him a good meal and a sound sleep, but it was not to be. As if in retribution for his stretching and patching of Catholic ritual that day, he was in for a veritable Purgatory of enthusiastic interrogation. Thus "the Prester sent the Ambassador and all the

Franks to go and dine, and ordered that I should remain alone with one interpreter." It seemed that the King, while much approving the ceremony in general, wanted to know why, in contradiction with Ethiopian church practice, laymen and even women had been allowed to stand in such proximity to the altar. (Apparently, several of the Abyssinian wives of the captive Franks had been present during the service.) Álvares' answer was spirited and unapologetic:

> I answered that the church of God was not closed to any Christian, and that Christ always stood with arms open for every Christian who approached and came to Him, and since he received them in glory in Paradise, how should we not receive them in church, which is the road to the church of Paradise[?] With respect to women, although in former time they did not enter the *santa santorum*, the merits of Our Lady were and are so great, that they sufficed to make the feminine gender worthy to enter the house of God.

Clearly our priest's desire to please had rediscovered its doctrinal limits, for this was in essence a pointed critique of the sexual apartheid that required the *Negus'* female subjects to hear mass at a church's side door and forbade them entrance to many ecclesiastical structures altogether.

The King let this pass, but immediately there were other questions concerning the number of priests that officiated at Catholic masses, the role of deacons, and especially the place in European Christianity of learned commentary upon the Bible, about which the Ethiopians were naturally wary. Álvares did his best to answer each query, but he also complains that through it all he was "not able to sit down, but only to lean upon a staff until the hour of Vespers" while the inquires, some in the mouths of messengers and others on paper, began to stack up in a disheartening backlog. Apparently everyone behind the curtains got into the act without any coordination, for "some answers went and other questions came, each in their own fashion, (and in much confusion)" until "two quires of paper would not suffice, [and] neither would memory keep them [straight] for they made me hurry." At last the exhausted man was reduced to begging for mercy:

> I answered as God helped me; [but] I was in such a state of weakness and hunger that I could not endure it, and instead of an answer, I sent to ask His Highness to have pity on an old man, who had neither eaten nor drunk since yesterday at midday, nor had slept, and could not stand for weakness. He sent to say that since he rejoiced to converse with me, why did not I rejoice too[?] I replied that old age, hunger, and weakness, did not allow of it.

This plea caused the Prester to reluctantly dismiss his witness, but as the priest was staggering back to his tent he heard pursuing footsteps and looked behind just as "a page reached [him] dead with running." Says Álvares, "when I heard him come I thought it was my sins come to make me turn back," and indeed though this messenger carried a belated apology from the *Negus*, he also carried a request that "as soon as I had eaten to come back at once, as he wished to learn other things from me." So great had been his ordeal that upon reaching the Portuguese tent, our priest was immediately "seized with giddiness," suffered a fit of temporary blindness, and found his teeth chattering with cold. Nevertheless, an hour and a half later he answered yet another summons to the royal apartments, bringing his makeshift choir with him to sing Compline — that is, the last prayers of the day before (one hoped) retiring to sleep — "because there was no room for more." To this encore "the Prester and the Queens were ... very attentive," and when it was over he was dismissed for the night.[6] The very last word he was given, however, was an admonition for all members of the embassy to be up early, for the Court would be traveling again come dawn.

If the Portuguese were getting used to such removals, however, this one was to prove very different from the last few, for the Court was now located at the foot of the vertiginous pathway that, on the way south, Álvares had heard called *ahya fajj*, or "Destruction to Donkeys." It was through this passage that the capricious *Negus* now meant to squeeze his entire capital, and once again the section of road was to live up to its name. In point of geographical fact, the *ahya fajj* consisted of the narrow cliff-hugging trail leading down from the top of the Shoan High Plateau to bottom of the gorge carved out by the River Wencha — a tributary of the Nile — and a similar ascent up the other side of the canyon. Such vast chasms, like those gouged out by the Jemma to the south and the Beto to the north, often have rims that are several miles apart, but each descent from those points to the river below invariably includes several gauntlets of vertical rock wall. As the embassy's stores were loaded up under the dour supervision of the Prester's captain, Dom Rodrigo quickly discerned that a bottleneck of nightmarish proportions was already forming at the trailhead, and took drastic action in order not to be delayed in catching up with his already vanished host. At De Lima's orders, "our people made way for us with their lances, and we traveled thus that day with lances in front and lances behind, and we in the middle, not allowing anyone to come in our midst[,] because otherwise we should never have got together again[,] such was the rush and the press and the crowd coming behind us." Apparently the Prester's official raised no objection — there was, admits a troubled Álvares, "no remedy for it" — for as it turned out the entirety of the city "spent more than three weeks getting through these gates." The exhausted and rattled Europeans caught up with the *Negus* on the opposite lip just as the sun set that day, but heard reports from behind that "there died in these passes men, women and many mules, asses, hacks, and pack oxen," including "a great lady" and her three attendants, all of whom "went over a rock [and] were dashed to pieces before they reached the bottom." Indeed, sighs our priest, "it could not be otherwise, because the cliffs are (as I said before) something unbelievable[,] and whoever sees them thinks them more like hell than anything else." Contrary to legend, the rocks of Prester John's alpine realm tended to possess deadly rather than healing powers.

As frightening as the *ahya fajj* had been for Father Álvares, he might have wished to remain perched over one of its precipices had he known what was awaiting him on the other side, though little of his new trouble would have caught the eye of a casual onlooker. After negotiating the great canyon, the *Negus* ordered his capital to stop in the vicinity of two major churches: Atronsa Maryam on December 28th, and then, farther to the northwest, Mekane Selassie on the first day of the European new year. (Even today the Ethiopian year begins on September 11 and contains thirteen months.) At both these places there was much to see, and Lebna Dengel wanted especially to know what our priest made of what he was beholding, to such an extent that there is simply no mistaking the pleasure that the King took in playing the role of tour guide and proud owner to his clerical guest. For his part, Álvares smiled and said all the right things, but as we shall see there is good reason to believe that one of the items he beheld during this week of sightseeing significantly increased his worries about the Ethiopians' doctrinal orthodoxy.

The glory of both churches lay in their decorations. The first, Atronsa Maryam, was a great round structure boasting a covered circuit upheld by "thirty-six wooden pillars," which were "very high, and nearly as thick as the masts of galleys." The doors were covered in gold and silver leaf—"very well put on" comments Álvares—while the interior walls were decorated either with "rich curtains, pieces of brocade ... [and] velvet and other rich cloths," or with "suitable pictures [of] very good stories," some of them by Brancaleone, most by indigenous painters. The inspection was conducted by the *Aqabe sa'at*, but the Prester was soon sending messages from his residence asking what the ambassadors thought of it all and whether the King of Portugal could boast anything like it. Álvares did his best to explain the difference between European and Ethiopian churches without unduly championing the former, a small feat of diplomacy which later that day earned him a private viewing of the large ceremonial umbrellas that were kept in the church's treasury. This was followed by a personal audience with the *Negus* during which he was forced to admit, much to his host's satisfaction, that King Manoel owned nothing to compare with the parasols either. On the surface, then, it was a day of leisured edification accompanied by the flattering attentions of the royal personage.

However, because it was also the first day on which Álvares was able to tour an ecclesiastical structure that was a major repository of, and in fact a canvas for, Ethiopian religious art, there is a good chance that it was also the first time he got a good look at an Abyssinian depiction of the Trinity. These painting of Father, Son, and Holy Spirit are like almost nothing found anywhere in the West.[7] In fact, to those unschooled in matters Ethiopian, such portraits of three *absolutely identical figures* standing shoulder to shoulder staring directly out at the viewer prompt the guess that they must be representations of the Three Wise Men, or of some unfamiliar family of pious triplets martyred in old age. For the European onlooker accustomed to seeing only God the Father depicted as a gray-bearded patriarch, with Jesus Christ usually appearing in much younger human form and the Holy Spirit cast allegorically as, say, a dove, it comes as a genuine shock to be told the intended subject of these paintings. If our priest did in fact first view such a canvass this day, and asked what it was meant to represent, one can't help but suspect that an unpleasant tingling began at the back of his skull as he absorbed the answer, for he well knew that in churchly art some doctrine or other drives every brushstroke of the painter. But was it really a dangerous and alien doctrine? After all, Roman Catholic orthodoxy insisted that the three persons of the Trinity were consubstantial and equally eternal. But of course when it came to the mystical, counter-intuitive, and precariously-balanced conception of the Holy Trinity, emphasis was everything, and even the subtlest shift in accent or stress could send one hurtling into heretical territory. Even if our priest didn't immediately put a name to the particular doctrine suggested by the painting before him, it was clear that this conception of the Trinity was anything but Western, anything but Catholic, anything but orthodox.

By January 2nd the Court was ensconced near the second church, Mekane Selassie. Álvares does his best to describe its adornments, but ironically the best account we have was penned by one of the Muslims who sacked it less than a decade later. This scribe of the jihadist Ahmed Grañ asserts that upon entering the structure, his companions "almost lost the power of sight" in contemplating the many "sheets of gold and silver on which had been placed incrustations of

A DEPICTION OF THE MONOPHYSITE HOLY TRINITY, UBIQUITOUS IN ETHIOPIA. Such images would have strongly suggested to Álvares the true nature of Abyssinian Christianity — a fact he was reluctant to accept.

pearls." The structure measured at least a hundred and fifty cubits by a hundred, its high-ceilinged interior decorated with many and various "golden statues." When the invaders' awe had subsided and the order to permit looting had been passed down from their general, "they set to work with a thousand axes ... from mid-afternoon till night," and even though "each man took as much gold as he wished for, and was rich forever," there was ultimately too much of the precious stuff to haul away and thus "more than a third of the gold was then burnt with the church."[8]

At present, though, the Prester's arrival was meant to coincide with the official dedication of this only recently completed cathedral, work upon which had commenced in his grandfather's time. And thus the previous day the Portuguese had witnessed Lebna Dengel being welcomed to Mekane Selassie by a massive crowd that included not only the familiar throngs from the roving capital but also thousands of priests and monks in from the surrounding countryside, many thrusting aloft the ceremonial crosses and umbrellas that announced their respective churches and monasteries. But even this outsized official pageantry had not prevented the *Negus* from again singling out our priest, for as soon as the greetings were concluded "he sent to call me" and wanted to know if the cleric had ever seen such a crowd greet a monarch in Europe. Clearly the *Negus* had developed a kind of addiction to Álvares' tactfully reassuring answers, and his supplier did not disappoint now, claiming that such a reception appeared to him "the best that could be made in the world," and that should he ever come to speak of it back in Europe "he would not be believed unless it were on account of the great fame which His Highness enjoyed in Christendom and in all the world." The Prester, in a happy and expansive mood, improved upon this flattery by opining that because the crowds in Portugal wore so much more clothing than those in Abyssinia, the former probably looked more numerous than their actual number.

Next day the King's pride in his new church was demonstrated by the fact that he was already in it when the official tour began, and under this royal supervision Álvares was again allowed to cast his eyes at leisure over walls that held the finest examples of religious subjects that Ethiopian painters could produce. The Prester asked for their assessments of it, of course, but mostly he wanted to discuss the prospects of getting some lead tiles for the roof from Europe to insure that all the brightly-colored tapestries, murals, and woodcuts they saw before them would not be damaged during the rainy seasons. And did this second gallery of masterpieces toward which the monarch contentedly gestured include any more of the distinctive and disturbingly identical images of the Father, Son, and Holy Ghost that had also been on display at Atronsa Maryam? Almost certainly it did, for the very name of the structure, Makana Sellase, translates as "Place of the Trinity," and to that illusive but indispensable Christian conception it was solemnly dedicated. It is surely ironic that just as

Seven. After Strange Gods

Father Álvares was drinking in images that would change his whole conception of Ethiopia and of his own purpose regarding it, he and that country's leader seemed to have reached their closest point of intimacy. Just the day before, as our priest had taken leave of the royal apartments, the Prester had made him the object of a friendly, if feeble joke, declaring that since it was customary for all who entered a newly-consecrated tabernacle to make an offering, that on the morrow he should donate his priestly costume to Mekane Selassie—and he could also tell that stubborn Dom Rodrigo to donate his precious sword![9] Now, as His Highness peered out from behind his portable curtains at the craning necks and whispered exclamations of his admiring guests, did he notice that his favorite among them wore an uncharacteristic frown and seemed weighed down with some private trouble?

But if this conjecture about what Father Álvares was thinking and feeling is correct, why didn't he, as was his custom, immediately commit his thoughts to paper in a way that could later be incorporated into his summative book? My guess is that a mixture of fear and growing affection held his hand. For one thing, he was an Iberian, and knew all too well that when you suspected people you cared about of harboring heretical opinions, the last thing you did was jot down your impressions. He knew how zealous Inquisitors operated, and what they could make from the most ephemeral slips of the tongue or the most casual of overheard remarks, let alone written evidence. In some way he probably couldn't yet fully articulate to himself, the Ethiopians were becoming his responsibility, his mission, even his congregation, and were therefore becoming a people to be protected from the harsh judgments of distant authorities who could not know them as he did. And then too, what he had just seen was not in itself an unambiguous proof of guilt but rather just a striking piece of evidence — one that would only become the key to a certainty when it was juxtaposed with other facts, especially the long talks he would soon have with learned Ethiopian churchmen. But even in the months to come, after all doubt had ceased and he knew for certain, he still would not write what he had discovered. A man who loves does not endanger the brother or the child who occupies his heart, no matter their sin or how plainly he sees it.

But that was all in the future — in the days that immediately followed, the new doubts gnawing at his composure would merely reveal themselves in some uncharacteristic behavior. Up until now Francisco Álvares had witnessed a continuous parade of odd and unsettling religious rituals performed before his eyes by Abyssinian priests, and yet throughout them all he had maintained a patient forbearance, an open ear to explanation, and a genuine traveler's curiosity that had been instrumental in winning him the friendship of the very King himself. He was soon to see more of the same fare, but this time an increasingly preoccupied Father Álvares would momentarily abandon his diplomatic equilibrium.

Eight

Divided We Fall

Why exactly would seeing a portrait depicting the Trinity as three identical figures push our priest closer to the conviction that the Ethiopians were monophysite heretics? Recall that the crucial difference between the Catholic and monophysite branches of Christianity involves the essential nature of Christ, with the former asserting that he is simultaneously both God and man while the latter insists that his fundamental substance is wholly divine. If, as in the West, one portrays Jesus in the likeness of an earthly man in the act of multiplying loaves and fishes, or raising Lazarus from the dead, then one is emphasizing the fact that he possesses two natures, one divine, one human. If, on the contrary — and perhaps even in defiant answer to such Western representations — one depicts him as indistinguishable from God the Father and the Holy Sprit, then one is drawing particular attention to his divine status as one of the three aspects of Almighty God and downplaying the fact that he once briefly walked the earth in the form — or was it perhaps merely the semblance? — of a human being. Indeed, at the Council of Trent in the mid-sixteenth century, Western Christendom banned images of the Trinity such as Álvares had just beheld, precisely because they were seen as encouraging monophysitisim and its near-cousin in heresy, modalism.

This leads to the question of why, back in the fourth century, the original monophysites objected to the emerging Catholic view of a two-natured Savior. For one thing, the idea of any sort of division within Christ struck them as impious, since in Classical thought unity is nearly always superior to division. The ancients disparaged divided conceptions, divided loyalties, divided polities, so seeing the Savior of the world as somehow riven at the core appeared to ontologically diminish him. Of course Catholics were careful to insist that the two natures of Christ — one divine, one human — were simultaneously unmixed, undiluted, and unchanged within his single personhood, making an actual unity out of an only apparent division. But, claimed the monophysites, such formulas couldn't overcome their own illogical nature, for once you started to talk about two *natures* in one person you were inevitably already talking about two separate *persons* because a rational being's nature is what *constitutes* him as a person: to affirm two natures was *by definition* to affirm two persons. And thus while it was true that Catholics at the Council of Chalcedon (451) officially declared the notion of a two-person Christ heretical (labeling it "Nestorianism" after its main promoter, one Nestorius), this was of no avail, since affirming two natures instantly made you into a Nestorian no matter how eloquently you denounced them. And once the Savior was indeed two distinct persons, then several unpalatable conclusions seemed to inevitably follow. To take just one, Christ's human person appeared to become utterly vestigial, a cipher or even a zombie, since obviously the divine person within him would in all ways control and overwhelm the human one — unless one made the blasphemous claim that a human being was the equal of God. It was much better, they concluded, to say instead that Christ's human nature was "absorbed into" the divine, or that his human flesh was a mere "garment" worn by His divine essence, for in this way the Savior could be imagined simply as God in the act of assuming human form or human appearance, but never human nature.

The proto-Catholics responded that bestowing upon Christ a unified divine nature meant either that God suffered pain on the cross, which was an impious absurdity, or that the crucifixion was a mere pantomime during which no real pain was felt by anybody. This last thought was especially troubling, for how could Christ redeem what he had not become, and if his human form was merely God decked out in a clever disguise, then how could you ask flesh-and-blood people to emulate his sacrifice, since it turned out to be no sacrifice at all? No, the only formulation which could underlie a truly salvific faith and inspire a life of good works was a doctrine of two separate natures within one person. In the words of Pope Leo the Great, "God was born in the undiminished and perfect nature of a true man, complete in what was His and complete in what was ours," and in such a way that "each nature kept its proper character without loss."

This, then, remained the heart of the contention: the Catholics couldn't find salvation in a wholly divine Christ; the monophisytes could not imagine a Christ who could be simultaneously both multiple and unitary.[1] At Chalcedon they parted company forever, with the latter retreating to their stronghold of Alexandria and its Egyptian hinterland of desert monasteries. From there, and later from other isolated monophysite communities in Syria and elsewhere in the Middle East, Christianity first reached Ethiopia in the fourth and fifth centuries — a bit later than the *Negus'* boast of 10 A.D., but no less decisively for all that. And so Father Álvares was now beginning to understand that the Abyssinians' Judaizing might be the least of it — that Prester John's kingdom might well be a nation of damnable heretics in the eyes of Rome. It was of course possible to be a priest without being a theologian, but it seems inconceivable that Álvares could have long remained oblivious to the fundamental nature of Ethiopian Christianity. After all, he had been specially chosen for a mission that everyone knew would put him into close contact with Muslims, Hindus, and various Christian sects. Furthermore, while waiting for successive Red Sea fleets he had spent half a decade in India, where, thanks to the vagaries of history, the indigenous Christians were nearly all *Nestorian* heretics. No, the fact that he never wrote about his Abyssinian hosts' monophysitism bespeaks something far more interesting operating within him than the chronic drone of an implausible ignorance.

During this time our priest's narrower worries did not diminish, for relations between the *Negus* and Dom Rodrigo continued to deteriorate. Even as the tour of Mekane Selassie was winding down, a pointed question from the Prester as to why the Portuguese sometimes traded with their common Muslim enemy (of course the Ethiopians regularly did so too) developed into another altercation over the paltry official gifts. De Lima began by making his usual mendacious excuses calmly enough, but when the *Negus* informed him that had the embassy shown up with such presents during his father's time they would not even have been received at Court, the Ambassador lost his temper. Pointing out to the King that "many injuries had been done to us in his countries," including "robberies" of food and clothing (there had in fact been several thefts from the Portuguese tent), he further claimed that the Ethiopians had "tried three or four times to kill us," but that "we endured all with patience, for the love of God, and of the King of Portugal, to whom we belonged." The *Negus* might have let this go by, but in passing De Lima noted that Matthew had been treated much better by King Manoel, which of course led to another vigorous royal denunciation of that supposedly great liar. Losing the thread of argument amidst his anger, Dom Rodrigo declared in reply that if His Highness thought the Portuguese were all liars, he should dispatch them homeward, forgetting that he had already been given permission to leave. The *Negus* replied tersely that they would all be gone soon enough. The donnybrook ended inconclusively, but the larger fact we can garner from this and other reactions of De Lima's is that, having discovered Ethiopia's strangeness to be different from the strangeness he had expected to find, the Ambassador had not managed to remain enchanted or even curious about the place. On the contrary, he was by now full of impatience and at least half full of disgust. It was a dangerous frame of mind for the expedition's leader to nurture, for a great disillusionment will sometimes manifest itself as aggression. Judging from subsequent events, he was not the only member of the embassy grappling with soured hopes.

The Prester's Court, by contrast, was in a buoyant mood, for as the first week of January ran its course, the festival of the Epiphany — or *Timkat*, as it is called in Ethiopia — was approaching. The word "epiphany" means "manifestation," and while in the West this holy day commemorates the arrival of the Three Wise Men at Bethlehem — that is, the moment at which Christ was first manifested, or shown forth, to the Gentiles (i.e., to non-Jews)—in all Eastern Churches, including the Abyssinian, it commemorates Jesus' baptism in the River Jordan, that event marking the first time he revealed himself to humanity in general as the Son of God. This was one of the holiest days in the Ethiopian calendar, at which the sacred *tabots* were removed from their guarded sanctuaries at the center of their churches, wrapped in brightly colored fabric, and paraded about before the joyously chanting and dancing populace on the heads of the priests. It was — and still is — also customary for the faithful to immerse themselves in a body of water to commemorate the baptism of the Savior, but this was a spectacle that our newly burdened priest would soon react to with uncharacteristic bitterness. Indeed, evidence that he was distracted and brooding emerges from the fact that, while usually an exemplary listener, he suffered a crucial misunderstanding when this ceremony was explained to him. He tells us that the *Negus* ordered the Portuguese to carry their residence and church tents to a point half a league from Mekane Selassie, where a large tank had been excavated within a field delimited by a hedge. It was within this pool, he claims, that "they were to be baptized at Epiphany, because on that day it is their custom to be baptized every year." But in fact nobody was being either baptized or re-baptized, for in the Ethiopian Church, as in the Catholic, baptism was bestowed once in childhood and was deemed sufficient for life — rather, the dunkings were to be a mere *commemoration* of Jesus' immersion under the hands of John the Baptist. This mistake, however, combined with his own countrymen's lax attitude toward the sacrament in question resulted in his viewing the entire ceremony in an angry mood.

> He [i.e., the *Negus*] sent to ask us if we were going to be baptized. I replied that it was not our custom to be baptized more than once, when we were little. Some said, principally the Ambassador, that we would do what His Highness commanded. When they saw that, they came back again with another message to me, asking that I should say if I were going to be baptized. I answered that I had been already baptized, and should not be so again.

As it was now the eve of *Timkat*, some combination of the embassy's personnel and the captive Franks asked for and were granted permission to put on a small pageant depicting the Adoration of the Magi, no doubt in order to demonstrate to the Ethiopians what events Westerners celebrated at Epiphany. One would have thought that Álvares would have been eager to promote what he considered an orthodox version of the holy day, but instead he sniffed at the European production, claiming that "it was not esteemed, nor hardly looked at, and indeed it was a dull affair." This seems to indicate that he himself was not involved in it, another striking turnaround from his recent eager showmanship in front of the altar — perhaps his refusal to direct explains why the play flopped. Meanwhile, the baptismal tank was being filled with water by means of a pipe connected to a nearby brook, a bag over its spout to strain out impurities. This artificial pond was three fathoms in length with a short flight of wooden steps and the *Negus'* enclosed platform side by side at one end, while its sides and bottom were lined with planks covered by waxed cotton cloth — a waterproof lining, in effect. The whole affair was roofed by a long, ridge-peaked tent decorated with red and blue crosses of silk, between whose walls and the edge of the water were arranged branches of lemon, orange, and other citrus trees, giving the entire space the feeling of an indoor garden. Once the sun had set, "all [that] night till dawn a great number of priests never stopped singing over the said tank, saying they were blessing the water." That single word "*saying*" succinctly communicates Álvares' glowering skepticism over the purported sanctity of the proceeding.

Although the ruckus of the priests kept him awake all night, it was only at "the hour of sunrise" when the ceremony was "in fullest force," that the *Negus* called him to witness it. He found the King stationed at one end of the tank inside his curtained box, but with his draperies parted about a hand-span so that he could observe his subjects both as they entered and exited the water by means of the wooden steps. "They placed me at the other end of the tank, with my face looking to the Prester, so that when he saw the backs, I saw the fronts." This anatomical precision is driven by our priest's shock at the naked condition of the celebrants, for while he says that the Prester, his Queen, and the *Abuna* were baptized before everyone else and allowed to "wear clothes over their private parts ... all the others were as their mother bore them." And, as he goes on to describe the scene, one can feel his dual objections to the immodesty and the spiritual irregularity of the ritual mutually reinforce each other:

> In the tank stood the old priest, the Prester's chaplain, who was with me on Christmas night, and he was [also] naked as when his mother bore him (and quite dead with cold, because there was a very sharp frost), standing in the water up to his shoulders or nearly so, for so deep was the tank that those who were to be baptized entered by the steps, naked, with their backs to the Prester, and when they came out again they showed him their fronts, the women as well as the men. When they came to the said priest, he put his hands on their heads, and put them under the water three times, saying in his language, "I baptize thee in the name of the Father, of the Son, and of the Holy Spirit": he made the sign of the cross as a blessing, and they went away in peace. (The "I baptize thee" — *I heard him say it.*) [italics mine]

After several hours of this immodest and unorthodox parade, during which he witnessed literally thousands undergoing immersion, Álvares was summoned to the royal box to be questioned about what he thought of it all. Once inside the confines of the smallish structure, and despite the ubiquitous curtain, our priest found himself in perhaps the closest physical proximity to Lebna Dengel he was ever to enjoy, for he, the *Aqabe sa'at*, and the monarch stood "so near that the Cabeata did not stir to hear what the Prester said, [or] to speak to the interpreter who was close to me." Given what he was feeling at the moment, however, this honor was clearly thrown away upon him. In times past, when confronted with other Ethiopian church ceremonies that he considered unnecessary, ill-conceived, or destructive of some religious principle, our priest had always begun his assessment (since he was always asked for one), with the same polite formula: "I said that their ceremony seemed to me good..." This time, however, his preamble was different, and what followed it was undiplomatically direct. "I answered him that the things of God's service which were done in good faith and without evil deceit, and for His praise, were good, but [that] there was no such rite as this in our Church, rather it forbade us baptizing without necessity on that day, because on that day Christ was baptized, so that we should not think of saying of ourselves that we were baptized on the same day as Christ; [moreover,] the Church does not order this sacrament to be given more than once." This uncharacteristically harsh response clearly surprised those in the royal box, which in addition to the *Negus* and the *Aqabe sa'at*, might have included the chaplain and other Chruch officials as well (including perhaps the *Abuna* Marcos himself). Someone apparently asked him to cite his text, a challenge he must have relished, since he could draw it from the Creed forged during their own beloved Council of Nicaea, i.e., "I believe in *one* baptism for the remission of sins." His questioners could only admit the truth of this, but apparently tempers on both sides were now running high, for what emerges is a confused exchange in which someone within the King's enclosure — likely the *Negus* himself— begins arguing as if the *Timkat* ceremony *did* effect actual re-baptisms. "But what [are we] to do with [the] many who turned Moors and Jews after being Christians and then repented," and what about those who may be baptized Christians but who "do not rightly believe[?]" How was that again?—*Self-declared Christians who wrongly believe?* Was this last question a jab at Álvares himself? Despite all the kind words that had followed his masses, was someone intimating that, from an Ethiopian perspective, all the Roman ritual he had shown them only painted the Catholics themselves as the actual heretics?

Whatever was intended, our priest answered in a way that seems contrary to all his fundamental instincts, and which jumps off the page of his book like shouted profanity in the midst of an otherwise temperate sermon. "I answered that [as to] those who do not rightly believe, teaching and preaching would suffice for them, and if that did them no good, *[then] burn them as heretics*" [italics mine]. As startling as this proposed solution — given its source — may seem to us, it was probably the partisan edge and lack of tact in Álvares' *next* answer that truly took his listeners aback. As for those, he continued, who had turned renegade against Christ's Church and then repented of it, their own

"Abima would absolve them, with penances salutary for their souls, *if* he had powers for this[;] if not, let them go to the Pope of Rome, in whom are *all* powers"[italics mine]. Then, as if for good measure: "And those who did not repent, [you] might take and burn, for that is what happens in France and the Church of Rome." One can only imagine how this outburst from their normally agreeable guest was met — it most likely occasioned several moments of stunned silence. Lebna Dengel's response, when it came, seemed a double reproach, both in its echoing of Álvares' formerly pacific tone and in its emphasis on Christian mercy: "all this seemed to him good, but ... his grandfather had ordained this baptism on the advice of great priests, in order that so many souls should not be lost, and ... it had been the custom until now." The King, seemingly in a tone of injured politeness, then wondered if the Pope might be persuaded to invest his *Abuna* with any powers of forgiveness he currently lacked. Álvares answered in turn, but reading the account gives one the distinct impression that the wounded (or offended) *Negus* was simply looking for a way to end the conversation on a calm note, for "to this there came no answer except that I might go in peace to say mass." The priest's own anger, however, had clearly not dissipated: "I said it was no longer time for saying mass, that midday was long passed. So I went to dine with our Portuguese and the Franks."[2] Though it was doubtful that he dared do it himself in the flesh, his language here rudely turns its back upon the sovereign.

Several issues need to be clarified before we leave behind this remarkable interview. First of all, it won't do to envision Francisco Álvares as a person who rightly should have professed anything like our own contemporary notions about the absolute wrongness of burning people at the stake over of their religious views. As stated before, he was a man from a time and a culture where many violent acts were perpetrated in the name of the Prince of Peace, and he could not escape his historical context any more than we can ours. Still, as we shall find in a later chapter when we peer forward from the time of the embassy to the Jesuit invasion that followed it, Father Álvares — when his fundamental temperament was not overwhelmed by cares — inhabited the latitudinarian end of a spectrum of Catholic attitudes toward the beliefs and practices of the Ethiopian Church. That is to say, while a handful of those clerics who followed him took pains to approach his usual example of patience, charity, and healthy self-doubt, many more arrogantly went after Abyssinian heresy with fire and tongs, leading to tragic results all round. Thus in drawing attention to the anomaly of our priest's suggestion of the stake as the shortest way with dissenters I am not holding him to some ahistorical standard of humanitarianism, but rather to one set by the vast majority of his own words and deeds as he sojourned through Ethiopia.

Another question that needs answering is why, when he came to finally write his book, he never corrected his mistake about *Timkat* representing a

EIGHT. Divided We Fall

yearly re-baptism of the Prester's people. Surely he had learned the truth by then, hadn't he? Well, to judge by the *Negus'* own words, it appears that no less an educated Ethiopian than the monarch himself was fuzzy on whether baptism was a renewable or a once-in-a-lifetime affair. And then too, his account of the chaplain's words to each bather—"'I baptize thee'—*I heard him say it!*"—suggests that he simply may never have ceased doubting Abyssinian assurances about what they were or weren't doing. Finally, there is the question of why he didn't edit out his own churlishness during the ceremony and its aftermath. Part of the reason is surely that same honesty of self-reportage that allowed his initial surprise concerning a black man's ability to be a gentleman to stand without emendation. But in this case there may have also been a motive at work that involved something other than forthright honesty. If, as I have been suggesting, Father Álvares was at this time slowly beginning to come to grips with a fact about his hosts' religion that was far more dire than any wrong-headed ritual, and if in the long run reasons of love and loyalty would stay him from writing the truth about it—then the *Timkat* immersions eventually provided him with the perfect retrospective opportunity to mask his obfuscation of a supposedly great apostasy by playing up his (genuinely at the time) angered reaction to a lesser one. Even basically honest people who must for some good reason abandon honesty still desire both to assuage their own consciences and to appear publicly plausible. Father Álvares was a conscientious priest who wanted to do his duty to his superiors in Lisbon and ultimately in Rome, even if that meant telling them some very bad news about the Realm of Prester John. But when he finally discovered that he couldn't bring himself to speak the worst of it I imagine he found it both personally comforting and politically advisable to include in full those incidents where he could at least show himself scrupulously denouncing that nation's more venial sins.

Whatever the *Negus* thought of Álvares' behavior, the priest was not made to forfeit a previously-scheduled interview with the *Abuna* Marcos the next day. The *Abuna*, recall, was always an Egyptian Coptic bishop appointed by the Patriarch of Alexandria who left his homeland to become the head of the Ethiopian Church for life—it's quasi-Pope, in practical terms. And, since the Abyssinians, despite their plethora of churchmen, had no indigenous bishops of their own, he was the only figure in the country who could ordain priests and deacons. In fact it was one of the *Abuna's* ordination ceremonies that Álvares was specifically invited to witness, a ritual that would wind up shaking him almost as deeply as the naked splashings of *Timkat*. His first hours in the aged metropolitan's company, however, were perfectly pleasant. He was warmly welcomed into the tent of a man he described as small, slender, and bedecked with a large blue turban and "a beard like very white wool, thin and of middling length." Our priest estimated that he was "getting to the age of one hundred and twenty," and claimed that this would be confirmed by anyone who "look[ed] at him well." To his relief, Álvares soon discovered he was having a sympathetic shop-talk with a fellow professional:

> When we were seated both together on a *catre*, the beginning of our conversation was to give thanks to God for bringing us together. Then he began to speak of the great pleasure he had received from what they had told to him about what I had said many times, and from what he had seen had passed with me at the baptism, and from the great clarity with which I had spoken the truth in the presence of the Prester, which he [i.e., the *Negus*] would not believe from him, the Abima, because he was alone; and that if he had an associate or two, who would help him in speaking the truth, he would free the Prester from many things and errors, in which he and his people were [sunk].

These errors to which the *Abuna* referred were the Judaizing practices of the Ethiopians, which the Egyptian Copts had long since sloughed off roughly in tandem with the Catholic West. And even if he could have offered no relief to Álvares' main worry, had our priest dared broach it — since all Copts were monophysites — Álvares must have been heartened to have it brought home to him that the head of the Abyssinian Church was, like himself, a foreigner. Indeed, for all his many years in the country, the *Abuna* Marcos spoke no Amharic. Things went on so swimmingly that by the time the visit was over, the two had even managed to hold a jesting conversation with one of the Patriarch's underlings about whether Jesus Christ had been circumcised or not. When a wine and fruit basket from the old man followed Álvares home to his tent that afternoon, he must have rejoiced in finding what appeared to be an important ally amidst his troubles.

However, when he accompanied the *Abuna* and his staff to the place of ordination the next morning, he was shocked to see literally thousands of people waiting for them in a large field, and remained mystified as the metropolitan began addressing the crowd in Arabic without dismounting from his mule. He asked one of the assistants for a running translation, and was told that the crowd was being warned that if any of them currently had more than one wife, that they could not be ordained, and that if they misrepresented their marital state and tried to sneak through, that they would bear the weight of the *Abuna*'s curse. It gradually dawned on Álvares that nearly everyone there was in fact a candidate for the priesthood. This was disconcerting, but he probably assuaged his unease by telling himself that surely only a fraction of the multitude would be found fit for holy orders. *Abuna* Marcos now sat himself down in front of a tent while a trio of priests with large books in their hands fanned out in front of him, whereupon the multitude began forming themselves into three great lines that stretched from each of these clerics far off into the sunlit distance. At a signal, the first man in each line stepped forward and directed his eyes toward a passage of text pointed out by his line's respective priest. This was apparently a literacy test, but to Álvares' dismay the *Abuna's* men only "examined them very briefly, for each one did not read more than two or three words." It was only after this hurried quiz, however, that the almost industrial efficiency of the process was finally made apparent to him, for "then they go to one who stands behind these [priests] with a basin of white ink and a stamp like a seal, and he puts this stamp on the flat of the right arm." The number of those wearing this mark of distinction rose steadily and rapidly, for as our priest noted with distress, "there were very few who did not pass."

The first stage of processing complete, the aged Marcos moved inside his tent to administer the finishing touches. "This tent had two entrances, and they put all those who had been examined in a line, one in front of another, and they passed before the Abima, entering by one door and going out by the other." As the file of aspirants passed before the bishop "he put his hand on their head[s], and said words which I did not understand," then took up a book and read from it while making "the sign of the cross over them many times" with an iron crucifix.

> This ceremony being concluded, a priest who was with the Abima went out to the door of the tent, and read from a book something like an Epistle or Gospel; then the Abima said mass, which was not more than as much as one might say the psalm *Miserere mei Deus* three times. And he gave communion to these priests, who were 2357, all mass priests .... They are not put down in a register, nor do they carry a letter, or other certificate of their orders.

Álvares had often mentioned the remarkable number of priests in the Prester's realm; now he understood that such was the case because they were turned out like sausage.

He does not record what he said to his new friend the *Abuna* about this mass ordination, but the next day — January 9th — he was summoned before the *Negus* and asked to give the Court his views. He had apparently composed himself a bit, for he merely remarked upon rather than denounced the sheer size of the affair, and managed to introduce his other criticisms in something like his old, agreeable way. "I answered that ... the rite seemed to me very good, but what did not seem to me good was the great indecency with which those priests came who were ordained," for many had "come almost naked and showing their private parts." This was bad enough, but worse was the fact that while those in holy orders were supposed to be sound in all their wits, senses and limbs, what had he seen? One aspirant had been "entirely blind," and so how could he "have learning, or administer the sacrament[?]" There was another who was "entirely crippled in the right hand, and four or five who were crippled in the legs," and yet "these also they made priests." Lebna Dengel, no doubt relieved at Álvares' regained equilibrium, replied "that he was very pleased that I looked at all things and told him of what did not seem ... right, so that they could correct them." As to the nakedness, the *Negus* "would see to that," while concerning the cripples he was directed to dine with one of the churchmen present. Over this meal the two priests agreed that candidates should be "complete" but sparred a bit over the meaning of that term. Before long, however, his unnamed host asked "what such as these would do if they had not alms from the church?" This question spoke to the fact that ordination in Ethiopia solved certain social problems that were handled by other means in the West. As one scholar points out, the Abyssinian priesthood was often "a refuge for misfits, physically and mentally and otherwise handicapped people, and a horde of parasites who shunned physical labour and opted for the respected, though economically unrewarding, membership in the church organization."[3] For his part, Álvares was honest enough to admit that the Catholic church also frequently took on the care of such people, but explained that back home they served as "organ players and organ blowers and bell ringers, and do other things." Let them be beadsmen and candle-snuffers, he urged, but don't *ordain* them. One can tell that his professional pride was engaged in this criticism of his hosts' customs.

Acting like a glutton for mental punishment, but probably feeling he was duty bound to do it, the next day Álvares followed the *Abuna* to a church to watch him create *zagonais*— the deacons or lay officials of the ecclesiastical establishment. It was a similar mob scene to the one before, except this time the mob was younger — some so young, in fact, that many were accompanied by a parent. "The children who can neither speak nor walk are carried by men in their arms, because women cannot enter into the church, and their wailing is like kids [i.e., young sheep] in a [barn]yard without the mothers." The age of these prospective deacons, who would many of them in later years go on to be fully ordained, underscored another aspect of Ethiopian priesthood about which Álvares may only now have been gaining clarity — that it was substantially hereditary. The truth of the matter was that the office of village priest would often be jealously monopolized by one family over several generations, another feature that insured the uninspired quality of the Abyssinian Church at the parish level, though in fairness the men at the top of the hierarchy were generally educated, competent, and committed. This ceremony, like the previous one, featured a brisk walk-through of the *Abuna's* tent to receive that worthy's blessing, and likewise culminated in a mass. The giving of the eucharist to some of the younger children, however, re-ignited one of our priest's *bête noires:* "they give communion to all of them, and the danger of the little ones is an amazing thing, for even by force of water they cannot make them swallow the Sacrament because it is of coarse dough, [and] because of their age and their crying."

When it was all over and our priest and the *Abuna* were sharing a cordial meal, Álvares finally asked him why in the world he had to ordain so many candidates at the same time; the answer he received was probably a salutary education in what it meant to run a national Christian church behind Muslim lines. The metropolitan replied that large ceremonies were necessary because he himself "was very old, and he did not know when they would have another Abima," for "he had been fifty years in the country, and ... had come as white as he now was." Indeed how could he or anyone know the date when his replacement would arrive from Alexandria, given the difficulty of procuring such a figure from the Christian Patriarch of a foreign country ruled by Muslims? There had, he continued, been a time within the memory of some at Court when Ethiopia had gone twenty-three years without an *Abuna*, during which time no one could be ordained and toward whose end what few priests remained above ground were as white-haired as he himself was now. And, since such a second spiritual winter could arrive the minute his own feeble heart ceased to beat, both he and the Prester agreed it was needful to store up human supplies against such an eventuality. Not that the *Negus* had been idle, for three years previously he "had sent 2000 ounces of gold to Cairo in search of an Abima," but "on account of the wars of the Soldam [i.e., the Sultan of Egypt] with the Turk, they had not sent [an *Abuna*], and they had taken the gold." Indeed, when one thinks about it, the question arises as to why the Muslim leaders of Egypt, be they Fatimid, Ayyubid, or Mamluk, hadn't at some point over the last eight hundred years refused absolutely to let the Coptic Patrirach dispatch an *Abuna*, and thereby destroyed Ethiopian Christianity from the top down? One answer might have been the mythical but widely credited possibility of the *Negus* cutting off the flow of the Nile in retaliation, but there was a more palpable reason why, despite some long interruptions, a metropolitan from Alexandria had always eventually made his way southward to Ethiopia in time. The fact was that while the Coptic Christians were a grudgingly tolerated religious minority in Egypt, Muslims were a no less perilously situated group amidst the Roof of Africa. Consequently, if no *Abuna* was forthcoming after the requisite payment had been sent, the reigning *Negus* would eventually begin to harass and persecute his resident Islamites, who would naturally appeal to Cairo for relief. In like manner, if any Ethiopian king outrageously mistreated his Muslim subjects, the Sultan would begin putting the screws to the Copts. Thus between Egypt and Ethiopia a kind of balance of terror existed, out of which a rough détente had eventually developed. Still, it was a long and treacherous — and now a war-torn — road from the mouth of the Nile to its source, and thus the *Abuna* Marcos felt obligated to ordain *en masse*.

After relating his elderly friend's explanations, he admits that in later years the Ethiopians' many reasons — religious but mostly economic — for desiring ordinations eventually got the better of his scruples, such that "after going on these two occasions ... I went endless times later to see them, for they were given nearly every day, and also on Sundays, because of the great crowds that came at all times." He even divulges with a sigh that once it became known that he and the *Abuna* were close, whenever the latter would take a few days off strangers sought out our priest "and begged me for the love of God to speak to the Abima, and ask him to confer orders, as they had nothing to eat." (I.e., they needed a job and that of priest would do.) And, as old and weary as *Abuna* Marcos was, "certainly I ever asked it but what he did it, for he had a very good will towards me."[4] Father Álvares was a man of principle who could flash into righteous anger when things he held dear were threatened, but in the long run he knew how to pick his battles.

During the next month, as the Prester's letters to India and Europe slowly took shape, the business of the embassy revolved around Mekane Selassie, from whose vicinity the Prester's capital never moved, and at which they witnessed a pair of ceremonies in quick succession. These were the consecration of the structure on January 14th and, three days later, the reburial within it of the bones of Lebna Dengel's father, the *Negus* Na'od. This latter occasion was marked by much vivid spectacle, beginning in the morning with the clergy designated to serve there performing "a great rite, with singing, and playing instruments, and dancing, and leaping" before a large crowd. Toward afternoon, the procession accompanying the royal remains approached the church, its number swelled by such Court luminaries as the *Abuna* Marcos — "very tired" and supported by a man under each arm — the Prester's Queen, the Queen Mother, and the dowager Eleni, all clad in dark robes and walking slowly beneath the black umbrellas that signified mourning. Only the dust of Na'od himself was exempt from such somber costuming, the bier encased in satin curtains and progressing beneath a canopy of gold. Álvares was impressed by the sincerity of emotion on display, as if the former King had died just the day before, reporting that the crowd carried on "so pathetically, that we, standing where we were, all wept."

This solemn occasion, however, possessed an odd coda. After the consecration ceremonies had finally wound down two nights later, the Portuguese found themselves conducted to a pavilion they had never seen before which had been erected inside the royal compound. According to our priest, "the whole of this tent was spread with very beautiful carpets, and it was large like a reception room, and [the *Negus*] sent to tell us that for his sake we should enjoy ourselves there and talk of our affairs." Moreover, "while we were in conversation they brought to us many different things to eat and drink." This fare was apparently extraordinary, for Álvares — who, recall, enjoyed the pleasures of the table — spent a half a page praising its quality and variety, remarking that some of the dishes were even cooked "almost in our style," and noting that all of it was accompanied with "many jars of wine." Was this feast then a reward of some kind? — an act of spontaneous largess? — was it yet another Ethiopian holy day? Suddenly, a suspicion began to run through the diners that, amidst all the pages coming and going with plates and goblets, they were somehow being spied upon, and that the Prester or his minions might be stationed nearby "to hear us and watch what we did." This spontaneous worry quickly hardened, without benefit of evidence, into a certainty for some among the party, who now "declared that he [i.e., the *Negus*] was there, and that nothing improper ought to occur among us." What was going on here?—were some Court officials actually eavesdropping, or were the Portuguese merely suffering a fit of paranoia? We can't know, but either possibility would have had its genesis in the likelihood (large or small) of the embassy's immanent departure. After all, Lebna Dengel had up till now seldom allowed any Frank to leave his realm: yet he said they would soon be released — and yet still the weeks dragged on. In truth the *Negus* probably would have given much to know what the squabbling and increasingly unhappy envoys really thought about his land, while for their part the Portuguese had good reason to suspect that their brawls had soured the King's attitude toward them. At any rate, the Ethiopian Court had this in common with its European counterparts — it was not a place where many heads slept soundly through the night.

    As the date of departure, however uncertain, appeared to approach, Pêro da Covilhã, who had intermittently been acting as translator and cultural liaison between the embassy and the Court, and who was present during much of the capital's residence near Mekane Selassie, felt the stirring of old desires within him. Of this man who had been so long in Ethiopia, who had prospered so richly under its kings, and who had founded a family with one of its women, Álvares says: "when he saw that we wanted to leave, a passionate desire to return to his country came upon him." Dom Rodrigo was certainly sympathetic to this wish, for who had served the Portuguese throne more diligently than De Covilhã, a man who would surely merit a hero's welcome even if he retuned thirty years later than expected? And so when the longstanding exile "went to ask leave of the Prester ... we went with him and we urged it with great insistence and begged it of him." But, as our priest flatly reports, "no order for it was ever given." Heartless as it may seem, it is not hard to fathom Lebna Dengel's motives for this refusal. On the one hand, while the *Negus* still had some power to shape the embassy's views of his country, Da Covilhã knew it inside and out and once home might perhaps report things His Highness would rather keep concealed. More importantly, if Dom Rodrigo and his company were merely the forerunners of a steady stream of Portuguese who would soon be arriving upon his coast, then he would need a go-between he could trust — or at least readily comprehend. Still, it must have been a bitter check for this man whose life had been sent spinning across three continents by one king and immobilized in luxurious amber by another.

    If it was not surprising that at least one of the captive Franks asked permission to leave, it was somewhat more unexpected that a member of the embassy requested to stay behind. This petition came from the physician, Joam Bermudez, whom we have so far seen tending the sick at the monastery of Bizam and escaping with a bloody head from one of the hostile villages on the journey inland. He is also briefly mentioned as one of the five men "who understood church matters and could sing well" whom our priest recruited as his makeshift choir for the Christmas mass. These are fleeting enough glimpses, but given his subsequent career of audacious impersonation, one can't help but search them for possible foretastes of his later escapades. His freeing of himself from captivity might indicate a modicum of cunning, though it could just as easily have been the result of dumb luck, but the fact that he "understood church matters" attracts one's notice given that years later, having suddenly reappeared in Europe, he would claim to be Ethiopia's duly consecrated *Abuna* as well as the trusted ambassador of a now-desperate and fugitive Lebna Dengel. One wonders — had he already eyed the aged Marcos, reckoned up his own knowledge of matters ecclesiastical (whatever that amounted to), and, like some Conradian villain, sketched in his imagination the outline of a fantastical future in an exotic land rife with possibilities for an unscrupulous foreigner? Álvares gives no hints as to what he thought of Bermudez's character, but it is interesting that he betrays not a hint of sorrow when reporting that his request to remain was granted.

By the second week in February, the *Negus'* letters in answer to the Portuguese King and his Governor were nearing completion. "They spent a long time over them," explains our priest, "because their custom is not to write to one another, [since] their messages, communications, and embassies [are] all by word of mouth." The Ethiopian scholars, in order to avoid some vulgar mistake and to emphasize their Christian bona-fides, covered the scriptorium tables with "all the books of the Epistles of St. Paul, of St. Peter, and St. James," and "those that they held to be the most learned studied them." This careful cross-referencing could not be done speedily, and a further desire to be diplomatically punctilious meant that separate missives were drafted for Manoel and Sequeira, and that each of these were written three times — once in Ge'ez (the literary language of Ethiopia), once in Arabic, and once in Portuguese — for a grand total of twelve outgoing pieces of meticulously wrought mail. Álvares was, "by order of the Prester," intimately involved in the tedious process of translation. First, Zaga Za Ab would read out what the *Negus*, after consultation with his advisors and churchmen, wanted to say, whereupon Pêro da Covilhã would translate a passage of it into Portuguese so that our priest and the embassy's clerk, Joam Escolar, could write it down on long scrolls of parchment. By this point Álvares had a solid handle on Amharic and possibly on Ge'ez as well, but still he complained that "it is very difficult to translate Abyssinian ... into Portuguese," for the former language was itself "very difficult and ... without rules." When they were all done, the letters were to be sewn up in brocade bags and carried to their addressees in special leather baskets lined with cloth.

What our priest discovered during this process of inscription, and what he undoubtedly kept strictly to himself, was the Prester's respective evaluations of Dom Rodrgo and himself. In his letter to the Governor, for instance, Lebna Dengel described the Ambassador as being "very good excepting his faults," which included the fact that he "does not speak much with his lips," and "is remarkable for making himself [i.e., thinking himself] ... better than all." He also made mention of "some quarrels" among the members of the embassy and hinted that the fault lay at De Lima's feet. Our priest, however, fared better in His Excellency's eyes:

> To Father Francisco give twice as many thanks, because he is a holy man, honest and of good conscience for the love of God: I know his character, and I gave him a cross and a staff of his lordship into his hand.... [Know from these signs that] he is an Abbot in our country: and do you increase him and make him lord of [Massawa] and Zeila and all the isles of the Red Sea, and of the limits of our countries, because he is sufficient for, and deserving of such an office, which he rejected.

So, had he wished, Álvares could have found himself titular ruler of the Dahlak Islands and of Kamaran — two pieces of geography he had no reason to love other than their being the gravesites of his former shipmates. And Massawa and Zeila too — especially embarrassing appointments those, considering that Dom Rodrigo had already nominated himself (in the Prester's hearing) to be their commander. It is a safe bet that our priest made sure the brocade bags were stitched up double-tight, and that he began scheming about how to be elsewhere when it came time for the letters to be read out publicly back in the *Estado*.

On February 11th the *Negus* summoned to his tent not only the members of the expedition but also the thirteen captive Franks who were then at Court to attend an official ceremony dismissing the embassy. In an act of calculated insult, His Highness proceeded to lavish gifts of gold and silken garments on the resident Europeans while giving the travelers nothing. The only exceptions to this were the cross and pastoral staff of silver mentioned above, which were delivered to Álvares along with his commission to rule the Red Sea, the latter of which our priest tried to assure his staring companions must be some kind of merely honorary title. Having thus made his point by means of selective largess, the King sent a message begging Dom Rodrigo to make up with De Abreu and to travel back to the coast in close company with him, implying that the embassy's share of the gifts would be released upon a favorable answer. To this overture, however, "the Ambassador replied that he was not going to be his friend, nor travel where he went, but rather begged of His Highness to keep him at his Court two months after his departure, because he was trying to kill him." Stubbornly rebuffed, the King announced that the supplies and money for the outward journey would be doled out proportionately to both De Lima and D'Abreu's camps, adding irritably that the Portuguese on their way out "were not to injure the peasants who were poor," for he had been told that on their trek hither "they destroyed the people of the country." Thus were Zaga Za Ab's sins transferred to the head of the *Negus'* least-favorite European.

Later that day, when Dom Rodrigo's portion of the traveling supplies began to arrive at his tent, they were accompanied by an object meant to convey the Prester's seriousness concerning his new alliance with Portugal — a large gold and silver crown. A message from the King instructed the Ambassador to tell his master

> that [such] a crown never passed except from father to son, and that he was his [i.e., King Manoel's] son, and [that] he took it off his head and sent it to the King of Portugal, who was like his father, and that he sent it now as the precious thing it was; [that] by it he gave and offered all favor and assistance and help in men, gold, and provisions which might be necessary for his fortresses and fleets, and for the wars he might please to wage against the Moors in these regions of the Red Sea as far as the Holy House [i.e., Jerusalem].

Despite the heavy strategic import of this pledge, several of the Portuguese began murmuring that they were still rightly due the same clothes and gifts that the captive Franks had received. This grousing was overheard by some Court officials who informed them that the *Negus* was "angry because [De Lima] would not be friendly with Jorge d'Abreu, and that he was dispatching us with great disgust, and that we were not to expect clothes, nor anything else." Gold crowns and high promises notwithstanding, such mutual displays of spleen seemed to cast a shadow of pettiness over all the Portuguese had ventured and endured.

The next morning Zaga Za Ab arrived with the sealed letter-baskets, formally entrusted them to Dom Rodrigo's care, and "said to the Ambassador that we might go whenever we pleased as we were fully dismissed." Not wanting to depart on such a sour note, however, De Lima asked for one further audience with the *Negus* — no doubt to explain yet again D'Abreu's perfidy rather than to acquiesce in making peace with him. The reply was that His Highness had already departed the capital, and that "he was very displeased with the Ambassador because he ill-treated men so, and because he would not be a friend of Jorge d'Abreu, and for other things that he kept to himself, [but] that we might depart in peace." Seeing no remedy, both sects of the embassy made ready to break camp. It was soon discovered, however, that although the necessary number of mules had arrived, the horns of wine had been delivered empty, ostensibly because it was now the start of Ethiopian Lent. Álvares describes the inauspicious farewell that ensued:

> Upon this some went to the market-place to buy what they needed for the journey,

and on this account we were putting off our departure till another day, as it was already late, when so great a wind fell upon us that it broke the tent ropes, and the whole of it came to the ground. When we saw this and how we were left in the open, all of us that were there began to call out: "Come, come, let us be going, since they send us, let us be off." So we set out from the Court this day, which was our Shrove Tuesday, and went to sleep in a field a distance of a league from the Court. There [went] with us and in our company Pero de Covilham, with his black wife and some of his sons who were grey, [while] the monk [went] with Jorge d'Abreu, almost like his guard, and they took up their quarters apart from us.[5]

A cynical observer might have chided Dom Rodrigo that the Prester's capital must in truth have proved the magical city of legend, for whereas only one Portuguese embassy had arrived there, two were now leaving it.

Álvares relates very little of the northward journey's day-to-day progress, in part because he was now covering geography he had already described, but also because his attention is focused upon the self-inflicted catastrophe that prematurely ended it. The premonitions of this disaster were not long in coming, for "on this second night of our journey, sin began to excite fresh quarrels." The immediate trouble arose when Joam Goncalvez, the embassy's factor (roughly baggage-master) began ferociously beating his servant, Fernandez, with a stick over some perceived blunder or act of insubordination. Both had apparently been traveling in Dom Rodrigo's camp, and when the Ambassador was called to intervene he took the servant's side against the master, a somewhat unexpected stance given his usual insistence upon the perquisites of rank. Though the combatants were separated, their animosity was not quelled, and some time later — how long, exactly, Álvares does not specify — Fernandez decided to ambush his master. Using a lance he was either given by or had stolen from Dom Rodrigo, he sprung upon Goncalvez and stabbed him twice, in the hand and the chest, delivering a wound that looked serious enough to prompt our priest to offer confession to what he thought was a dying man (though he later recovered). For his part, Fernandez fled to the imagined safety of his earlier partisan, De Lima, but when the Ambassador had him arrested and bound, he managed, perhaps with someone's help, to get free from his ropes and escape altogether to D'Abreu's camp. Up till now the two columns had been shadowing each other, the Ambassador's being led by the Prester's Master of Pages, De Abreu's by Zaga Za Ab. (Da Covilhã, after riding with Dom Rodrigo for awhile, had apparently turned aside to his estates, obeying the *Negus'* insistence that he remain in the country.) They could see each other plainly during certain stretches of the road, and when Fernandez fled to D'Abreu the rival campsite was clearly visible farther down the nearly dry riverbed on which they had both pitched their tents. The two factions had reason enough to be wary of each other, but after this defection Álvares tells us that "the Ambassador became doubly frightened."

The *Negus*, however, had not yet despaired of his efforts to reunite the embassy, for while the Portuguese were re-traversing the territory of the *Tegremakuannen* they were overtaken by a pair of Court officials charged with forcing the two warring halves back into a whole, no matter how jury-rigged or unstable the resulting aggregate might be. The King's intense nervousness about how a continuing split would reflect upon himself and Ethiopia was clearly detectable in the set speeches of the two officials, who insisted that De Lima and D'Abreu should "not keep apart before the [*Estado's* Governor], as it seemed a very scandalous thing." Though our priest is maddeningly uninformative about how the feat was accomplished, he declares that eventually "we made them become friends and meet together." Perhaps Álvares managed to convince both *fidalgos* that it would indeed be unseemly to re-emerge from the Prester's realm and present themselves to the Governor at the head of two bickering cliques; perhaps the two men's growing awareness that they would soon have to give an account of themselves to their superiors made their disagreements seem suddenly less significant. However it was arranged, and however shaky the truce, the recombined embassy continued north under the direction of the two new officials, in part to ensure that there would be no backsliding into discord, and in part so that the pair could greet the arriving Portuguese fleet in the Prester's name, since the *Bahr-nagas*, who would usually have that honor, was detained back at Court.

When the Portuguese reached Debarwa, that capital of the *Bahr-nagas'* territory where they had impatiently negotiated for mules and camels on the inward journey, they were instructed to hunker down and wait for news of their armada's arrival at Massawa, some several days march to the northeast. Although the embassy had been making good time both apart and then together, they apparently did not press on to the coast because at Debarwa there was abundant water, food, coolness, and a Christian majority, amenities which the heat-blasted Massawa could never boast. Better, they were told, to linger a while longer atop the temperate Roof of Africa. And so they waited, but throughout that spring no encouraging word from the sea ever reached them — no Portuguese galleons appeared upon the Lake of Fire. Our priest mentions this unsettling disappointment almost in passing, perhaps because by the time he came to write his book it had recurred so many times, but it must have been a hard fact to digest, especially as there would have been no hint as to the reason for it. Had the Governor's ships met with some mishap on the water; had India come under attack from the Moors; had they perhaps been forgotten altogether? The last was of course a wildly unlikely conjecture, given the import of their mission, but complete uncertainty magnifies even the remotest possibilities. And it must have been daunting to imagine what they would do with themselves for the space of another year, given that they were stranded in a foreign land where their work was already finished. How would they pass the time, and how would the time that passed feel to them?

If any of the Portuguese were looking forward to a long spell of monotonous leisure and sedentary calm, however, the passions of their leaders betrayed them, for those passions took license from the empty days to grow furious and brazen once again. Once they had finally given up on the fleet, the embassy had apparently fallen into a living arrangement at Debarwa that featured the worst aspects of both their previous divorce and their recent re-marriage, for D'Abreu and his followers had again physically separated themselves from the Ambassador's faction, and yet Dom Rodrigo was apparently once more the sole receiver and distributor of food and supplies provided by the Ethiopians. Why this explosive situation did not immediately come to the attention of the pair of Court officials still overseeing the Portuguese is unclear, but they seem to have grown complacent after their earlier success at peacemaking. Be that as it may, sometime in the late spring or early summer the Ambassador, probably at the instigation of some insult, cut off food deliveries to his lieutenant's camp. In response, D'Abreu sent the runaway Fernandez to demand that the distribution be continued, an odd choice considering that servant's history with Dom Rodrigo, and indeed the latter merely chased him away. As Álvares reports, "thereupon Jorge d'Abreu sent to ask me to come to a church, and there he told me to tell the Ambassador to order food to be given for him, and those that were with him; otherwise he would take it by force." Our priest duly relayed this ominous message, but De Lima replied that "he would give nothing, as they were traitors to the service of the King of Portugal." Momentarily showing a cooler head than was usual for him, D'Abreu then took his complaint to the two officials, who immediately convened a parlay in an open field, much as the Prester had attempted some months before.

Once all the parties were situated in the knee-high grass, one of the courtiers proceeded to give the Ambassador a rather condescending lecture on good leadership skills and then asked him to

> consider how much displeasure the Prester John would feel at his so ill-treating his company; and that if he would treat them in another way, he himself would be treated differently, and would be more pleased than he was; and he asked him to give [his rivals] their own, and not break the friendship which he had already promised in his presence to keep with Jorge d'Abreu. The Ambassador replied briefly, and almost angrily that he was not going to give it him, [because] they were traitors to the service of the King of Portugal for which he came. Jorge d'Abreu said that if he did not order [the supplies] to be given him he would take [them]; and so we arose all of us dissatisfied, and each one went to his quarters.

Whatever the Ethiopians believed about the special efficacy of negotiating out-of-doors, the practice had now failed them twice.

Goncalvez, the embassy's factor, who had physical possession of the food, and who justifiably dreaded an immanent attack by D'Abreu's people, immediately moved himself and the stores into the Ambassador's dwelling since it was the most substantial in their compound, "good and strong as they go in this country." He hadn't long to wait for what he feared. That very night, Álvares, who was asleep in another building with his (infrequently-mentioned) nephew and Escolar the clerk, reports that he was awakened by "shouts of, 'Fire here, fire there,' and then muskets." Rushing toward the source of the commotion, our priest and Escolar saw by moonlight D'Abreu and some of his followers crowded outside the front door of the Ambassador's residence, "knocking down the houses as if with rams, and firing muskets, and it seemed to us that those that were inside must be dead, so great was the uproar." Realizing that, unarmed (in Álvares' case, un-croziered), they could do nothing themselves, they "went running to the houses of the Barnagais, where the [two] lords were lodging, to tell them to come to our assistance." Just as they were bursting in one door of the *beta Negus,* however, "the Ambassador and his companions [ran] in at the other, ... bringing with them the basket with the crown and letters of the Prester John, and what few goods they could." They had apparently escaped their own besieged structure by a small side door, but not unscathed, for "one of the Ambassador's men came wounded by a musket in the knee, which made four of five wounds, as they carry shot." The Court officials, quickly forming their guards and retainers into a posse, set out for the scene of the battle, where they came upon D'Abreu and his men "still knocking down the house, thinking that they had caught the people inside." No doubt envisioning their own heads already rolling before the Prester's feet, the lords let their men vigorously beat all the combatants on both sides into bloody submission and thereupon arrested every Portuguese in sight.

Subsequent to this squalid debacle there was a good deal of discussion between the two doomed courtiers about what to do with their Frankish prisoners, at whom their anger can only be imagined. There were strict prohibitions against arriving at the capital without orders, and yet to just stay put after such outrages might suggest an attempt to cover them up. As Álvares sympathetically remarks, they "did not dare to leave us or to take us, nor to return themselves, neither could they make peace between us, and at length they made up their minds to send us back to the Court and lay themselves open to any punishment which [the *Negus*] might please to give them for this." Clearly the Portuguese had marred more futures than merely their own. And so, runners were sent ahead with the scandalous news and the southward march began. The whole dispirited troupe had only gotten a few leagues beyond Manandelay, however, before they were intercepted by a grandee heading north who bore a familiar face to those in the embassy, though not necessarily one they remembered with affection. It was none other than the *Bahr-nagas,* returning from Court to his home province athwart the Red Sea. He had already heard the news, was at a piping boil, and had something to say to all of them.

We all took our places in a tilled field at the foot of a big tree, as many as there was room for there. These gentlemen were much reproved by the Barnagais for having brought us without leave, and he also shouted a good deal at the Ambassador and at Jorge d'Abreu: and he told the Ambassador to give up to him at once the crown of the Prester, and the letters which he was carrying for the King of Portugal and the [Governor]. Between the Ambassador and Jorge d'Abreu some very ugly words passed. Then the Barnagais told the others to continue on their way to the Court, and there they would have their punishment.[6]

As for the members of the embassy, they were to accompany him back to the precincts of his capital at Debarwa — as prisoners of himself and the *Negus*. Once the particulars of their confinement had been seen to, their own punishment would also be handed down by His Highness. It seemed a farcical end to an enterprise once burnished by diplomatic courtesy and elevated by hopeful idealism. If there was even one bright thought that day, it must have belonged to the *Bahr-nagas* congratulating himself on all the daylight he had managed to put between himself and these Frankish imbeciles so soon after their arrival, though one suspects that his blinding migraine had also returned. As the weary line of Portuguese inmates trudged northward once again, the downpours of their second rainy season under Ethiopian skies pelted them as if in derision.

NINE

The Magic Mountain

That the arrest of the Portuguese marked a decisive turning point in their fortunes, a bright line separating their life before it from the very different life that followed, is attested to by the fact that immediately after telling us of it, Álvares (or perhaps one of his editors), announces at the bottom of the page that "here the author ceases to speak of his journey." Luckily for us, this assertion is true only in a very limited sense. What our priest does in fact give up is any attempt to record the events of each succeeding day, since any given Tuesday spent in captivity closely resembles the Monday that preceded it and the Wednesday that succeeds. And then too he could no longer speak of their "journey" because for a long while their existence became too sedentary to merit such a term in its usual sense, though it is clear that Álvares' own spiritual odyssey never paused for long. What he continued to write about was the Ethiopian people — their customs, their aspirations, and their character. And, when he or other members of the embassy did manage to cover significant ground once again, he took care to record the high points of that renewed traveling in roughly chronological order. Thus our priest by no means fell silent — it was just that the moving canvas of images and incidents he had once scrambled to narrate now passed before his eyes at a much more leisurely pace, and if he had fewer things to relate in an absolute sense, he now also possessed the leisure to contemplate them within a wider perspective.

The immediate circumstances of the embassy's imprisonment were humiliating enough, for like two spoiled children who cannot play peacefully together, the factions were permanently separated by the grownups they had angered. The Ambassador's followers were put under a kind of loose house arrest at Debarwa, the *Bahr-nagas'* capital, while D'Abreu's band was quartered some four leagues distant from them at a town Álvares refers to as Barra. Ominously for Dom Rodrigo, the Ruler of the Seacoast renounced his usual provincial seat and dwelt in the latter town with the rebels, a precaution he reportedly took "in order not to quarrel with the Ambassador," whom he had long considered a tedious fool. Furthermore, though both sides in the dispute were "very badly supplied with all things," it appeared to those in the Ambassador's camp that "Jorge d'Abreu and his companions were better supplied than we were," a discrepancy that no doubt reflected the biases of both the nearby *Bahrnagas* and the distant Lebna Dengel. As it fell out, though, such a meager dole proved an unexpected boon to the sportsman Álvares, for it created a situation in which "a great deal of hunting and fishing [became] valuable to us," activities he took up with enthusiasm upon the river and small hunting ground the prisoners were allowed to make use of to supplement their diet.

But our priest was fortunate in another way as well, for it seems that his movements were in general far less restricted than those of his fellow prisoners from either faction. We know this because he mentions that during the eighteen months that the embassy was immobilized in the precincts of Debarwa — summer 1521 until early in 1523 — he "often" visited the monks of Bizam, "leav[ing] home in the morning on my mule and reach[ing] the monastery at Vespers" (that is, in the late afternoon or early evening). This degree of freedom could only have come at the express order of the *Negus*, who was obviously aware that Álvares had always done all in his power to cool the embassy's brewing feuds, and who simply held our priest in far higher regard than he did the rest of the Portuguese. Álvares says that during this season he visited Bizam "many times, because [he] came there to pass time with the monks, principally on feast days" and "in this way [he] learned about them and their property, and revenues and customs." And therefore it was surely during this year and a half of intermittent discussions with the learned anchorites that our priest came to comprehend the full truth concerning the Ethiopians' monophysite heresy. After all, he came to know equally esoteric, if less dangerous doctrinal information, such as that the monks of Bizam were "the most Judaizing of [any in] the kingdoms of the Prester John," understanding well the religious controversies that had divided those Ewostatewosian monks from those of the order founded by Takla Haymanot.[1] And so the more vital issue of the nature of the Holy Trinity cannot have been wholly avoided by clerics from two disparate Christian lands competent to, and intent upon, comparing theological notes. Sadly then, the eighteen months that saw his daylong rides up to the heights of Bizam undoubtedly contained somewhere within them the *terminus ad quem* of whatever starved hopes he still held out for the nation's orthodoxy. If, however, it was during this time that he came at last to know the worst, it is not at all clear that he had yet decided what to do — or rather what *not* to do — in reaction to this disconcerting truth he could no longer deny. As a Catholic priest Álvares had a clear duty in this regard, but it may have happened that, amidst a land so alien and yet so obviously Godly, he was beginning to feel that the noun in his title entailed responsibilities that outweighed those implied by the adjective: namely, to protect the flock from those who would ridicule their beliefs, and to cherish whatever spiritual expressions naturally arose from the hearts of his chosen congregation.

We know this much, at any rate: instead of detailing the content of his theological discussions at Bizam, he chose to expatiate upon the remarkable acts of piety continually performed by the Ethiopian people. As he begins to list their various fasts and self-scourgings, however, it is difficult to determine exactly how he feels about them, for his prose seems to waver at a point of unstable equilibrium between genuine admiration and revulsion in the face of excesses. For instance, after informing us that the beginning of Abyssinian Lent entails "three days of severe fast[ing] universally, [for] clergy, monks, and laymen," during which time many anchorites "do not eat more than once, and ... [then] only herbs" and even doting mothers only suckle their infants once a day, he immediately complains that if the Ethiopians had *wanted* to eat fish during this fast as Catholics do there would have been plenty to be found in the rivers, but that perversely they possessed "very little skill in catching them." (Álvares was a mighty evangelist when it came to angling.) In like manner he seems at first to extol the religious fortitude of a monk he came to know who never touched bread to his lips at any time of year but rather sustained himself entirely upon thin soups consisting of boiled kale, nettles, mallows, and watercress, all made without benefit of salt or oil "or anything else." But when our priest sampled this spare broth for himself his gourmand's palate overcame his appreciation of its pious purpose, for he pronounced it "the most dismal food in the world." Re-encountering this same monk at a later date, he embraced the man only to discover that he was wearing "an iron girdle four fingers broad" which was "joined on both edges on the side towards the skin with thick points of the size of those of a saw for sawing wood, badly sharpened (and all this not in Lent)." He dragged the man to his tent that he might show this feat of mortification to his nephew, but something in Álvares' demeanor must have communicated other sentiments than spiritual envy, for "this monk was offended by this, and he never visited me again, and on my account he went away from that town." Of course we have already heard enough heartfelt complaints from our priest about his being wet, cold, hot, and hungry to understand that he himself felt no calling to further mortify his own sinful flesh.

Nevertheless, his catalog of deprivations continues, including more and more (to Western eyes) outlandish practices. Hearing word of monks who remained standing during the whole of Lent, and learning that "there was one doing that penance at a distance of two leagues from where we were, in a cave," he rode out to see the fellow. This penitent was discovered to be living inside a narrow upright coffin scarcely bigger than himself and "much plastered with clay and dung." Not that this narrow "tabernacle" (as Álvares calls it) was completely free of amenities: "where the buttocks reach there is a ledge three fingers wide, and where the elbows reach, for each of them there is another such ledge;

and on the front was a shelf on the wall with a book." For good measure the occupant of this premature grave was sporting a hair-shirt and his own version of an inwardly-spiked cummerbund. And it was not only the monks who indulged in inventive penances, for years later while residing at Axum he came across a "multitude of people" who were spending the night submerged to the neck in a tank of water even though the Lenten season thereabouts featured "hard frosts and cold" once the sun went down. Some of the laity even chose to honor God during the run-up to Easter by suppressing their own habitual gregariousness, a feat which was certainly felt as a hard penance by the remarkably affectionate Ethiopians. As Álvares explains, "it is the custom for them to greet one another ... when they meet by ... kissing each other on the shoulders; one kiss[ing] the right shoulder and the other the left; [but] during Holy Week they do not give this salutation of peace to those they meet, nor do they speak, but pass one another as if they were dumb, and without raising the eyes." He ends his list of mortifications by recounting how on the day before Easter it was the custom for worshipers to drop to the floor of the church for a frenzied, two-hour lamentation during which they "buffet one another, and knock their heads against the walls, ... and punch themselves," all the while weeping "so bitterly that a heart of stone would be moved to tears of devotion." This orgy of grief completed, the parishioners exited the church "stripped from the waist upwards" through doors manned by priests wielding whips, before whom they voluntarily stooped while "those with the scourges keep striking them as long as they are still. Some pass quickly, and receive few strokes; others wait and receive many. Old men and old women will remain half a hour, until the blood runs."[2]

Clearly the Abyssinians' various imitations of Christ did not end with good works, but extended as far as possible toward a re-creation of their Savior's final agony. In writing at length about such things, one can feel Álvares beginning to build a compensatory case for Ethiopian Christianity, no matter how ambivalent he felt about particular acts of fleshly contrition. When he had so sharply denounced the *Timkat* immersions, he had essentially been covering the tracks of his own growing sympathy toward probable heretics, but here he appears to be concerned not with how he himself will appear beneath the eyes of his superiors, but how the Abyssinians might fare under the same cold glare. He seems here to be groping toward an argument that presents his hosts as people who, through the startling extremity of their devotion, practice a kind of orthodoxy of the spirit rather than of the letter. No doubt it was an argument he could not yet bring to conclusion in his own mind, since hair-shirts and whips were not the kind of evidence that could wholly convince even himself. It was a brief he would probably only become certain of once he had encountered the most positive expressions of the Ethiopian religious spirit — that is, once he had beheld and wandered among the rock-hewn wonders of Lalibela.

As best one can determine, Álvares again took interesting advantage of his relative freedom to briefly join a caravan of pilgrims headed for the Holy Land in January of 1522. His purpose was never to effect an escape from the country alongside this party (though there must have been some temptation), but rather just to ride in their midst for two days in order "to see their customs." Most of his remarks betray bemusement at how slowly this party of 300-odd monks, priests, and nuns managed to proceed, what with their frequent stopping for religious devotions, a hindrance to progress exacerbated by their desire to outdo one another in visible acts of piety. However, his report of their usual route toward Jerusalem — where, as previously mentioned, there had been a small but uninterrupted Ethiopian presence for centuries — is clear and businesslike. They left the province of the *Bahr-nagas* heading north along the Red Sea coast until they reached the port town of Suakin, where "Egypt begins." From there, the direction changed to westward for a fourteen-day journey over the desert sands to Rifa on the Nile, a leg which entailed at least "two days where there are no settlements or water." From Rifa it was an eight-days' float down the great river to Cairo, and from there at least another week's travel overland to Jerusalem. He notes that there was a much easier route that involved simply sailing to the Red Sea's northern extremity at Tor ("which is near Mount Sinay" [sic]), a seaport located only eight days distant from the Holy City, but he also mentions that this expedient was rarely used because the Ethiopians were such hopeless sailors. This last fact was so undeniable that even Queen Eleni had not attempted to whitewash it in her letter offering alliance to Albuquerque.

Either of these routes necessitated the Christian travelers putting themselves into the hands of Muslim guides for long stretches of the journey, a process which had seldom led to trouble both because of the fees that were charged and because of the *Negus'* previously-mentioned ability to punish his Islamic minority in response to any Egyptian depredations. Now, however, things were different, for two related reasons. First of all, the Portuguese presence in the Red Sea, beginning with Albuquerque's initial penetration of the Gate of Tears in 1513 and continuing through the disembarkation of the embassy at Massawa less than two years previous, had alarmed Saracen observers from Cairo to Aden. Ethiopia had in recent decades been only fitfully attacked by Muslim forces, mostly at the spontaneous inclination of local tribal leaders such as the unfortunate Mafouz, because its obvious isolation from the main body of Christendom had rendered it no threat to vital Islamic interests. If, however, the Prester's nation was about to make a firm alliance with the unbelieving European country that had already captured India and nearly monopolized the spice trade, that prospect suddenly painted a large target over the Roof of Africa.[3] Secondly, just four years after Albuquerque had sailed into the southern end of the Red Sea the Ottoman Turks had descended upon its northern end, and in the time since they had gained control of most Muslim territories surrounding that nearly inland sea. Whereas the region's previous masters, the Egyptian Mamlucks, had been complacent and languorous, the Ottomans were zealous and in a hurry; the doctrine of live-and-let-live was over. Hence, somewhere past Suakin the pilgrims whom Álvares had waved good-by to the previous month were attacked and almost all of them were either slaughtered or sold into slavery. When a handful of survivors straggled back into the territory of the *Bahr-nagas,* Álvares talked to three of them and found that they were well aware of the politico-religious shifts responsible for their misfortune. These victims "related to me all their troubles, and told me that that had happened to them because they were friends of the Portuguese; and in truth it is so, because they receive bad treatment from their neighbors for our sake."[4]

But it was even worse than either Father Álvares or the pilgrims understood, for the Ottoman takeover meant that anyone who decided that the time was ripe for a full-scale *jihad* against Ethiopia, any zealot willing to dedicate himself and his fortune to such a purpose, any leader geographically well-positioned to strike at the Christian highlands, would be likely to receive money, arms, and supplementary troops from his Turkish overlords. After Lebna Dengel's defeat of Maufouz the lands between the Christian highlands and the Somali coast had devolved into chaos, but in the lowland city of Harrar an extraordinary man who would eventually become all these things was even now making plans to convert Ethiopia to Muhammad by force of arms. He was patient, and he had many homegrown obstacles to overcome on his ascent to power, but the time would soon come when his forces would break over the Prester's mountains like a terrifying and unstoppable tsunami, dwarfing the massacre of Christians that Álvares now mourned. Already in the dream of a pious Muslim this man's face had appeared, toward which the Prophet gestured and declared that he and no other had been chosen by God to bring Abyssinia, so long a nest of infidels, into submission to the true religion.[5] The members of the embassy, whiling away their soft confinement in and about Debarwa, thought themselves a secure day's ride from the escarpment that plunged downward to the surrounding Moorish deserts, but historically speaking the entire wide prison in which they loitered was perched upon the crumbling edge of a precipice.

As it happened, the Portuguese were also ignorant of an even more immediate fact: that they were now prisoners in Ethiopia. Of course they understood that as a result of their internal squabbles they were not free to roam about the countryside at will (the good Father excepted), and that they continued to languish in the bad opinion of the *Negus.* But, that having been admitted, they found themselves detained at a town quite close to Massawa and thus they fully believed that as soon as a Portuguese fleet showed up at that port they would be released to join it and resume their journey homeward. And while it was true that in the spring of 1522, just as in the previous year, no rescuing armada had appeared off the Prester's coast, and that this had been a daunting blow to their already-deferred hopes, it was still their understanding that the first appearance of a Portuguese sail upon the Red Sea would restore their every freedom. But in this they were sadly mistaken — Lebna Dengel, morbidly worried about how the divided embassy would represent him to European ears, had no intention of ever letting them leave; in his eyes, they were already destined to become his next generation of Da Covilhãs. This decision of the *Negus* and his advisors must have emerged from a mood of profound paranoia, given that in detaining the embassy indefinitely they were in effect chucking away the alliance that they themselves had envisioned as leading them out of their centuries-long isolation, but such was their perverse resolution at the time.

That between 1521 and 1523 Lebna Dengel was indeed intent upon keeping the embassy his prisoners becomes clear once we realize that he had timely knowledge of something his detainees did not: the passage of any Portuguese fleet through the Gate of Tears. How could such knowledge have reached his mountain fastness with alacrity? The answer involved the fact that at the Prester's capital it was Muslim merchants who handled all the international trade. Given the voracious demand of that mobile metropolis for manufactured goods only to be found outside the Highlands, the caravans of those entrepreneurs arrived daily at the tent city from all parts of the Muslim plains, including the Somali coast, so that along with silks and the occasional musket, information was for sale. Then too, Lebna Dengel received annual tribute from restive Islamic vassal states that stretched almost all the way to Zeila, just outside the Gates. He had salaried spies aplenty in those lands and good reason to listen to their reports as soon as they arrived. Once the Prester's advance knowledge of all approaching Christian armadas is accepted, we can discern a telling pattern by connecting some chronological dots. We see that for eighteen months following their arrest the embassy was confined at Debarwa, which they believed had been chosen for them because it was a handy jumping-off point for their return to India and Europe. Now recall that because of the pattern of monsoon winds, Portuguese ships could only reach the Prester's coast during early spring. In the spring of 1522 the *Negus* was perfectly content to let them remain at Debarwa because he knew that, as in the previous year, no Christian fleet had entered the Red Sea. However, at the beginning of 1523, when an armada was in fact on its way to pick them up, the *Negus* ordered that the Portuguese return hundreds of miles south to his Court, insuring that they would miss their rescuers' short season of safe anchorage at Massawa. Of this suspicious summons Álvares only flatly reports that "we happened to keep one Lent [thus, one Spring] at the Court of the Prester John," as if reluctant to impute a sinister motive to the monarch who so favored him, especially since the action deprived his companions of their dearest wish.[6] It is clear, however, that in January of

1523 Lebna Dengel had suddenly demanded to see his Portuguese visitors again precisely because he no longer thought of them as visitors and intended them to become residents of Ethiopia for life.

What the individual members of the embassy made of their forced removal from the confines of the coast at this crucial season Álvares does not relate, but any resistance would have been less than futile since the Portuguese were dependent upon the *Bahr-nagas* and his lieutenants for food, and their captors would never have endangered their own lives to cater to Frankish desires in the teeth of their *Negus'* direct order. As for the journey inland itself, our priest has nothing to say, only reporting that the Court was now situated even farther south than it had been on their initial visit, "in the furthest part of a country of pagans called Gorages, a people (as they say) who are very bad." We also do not know what pretense the Prester gave to the Portuguese for pulling them away from proximity with the Red Sea in such an untimely fashion, or whether he bothered to promulgate any at all, or whether Dom Rodrigo even asked for an explanation. Clearly, though, the King did not reveal to them his real reason for the summons. However, perhaps as a result of a guilty conscience over his thwarting of the embassy's hopes and his rather cowardly refusal to inform them about what he intended, he seems to have ordered his prisoners to be well-fed during the fasting season, for Álvares reports that "all this Lent we were very well provided with food and drink, and much fish and plenty of grapes and peaches which there are in this country." One wonders just when they began to comprehend the bad faith that was larding their tables.

At the end of Lent there transpired an odd incident that might or might not have been the gambit of some courtier looking to assuage the *Negus'* conscience about incarcerating the embassy. Lebna Dengel had made it known that as part of the Easter-Day observations he wanted to witness the Portuguese say mass in their own manner. Álvares was amenable to this, but pointed out that the church tent they had been given had become tattered by rain and travel during the last two years, whereupon the Prester said that he would have a new one pitched for them close by his own apartments. Come the holy day itself, the Ethiopian side of the ceremonies constituted a grand spectacle, with six thousand candles (by our priest's count) illuminating the enclosed royal compound, which was crowded with innumerable spectators and churchmen from far and near. The King emerged from his residence preceded by capering horsemen, whose mounts "were so caparisoned and adorned and covered with brocade that in the [candle]light they looked as if they were sewn up in gold." The *Negus* himself was seated upon "a dark bay mule like a raven, as big as a large horse," resplendent "in a mantle of brocade which reached almost to the ground, and the mule too was all covered over." Proceeding from his own pavilion to the church tent of the Holy Cross, he insisted that the Portuguese walk close behind him in a position of prominence, and later when it came time for a great procession around the royal enclosure "they put us at the head of it with the most honoured dignitaries." But, when the overflow Abyssinian mass was concluded and the Portuguese went to prepare for their own ceremony as instructed, they found that the ecclesiastical tent which had been reared for their own use was entirely black. The immediacy and unanimity of their response is interesting, for Álvares says that "we, seeing the black tent, said: 'They have pitched this tent for us in mockery.' Then the Ambassador said: 'Father, you will do well not to say mass, because this is done to put us to the test.' [And] I answered him: 'Neither do I wish to say it.'" They had apparently now been in Ethiopia long enough to have strong opinions about which configurations of hemp and canvas were fit to act as churches and which ones were not.

The Europeans returned to their lodgings, which soon brought an angry query from the King as to

> why we had omitted to say mass on so great a feast. I answered that I did not want to say mass because of the great insult which had been offered — not to us, but to God and His holy Resurrection, as they had pitched a black tent for us to say mass in, such as they [i.e., the Ethiopians themselves] do not pitch, except for horses and fugitives from justice. They returned with another message, asking what tent they were to pitch. I answered that it must be a white one to represent the splendour of the Resurrection and the purity and innocence of Our Lady, and that a red one might well do, as it would represent the blood which Christ shed for us and that the Apostles and martyrs had shed for Him.

The *Negus* replied that he would find a replacement, but that for now even if they could not say mass in the black tent they should nevertheless return to it and eat their dinner there. Characteristically, this appeal to the appetite found no objection from our priest, and having arrived back at what was now their pitch-colored dining hall, the Portuguese found the Lenten bounty continuing to flow, for "they sent us a very good meal of many good dishes of different kinds of meat, and good wines, among which were grape wines of good flavor, and very red." Over this repast, Pêro da Covilhã, who was once again at Court, declared that Álvares' refusal to say mass had caused him "such great pleasure as he had never [yet] felt in this country, or had expected to feel," since the offending pavilion had obviously only been erected "to test the respect we had for the things of God and the church, and that now they would respect us as good Christians." But was this true? Had someone at the Court in fact attempted to trap the embassy into performing a public act of blasphemy that would have discredited them in Abyssinian eyes and thus tacitly justified the *Negus*' proceedings toward them? We cannot know, and no more is said of this puzzling issue. Thus, like the previous banquet where the Portuguese suddenly felt they were being spied upon, the brief appearance of the black tent can at best suggest what courtly intrigues might have been surreptitiously playing out behind the thousand opaque curtains of the Prester's roving capital.

NINE. The Magic Mountain

It had been a memorable Easter Sunday, then, but even more memorable to the Portuguese would be the Sunday following — April 15th 1523, by Álvares' reckoning — for this day saw the arrival at Court of messengers hastening from the seacoast bearing letters. These missives had been written by Dom Luis de Meneses, brother of the man who had succeeded Sequeira as Governor of India, and who was even then anchored with a small fleet of ships in the harbor of Massawa intending to pick up the embassy his predecessor had landed three years ago that month. His communication addressed to the *Negus* "begg[ed] him to send us at once" while the one directed to Dom Rodrigo appealed for them to make all possible haste northward, since "because of the monsoon ... and because he was required in India" he could only linger at Massawa until — *April 15th!* The rapid alternations of frustration, despair and resurgent wan hope among the embassy at hearing this news can readily be imagined. And allied to these wracking emotions was also the dawning realization of how Lebna Dengel had plotted their continued stranding, for it now became evident to them that "the Prester knew the news of India more quickly than we did, by the Moorish merchants who came from there daily." And if this was not enough, the letters also carried the sad news that King Manoel I, the messianic *primum mobile* of their improbable enterprise, had died back in December of 1521 and been succeeded by his son Prince João, now King João III. As anxious as they were to get on the road no matter how remote the odds of still catching De Meneses at Massawa, they decided that they were still obligated go through the official motions of national mourning, and to appraise their royal jailer of the change in their country's leadership.

Just as their balking at the black tent betrayed two years of acculturation to Ethiopian ways of thought, so too did their manner of grieving for the departed Manoel. Since it was the Abyssinians' custom upon the death of kings "to shave the head with a razor, and not the beard, and to dress in black, we began to shave each other's heads, and to dress in mourning." This behavior was noticed before they could make an official announcement, and soon monks arrived at the Franks' tents asking what was going on. Since "the Ambassador said that someone should answer the monks, as he could not for weeping," our priest took on that duty, doing so again "according to the usage of the country":

> Tell His Highness that the stars and the moon have fallen, and the sun has grown dark and lost its brightness, and we have no one to shelter or protect us; we have neither father nor mother to care for us, except God, who is the Father of all: the King Dom Manuel our lord has departed from the life of this world and we are left orphans and unprotected.

Whether Lebna Dengel was naturally touched by the death of a fellow monarch or whether he was merely continuing his recent indulgence of the Portuguese in all things save their desire to leave, he immediately declared a three-day period of mourning in which all the capital's shops were to be strictly closed.

He also sent to the embassy's tents to ask who would succeed Manoel, and when told the answer he replied, "Do not be afraid, for you are in a Christian country[;] the father was good, the son will be good, and I will write to him."

This last promise quite rightly filled the Portuguese with dread. A smooth-pated Dom Rodrigo hurriedly "explained to him how they were waiting for us at sea," and that thus the embassy "begged his leave to go away, as now it did not seem a good thing for us to be in his country." Yes, yes, undoubtedly, replied the *Negus*, just as soon as De Meneses' letters to him and his own reply to that personage and his brother the Governor—and to the new King João as well—had all been properly translated. The prospect of another scriptorium being erected athwart their road to the sea propelled the embassy's leaders to take pre-emptive action: "As we already knew what his dispatch was like," before that very Sunday was over they had "sent off Aries Diaz, a Portuguese of our company, and with him an Abyssinian, to go with our letters to the said Dom Luis De Meneses." It was unlikely that Lebna Dengel could have been ignorant of this ploy, but he was apparently already confident that his scheme had worked its desired end. Then Father Álvares and Da Covilhã, turning to with a passion and working through the night, "the next day ... took the letters to the Prester in his language," though that very morning "he left for another place with his Court, and we with him." As delay predictably followed delay, the Europeans repeatedly asked to be released, but all the *Negus* would allow was that the factor Joam Goncalvez might go on ahead atop a good mule with rough drafts of His Majesty's precious replies. It was all a charade, of course—the Portuguese now knew they were being purposely delayed and Lebna Dengel probably knew they knew it, but no one was going to call the King on his real motives. Sighs Álvares, "we stayed, and however much we importuned the Prester and made request to him, he kept us waiting yet a month and a half." Finally, when reasonable hope had all but evaporated, he sent them on their way loaded down with presents of clothes, gold chains, silver crosses, and more mules than they needed. Like soldiers setting out to relieve an already-sacked city, they departed in dull spirits and "did not travel long before we got a message from our people whom we had sent to the sea, that Dom Luis had been gone a long time." Taking council at this expected but still disheartening news, they nevertheless decided to push on, if only to see what had been left for them on the beach; besides, none of them had any desire to return toward the King who had ruined their hopes of seeing home.

Once at Massawa they found bales of pepper and fabric left by De Meneses in order that they might pay their way for another year, as well as letters directing them for God's sake not to venture far from the sea so as not to miss the fleet next spring. There then ensued "a council among us [considering] what we should do with that pepper," and while some were in favor of keeping it all and settling down somewhere near the coast as per instructions, the majority decided that they should give half of it to the *Negus*, no doubt seeing it as a kind of bribe that might persuade that monarch to allow them to leave if the opportunity to do so ever again materialized. Furthermore, it was agreed that the factor Goncalves and Álvares would make the journey back to Court alone, since it was the former's job to transport goods and because everyone knew that the latter had the best chance of giving over the spice to good effect. But then Dom Rodrigo decided to overrule their conclusions:

> That morning the Ambassador came to me saying, "Father, I wish to give you another companion to go with you to the Court." When I said, "Let it be whoever you command," he replied to me: "Would you like my company? I intend to go with you, and we will take all the pepper." And though I opposed him, saying that nothing would be left for the others to spend, he still said that he was going to go and take all the pepper. He did this expecting great rewards and all for himself, as it is the most highly valued thing that can be carried in these countries. So the Ambassador insisted on taking all the pepper to the Prester; and we set out at once.[7]

Several conclusions can be drawn from this interesting exchange. First of all, the mere occurrence of councils among the Portuguese seems to indicate that Dom Rodrigo's power to command was beginning to give way to a rough democracy, though as we see he still possessed the authority to overrule such conclaves when he wished to. But furthermore, both the fact that a peaceful council could take place among the travelers and that the Ambassador could nullify its decision without sparking a revolt suggest that D'Abreu was not present with the party that journeyed to Massawa in that late summer of 1523. Indeed, those same facts also suggest an explanation for De Lima's desire to take all the pepper back to Court and Álvares' criticism of that plan as selfish. In sum, it is likely that D'Abreu and possibly several of his cronies had remained behind at the Prester's capital, where — and because — they were there enjoying the favors of Lebna Dengel in a way that the Ambassador never had, a situation Dom Rodrigo hoped to rectify by personally presenting the sovereign with a big load of pepper. We know from odd phrases here and there that the *Negus* was already much taken with D'Abreu's horsemanship and demonstrations of swordplay, and that he had nicknamed the deputy "my own Abyssinian." We also know that come the following year D'Abreu would go so far as to follow the *Negus* into battle against his Muslim foes. It thus appears that, in Dom Rodrigo's mind, the prospect of reversing this royal preference for his despised lieutenant outweighed his concern for the welfare of those men whose allegiance he still held.

During the return journey southward, which began on September 1st and concluded sometime in late November, two remarkable incidents occurred. The first happened near the beginning, when Álvares and the Ambassador were apparently still getting the bulk of the embassy re-settled around the town of

Debarwa.[8] One morning the rising sun "became yellow, and the shadow on the earth too, and the people were all dismayed." This discoloration of the sky was the warning sign of an approaching locust swarm, for as Álvares explains "these locusts are like large grasshoppers, and have yellow wings; when they are on the way it is known a day before, not because the people see them, but because they see the sun yellow, and the earth yellow, [for] that is the shadow which they cast over it." In other parts of the country our priest had already come across the aftermath of such infestations, areas in which crops had been eaten to the root, amid which stood "trees without any leaves, and the tender twigs all eaten [too]." Sometimes the devastation was eerie in its completeness, such as the zone of destruction three leagues wide in which there remained no "bark on a tree, and [in which] the country did not look burned, but very snowy with the whiteness of the [uncovered] wood" and "the ground [which] was left quite clean." Now, with just such a ravenous juggernaut bearing down upon them "the priests of the town came to ask [Álvares] to give them some remedy for it." At first he could imagine no antidote but prayer, but after some private reflection he approached Dom Rodrigo with the idea that they might all mount a religious procession against the locusts that would culminate in a kind of exorcism or statement of anathema. No doubt unnerved by the increasingly unnatural hue of the heavens, the Ambassador readily agreed to this rather unorthodox idea, and soon Álvares had mustered "all the Portuguese and the greater part of the townspeople" into a snaking line, he carrying his alter stone, the village priests hefting their sacred *tabots*. As the first of the swarm began to land upon their clothing and hair, Álvares urged the terrified marchers forward, exhorting them "not to go in silence, but to cry out like us saying in their own language … Lord Jesus Christ have mercy upon us." One can do no better than to follow our priest's own description of what happened next:

> With this cry and litany we went through a plain of wheat fields for the space of a third of a league to a small eminence, and there made a denunciation which I had brought already written out that night with a requisition and denunciation of excommunication besides, that within three hours they should begin to set out on their way, and go to the sea, or to the country of the Moors, or to mountains of no profit to the Christians: and should they not do so, it called upon and invoked the birds of the air and the animals of the earth, and the stones and tempests to disperse and break and devour their bodies. For this, I commanded a quantity of the locusts to be caught, and thus made this denunciation to those present, in their names, and those of the absent ones, and ordered them to be let go in peace.... When we were returning to the town, because [the insects'] road was to the sea from whence they came, there were so many coming after us, that it seemed as though they wanted to break our ribs and heads by pelting us with stones, such were the thumps they inflicted on us.

Our muscular St. Francis having delivered his petition, relief from On High was not long in arriving, for "meanwhile a great storm arose from the sea, which met them, confronting them with violent rain and hail, which lasted quite three hours." Back at Debarwa, those who had remained behind and taken to their housetops for a better view of the epic battle began "giving thanks to God for the manner in which the locusts went flying before us." During the ensuing downpour "the river and streams welled very much," and when it was over the carcasses of the dead locusts "measured two *covados* deep" upon their banks, such that "the next ... morning there was not a single one alive in the whole country." The local reaction to this deliverance was predictable:

> The towns all round whence the locusts had arrived, hearing of this, came to see what had happened; some said: "These Portuguese are holy, and by the power of God they have driven away and killed the *Ambatas* [i.e., locusts]." Others, and chiefly the priests and monks of the neighborhood (not those of this town) said: "Rather they are sorcerers, and by sorcery have cast out the *Ambatas*; and so they have no fear of the lions and other animals, on account of the sorceries they work."

Father Álvares' explanation was simpler, and altogether in character: "It pleased Our Lord to hear [us] sinners."[9] But who knows — had he remained in Ethiopia indefinitely, perhaps our priest would have eventually acquired the title of saint, leaving Lebna Dengel to argue with the Catholic Church over whether he fell to the European or Abyssinian side of the (as the King saw it) competitive ledger of the blessed.

It was apparently farther along on this same southward journey that Álvares had his closest physical encounter with the mountaintop prison of *Amba* Geshen and its royal inmates.[10] He, Dom Rodrigo, and a handful of companions were passing along the foot of the massive, broken plateau — atop one of whose isolated, flat-topped pinnacles the prisoners abided — when their guide made the mistake of trying to stop for the night at an unfriendly village full of talented stone-throwers. Amidst the ensuing melee this panicked official spurred his mule forward so vigorously that the Portuguese members of the party were soon left behind, whereupon they proceeded to get separated from each other as darkness fell. Riding blindly into another village where again "many stones rained upon us, and the darkness was like having no eyes," Álvares abandoned his mule and was about to make a run for it into the fields when "God was pleased that an honorable man, a guardian of the mountain, should come upon me and ask who I was." Hurriedly explaining that he was a *gassa Negus*— that is, one who walked under the protection of the King's shield — he quickly found rough shelter in the person of this very tall Samaritan: "he took my head under his arm, for I did not reach any higher, and so he conducted me like the bellows of a bagpipe player, saying *Atefra, atefra,* which means 'Do not be afraid, do not be afraid.'" Safely stashed in this guard's potting shed, our priest hunkered down for the night while his rescuer sallied out to bring in others of the Portuguese before his neighbors succeeded in hunting them down. The next morning, when order had been sufficiently restored and the traveling party was getting reassembled, this unnamed benefactor took Álvares to one of the locked gates — situated between encroaching rock walls — that blocked access to the mountain and explained some of the duties of his office:

> This host said to me: "Look here; if any of you were to pass inside this door, there would be nothing for it but to cut off his feet and his hands, and put out his eyes, and leave him lying there; and you must not put the blame on those who would do this, neither would you be at fault, but ... if we did not do this, we should pay with our lives, because we are the guardians of this door."

Given that the vertiginous trail beyond that bolted threshold culminated, after a score of miles and a 5000-foot ascent, at the base of the *amba's* two-hundred foot-high capstone, up whose sheer sides there was only one (also heavily guarded) footpath, the royal nephews and cousins sequestered there might have seemed hermetically cut off from all doings of the outside world. Indeed, as Álvares was informed concerning this mountain's final granite rampart, "it is a rock sheer like a wall, straight from the top to the bottom; if a man goes to the foot of it and looks upwards, it seems that the sky rests upon it."

A VIEW OF THE TOWERING AMBA GESHEN. This prison-house, in the time of Álvares' journey, held all members of the Ethiopian royal family who might have challenged the legitimacy of the reigning *Negus*. This view is from a point already thousands of feet above the valley of the Bashilo River.

NINE. *The Magic Mountain* 193

However, because the flat tops of these summits were chosen precisely because they encompassed enough acreage to support what amounted to a miniature society—the social status of whose members entitled them to a steady supply of goods and even luxuries from below—they also sustained miniature versions of all manner of things found in human society at large, such as espionage, bribery, and an unquenchable desire for freedom. It may well have been that the incarcerated royals knew of the Portuguese presence in the country soon after the 1520 landing and that the tantalizing passage of Álvares' party in 1523 inspired someone inside to risk everything in smuggling out a rescue plea to the Europeans.

This desperate scheme came to our priest's attention only after he had arrived back at Court, when a monk accused of having carried a letter off the mountain was hauled before the King's justice along with fully two hundred guards whom the *Negus* collectively held liable for letting him slip by. Our priest relates that "it was a common rumor and report through all the Court that this monk had brought letters to the Portuguese from the princes of the mountain in order that we might take them out of it," so he and the Ambassador could hardly have remained detached viewers of what now transpired. "The

THE NEAR VERTICAL CAPSTONE OF AMBA GESHEN PREVENTED ESCAPES BY ANY OF ITS ROYAL INMATES. However, upon the death of a reigning *Negus* or the outbreak of civil war, a summons might arrive for one of the prisoners, calling him to rejoin the wider world below—and immediately assume the mantle of King.

wretched monk said that it was sixteen years since he had come out of the mountain, and that they had then given him that letter, and that he had never returned there, nor had dared to give the letter except now, that sin had caught him." Álvares believed this story, but even if it were true it might not have changed the *Negus'* mind about the substance of the case, since the monk's dating still suggests that the letter might have been written to Da Covilhã when he first arrived, and that the monk only got up the gumption to deliver it once a larger group of Franks had entered the country. At any rate, the accused and his dozing jailors underwent a cruel and extended ordeal that was a combination of interrogation and punishment, for "they flogged this monk every two days, and they also flogged these men, dividing them into two parties. On the day they flogged the monk, they flogged half of the guards," and on the monk's day off they whipped the remainder. As the blows fell "they put questions to the monk, asking who gave him that letter, for whom, and if he had brought more letters, and what monastery he belonged to, and where he had become a monk, and where he had been ordained for mass." From the sound of things, it appears Lebna Dengel was ready to hunt down the man's childhood catechist for the sake of completeness. Meanwhile, "to the guards they did not put any other question, except how had they let this monk get out." Only pausing on the dual Sabbaths of Saturday and Sunday, this rotating schedule of abuse dragged on for two excruciating weeks.

While narrating this incident, Álvares also describes the subtleties of corporal punishment as it was doled out at Court. "The method of flogging is this: they throw the man on his belly, and fasten his hands to two stakes, and a rope to both feet, with two men both pulling at the rope; there are also two men like executioners to strike one at one side and the other at the other." However, when bringing their scourges into play these thrashers "do not always strike the flogged man," and in fact "many blows fall on the ground." This was because, when it came to whipping, there were almost always two sentences handed down — an official one mandating a quantity of stripes certain to prove fatal, and a second, secret one delivered *sotto voce* from the Prester's own lips directing that only every second, or every third, or even every fourth blow actually land on the accused's back. It was a savvy political tool, allowing the *Negus* to appear draconian and merciful simultaneously, though our priest was present on occasions when Lebna Dengel ordered no deflections whatsoever, ordeals which resulted in an agonizing death for the accused, for "when orders came from the King to strike, the blow reache[d] the bones." Curiously, he does not tell us whether the monk lived or died.

But whatever this particular man's fate, as far as Lebna Dengel and his courtiers were concerned, any breech of the *cordon sanitaire* surrounding *Amba Geshen* was a deadly serous matter. At any given time a portion of the "great Captains" and "great guards" who patrolled the mountain were recalled to

Court, perhaps to have their soundness tested, and while there, says Álvares, they "lodge apart by themselves, and no one approaches them, nor do they go near others, so that no one may have an opportunity of learning the secrets of the mountain. And when they approach the door of the Prester, and he has to receive a message or speak to them, they make all the people go away, and all other affairs cease while they are speaking of this." The mountain's prisoners themselves were familiarly referred to as "Israelites," an evocatively subversive nickname for the state prisoners of a nation that explicitly proclaimed itself a Second Zion. The following year Álvares had the unsettling experience of glimpsing one of these Israelites — it was in fact Lebna Dengel's brother — who had been captured after escaping from Geshen. Accompanied by stout bailiffs escorting him to Court for judgment, "he and his mule were covered with black cloths, so that nothing of him was seen, and the mule showed only its eyes and ears.... They did not allow any person to approach or speak to this brother of the Prester John, except two men, who went close to the mule. Everybody said that he would die, or that they would put out his eyes. But I do not know what became of him."

When summing up this peculiar institution of the Ethiopian monarchy, Álvares was willing to look beyond its immediate cruelties and appreciate the larger mercy of order and stability that it seemed to bestow upon the land:

> Truly, whoever considers this way of keeping such a great kingdom at peace, without bloodshed, for so many centuries, and that the sons and brothers have not revolted against each other, and that nevertheless that lineage has never failed, will recognize that it is indeed a divine and not a human thing, a felicity which it has never been possible to have in any kingdom of Christendom.[11]

The English poet John Milton, a likely reader of Álvares' account, also seems to have agreed that Geshen's general benefits outweighed its particular evils, for in *Paradise Lost* he affirms that the *amba* was at least a reasonable wrong guess as to where the Biblical Eden might have lain:

> Nor where *Abassin* Kings their issue Guard
> Mount *Amara*, though this by some supposed
> True Paradise under the *Ethiop* Line
> By *Nilus* head, enclosed with shining Rock,
> A whole day's journey high... [Book IV, ll. 280–84]

But of course no appreciation of political expediency could prevent our priest from sympathizing with the harsh plight of the Isrealites themselves or of the "wretched monk" who might or might not have been guilty of trying to help them. Indeed he must have felt a doubled pity for the accused anchorite, suffering so sharply for undertaking a fool's errand, for what could be more futile than begging aid for a prison break from a group of strangers who were no better than prisoners themselves?

The fortunes of the embassy, however, were about to undergo a startling change for the better, and oddly enough, this transformation was to commence with Lebna Dengel becoming more disgusted with the Portuguese than he had ever been before. Álvares informs us that once he and Dom Rodrigo had arrived at Court, they officially presented their pepper along with translated copies of De Meneses' greetings to His Highness, but that he returned "no answer whatsoever." Merely one more piece of evidence that the King did not envision them ever leaving his country, one would think. But soon after this, Lebna Dengel *did* return something to the pair — "a map of the world, which we had brought to him four years before," asking that the names of the countries printed on it be translated into Amharic. Just what whim of the *Negus'* caused him to suddenly take an interest in one of the embassy's original presents to him — all of which he claimed to heartily disdain — we will never know, but to consider the long-term consequences that sprang from this random impulse is to tremble before the terrifying contingency of all historical events. In the moment, though, Álvares and Zaga Za Ab "at once set to work" upon complying with the Prester's request, a process which occasionally involved some tight calligraphy, since on this particular map "our Portugal [was] mixed with Castile in a small space, and Seville [was] very near Lisbon." Still, the process was completed in good time and "when the whole of the map of the world was finished and nothing was left they took it away." The *Negus*, however, was incensed at the result, so much so that "the following day he sent to call the Ambassador and all of us that were with him, and immediately in the first conversation he sent to say that the King of Portugal and the King of Castile were lords of few lands, and that the King of Portugal would not be strong enough to defend the Red Sea from the power of the Turks." In other words, he felt he had been deceived by the big talk of the Portuguese into thinking that Portugal was a large and therefore a powerful country, when the map clearly showed that he had been suffering the outrageous behavior of unruly ambassadors from a two-bit backwater, alliance with whose tin-pot monarch would buy him exactly nothing.

Dom Rodrigo immediately attempted to correct the *Negus'* genuinely mistaken equation of geographical size with geopolitical power, but did so by means of a scattered argument that made his previous explanations of the shoddy gifts seem eloquent by comparison. Its exquisite lameness must be quoted at length:

> The Ambassador replied to this that his Highness was deceived or ill informed, and if any one had told him so, he had not told him the truth; and if he judged of it by looking at the map of the world, he would not acquire a right knowledge of the countries, because Portugal and Spain are in the map of the world as things that are well known, and not as things requiring to be learnt: and he should look in the map of the world how the cities and castles and monasteries

were, and also how Venice, Jerusalem, and Rome were, like things well-known and in small spaces, and let him look at his Ethiopia, how it was an unknown thing, very large and much spread out, full of mountains, and rivers, and lions and elephants and many other beasts, and also many mountain ranges, without the map showing the name of any city, town, or castle.

In his defense, Dom Rodrigo must have been the victim of one of those Renaissance cartographers who had optimistically represented Ethiopia as monopolizing most of Africa, but his bumbling attempt at explanation only hardened the Prester's mistrust. "To this there was no answer," and the two Portuguese were soon dismissed to their tent, there to anxiously consider what other penalty besides perpetual imprisonment the *Negus* was going to impose upon them as his angry silence stretched across four days, and then into five.

But when our priest and the Ambassador were again finally summoned to the royal pavilion they received a genuine surprise, for instead of threatening and abusing them, the Prester "sent to say that he wished to write to the Pope of Rome ... and he desired that [Álvares] should write the beginning of the letter, because they were not accustomed to write, and did not know how to write, and that [Álvares] should take these letters to the Pope." As pleasantly surprised as he may have been by the *Negus'* lack of anger, Dom Rodrigo did not react well to this suggestion, asserting that they "had not come to write, nor was there any one among us [competent] to write to the Pope." The Ambassador was seeing the Prester's new desire in the context of his earlier insistence on composing fresh letters to the recently ascended King João III — that is to say, as a make-work delaying tactic from a monarch too duplicitous to tell his prisoners outright that they were indeed prisoners. After all, it was now January of 1524, and if De Lima and Álvares were going to be meeting any Portuguese fleet that might land at Massawa that year, it was almost time for them to be leaving. But in taking things this way he was missing the utter revolution which had occurred in Lebna Dengel's thinking during his five days of brooding. True, he had been furious to learn of Portugal's actual size and still believed he had been flim-flammed, but once he had convinced himself of that nation's obvious marginality, it had ceased to be a concern to him what the self-warring embassy would say about him once they were back in Lisbon. In other words, when Portugal ceased to loom large in his imagination, slanders about himself before the Portuguese throne also lost their significance. Indeed, if the map was at all accurate, many of the other highly touted European nations he had heard so much about seemed equally smallish polities when compared to his own. So, if he wanted aid and alliance from Europe, it was now clear to him that he would have to seek it from *all* of Europe collectively, and there was only one truly pan-European figure that he had ever heard of: the Pope. Thus it was to that one supreme churchman, toward whom all the kings of Western Christendom piously bent their knee in submission, that he must direct his appeal. And luckily there was one member of the embassy who was both a priest in the Pope's church and whom the *Negus* trusted to fulfill his own purposes as he trusted no other Portuguese: Father Álvares. And since Father Álvares would never return to Europe without his companions, the embassy as a whole must return there too, and at the first possible opportunity. Dom Rodrigo didn't realize it yet, but he was once again a free man.

Our priest, though no more cognizant of the *Negus'* change of heart than his leader, dove into the new project with cheerful energy and a determination to circumvent the Court's usual constipation when it came to composing diplomatic correspondence. "There came a message that we should go and dine, and [that] afterwards the monk and I should come back, and that I should bring all my books to prepare the letters.... When we came [back] we found all those whom they hold to be most learned assembled together with many books; and they asked me for my books. I replied that books were not necessary, but only to know His Highness' meaning, and by that we should be ruled." This struck the Prester's brain trust as a reckless and unsound way to proceed, but Álvares pushed ahead anyway.

> I settled down to writing and shortly made a small beginning, which was then taken in my handwriting to His Highness, and was brought back at once, and in that hour we put it into their language and sent it back again. There was no delay with it, for the page came back at once, saying that the King was much pleased with the writing, and amazed it had not been taken out of books: and he ordered that it should at once be written in good writing [i.e., in an official hand].

It appears that Álvares was not the only person minding the calendar, since Lebna Dengel could certainly have dallied and delayed once again had he still wanted to. Even Dom Rodrigo adopted a new attitude once he discovered how quickly things were proceeding, offering the priest something that approached an apology: "Father, I regret very much what I said to-day to the Prester John that there was no one among us who knew how to write to the Pope, because he will take us for men with little knowledge; I entreat of you to put all your efforts into this, and do for him all you know." When, a mere three days later, the missive was complete, it boldly and plainly expressed the *Negus'* new view that all of Europe must come to his aid and that only the Pope could make that happen: "I am daily annoyed to see the enemies of the Christian religion united in fraternal charity and rejoicing in mutual peace, whereas the Christian Kings, my brothers, do not agree to give me succour as Christians should." The Prester was careful to say that he was asking for no soldiers from His Holiness, but rather entreating him only to rally the squabbling states of Christendom behind Ethiopia's cause. "I pray you to make a good peace between them, exhorting them to give me aid, because on all the confines of my realms I am surrounded by enemies of the faith, who nevertheless preserve some fidelity among themselves, aiding each other, allying kings with kings, lords with lords, in great loyalty and constancy against us."[13] Working together with a swiftness made possible by minds in sympathy with each other, Francisco Álvares and Lebna Dengel had by week's end completed a punchy and eloquent appeal to the ideals of Christian unity, asking Pope Clement to preach a new Crusade, a renewed battle against Islam that would at last include Christendom's long-lost bother-nation in its ranks. This accomplished there was little more to do, and indeed our priest could have left for the Red Sea that very minute with the Prester's blessing except that, as he complains, the Court artisans "spent fifteen days in making a small gold cross, which weighs a hundred *cruzados*, and which is also going to the Pope." During this delay an afterthought apparently occurred to the *Negus*, whereupon a second letter was quickly hammered out.

Nothing testifies to Lebna Dengel's change of heart toward the embassy's proposed departure than his immediate decision to send an ambassador of his own to Europe along with the returning Portuguese, something he had not thought to do even when he had previously intended them to leave back in 1521. Now, however, he hoped to insure that "his wishes might be met sooner, his representative being there," and asked Álvares and Dom Rodrigo if Zaga Za Ab would be a good candidate for the office, "inasmuch as he could speak our language and had already been to our countries." Whatever worries our priest still had concerning the monk's violent temper, he gladly embraced the idea, replying that Zaga Za Ab "was a man who got on well with us, and we with him, and [who] had no need of an interpreter." Still mindful of how angry the King had recently been at what he thought were the Franks' false representations of themselves, our priest further opined that "now His Highness was doing what he ought to do, because when [Zaga Za Ab] came back he would rather believe what his own countrymen saw and heard of foreigners, than what foreigners said of themselves." It was in fact a very reasonable choice, though as we shall see, not an ideal one in the long term — and Zaga Za Ab's second sojourn in Europe was to be a long one indeed.

This appointment did occasion some additional delay, in that Zaga had to be outfitted with credentials, money, presents, and other gear. Then too, the Chief Justice was also to be sent north, for De Meneses had complained in his letters that some of his shore party had been killed in a scuffle with Ethiopians, and thus there were capital floggings to be meted out. Still, the *Negus* made no objection whatsoever when Álvares and De Lima asked if they could start their own journey immediately, and so "after all we set off without them, saying that we would go on slowly: this was because we had often seen his dispatch." They needn't have worried, though, for the Prester was now a new man in this regard, and soon enough the two officials "caught us up on the road, each in his turn, and we traveled until we reached [Debarwa], which is near the sea."[14]

In the short term all this newfound expeditiousness appeared to be somewhat thrown away, since no Portuguese sails appeared off Ethiopia's coast during that spring of 1524. But in the long run, what it represented was nothing short of momentous. Just consider what would have happened if the *Negus* had not changed his mind about letting the Portuguese go. If De Lima's embassy had disappeared into Ethiopia without a trace, or if it had somehow become known in India and beyond that they were being held prisoner against their will, what would have been Portugal's subsequent attitude toward the realm of Prester John? What would have been her eastern *Estado's* response when, years hence, a desperate and dying Lebna Dengel sent out an urgent plea to his Portuguese allies for rescue as his nation tottered on the brink of collapse? It was only because the embassy eventually did re-emerge, bringing confirmation that Abyssinia, despite its lack of magical wonders, was indeed a Christian country on the other side of the Moorish enemy — and one which had fought that enemy valiantly for centuries — that Portuguese *fidalgos* responded to his call for help with men and arms sufficient to eventually turn the tide of war. And looking back toward the past, what had made the *Negus'* reversal of heart possible? His mistake about the map, to be sure. But it was only because he respected Father Álvares' abilities that he felt he could *do* something about his new (erroneous) perception of Europe; it was only because he liked and trusted the cleric that he determined to send him to see the Pope, sweeping the benighted embassy out of Ethiopia in his wake. Two years previously our priest had managed to transform a haughty foreign monarch whose face was perpetually hidden from him into someone resembling a friend. In doing so Francisco Álvares — though he did not know it, though he would never know it — had, by nothing more than the exercise of his temperate judgment, his generous empathy, and his natural intelligence, saved the country he had come to love from utter destruction.

TEN

The Last Crusade

Although the *Negus'* fortuitous misreading of the world map in early 1524 convinced him that the embassy must be allowed to return home as soon as possible, the non-appearance of a Portuguese fleet at Massawa that spring — and the next one as well — meant that Álvares still had another two years to spend in Abyssinia. This was to be a crucial time for our priest, during which he beheld stone-chiseled works of the spirit so wondrous that when placed beside them even the Ethiopians' apostasy dwindled into a mere distraction — and thus into something he felt he could ethically conceal from his superiors. We will take up the story of this period soon enough, but in order to fully understand the cascading effects of Father Álvares' relationship with Lebna Dengel — how its freeing of the embassy from imprisonment in turn made possible Portugal's eventual rescue of Ethiopia in the latter's darkest hour — it is first necessary to skip ahead a decade or two. Luckily for us, any account of Christian Abyssinia's near-death experience and the small band of Portuguese adventurers who battled to bring it back to life must rank as one of those rare instances in which the facts of history seem to have been dictated by a screenwriter. Furthermore, as if springing from some conscious intention to provide comic relief, this real-world instance of chivalry and idealism in action is punctuated throughout by the clownish antics of one of history's most audacious con men — a figure already known to our priest, and to us.

But no less remarkable than any hero or jester who eventually made his appearance upon the stage was the man who, from the perspective of Ethiopia's Christians, figured as the villain of the piece. Born in 1506, Ahmad ibn Ibrahim al-Ghazi was, by the time of the embassy's oft-delayed departure in 1526, already the undisputed master of Harrar, the most important Muslim city between the Ethiopian highlands and Zeila on the Indian Ocean coast. He had emerged from the chaos following upon Mafouz's defeat at the hands of Lebna Dengel in 1517 by killing Harrar's reigning sultan and installing the man's brother on the throne as his puppet. Having taken Mofouz's daughter for his wife and thereby gained the support of that previous jihadist's surviving followers, he then imitated his father-in-law by conferring upon himself the religious title of Imam and setting his sights upon the conquest of Abyssinia. His name first became worrisome to the Prester's roving court in 1527 when, after ordering Muslim towns within his sphere of influence to stop paying their annual tribute to the *Negus*, he decisively defeated the general whom Lebna Dengel sent down to the desert plain to collect those overdue taxes. This initial victory was soon followed up by a series of offensive raids which penetrated far deeper into the Prester's realm than any recently attempted, and which, unlike those of Mafouz, occurred not just predictably during the starving season of Lent but at any time of the year the Imam found congenial.[1] It was not long before the terrified villagers of Ethiopia's eastern escarpment, who saw their menfolk put to the sword and their churches looted, were calling the invading general after a physical feature that became apparent whenever he waived his sword aloft to direct his ravaging troops: he was now known in Amharic as Ahmed Gran — that is to say, Ahmed the Left-Handed. No doubt this characteristic was, to his Christian victims, just one proof the more that the Imam served the powers of darkness.

It wasn't merely the case that Ahmed Gran's raids were more effectual than Mafouz's; rather, his agenda stretched beyond such smash-and-grab operations toward a full-scale *futuh* — the decisive conquest of an infidel territory that would bring it permanently into the house of Islam.[2] As he warned Lebna Dengel early on in a letter proposing an exchange of prisoners, one "should not think of us as we were before, making an incursion and then going home. This time we shall not return until God has conquered the country for us — if it be God's will — or we have died."[3] At this point such was only a personal ambition he had not yet fully articulated even to his own lieutenants, but as his well-disciplined and well-motivated forces began to win major victories against numerically superior Ethiopian armies, the facts on the ground began to favor his grand dream becoming a reality. By March of 1529 the Gran's forces had dealt their Christian enemies a stinging defeat at a place known as the Swamp of the Chickpeas, and just over a year later his troops were setting ablaze the religious center of Debre Libanos, located deep within the high Shoan plateau not far from where Álvares had first seen the Prester's tented capital almost a decade before. When one of Ahmed's officers complained that such a wanton act of destruction was uncalled-for, the man was upbraided by the Imam, who replied that "there was nothing wrong in burning it down," that indeed such was a necessary step in breaking the Ethiopians' spirit, since the artistic glories of Debre Libanos "meant much more to them than anything else."[4] If such chilling clarity of purpose was a potent psychological weapon in the Gran's arsenal, a battle fought south of Lake Hayq in the spring of 1531 showed that he also possessed material arms superior to those of his foes. The Ottoman takeover of the Red Sea meant that the Left-Handed had access to state-of-the-art cannons and Turkish experts in their use and deployment. During this engagement an opening bombard from one of these engines neatly halved an olive tree that stood close by the Ethiopian front line, a terrifying omen which sent the superstitious Christian troops into a headlong retreat at the first sign of an ensuing Muslim charge.[5] As the decade proceeded and Ahmed Grañ swallowed up province after province of a formerly impregnable Abyssinia, it must have seemed to Lebna Dengel as if God, or at least the god of war, had deserted his camp.

Not that the Grañ's troops were infallible. On one occasion the Imam, at the head of a small group of cavalry and foot soldiers, spotted the massive white tent of the *Negus* perched upon a mountain some distance before him. (In fact the chronicler claimed it was visible across a space of two day's ride.) Rather than let such a golden opportunity slip by Ahmed ordered his party to masquerade as Christian troops returning to the Court from some distant battlefield, and to either keep silent or, if they were able, to speak only the local dialect so as to mask their true identities as long as possible. Under such deceptive flag they made good progress toward the King's sunlit headquarters. On their final ascent of the hill, however, one of Ahmed's men who was jacked up on *khat* impulsively set fire to a church that was close by the trail. When the denizens of the royal camp looked down and beheld the burning structure being passed by men-at-arms who seemed unconcerned about saving it, the jig was up. The Grañ, after a laconic prayer that God would see fit not to bless the jittery arsonist, ordered an immediate charge across the remaining distance, the result of which was a desperate combat just outside the doors of the King's apartments. Lebna Dengel, spilling out of his silken cloister to join the fray, recognized the officer wielding a sword in his left hand as his great enemy and shouted to his men: "Look, Satan has come in person!" The *Negus* eventually effected a narrow escape and retreated across broken country to *Amba* Geshen, where he was no doubt met with some consternation from his kinsmen imprisoned there precisely so that they could never approach him. This choice of refuge, though, underscores the fact that Lebna Dengel possessed a powerful ally in the extraordinary geography of Ethiopia itself. The Imam's forces, for instance, attempted on three separate occasions to assault the isolated, upthrusting pinnacle of Geshen. After the first assault the Grañ's exhausted lieutenants eventually talked him into walking away. On the second try, he had his cannons dragged up the steep road that wound toward the prison's capstone and tried to lob some ordinance onto the sky island above, but every ball was answered with a tumbling boulder, until the Imam admitted that "fighting on this mountain serves no useful purpose." It was not until 1539 that one of the Grañ's viziers finally broke through the peak's natural defenses, his men slaughtering every last inmate of the aerie, though by that time Lebna Dengel had long since fled to other precincts of his steadily shrinking kingdom.

In the summer of 1532, with much of the eastern and southern sections of the highlands under his control, with much of the defeated population reluctantly converting to Islam, and with major churches such as Antronsa Maryam and Makane Sellase reduced to ash, the Imam decided to make his vision of a permanently Muslim Ethiopia manifest to his brother campaigners. Calling all of them before him, he announced what some of them had already guessed — that it was his will that the green mountains of Abyssinia should become not just their bivouac, but their new homeland. "Praised be God who has conquered the whole of the land of Abyssinia. Now let us send to the land of Sa'd as-Din, to bring up our wives and our children. Let us make our homes in Abyssinia. It is no longer possible for us to go back down to our country, or to leave this one."[6] In the end they agreed, for most of them had been following the Imam's wildly successful *jihad* for five years now, and thus saw their leader as a man inspired by God to always choose rightly. And then too, after stripping so many churches and looting so many monasteries the accumulated booty was simply getting too weighty to drag around behind them; it was time to put down new roots. But while Ahmed Grañ's appeal was an assertion about what Ethiopia would look like after the war, it was not a declaration of victory in that conflict. There was much fighting yet to do, and the Imam now wheeled his columns to the northward, subduing Amhara in 1533 and Tigre in 1535, pushing Lebna Dengel into ever-more-remote fastnesses, from which the King mustered what resistance he could amid his increasingly fearful, dispirited, and scarce subjects.

It is at this moment that Joam Bermudez, or "Mestre Joam," as Álvares had always called him — the physician who had asked and received permission to stay behind in Abyssinia when the embassy first attempted to leave — re-emerges into the historical record. Apparently he had managed to keep himself within the good graces of Lebna Dengel since the embassy's actual departure in 1526, and had been granted some estates by the ever-retreating *Negus* in territory not yet conquered by the Grañ.[7] Then, at some point in the mid 1530s, the King finally decided that his country's deteriorating situation required that he swallow his considerable pride and appeal to his Portuguese allies for aid in the form of troops and weapons, and that Bermudez should be his messenger. The choice of envoy makes some sense given the doctor's nationality, and Lebna Dengel must have had little clue as to what a mischief-maker he was now loosing upon the world. For instance, the King would have been furious had he been able to foresee Bermudez's claim that His Highness had done much more at their interview than merely entrusting him with an urgent distress call. According to Mestre Joam, the *Negus* also escorted him to the deathbed of the *Abuna* Marcos and begged the Coptic archbishop "before his death to institute [Bermudez], in accordance with his use, as his successor, and as Patriarch of that country." Had such an unlikely thing actually occurred, it certainly would not have been "in accordance with his use," since as we have seen the *Abuna* of the Ethiopian Church had for centuries been appointed by the Patriarch of Alexandria, a practice that would in fact endure until as recently as 1959. But the physician goes on to say that he was not even willing to accept this honor unless he could extract some concessions from Lebna Dengel that would lead Ethiopia toward conformity with Catholic orthodoxy: "I accepted this on the condition that it was confirmed by the High Roman Pontiff, successor of St. Peter, whom we all have to obey. The said Emperor replied that he was well content, and further asked me to go to Rome to yield obedience to the Holy Father on my own part, for him, and for all his kingdoms." Lebna Dengel may have been at this time an increasingly desperate monarch, but the idea that he would have agreed to alter the religion of his country as the price for having Bermudez (as opposed to some other resident Frank) carry his S. O. S. is simply ludicrous. Although the memoir which brings together all the cumulative fantasies of Mestre Joam's heated imagination did not appear until 1565, we will in what follows attempt to keep track of just when the erstwhile bone-setter added each successive apocryphal title to his *curriculum vitae*, thus tracing an extraordinary career of escalating imposture.

Bermudez, surely possessed of no other actual office than that of the beleaguered *Negus'* messenger to King João III, made his way toward Europe by means of Egypt and the Mediterranean, a much shorter, if more hazard-prone route than that which arced through Portuguese India and around the Cape of Good Hope. In fact this journey was not completed without mishap, for the doctor claims that he was captured and detained by the Turks, who cut out part of his tongue. (Perhaps they knew a congenital liar as soon as they heard one.) This story, at any rate, can be believed, for subsequent witnesses claimed that because of this injury Bermudez spoke with a slight impediment for the rest of his life. Of less certain veracity is Mestre Joam's claim to have stopped off in Rome for an audience with Pope Paul III; certainly the titles he later claimed had been bestowed upon him by the Pontiff strain credulity to the breaking point. At any rate, he did successfully reach Portugal sometime in 1536 or 1537 and duly reported to King João on the direness of the Prester's situation and his appeal for an expeditionary force to save his country, news which was met with sympathy, alarm, and at least some measure of practical action. Incidentally, he also claimed to have been charged by Lebna Dengel to "arrest" Zaga Za Ab, who had now been in Europe for a decade "without negotiating anything, through his own mere neglect." (We shall later see that while the lack of progress was undeniable, the fault for this inaction scarcely lay with Zaga Za Ab.) He also claimed that the *Negus'* previous ambassador "acknowledged [him] as his Patriarch and superior, and kissed [his] hand, and resigned to [him] his office without another word," though when the doctor fell sick on the eve of starting back for India with a Portuguese fleet in 1538 — which caused him to miss its sailing—he darkly hinted at having been poisoned by the supposedly submissive Zaga Za Ab.

Bermudez is eager for us to understand that while he remained in Portugal he enjoyed frequent hobnobs with King João and that at palace functions he "was also given precedence next after the [Papal] Nuncio, as befitted [his] dignity." Such bragging is trivial, but his account of the actual material aid he carried back under his command to Ethiopia is a boast more pertinent to our concerns, if no easier to confirm. He says that he was granted "four hundred matchlockmen and pioneers"—i.e., riflemen and foot soldiers.[8] As it turned out, about that many troops did eventually disembark at Massawa, but the truth of the matter is that they had been initially sent into the Red Sea for another purpose, their decision to aid Ethiopia was more or less spontaneous, and they were certainly not under Mestre Joam's command. Here is a case, then, of the doctor attempting to make himself out as the central actor in a drama in which he played at best a supporting role. In all probability what he carried with him when he finally pushed away from the Lisbon quay in late March of 1539 were general instructions for the *Estado's* Governor at Goa to do what he could for the Abyssinian monarch as long as it didn't sap vital resources from wider Portuguese projects. After all, such would have been in keeping with what King João had by this time learned from Dom Rodrigo and Álvares—that Ethiopia, while indeed a Christian kingdom beyond the Moors, was in no way the salvific superpower of the Prester John legend.[9] The *Estado* would do what it could, but the golden age of chasing myths was over, and there would be limits.

Accompanying Bermudez on his return to the East was Zaga Za Ab who, after ten frustrating years in Portugal, was no doubt anxious to see his homeland again. This was not to be, however, for he died at the Indian port of Cochin in 1540. There will be time in due course to tell the story of Zaga's sojourn in Europe (the second in his eventful life), and especially of how the Catholic Church was able to extract from him the secret about Ethiopia that Álvares had struggled with himself to conceal. For now, though, we need only triangulate his death with Mestre Joam's career as a prevaricator, since it was only after the former's demise that the latter began to put it about that Pope Paul III had consecrated him the Catholic Patriarch of Ethiopia. Since Zaga Za Ab was the only other person fresh from Portugal who was also knowledgeable about Ethiopian affairs, and who thus could have readily informed any interested party that he had heard nothing of any such appointment, the coincidence of the death and the fib is explained. It would not be the last time that the passing of an inconvenient witness prompted the good doctor to a new and brasher impersonation.[10]

Whatever instructions for the Viceroy Bermudez brought to India, that official's fatal illness prevented any full-scale assault on the Red Sea from being attempted in 1540. Rather, a single foist — i.e., a light and speedy ship employed for reconnaissance — was dispatched to Massawa in order to check on conditions in the Prester's realm. From that port letters were dispatched inland, which found Lebna Dengel at his *amba*-top refuge of Debre Damo, not many days ride from shore. This fortress-monastery was even more impregnable than *Amba* Geshen, for its vertical capstone, in addition to being set atop its own steep-sided mesa, actually curved outward in its last hundred-or-so feet, such that access to the top could only be had by being hauled up in a bucket lowered by the monks above. The *Negus* was there with his wife, Sebla Wangél, and had been for some time, for the territory where his writ still ran amounted to little more than small pockets of land wholly separated from one other. The Grañ had once laid siege to the mountain, but the impossibility of scaling the more-than-sheer ramparts had eventually sent him off to other business, which by then might have been justly called mopping-up operations. The *Negus* wrote back to the Portuguese reiterating his sorry condition but also his willingness to fight on if their troops arrived to aid him in a timely manner. He also wrote to Bermudez, thanking him for his efforts, but referring to him as nothing more than his messenger to the Franks.[11] These were to be the last letters Lebna Dengel would ever write to his European allies, for soon after sending them he succumbed, at the age of thirty-nine, to natural causes upon the heights of Debre Damo, leaving his shattered empire to a son equally harassed by encircling foes hundreds of miles to the south. He was, as we have seen, a flawed man and a sometimes mercurial king, but ever since the time of his friend Álvares' departure fourteen years before he had fought bravely and tirelessly to preserve his nation and its religion from destruction. He had suffered much both as a monarch and as a man, seeing one son killed by the Muslims and another taken into captivity, and yet he had hung on long enough to keep his country's heart beating until European Christendom could come to its aid.[12] Though he would not live to see it, the cavalry he had summoned was about to come charging over the hill just in the nick of time.

By the time these final missives of Lebna Dengel had reached India, the previous Viceroy was dead and the *Estado* had a new master — none other than Estêvão da Gama, second son of the man who had first slashed and burned a passage to the East for the Portuguese over forty years before. As Da Gama interpreted King João's instructions, he was to proceed with an armada into the Red Sea in order to destroy Turkish galleys in their home ports at its northern end, and only secondarily to render what aid he could to the Ethiopians as time and circumstances allowed, including dropping off Bermudez on the Prester's shore. This he promptly undertook to do, and by February 10th of 1541 his fleet had passed safely through the Bab-el-Mandeb and pulled into Massawa for repairs. Here the Portuguese learned of Lebna Dengel's death and received letters from his surviving son Galawdewos, letters "that were more than piteous and miserable, on all of which above his signature was depicted Our Lord Jesus crucified."[13] By this point almost all the patricians of Ethiopia had gone over to the Grañ from an opportunism born of despair and the young *Negus* found himself heavily outgunned, nearly friendless, and increasingly encircled.

As compelling as this news was, Dom Estevão had his orders, and thus he determined that the Turkish ports to the north must be attacked before anything could be done about the Ethiopian situation. On February 18th he departed toward Suez with the lighter vessels (he would need nimble ships inside the enemy harbors), leaving the heavier hulls to await his return at Massawa under the command of his relative Manuel Da Gama, to whom he gave strict orders that no one was to attempt any adventures ashore until the fleet was reunited. Unfortunately for Dom Manuel, two factors were to make these instructions impossible to enforce: the dismal conditions prevailing in Massawa's harbor and the glittering lies emanating from Bermudez's mouth. As to the first, this costal section of Abyssinia was one of those territories that had passed into the hands of the Grañ's allies, and thus while the locals mounted no direct attack upon the Portuguese fleet neither did they offer any barter or assistance. As a result the considerable complement of sailors were condemned to eat ship's biscuit under a broiling sun within the narrow, insalubrious walls of their vessels — sickness soon began felling many. As for the doctor, we hear nothing about him healing the crew's ailing bodies but much about him heating their already susceptible brains with irresponsible talk. First of all, with Lebna Dengel now safely dead he began to claim that he was not only the country's Catholic Patriarch, but also the Ethiopian *Abuna*, duly consecrated as such at the insistence of the late *Negus* himself. Thus self-credentialed to talk authoritatively concerning all things Abyssinian, he proceeded to paint the same country that had been a shambles when he had left it six years ago as a current paradise ripe for any men of spirit bold enough to grasp its low-hanging riches in pursuit of honor and glory. He even went so far as to issue "written promises of large allowances and salaries" on the supposed authority of his two holy offices, because of which "many men were fired with the desire to go."

It was the Prester John legend all over again, and like the first time around it found numerous believers among the credulous. More and more men asked permission to go ashore and sign up for service under the beleaguered Christian king, and when Dom Manuel refused them they began slipping away under cover of darkness in ones and twos. Even the Commander's summary hanging of five men he caught on dry land without his permission could not stop the defections, and before long an organized band of one hundred mutineers were able to gain the beach and scamper to freedom when those left behind ignored Manuel's orders to shoot them down. (Bermudez, the prime instigator of this brave venture, inexplicably declined to join it and instead remained within the safety of his cabin.) This deluded band's career of adventure and profit under a foreign monarch was to prove short-lived, however. A willing and helpful guide soon appeared offering to direct them to the *Negus'* capital — a by-now non-existent destination — but instead merely lured them out into the arid hinterland where they parched from lack of water and then, when sufficiently weakened, were set upon by Muslim attackers and nearly wiped out. A pair of stragglers returned to tell the tale, forcing Dom Manuel into the absurd position of having to mount a punitive expedition to attempt to kill the people who had killed the people he would have earlier killed himself if only his orders had been carried out.[14] When, on May 22nd, Dom Estevão returned to Massawa from his campaign against the Turkish ports, everyone had a lot of explaining to do.

Once Da Gama heard the full account of what had gone on he understandably "waxed very angry" at those who had defied his deputy, but realized that quelling the still-simmering mutiny was his first order of business. Perhaps unexpectedly for a son of the fearsome Vasco he decided upon a psychological ploy rather than indiscriminate floggings and accordingly "dissimulated ... with great prudence, throwing all the blame on Manuel da Gama, and rating him in public to content and pacify the hearts of those who merited punishment." He then ordered increased rations for everyone and betook himself to his cabin to rest from his labors for a few days. Once refreshed, he summoned Bermudez to an interview, whereupon the doctor spread before him new letters he had received some weeks ago from the new *Negus* Galawdewos far in the interior (and which Bermudez had already made public to the dangerously restive *fidalgos*), which begged Dom Estevão "most earnestly, and with pious entreaties, to send help before his kingdom was entirely lost, as he was [as good as] a captive and blockaded by the Moors." His main mission having been successfully accomplished, the Governor now saw no objection — beyond its sheer difficulty and small likelihood of success, that is — to aiding a Christian monarch in distress. Calling a general council at which, predictably, "all the *fidalgos* agreed that under any circumstances help must be sent to the Preste[r]," he found himself besieged by volunteers importuning him to let them command this latter-day Crusade.

In the end, his choice of a leader for the relief expedition was exactly the right one, though at the time it certainly gave off a strong odor of nepotism:

> Several honourable *fidalgos* at once begged for this employment, but the Governor excused himself, saying that he would send none but D. Christovão, his brother, whom he would sacrifice for the King in this service, but that he would not adventure another's son; for none could tell how the enterprise would turn out, and it was very doubtful if any would escape death, because the country was so ill-minded that the very native born vassals were traitors and rebels to the Preste[r].

In point of fact, the youthful Christovão da Gama had much more than brotherly affection to recommend him. He had already twice saved ships at sea by showing a cool head in the midst of emergencies, and had distinguished himself well in battle, both at far-off Malacca and in the just-completed action against the Turks. Dom Estevão must also have had some inkling that the undiluted fund of storybook romanticism his younger sibling still possessed might prove just the quality that was needed on a mission displaying such daunting obstacles to success. Still, he meant to shorten the odds against Christovão by making sure he was supplied with all the weaponry he could reasonably hope to transport. The four hundred men that would accompany him would therefore leave toting "one thousand matchlocks, one thousand pike-heads, and much powder, bullets, and lead, and four falcons [i.e., small cannons], swivel guns, twelve bases [another kind of light artillery] with their carriages, ten very good bombards, and much powder in cases, and bullets, and all the necessary munitions in great quantity." Prester John's relief column would in fact be armed to the teeth.

Mixed in among this acutely martial company were "over seventy persons trained in all trades, namely, crossbow-makers, blacksmiths, carpenters, masons, shoemakers, armourers, and other handicraftsmen, whom Bermudez had engaged in India."[15] This comes from an objective source, so we can be reasonably sure that the doctor did in fact exercise some sort of leadership over this gaggle of craftsmen, but in his own account Bermudez, in typical fashion, makes the larger claim that King João had bestowed upon him and him alone the right of choosing the expedition's overall military leader, and that he had already promised the job to someone else when Dom Christovão's name was put forward. Also typical of Mestre Joam's memoir is the fact that in what happens next everyone comes off looking small except himself. He asserts, for instance, that Dom Estevão recognized his authority to appoint the leader but petulantly informed him that if his little brother was not given the captaincy then "The Patriarch" (as he always refers to himself) could only expect two hundred men to be assigned to the force. Bermudez claims that at first he high-mindedly refused to go back upon his previous promise, but that at last he reluctantly gave in for the good of the holy enterprise after many concerned *fidalgos* came groveling to him. Given this relentless habit of unsubstantiated self-promotion on Bermudez's part, we shall rely for the facts of the subsequent rescue mission itself on the writings of Miguel de Castanhoso, a plain-spoken soldier who marched alongside Dom Christovão, who was an eye-witness to all that passed, and whose accounts have never been contradicted by other available sources. Only now and again will we circle back and review the very different picture of events and personalities that Bermudez presumes to paint — a panorama in which "The Patriarch" is always centered in the foreground.

At some point after the Portuguese established at least a temporary

Christian beachhead at Massawa the current *Bahr-nagas* turned up, bringing additional information about conditions in the interior. The news continued bad, but in point of fact the man himself was probably the best indicator of the sorry pass to which things had arrived. The current Ruler of the Seaboard, who had until the fleet's arrival not actually seen the Red Sea shore for some time, was one of the few Ethiopian nobles who had remained loyal to the Solomonic Christian dynasty of which the distant and isolated Galawdewos was now the imperiled embodiment. But despite such personal steadfastness he was nevertheless eaten up with shame, for as he tearfully confessed to the assembled Franks his own father had seen the writing on the walls and gone over to serve the Moors, as had so many other of the *Negus'* governors, generals, and courtiers before him. Shamefaced and weary as the *Bahr-nagas* was, however, he was still eager to help, and unlike Álvares and De Lima twenty years before the Da Gamas could not afford to decline the offered services. But when, after several weeks of scouring the enemy-infested hinterland for sufficient mounts, the official understandably came up short, the column's youthful leader first exhibited that lack of concern for his own comfort and privileges of rank that was to become the morale-sustaining hallmark of his command. Dom Christovão, "finding that there were not riding animals for all, settled to march on foot, and the others followed his example."[16] Thus on July 7th 1541, after some brave speeches and heartfelt embraces upon the beach, the 400-man Portuguese expedition that meant to save Ethiopia from the Muslim scourge turned their faces from the sea and began marching toward the mountains that rose like a wall across the southern horizon. It must have been clear to Dom Estevão that he would probably never see his younger brother again.

The heat upon the coastal plain was so intense that at first the column decided to march at night, but once they ascended the escarpment — which proved "so lofty a mountain that [they] spent from morning till evening in getting to the top"— they found stretching before them "extensive plains, and a country very level and very cool, with good air and good water." By the end of six days they had reached Debarwa, but the town where Álvares and the embassy had spent so many months in comfortable captivity was now a shattered ruin, most of its population having fled to the surrounding hills to avoid the Grañ's marauders. When the Portuguese marched in behind a large cross held aloft on a standard, however, its citizens began trickling, then streaming back in, catching the scent of hope for the first time in years, including a large group of monks who tearfully declared Dom Christovão "the apostle of God come to deliver them from captivity and subjection." He replied consolingly that "with the help of our Lord they would quickly return to prosperity, as he had come to that land only to expel the Moors, and die for the faith of Christ." As eager as Christovão and his men were to begin accomplishing this goal, however, a conference the next day with the *Bahr-nagas* and several other officials who had begun emerging from the bush convinced them that the rainy season, which was already in full throat, would require them to hold fire for some months. The obvious strategy was for the Portuguese to move south and link up with the forces attached to the *Negus* Galawdewos, who would themselves move northward from Shoa to effect the rendezvous as soon as possible—indeed, it was so obvious a plan that they could certainly count on the Grañ anticipating it and doing everything in his power to prevent it. There was no remedy for this, but also no way for either Christian or Muslim to begin moving in earnest until October, so hunker down they must. The one positive thing the Portuguese could do in the meantime, besides drilling constantly, was to fetch Lebna Dengel's widowed queen to their side, for her presence would double their ability to rally Ethiopia's defeated citizenry toward one final act of resistance.

The honor guard which Dom Christovão sent to Debre Damo waited at attention along the steep, narrow trail that dead-ended at the perpendicular capstone's foot while the Queen, her daughter, her ladies-in-waiting, and her servants were lowered down in baskets by the monks from the mesa's ample roof. Whatever dangers loomed, it must have been for Sebla Wangél an almost giddy moment of liberation, given that the isolated monastery had been her home for the last four years. Nor had the view from the summit always been pleasant, since as Castanhoso notes, the Grañ "came against it with all his power for a year, ... and this not out of desire for the treasures that were in it, for there were none there and he knew it well, but to get the Queen into his hands, whom he much desired, as she is very beautiful." The first meeting between this empress of a defeated nation and that nation's would-be savior was in no way denuded of pageantry by the exigencies of the hour. The Queen rode into the Portuguese camp at the head of her considerable retinue sidesaddle on a mule, a silk canopy borne by servants protecting her from general scrutiny, but open slightly in front so that she might view her rescuer's face without impediment. The *Bahr-nagas* led her mount by the bridle, himself bare-chested but for a lion's-skin that draped over one shoulder in the approved Abyssinian manner for approaching a royal personage. As for the Frankish soldiery, they were "in full dress and in ranks," bristling with swords, guns, pikes, and "the best equipment they had," while above them ad-hoc regimental banners of blue, white, and red, all displaying the cross, rippled in the breeze. Dom Christovão himself was decked out in "hose and [a] vest of red satin and gold brocade with many plaits," a "French cape of fine black cloth all quilted with gold," and a black cap adored with a shining medallion. The Queen's arrival was formally acknowledged by a double salute from both the matchlocks and artillery, whereupon Da Gama and his lieutenants approached her mule to deliver their compliments and receive her requests. Responding "with honor and good grace she ordered the canopy in which she traveled to be opened, and she lowered her muffling a little, showing much pleasure while [they] spoke."[17] Given the death sentence which seemed to hang over both of them, Christovão and Sebla Wangél's insistence on as much gaudy pomp as they could each manage was itself an initial act of defiance against their common enemy.

It was to be only the initial step in the increasingly intimate meeting of their minds, for it soon became clear that the two of them had become important to each other in a way that transcended mere political expediency. Did they actually fall in love? Sharing the rigors of a perilous enterprise with someone is widely understood to be a straight and fast road to emotional intimacy, regardless of either's party's previous experience. Still, as we have no access to diary entries or whispered confessions to friends, it is impossible to say whether the pair developed genuine romantic feelings for each other, though no one can read Castanhoso's account of the campaign without having that possibility thrust readily and charmingly into his or her view. What we can affirm with certainty is that the two fell into Courtly Love with each other. That is to say, it is clear that Dom Christovão almost immediately began to act the part of Sebla Wangél's chivalric champion, dedicating his every action to her service, laboring indefatigably for her welfare, inverting her actual helplessness into a costume mastery over himself, playing the lover with little hope of physical consummation. And if the part of the feudal knight's Liege Lady was at first a culturally distant one for the Ethiopian Queen, she proved a quick study. Before long her outbursts of panic at the thought of harm coming to her hero, as well as her submissive calming at the sound of his gentle remonstrance, hit the marks laid down by European troubadours exactly, as did her effusions of solicitude for wounds and gratitude for victory at each battle's end. Of course there was one anomaly — in Courtly Love the Lady was supposed to be married, and thus unattainable. Perhaps the fact that Sebla Wangél was widowed and thus technically available just added amperage to the whole *pas-de-deux*. Or perhaps her color substituted for the insurmountable blockage to sex usually represented by the husband. But whatever the real truth of this matter, it is clear that Dom Christovão da Gama was, during the months that followed, a man in the happy position of living out a vivid cultural ideal that in reality had only ever been open to the merest few. To march to the defense of a stricken Christian nation was a fine thing — to be kissing the hand of its grateful, beautiful, exotic queen while doing so must have been the very stuff of heaven.

Certainly Christovão threw himself into the final preparations for war with an impressively disciplined zeal. While the rains still fell he ordered the construction of carts sufficient for carrying the army's matchlocks, artillery, and cannon balls, and in this project Da Gama himself was "master of the works ... as if he had been a carpenter all his life, and it was his pleasure to spend all his days at it." So well supplied with arms were the Portuguese that any gun-barrels not up to snuff were hammered into skids and racks for these vehicles. Though no additional spur to action was needed, during this wet summer of logistical preparation letters arrived from Galawdewos agreeing on matters of strategy, and recalling "a prophesy, made many years before the kingdom was overrun, that it would be recovered by white men come from far, who were true Christians." Christovão thus possessed, like the men of De Lima's embassy before him, hints and portents enough to feel himself the Heaven-destined grasper of that hand the Bible asserted Ethiopia would soon be reaching out unto God. And so when the skies at last cleared — much later than usual that year, but no matter — he left nothing to chance as the southward march began anew. Each day he rode up and down the column on "fast free-trotting mules," rotating his captains through the various needful assignments so that all might take each other's places if pressed by losses to do so. Only our chronicler Castanhoso received an unchanging duty, that of guarding the Queen and her entourage at the army's rear with fifty "arquebusiers, with their arms loaded and matches lighted, for such were my orders." At some points in their journey the Abyssinian geography threatened to render useless the wagons they had so carefully fashioned, but their commander balked at no exertion, no matter how Herculean:

> D. Christovão, seeing that the carts could not be dragged over [the mountain], ordered us to take every cart to pieces, and remove the artillery and munitions from them. We then carried all these things on our backs, little by little, with the very greatest labour; D. Christovão was the first to carry on his back whatever he could.... [A]nd such was our labour that ... as much could have been written of it as of the labour of Hannibal in crossing the Alps.... After this, the Queen believed that there were no people equal to the Portuguese.

One imagines that this last pronouncement was payment in full for all Da Gama's aches and bruises.

Their first substantial engagement came some fifty miles west of Axum (their march roughly, though not exactly, duplicating that of the embassy's original penetration) when they discovered that a high hill athwart their path — *Amba* Sanyat — was occupied by a substantial Muslim garrison. To say that topography seemed to favor the defenders is to understate the case, for like most heights in Ethiopia its approaches were steep and in this instance access to the summit was only to be had through three narrow defiles that were subject to fire from those higher up the final slope. It was tempting to bypass the place altogether, but Dom Christovão wanted to leave no harassing enemy forces in his rear and determined to attack, a decision that alarmed Sebla Wangél:

> When the Queen heard of D. Christovão's intention she sent for him, and told him that he should not think of daring such a great deed with so small an army; that they should march and join the Preste[r], and then they could do everything — that it was less difficult to fight twelve thousand men in a plain, and

destroy them, than to capture that hill. To this D. Christovão replied that she should fear nothing, as they were Portuguese, and they hoped to be able, with the help of God, to capture it with very little loss; that she should be at ease, for they would all die before any harm came to her. With these words she and hers were somewhat pacified, and agreed that D. Christovão should act in the matter as he pleased, but [remained] very doubtful that the attempt could be satisfactorily prosecuted. All this while we were approaching the hill.

Both here and later, Da Gama acted from a conviction that when an enemy's position appeared overwhelming, the only viable strategy was to quickly turn their complacency into panic by an unexpectedly direct attack. Which is not to say that he lacked strategic cunning. On this occasion, he first organized a feinting advance intended to probe the hill's defenses, and when he discovered what kind of weapons the Moors possessed (rolled boulders being not the least of them) and where their fire would be concentrated, he ordered his men to withdraw in a manner that looked like a disorderly retreat. When, later that evening, he heard the celebratory clamor of "many trumpets and kettledrums" waft down from the heights, he knew he had them where he wanted them. Equally misled by his performance had been the Queen, who was sorely disheartened, but he reassured her "that in the morning her highness would see how the Portuguese fought, and what men they were." The next day Da Gama set his artillery to playing steadily but randomly along the edge of the mountain-top to keep the defenders back from it and broke his men into three squads who each attacked one of the natural gates leading to the summit. It was no cake-walk: Castanhoso says that the Muslims dealt the Portuguese "evil treatment," and "attacked the ascent very briskly," such that the Franks only followed their commander upwards "with our lives in our hands." Dom Christovão, however, "gave [that] day proof of his great courage," gaining precious elevation at times only "by the help of his pike, and of fissures in the rocks." And eventually the reversal of battlefield psychology he had been counting on came to pass, for once even one of the Portuguese columns broke through its assigned defile it became clear that the enemy had not bothered to devise any coherent fallback plan to defend the summit itself, and organized resistance quickly crumbled. "When the Moors saw the passes were occupied they retreated, the one body on the other, neither knowing of the other's defeat; thus they all collected under our swords and pikes and remained in a trap whence none escaped." By afternoon Dom Christovão could boast of an unlikely victory at the cost of only eight Christian dead and forty-odd wounded, and bask in the Queen's assertion, overheard by Castanhoso, that "indeed we were men sent of God, and she thought all things were possible to us."

Before the army pushed on from the battle site, two Portuguese arrived from Massawa with letters, for now that it was February of the new year Dom Estevão had been able to send some foists into the Red Sea to discover how

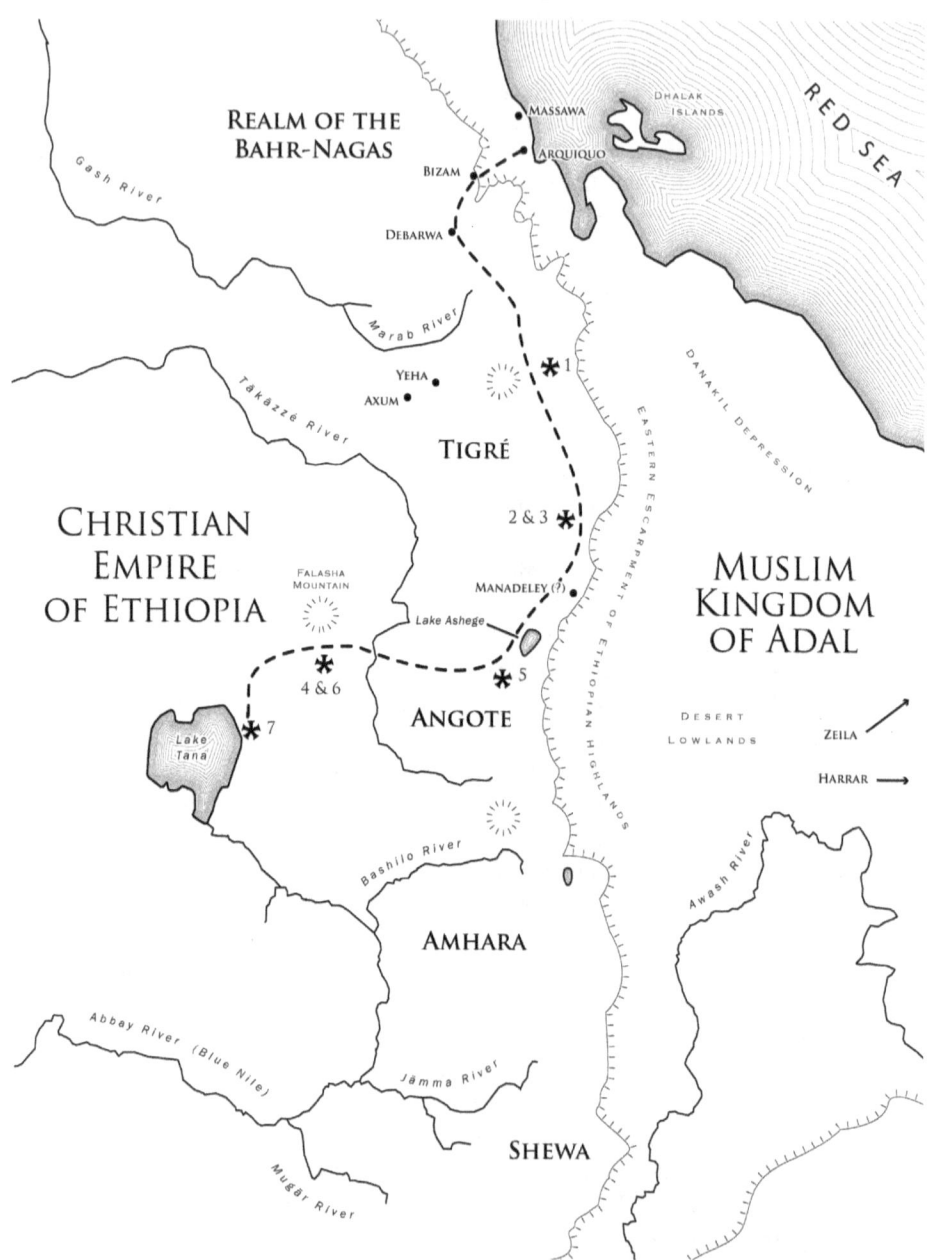

ROUTE AND MAJOR ENGAGEMENTS OF CHRISTOVÃO DA GAMA'S RESCUE MISSION INTO ETHIOPIA OF 1541–43. (1) Battle of the Mountain of Three Gates; (2) Battle of Ahmed Grañ's wounding; (3) Battle of the Powder Explosion; (4) Battle of the Falashas' (i.e., Jews') Mountain; (5) Battle of the Portuguese Defeat; (6) Retreat to the Falashas' Mountain; (7) Ahmed Grañ defeated and killed.

his younger bother was faring. Assigning fifty soldiers to return with these men to the coast and collect another load of guns and powder, Dom Christovão, after proudly writing to his sibling that he had so-far returned forty leagues of Abyssinia to the banner of Christ, resumed his southward march. It was not many days before the forward scouts of the Portuguese and those of the Grañ had each other in sight, the former of whom brought back dispiriting news about the size of the Muslim host: 15,000 foot soldiers, 1500 cavalrymen, and, most worrisome of all, two hundred Turkish arquebusiers (that is, men carrying muskets). A tactical retreat was considered, but the fickle nature of the Ethiopian populace argued against it. All along the line of march the locals were rallying to the banner of Portugal and the Queen, but their allegiance was fragile and fed entirely off the momentum of victory—one step backward and they, as well as the supplies the people provided, would melt away. Da Gama understood that he was marching down a narrow political alley in which straight ahead was the only possible direction. Therefore, having come upon a suitable piece of rising ground in the midst of a large plain, the Portuguese and their Abyssinian allies pitched their tents, began digging earthworks, and awaited the arrival of the Left-Handed.

The next day Imam Ahmed himself was visible on a nearby ridgeline between banners displaying the crescent moon, examining his unexpected foe's position with a curious eye. He must not have been very impressed with the almost ludicrously small force presuming to oppose him, for on the following morning he sent a messenger under white flag to the Portuguese camp to express his belief that Dom Christovão must be the innocent victim of some very bad advisors. Indeed, he "marveled greatly how [Da Gama] had the audacity to appear before him with so small a force; that indeed he seemed to be a mere boy, as rumor said, ... innocent [and] without experience." But, opined the Grañ, he understood what had happened—the locals had lied to him about the true state of affairs and about who now ruled in Abyssinia, but that such riff-raff "were of small account, for they were disloyal to their own King." Waxing avuncular, the Imam hinted that it was also too often the case that young men of admirable spirit thought with their groin rather than their head, "that he knew in fact that that woman had beguiled him, but that he should pay no more attention to her," for she had merely "deluded him by telling him that in those countries there was some other King" than Ahmed Grañ. Of course he himself admired the youthful Frank's boldness, really he did—so much so that he would magnanimously grant him the option of either joining his own army or departing the country in peace. Accompanying this condescending message was the insulting gift of "a friar's cowl and a rosary of beads, making us all out [to be] friars."

Such polite banter between men bent upon murdering each other was also part of the courtly code, and Dom Christovão knew how to reply in kind.

He soon sent his own messenger to the Muslim camp declining the Imam's generous offers and suggesting instead that he would do well to prepare himself and his men to become the subjects of His Most Catholic Majesty King João of Portugal. Along with this reply he forwarded a mirror and a pair of tweezers, implying that the Left-Handed was a woman. It was a snappy comeback alright, but Da Gama was to encounter that same pair of tweezers again under circumstances less amusing.

Having an overpowering advantage in numbers, the Grañ simply decided to surround the hill where his enemies were encamped, deprive them of food and supplies, and harass them just enough to keep them from sleeping day or night. As we have seen, however, it was just from such a seemingly impossible position that Christovão liked to take the offensive. Therefore at dawn on April 4th, 1542 the Portuguese attacked their besiegers. As Castanhoso reports, "when the Moors saw us advancing towards them, they raised such a noise of shouting, trumpets, and kettledrums, that it seemed as if the world were dissolving; they showed great joy, thinking they had us already in their net." Given his previous victory, this racket must have been music to Da Gama's ears. "At this we began to do our duty with matchlocks and artillery, which played continually on all sides, so that we cleared the plain as we advanced. The Turks, who were in our front, seeing the damage we caused, advanced close to us, and the battle began to rage." Technology was crucial in this contest, for the Portuguese artillery kept the Muslim cavalry at bay by terrifying its horses while the Turkish matchlock-men, on loan from an Arabian emir, were the only unit to successfully halt the unexpected Christian advance. At one point Dom Christovão led a charge toward these arquebusiers which resulted in fierce hand-to-hand combat and numerous Portuguese casualties, including Da Gama himself, who took a musket-ball through the leg but kept on fighting regardless. It was at this point, however, that a lucky shot from one of the Christian gunmen turned the tide. So confused had the melee become that although "it appeared to us that we had the worst of the battle," just the opposite seemed true to the Grañ, whereupon he "advanced to encourage his men, and came so close to us that he was wounded in the thigh by a matchlock bullet, that pierced his horse, which fell dead under him. When they saw him fall, his ensigns lowered the three banners which accompanied him," something they probably let happen because they were rushing to help him, but which also happened to be the agreed-upon signal for retreat. Some moments later, when the Moors saw their captain being borne away injured from the field, their orderly withdrawal turned into a headlong rush with the Portuguese cavalry in hot pursuit and "slaying them as if they were sheep" until their horses gave out.[18] Once again, an audacious roll of the dice had won Dom Christovão a long-shot victory.

The aftermath of this battle again threw Da Gama and the Queen together, and this time the realities of war swept aside any courtly posturing, though both rose well to the occasion. As Castanhoso explains, "while we were in pursuit, the Queen had had a tent pitched and placed the wounded in it; she and her women went about binding up the wounded with their own headgear, and weeping with pleasure at the great mercy our Lord God had done them that day, for truly she had found herself in great fear and tribulation." When Christovão made it back to this makeshift hospital he "laboured much" by "attend[ing] to all the wounded himself" since the only surgeon in the force had been stabbed in the right hand (apparently the "Patriarch" Bermudez no longer stooped to medicine). "After tending to all the others," the Commander "tended his own wound last of all." The sight of the new casualties (eleven dead and forty injured) must have troubled Da Gama, for though he had been both shrewd and lucky so far, attrition was his greatest enemy. Even though Ethiopian men of fighting caliber were now joining his ranks in increasing numbers, the Portuguese contingent was always going to be the vital heart of the army — just as the Turkish gunners would be to the Grañ's — and when they dwindled below a certain critical mass, the whole campaign must collapse.

Dom Christovão was understandably anxious to press his temporary advantage and therefore after giving the casualties a few days to rest up, he actively sought out another battle with the Left-Handed, whose army was still within sight. If anything, though, the Muslim force had grown in size since the last engagement, for "there had joined him a Captain with five hundred horse and three thousand foot." This was dismaying, but had the Portuguese delayed because of it "more would have come to him," for his lieutenants and viziers, who were "scattered over the country ... joined him daily" at his call. The Franks advanced brazenly upon the Muslim formations, and the latter responded by going on the attack. The wounded Imam was carried into this latest battle on a bed lifted onto his ensigns' shoulders: "he came to encourage his men, but this was hardly necessary, for they were so numerous that merely seeing how few we were encouraged them." One of Ahmed's newly-arrived captains, incredulous at the small number of the Portuguese he had been summoned to help annihilate, impetuously led his own contingent of cavalry into an immediate charge. At first the Christian artillery kept most of them in check, but soon more and more horsemen from other units joined the advance and it looked as if Da Gama's lines must surely be overrun. Then, without warning, a second stoke of luck descended as if from heaven, or perhaps more accurately, erupted from hell: "at this time, a little powder accidentally caught fire in the part where we were weakest." Two Portuguese were killed outright in the terrible blast and eight were horribly burned in the ensuing fire, but the carnage and confusion sown among the Muslim cavalry was far worse, for the clearing smoke revealed the ground to be strewn with shattered corpses over which panicked horses hurtled with their helpless riders every which way across the plain. As before, Christovão ordered his own cavalry in pursuit, though the few horsemen he possessed could not fully exploit the situation. Still, the end of the day saw the Portuguese in possession of the Muslim camp and the bedridden Grañ ignominiously bouncing over the next line of hills in retreat.

By now the clouds of the annual monsoon were once more gathering overhead, compelling both armies to stake out camps in which to sit out the coming season of downpours. As he prepared to do so, Dom Christovão was joined by the returning two-score of men he had dispatched to Massawa, who brought with them several hundred Abyssinian recruits. These comrades arrived doubly disappointed, however, both because they had missed out on the recent battles and because they had found no foists at Massawa bearing needed munitions. (The vessels had apparently been chased away by Turkish galleys, and the hard truth was that with Portuguese resources stretched thin from Brazil to China, the Red Sea had been gradually reverting to a Muslim possession for some time.) Resolving to make do with what they had, Da Gama chose as the spot for his army's long encampment a hill to the south of the strikingly beautiful Lake Ashege. The land round about was abundantly supplied with food (which the citizenry now donated in bulk) and also lay along the likely route that Galawdewos would follow up from the south. It was also close enough to the summer "wintering"-ground (as the Abyssinians would have called it) chosen by the Grañ that the Portuguese scouts could just manage to keep an eye on their enemy. For his part, the Imam had also settled his troops upon a substantial hill, located along roughly the same latitude as Christovão's but on an eastward-thrusting arm or foothill chain of the Ethiopian escarpment. This was a sage decision, since it placed him at the closest elevated point to his main Red Sea port at Zeila, from whence he could receive substantial reinforcements. While Da Gama had to scrape by with the return of his forty Portuguese and the arrival of local volunteers, Ahmed sent word to his Turkish allies in Arabia that he urgently needed more trained arquebusiers if his *futuh* was not to be wholly reversed. By the end of summer he had received no less than nine hundred of them into his ranks, in addition to ten field cannons and a dozen armored cavalrymen whose steeds were plated as well. Only food was in short supply, since the Ethiopian peasantry had begun withholding their produce at the first whiff of a Christian victory.[19]

Sometime in early August, however, an opportunity presented itself to Dom Christovão that also promised to provide him with some crucially needed materiel. There came to his camp an Abyssinian Jew — or Falasha as they are known in Ethiopia — the homeland of whose people lay to the west of Da Gama's current position in the high Simien mountains. The Falashas had been residents of the Horn of Africa for centuries, and though the time and means of their actual arrival there is still disputed today, legend looked upon them as the ancestors of the Hebrew companions who had accompanied Menelik to Ethiopia along with the Ark of the Covenant, but whose descendents had never converted to Christianity. And just as Abyssinian Christianity retained many ancient Hebraic elements that the religion had elsewhere shed, so too did the Falashas cling to Jewish ceremonies which suggested their departure from the Holy Land many centuries before the end of Biblical times.[20] This particular Falasha claimed to be the former "captain" of a mountain that had been overrun by the Muslims, and which commanded a road by which Galawdewos might well have to travel to reach the Portuguese camp. Furthermore, he claimed that it pastured many fine horses, of which Dom Christovão's army was in dire need. Da Gama's first impulse was to let Galawdewos capture this prize on his way northward, but here the Jew dealt a severe blow to the Commander's spirits by informing him that, contrary to his long-held assumption, the *Negus* had far too few followers left to accomplish such a thing.

> When D. Christovão learnt how small a force the Preste[r] had with him, he became very dispirited and disquieted, and went to the Queen to learn if it was true that her son had so small a force; when it was confirmed by her he became still more downcast, without, however, letting her know it, because until then he had not heard this, but had hoped that the Preste[r] would quickly join him, as the winter was already verging to an end. That [the Prester] might not find that obstacle in the way, and because he himself wanted the horses, he determined to go there personally, as the Jew told him that with one hundred good fellows he might with skill recover the hill; that he required but few days for this, and that he could return to his camp with many horses without his absence being noted [by the Grañ].

Accordingly, Da Gama picked a hundred men for the assignment and marched them out of camp under strict silence at the hour of midnight, "carrying with him many skins necessary for crossing a river near the hill." This torrent, which they found quite swollen by the rains, seemed a formidable obstacle, but they "quickly cut a quantity of wood and branches and with these, and [causing] the skins [to be] filled with air, made rafts ... which they bound strongly together.... They crossed a few at a time, taking their matchlocks, powder, and matches inside other skins, lest they should be wetted; thus they all got over, some by swimming" (a much rarer skill then than now). This fording was followed by another silent all-night march, with the Jew acting as guide, which brought both horse and foot to within striking distance of the mountaintop fort. At first light Christovão sounded the charge, and once again the Portuguese fell upon their unsuspecting enemies like thunder from a cloudless sky. Before many minutes had passed the Moorish captain was dead, whereupon his soldiers, seeing that "there was none before whom they could feel shame, nor from whom they could receive orders, took flight, and many died, for the very Jews slew them, and few escaped." Quickly rounding up over ninety precious horses, three hundred mules, and many head of cattle, Da Gama immediately began marching his men back toward the monsoon camp at a steady trot. Suddenly beset by a gnawing premonition that his main force was in immediate danger, he went so far as to split the column into two groups, one to hurry ahead toward the wintering ground, the other to follow along with the captured animals as swiftly as they could manage.

He had good reason to worry, for the morning after his return the Imam's army was out in force, displaying beneath the alarmed eyes of the Portuguese squadron after squadron of their newly-arrived matchlock-men. Again there was talk of withdrawal, but again the sunshine patriotism of the populous made such an otherwise reasonable response unwise. As Castanhoso relates,

> he knew that, if we struck our camp that night, the very people would rise against us, and we should have nothing to eat; for this reason we were bound to fight and retain what we had gained. He sent an urgent message to those with the horses, to march as quickly as possible, as the Moors had been reinforced by the Turks, and a battle appeared immanent. We kept careful watch all that night, which was not good refreshment for those who came weary from their journey. All that night we were under arms.[21]

Fortune, skill, and daring had taken them far, but they would surely need all three and more to survive this latest onslaught.

The next morning "the Moor came out with all his power, with one thousand Turks in advance, to give us battle." During the preceding months some rude palisades had been set up at the foot of the hill on which the Portuguese camped, and this thin and broken defensive perimeter soon became the focus of most of the fighting. With Turkish artillery matching the Portuguese ball for ball, and with a fresh multitude of Turkish arquebusiers doing deadly work against those who were attempting to make a stand at the palisades, Dom Christovão once more decided that the best defense lay in mounting an attack. He therefore ordered alternating cavalry sallies to gallop out from the left and right flanks of the Portuguese position in an attempt to scatter the enemy matchlock-men approaching closest to the stockade wall. Each of these charges proved successful in its initial phase as the Turks were mowed down, then scattered and ran before the Portuguese horsemen, few as there were of the latter. When, however, such advances reached the much more numerous main body of Moorish troops beyond and of necessity had to wheel about and race back to the camp, a deadly volley of bullets from the recovering arquebusiers would inevitably follow them, picking off a few men each time. Da Gama himself was wounded in the leg his first time out, and all of his comrades returned with some kind of injury received after turning their backs to the enemy. Had the Portuguese possessed more soldiers and horses (those from the Falashas' mountain still being in transit), this tactic might eventually have broken the momentum of the Muslim assault, but every man lost was, proportionally, a decrement the Franks could ill afford, and at the conclusion of each sortie three or four *fidalgos* the less regained the precarious shelter of the palisades. As the day dragged on, the world of the Portuguese became increasingly smaller, louder, and lonelier.

> D. Christovão, wounded as he was, went round the positions, encouraging the men: for these are the days when leaders are [revealed.] I have no words wherewith even to express his courage, when[,] looking at the positions and the camp, he saw his men very weary, and the greater number wounded. The Queen was in her house in the direst trouble, weeping for the hour that had come to her. The house was filled with men too wounded to fight, and she, with her women — who that day did their duty in this well — bound up their wounds. They fired many shot into her house, and wounded two of her women.

Grasping the crucial weakness of his strategy, Christovão ordered the interval between the sallies shortened, such that one charge might cover the retreat of the previous one, but by now his men were too exhausted and too few to keep up that kind of continuous riding. Nevertheless, as if welcoming the heightened peril, Da Gama gathered a column from among his decimated cavaliers and charged out once more, only to have his right arm shattered by musket fire, which sent him back to the Portuguese lines in agony. From that point on he became the unfortunate double of his antagonist, waving his sword aloft in his left hand, though his encouragements now began to be ignored. Castanhoso notes, for instance, that "when the patriarch saw affairs in this state, he mounted a mule, and retreated to a hill on our flank," a rare mention of the imposter Bermudez in the old soldier's businesslike narrative. Still, it was now high time for the bravest men to do likewise, if with somewhat more dignity:

> By now many of the Moors were inside the palisades, and of ours there was none to fight, the greater part being wounded or dead. We were compelled to retreat up the hill, which D. Christovão refused, being determined to die. Our men, seeing that it served no purpose to delay, as there was none to fight, made him retreat, telling him that he could see that all the Portuguese were withdrawing, and that those around him were too few to resist the enemy; that for all this, they would all die with him, as honour bade them, but that it would be wiser to join his own men, as the Lord God was pleased to give them that punishment for the sin of all. With this they made him retreat, riding a mule; the Queen preceding him, ready to share whatever fate befell us.

The steepness of the hill up which they withdrew, impossible for horses to negotiate, as well as the desire of the Turkish troops to plunder the Portuguese camp, combined to effectively cover their retreat. At one point a massive explosion turned all heads back toward the scene of their defeat, where one of their mortally wounded comrades had managed to set off the collected bags of gunpowder, rudely interrupting the victors' looting spree. However, between the darkness which had now fallen, the unfamiliar, difficult trails, and the dazed senses of those who stumbled over them, the survivors could not keep together, soon dispersing into isolated bands weakened by pain and thirst.

The next morning Dom Christovão and two dozen other Portuguese took refuge at the bottom of a deep valley among some camouflaging thickets. Here they found a trickle of water and began attending to their wounds. As they had no ointment or bandages, they slew the mule their leader had been riding and used its fat to dress their punctured and mangled flesh. From this hiding place they could occasionally see or hear their pursuers in the distance, but for a while it looked as though they might well evade all patrols. Then, an elderly Abyssinian woman, frightened by the Turks and Arabs who were beating the brush, rushed into the thicket in an attempt to evade them, bringing the Grañ's men directly upon their principle quarry. (The hag escaped, leaving Castanhoso to surmise that she was none other than the Evil One in disguise; one of the more lightly wounded Portuguese also got away, which is why we know the details of Da Gama's capture.) The Commander was seized and brought before Imam Ahmed without delay, who was delighted with the prize, and whose first act was to show his defeated adversary the pile of one-hundred and sixty severed genitals that his men had so-far collected from the Christian dead scattered about the battlefield. He then began to inflict various tortures and humiliations upon Christovão, which included whipping him with gusto, waxing his pointed beard into a candle and lighting it on fire, and having slaves buffet his face with the soles of their shoes. Then, with no doubt supreme satisfaction, he produced the tweezers that the *fidalgo* had sent him some months before, stating that since he and his men never employed such instruments, he had saved them for Da Gama's own use. He then ordered that every remaining hair on his prisoner's face — beard, eyebrows, eyelashes — be individually plucked out. This amusement concluded, Dom Christovão was dragged around by a rope to the tents of the Grañ's various lieutenants, where each dealt with him according to his humor.

Another Portuguese prisoner in the camp who later escaped reported that through all these ordeals Christovão stoically displayed "much patience, giving many thanks to God for bringing him to this, after allowing him to reconquer one hundred leagues of Christian country."[22] This admiring account is quite believable, for even after granting every particle of physical agony that Da Gama suffered its appalling due, one has to admit that in the midst of such torment he was also living out the denouement of his own chivalric dream. There was no glory to be had hiding from one's pursuers in the bushes, but to be tortured to death by the enemies of God — well, that was according to script. It could even have been the case that he found a kind of heavenly equivalence in his final extremity — after all, so much of his courtly dream had been rendered flesh in moments of pleasure, dalliance, and victory; perhaps it seemed fitting that the physical incarnation of its climax be endured in pain, sinner that he knew himself to be. Whatever his thoughts, it appears that the persistent beatific look on his burned and bleeding face finally got on the Imam's nerves, for when Christovão was returned to his tent Ahmed impulsively cut off his head with his own sword rather than sending him back to the Grand Turk as a token of thanks, an act which cost the Left-Handed much good will with his arms supplier.[23] And though the body of this young and impetuous Portuguese knight wound up being flung into an unmarked grave accompanied by the carcass of a dog, one must admit that his life, taken as a whole, seems to defy the moral entropy that usually besets those worldly enterprises — such as the Portuguese conquest of the East — that loudly trumpet their supposedly idealistic motivations. Too often they follow the trajectory of the Crusades — their first act almost attaining the altruism and nobility of their self-advertisements, their second and subsequent phases devolving into cynical scrambles for quick wealth and tyrannical power. But with the Da Gama family the story is reversed: it is the father's undertaking which seems the whited sepulture masking insatiable avarice and egoistic brutality, while the son's appears by comparison to glow with the natural light of higher purposes and genuine self-sacrifice. Dom Christovão was no Gallahad — he could kill an inconvenient prisoner as blithely as any Portuguese who had rounded the Cape — but to compare him with his father is to witness the apple roll uphill from the tree.

Among those of Da Gama's followers who survived the disaster there ran a mixed vein of despondency and determination. Sebla Wangél, for instance, whose fears Christovão had often been obliged to talk into remission, did not, as one might have expected, crumble or cringe when she learned of her champion's death. As Castanhoso relates, she and her ladies

> felt the greatest grief at the fate of D. Christovão, whom they lamented as if he had been her son. The following day she sent for us all, and made us a speech, consoling us for our great loss, and for our contrary fortune; and this in very discreet and virtuous words. We asked the patriarch to reply for us all, encouraging her; and she was pleased, saying that the courage of the Portuguese was very great.

The largest contingent of Da Gama's troops fled westward, linking up with the thirty men who had been fatally slow in bringing the horses from the Falashas' mountain, whereupon this combined group, now numbering close to a hundred, determined to repair to the relative safety of that sky-high fortress to recover themselves and plan their next move. They had not been settled there more than ten days before Galawdewos at last arrived from the south, bringing with him a paltry contingent that would indeed have been far too small to conquer the Jews' massif without assistance. The young *Negus*, "hearing of the death of D. Christovão and of our defeat ... showed such affliction as was to be anticipated, for he came full of desire to see D. Christovão from the fame that had reached him." At first there didn't seem much that this small band of loyal Ethiopians and the reduced remnant of the Portuguese could do other than hide out, but soon something unforeseen began to happen. Apparently, while neither the King alone nor the Franks by themselves could inspire sufficient hope or allegiance among the populace, the presence of the two side by side constituted a patriotic critical mass that could and did, and thus Castanhoso was agreeably surprised by the number of men fit to bear arms "who daily flocked" to their suddenly swelling ranks. Seeing this, the Portuguese decided that revenge against the Grañ might just be possible and began taking several practical steps to facilitate it. Months earlier they had stashed their surplus weapons at Debre Damo, and these were now sent for. Messengers brought news of about thirty soldiers who had fled northward toward Massawa, and orders were given to gather them back. Finally, the Jews' mountain was discovered to be rich in sulphur and saltpeter, and the army's chemist, who had luckily survived, began manufacturing gunpowder at a steady clip.

The question naturally arose as to who was now going to lead the Portuguese in this new and — one way or another — final campaign. Galawdewos offered to appoint one of them to the captaincy, but in the end they opted to march under no new leader from their own number, but rather to simply carry into battle before them "the banner of Holy Compassion." As they informed the *Negus*, "we desired none save the banner or himself to lead us, for it was not to be anticipated that we should follow another, having lost what we had lost." In this poignant manner did Christovão da Gama's former comrades, "bent on vengeance or on death in the attempt," elevate their fallen general into posthumous command of the wounded army that had survived him. By early February of 1543 they were on the march, numbering "eight thousand footmen with bows and bucklers, and five hundred horse, all very fine and well-found men, and one hundred and twenty Portuguese, some maimed, with wounds still open, who refused to stay behind." Their first skirmish — a victory against a relatively small force under one of Ahmed's vassals — provided them with the intelligence that the Left-Handed and his army were enjoying a season of rest on the shores of Lake T'ana, and toward that inland sea they immediately turned their steps.

The landscape encompassing the shoreline of Ethiopia's largest body of water stands in clear contrast to the usual geography of vertiginous cliffs and deep-plunging gorges that makes up the rest of the highlands. Here the plains that lead away from the lake are broad and gentle, the vistas across them long and hazy, and even the tallest and nearest mountains appear only as bluish undulations on the horizon. The relative flatness of the land allows for larger fields of crops than are possible elsewhere in the country, and the whole region is low enough in elevation for the occasional palm-tree to flourish, giving the place a lush and slightly tropical feel. As the lake itself is far too wide to allow one to see its opposite shore from any vantage point near the water, the effect is of gazing out over a strangely placid sea. In short, whereas the rest of Abyssinia seems to have been fashioned by an intention of violence, the precincts of Lake T'ana appear to have been created in a mood of peace. It was thus not surprising that the Grañ had chosen such a spot to rest himself amid the company of his wife and sons after his year-long struggle against the interloping Franks. But he must have choked on his hookah when his viziers anxiously directed his eyes to the mixed force of Ethiopians and Europeans who were emerging from the hills and making a bee-line for his own encampments. When it came to understanding when you were beaten, both the white and black varieties of Christians appeared to be equally clueless.

What may have given Ahmed some small anxiety was the fact that the bulk of his Turkish arquebusiers had gone home, leaving only the two hundred or so attached personally to himself. His opponents did not immediately exploit this advantage, however, since after raising their tents in clear view of the Muslim army they decided to postpone an all-out attack until the contingent of Portuguese who had made for Massawa could join them, for as Castanhoso chauvinistically puts it, "in that country fifty Portuguese are a greater reinforcement than one thousand natives." Neither did the Imam mount an attack, apparently counting on the distinct possibility that the Ethiopian volunteers would begin melting away after a few days of watching his battle-hardened troops ready themselves for combat. As both armies hesitated, there occurred daily skirmishes in the no-man's land between their front ranks, with small contingents, usually of cavalry, venturing out to engage in showy duels with each other. For a few days running the Ethiopians and their allies got the better of these contests, with one Abyssinian general in particular delighting his comrades by demonstrating that one of the Prester's people could kill Muslims from horseback with just as much ease and panache as any Portuguese. Indeed, this officer was so successful that the Muslims decided to lure him to his death by putting out a false white flag and pretending that they wanted a parlay with him. Thinking that some of the Moors had lost heart and were attempting to defect, he rode into the trap and was shot down by matchlock-men secreted in some nearby bushes. However underhanded this maneuver, it worked the intended trick, for upon seeing their most popular general carried back dead into camp "the Abyssinians began to lose their courage, so much so that many advised retreat, victory seeming impossible." Galawdewos was realistic enough to understand the limits of the loyalty he inspired, and so after a quick consultation with the Portuguese he decided not to wait for the last contingent of Franks but rather "to give battle the next day, as he felt that if he waited longer, all his men would disperse through fear."

The martial contest that began the following morning played itself out very quickly, and in an eerily familiar manner. One would have thought that the Imam, having once already taken a Portuguese bullet as a result of encouraging his troops from too near the skirmish line, would have taken care to hang back once the matchlocks started firing. In fact, however, a combination of bravery and exasperation undid him:

The Portuguese, seeing that the Turks were defeating us, charged them, slaying many and driving the rest back; for the Portuguese horse, who were sixty, worked marvels, and the Abyssinians, ashamed to see them fight thus, threw themselves in so vigorously that they left a track as they went. When the King [i.e., the Grañ] saw that his men were losing ground, he in person led them on, encouraging them, and with him was his son, a young man, helping him; they came so near that he was recognized by the Portuguese, who, seeing him close, fired at him with their matchlocks. As all things are ordered by the Lord God, He permitted that one ball should strike him in the breast, and he fell over his saddle-bow and left the press; when his followers knew that he was wounded to the death, they lost heart and took to flight.[24]

As the Ethiopians' own royal chronicles put it, the Imam's army "dispersed like smoke and like the cinders of an oven."[25] Nor was this a mere tactical retreat until such time as a trusted lieutenant could regain command of Ahmed's columns — without the charismatic and visionary leader who had led them from victory to victory over a span of fifteen years the Muslim forces lost the will to fight on, and soon many were headed for the desert lowlands carrying what treasure they could. Perhaps in the end it was only the Grañ himself who had been at peace with the idea of making a home in the mountainous country he had conquered. At any rate, in his absence the people who had helped him subdue it answered their long-suppressed desire to live out their lives amid the familiar heat and flatness of Harrar and Zeila. Galawdewos would have labor enough in years to come mopping up Muslim pockets of resistance here and there about his kingdom, and he would face new challenges as well, but he would never again be threatened with the prospect of becoming the last *Negus* of Christian Ethiopia. Four hundred Portuguese, over half of whom now lay beneath Abyssinian soil, had seen to that.

Our chronicler Castanhoso, after a sort of victory lap around the reawakening country at Galawdewos' side, and after participating in the joyous *Timkat* celebration which capped it all off in early 1544, departed for India in April of that year. In his account of the heroic campaign through which he fought and suffered, there appears from time to time the odd figure he deigns to call "the Patriarch," whom we glimpse always at the periphery of the main action — gossiping with the Queen, leading the occasional public prayer, fleeing a battle on mule-back. This dubious *Abuna*, however, has left us his own narrative of the Portuguese rescue of Abyssinia, though one very different than Castanhoso's in its relentless focus upon the personage it casts as the actual protagonist of the enterprise: none other than Bermudez himself. Indeed, to peruse Mestre Joam's chronicle is to enter an alternative world altogether, wherein an all-wise and utterly sincere man of God just barely prevents a reckless and incompetent Dom Christovão from delivering Ethiopia into the hands of her Moorish despoilers at his first and every opportunity. The onetime physician first claims to have prevented disaster as early as the rescue column's initial march inland from Massawa to Debarwa, during which he asserts that a neurotically prickly Da Gama supposedly "wanted to make the Bernagaiz prisoner, on the ground that he did not give him as good a reception as he desired." Not to worry, though, for Bermudez reassures us that he "did not consent" to this mad scheme of Christovão's, implying that his disapproval could stop the youthful Commander in his tracks. On other occasions, though, Bermudez says he found it necessary to enlist the aid of the expedition's lieutenants in his efforts to prevent Da Gama from doing something stupid. Just before the battle in which the Grañ was wounded, for instance, he says that "D. Christovão did not wish to take [his] advice, but his captains and *fidalgos* told him that he would commit a great error and would ruin himself if he did not follow it," against which consensus the headstrong boy could not hold out. (For good measure, Bermudez also claimed that it was he who directed the shot of the matchlockman who injured the Imam the following day.) On the eve of the next engagement — the one resolved by the sudden explosion of powder — Da Gama was again on the brink of rejecting the Patriarch's sound suggestions concerning strategy until his comrades "told D. Christovão that he ought to agree with it, and follow my judgment, which was that of a father." Thank heaven there was an adult present.

When the tide of battle eventually turned against the Portuguese, however, it had nothing to do with the Patriarch's military advice; rather, it was the result of the Commander's scandalous sensuality. Da Gama first brought dissention to the ranks when, after conquering the Falashas' mountain, he appropriated for himself "the very beautiful wife of the [Moorish] captain." When he then discovered that two of his lieutenants also "desired her greatly, there were jealousies about her," prompting Christovão to "depos[e] them from their captaincies," though, says Bermudez, the lascivious general later "came to my tent, and begged me as a kindness to call the two captains" and "to reconcile him with them." Bermudez did so, but it was sadly too late, for God had already been mortally offended by such antics. And thus when, on the eve of Da Gama's final battle, the misguided leader again rejected the *Abuna's* advice on how to fight it, the mistake was allowed to stand because "God intended to put an end to the sensualities which should not be remembered of Christian men at such time." The wages of sin were all too predictable, and after the disaster played itself out a sorrowful but never-vindictive Bermudez did not hesitate to console the distraught and weepy Christovão, urging him to "remember the victories that God had given him, and [to] thank Him and not go to extremes because of the chastisement He had given us for our sins." The Patriarch was perfectly willing to stay with the wounded man, but the Commander would not hear of it, asserting that the *Abuna's* personal survival "was necessary for the governance of those people, lest they should be entirely lost, and with them all that country." Left alone, Da Gama was soon captured by the Grañ's men, who were happy to have him but naturally wrung their impious hands at the thought of the Patriarch having eluded their grasp. Bermudez's unwavering generosity toward the young man who never appreciated his genius is exemplified in the title of his chapter recounting the Commander's capture: "Of how D. Christovão hid in a Thicket."

Once this great impediment to victory was dead, Bermudez was finally allowed to come into his own. He appointed a new leader of the re-grouping expedition on the basis of merit, though the haughty, blue-blooded *fidalgos* caviled at his choice. But this new general actually turned out to be something of a cipher, for the Patriarch basically designed and executed the final victory against the Grañ from that point on. He was occasionally distracted from his brilliant and wonderfully intuitive war-planning, however, by the necessity of dealing with the late-arriving Galawdewos, whom he depicts as a selfish and ungrateful coward throughout. Eventually, though, he managed to maneuver the unwilling *Negus* into giving battle to the Left-Handed at Lake T'ana, knowing that he himself absolutely had to be on scene "to restrain the King and encourage the people." Indeed, such was his spiritual stature that his mere appearance fired the morale of Portuguese and Ethiopian alike, for "when the people on the hill-tops saw me they raised a great shout, and said: As the Abuna comes, the victory is ours." It is perhaps surprising that Bermudez does not take credit for squeezing off the fatal shot at the Imam himself, but as the Left-Handed's troops flee in disarray the reader is left in no doubt that the real savior of Abyssinia was not the spoiled scion of a famous explorer, but the lowly physician elevated by both innate genius and heavenly Providence to lead a people out of darkness.

Bermudez stayed on in the realm of Prester John for some years after the tumult of war had quieted down, but his subsequent career there was not a particularly happy one. For one thing, Galawdewos (who was anything but cowardly or easily manipulated) did not believe that his father had appointed such a person Ethiopia's *Abuna*. In fact, he didn't believe most of the doctor's claims and eventually wrote a letter to King João asking him to clarify what he felt to be this annoying man's outrageous pretensions. (Eventually Mestre Joam complained that the *Negus* and his court "had treated [him] as the Jews had treated Jesus Christ" by "crucif[ying] Him as a recompense for redeeming them," and that such ingrates "deserved the chastisement of God.")[26] As a result of this royal skepticism, Bermudez was forced to begin shedding his self-appointed titles. Galawdewos, reverting to the age-old custom of his national church, asked Alexandria to send him an authentic *Abuna*, and when one arrived in the late 1540s Mestre Joam had to fall back upon calling himself merely the Roman-appointed Patriarch of Abyssinia, with spiritual jurisdiction over only the Portuguese Catholics who remained in-country. With this in mind, imagine his chagrin when, in 1555, a ship arrived at Massawa bearing a Jesuit who in turn bore the news that the Pope had appointed his own, genuine Catholic Patriarch for that country, who was even now poised to take ship in India. His fantasy world having thus shrunk to claustrophobic proportions due to the incursions of serious people possessing bona-fide credentials, Bermudez finally bid goodbye to Ethiopia and sailed for India and Portugal in 1556, though in psychic compensation he began telling his shipmates and anyone else who would listen that he had actually been consecrated by Pope Paul as the Patriarch of Alexandria, which audacious and unintelligible fiction (Alexandria's Patriarch being a Copt) he maintained until his dying day. Voluble liar though he was, he did not publish his history until 1565, after the release of Castanhoso's the previous year left him apoplectic over that author's scandalous understatement of Joam Bermudez's proper place in history. The doctor's own account, in righting this glaring omission, heaped slanders upon the old soldier who still bore the physical scars inflicted by his desperate battles twenty years before.

When set against the larger drama of Portugal and Ethiopia's entanglement with each other, there appears a kind of imaginative circularity at work in the bright arc of Mestre Joam's audacious impersonations. The Land of Prester John was for so long a repository for European fantasies of outsized riches, supernatural wonders and millennial victories that it seems fitting that Ethiopia should in turn have transformed one of its first European pilgrims into such a fraudulent and self-deluded figure. And yet if Abyssinia somehow initiated the process which turned a barber-surgeon into the Patriarch of three denominations, it must have been the actual nation and not the fantasized one that accomplished it, for Bermudez witnessed the reality with his own eyes for the space of thirty-five years. This realization leads us to the possibility that, in his own way, he might have loved the place. His seamless self-regard is obvious enough in every line of his writing, but that doesn't mean he couldn't have been enamored of a land and a people as well. Perhaps it was precisely his narcissist's passion for Ethiopia that nurtured his fantasies of guiding it, ruling it, shaping it to his own satisfaction. But even if we grant Bermudez his affection, he still stands in stark contrast to that other admirer of the nation, Francisco Álvares. Our priest's love was less audible, for he never possessed a desire to lead or dominate anything Abyssinian—by the end he didn't even want to change the place very much, though it was his sworn duty to do so. No, in the end he just wanted to protect it; and given his office and his duty, that meant in a sense protecting it from himself. It is difficult to imagine a love less contaminated with egoistical considerations than his. And, as we have already seen, in the end it was not the loud and showy suitor who managed to rescue the nation, but rather the quieter man who, in the midst of his own deepening love affair with Ethiopia, possessed the capacity to make a friend or two along the way.

Eleven

Sermons in Stone

The failure of a Portuguese fleet to appear at Massawa in the spring of 1524 cast most of the embassy deeper into a frustrated gloom. The combination of anxiety and fading hope as they waited once more in vain at Debarwa for some news from the sea, the hard truth that their next hope of rescue would not come for another year, and the impossibility of receiving any explanation for their continued stranding must have taken its toll on mind and body. As our priest grimly reports, come June they had no choice but to send a messenger to the *Negus* admitting that "the Portuguese had not arrived, and that we were helpless." In a clear sign that Lebna Dengel was now desirous that the embassy somehow make it back to Europe, he ordered them only as far south as Axum, there to be quartered in relative comfort for the coming year. And, providing an equally clear signal that his anger toward them had been overtaken by more politic considerations, he plumped their larders by granting them "500 loads of wheat ... 100 cows, ... 100 sheep, ... 100 earthenware jars of honey, and another 100 of butter." And, if the coming year of suspended animation thus promised to be one without physical hardship for the Portuguese, it also seemed likely to be passed without internecine strife, for with D'Abreu and his partisans sticking close to their royal champion at Court, Dom Rodrigo held undisputed sway over the bulk of the party quartered at the ancient capital. For his part, Father Álvares took advantage of the relative calm to continue looking about him with keen interest, crucially deepening his understanding of Ethiopia and its inhabitants, especially as to their remarkable expressions of spirituality. But during this time we can also detect a shift in his mood, for as we shall see he began at times to speak like a man who was coming to terms with the idea that the profoundly foreign land in which he still found himself might well become his home for life.

Axum, though much declined from its former glory, was by no means just another Abyssinian town, and our priest even entertained the possibility that Lebna Dengel's purpose in settling them there might have been in part

LARGEST OF THE STANDING STELAE AT AXUM, being cleaned and stabilized at the time of the photograph. These funerary monuments date from the Axumite period between the third and tenth centuries.

broadly educational: "it seemed to us that the Prester John had sent us here, in order that we should see these buildings, and we ... rejoiced at seeing them, as they are much greater than what I write." If, as we shall soon find, Lalibela is the Ethiopia's smaller version of Jerusalem, then Axum is its miniature Rome, and thus Álvares would have walked under the shadow of monuments that were for the most part celebrations of worldly riches and achievements, and which, when they did pay homage heavenward, sometimes reflected a faith that pre-dated Christianity. Indeed, the towering stellae that are the city's most arresting feature are examples of that most profligate and egoistical of architectural genres, the funerary shrine. They bore witness to a time when Axumite emperors oversaw a nation respected by both Roman Caesars and Sassanid Kings, and whose control of the Roof of Africa was rarely in dispute. In Axum's main stelae field the celibate Álvares beheld the results of a social competition whose phallic dimension was clearly visible as column competed with previous column for the honor of being the highest and most satisfyingly ornate. Each king apparently felt obligated to erect one, leaving unambiguous proof that he had outdone his predecessors and (sadly for the state) his successors in commanding the labor of slaves, artisans and engineers to proclaim his glory.

Not that our priest or any of the town's residents could have conclusively

FALLEN STELA AT AXUM THAT MIGHT HAVE TOPPLED DURING ITS ATTEMPTED ERECTION. **It is the largest free-standing piece of stone ever worked by human hands, and may have provided Álvares with a ready-made sermon on the perils of hubris.**

matched the name of a particular emperor to a particular pinnacle — there is great doubt about many of them to this day — but perhaps our priest found this a satisfying object lesson in the transitory nature of worldly splendor. If he did, there was an even starker such homily close to hand, since the most massive — and what would have been the highest — of the stelae was not upright at all but tragically prostrate and broken into several immensely heavy pieces, forming a visually arresting example of prideful overreaching receiving its comeuppance. Whether this immense monolith shattered under the stresses of its attempted erection or whether it was cast down later by an offended Deity remained to Álvares a question lost to the ages.

Given that our priest was housed there for eight months, he must also have had a chance to examine coins from the Axumite apogee that continued to emerge more or less regularly from the local soil. As mentioned before, it is from these delicate but expressive pieces of specie that we can date the actual — as opposed to the legendary — arrival of Christianity in Ethiopia to the reign of King Ezana in the mid fourth century. The process that changed the figures on this emperor's coinage from moons to crosses began when two Tyrean cabin-boys, Frumentius and Edesius, became stranded at the port of Adulis after their master was killed there in a commercial riot at the docks. Brought to Court at Axum, the two young Christians became favorites of the King and, when he died, were asked by the widowed Queen to help her educate her young son, the future monarch Ezana. Frumentius thereafter took a large hand in managing the regency government, simultaneously spreading his faith by organizing the country's small population of resident Christian merchants and by proselytizing both within and beyond the royal household. When Ezana came of age and declared to his tutor his desire to convert the nation to Christ, Frumentius traveled to Alexandria to ask the Coptic Patriarch Athanasius to send Ethiopia a proper bishop. Athanasius, however, after hearing Frumentius' presentation and learning what works of the spirit he had accomplished already, pointed to the young traveler, declaring "Thou art the man!" and consecrated Frumentius himself as Abyssinia's spiritual leader, beginning the tradition whereby Ethiopia's *Abunas* were always procured from Alexandria. Frumentius returned to Axum where he began building a cathedral and baptized Ezana, after which the two of them collaborated in the work of national conversion. Hard on Frumentius' returning heels, however, came an angry letter from the Byzantine Emperor Constantius II addressed to Ezana, demanding that "the same [religious] doctrine be observed equally by Romans and yourselves" and that the Axumite monarch therefore ignore the teachings of Frumentius, who had learned his peculiar brand of Christianity at the feet of that "most wicked Athanasius."[1] The problem was that while Athanasius was a monophysite, Constantius was an Arian, and if Catholics abhorred monophysitism, the Arians — who believed that the Son, far from being consubstantial with the Father, was a separate, later, and lesser creation of God — despised it with a burning passion. At the time, however, Axum was at its zenith and thus largely immune from bullying by the Byzantines, who anyway had problems enough elsewhere. Ezana ignored Constantius' imperious demand, and Ethiopia has continued monophysite to this day.

In fact, though he may not have fully realized it, in walking about Axum Father Álvares could within a short span have put his hands upon stones that represented an impressively wide swath of Ethiopia's history up to that point. From the stelae field it would have been a pleasant stroll uphill past a small reservoir reputed to be the Queen of Sheba's bath to "the two houses under the ground, which men do not enter without a lamp" — that is, to the two large subterranean structures said to be the tombs of Ezana's successors from the sixth century, the emperors Kaleb and Gabra Maskel. From there he could have rounded one of the two promontories that shadow the town and encountered the Church of Abba Pantalewon, almost comically monopolizing the small summit of a very steep hill "ascended by 300 steps" from whose top "men are afraid to look down." This "very elegant small church of great sanctity" was associated with one of the Nine Saints, those Syrian refugees who completed the missionary work begun by Frumentius two centuries before. Circling back toward the stelae field would have brought him in sight of the Cathedral Church of St. Mary of Zion, that same one built and consecrated by Frumentius with his former pupil King Ezana standing by his side. Álvares, swallowing whole the nationalist legends, attributed its construction to Queen Candice (who, recall, was supposedly converted in 10 A.D. by her eunuch, who had himself been instructed by St. Phillip), but he was still probably accurate in calling it "the first there was in Ethiopia." He reports that its name derived from the belief that its altar stone, reputedly a collective gift from the Apostles, originated on Mount Zion, and goes on to say that the structure was in fact "very large," boasting "seven chapels" with "their altars well ornamented," five aisles "of good width and of great length, vaulted above," and walls brightly painted with religious subjects. Furthermore, the cathedral itself was merely the centerpiece of a much larger religious complex that included a pair of "mansions" for the two rectors as well as other structures housing a large number of resident canons and monks. Álvares always got tongue-tied and bogged down in tedious technical measurements when he tried to describe architecture, and he knew it: witness his remark that the wonders of Axum constituted something "much greater than what I write."[2] Could he have foreseen the future, though, his position on the cusp of historical events would have provided him with even more reason to deplore his descriptive failures, for his stumbling account of St. Mary Zion is the only verbal picture of it by a Westerner that survives. Eleven years later the Grañ would reduce the great and ancient cathedral entirely to rubble.

Álvares does not give us much information about his daily routine during the more than half a year he resided amid such doomed or enduring splendor, only mentioning that on one occasion he heeded the locals' assertions that there was gold in the nearby streams and tried to pan for it, unsuccessfully as it turned out. When he came to leave the town at the very end of 1524, however, he did not do so at the request of the *Negus*, but of Zaga Za Ab, who learned that he had just lost a valuable piece of property due to some sharp legal practice and who "begged [Álvares] to go with him to the Court to ask justice for him." This motive for traveling is significant, for it is the first we hear of our priest hitting the road for purposes that were neither diplomatic nor an exercise in amateur anthropology. This willingness to ride for weeks in order to perform a personal favor for someone who was asking his assistance as a friend bespeaks a man who was no longer exclusively a member of a foreign mission, no longer unambiguously a stranger, but rather a person becoming immersed in the mundane purposes natural to someone who just happened to live in Ethiopia. Continually curious about and sympathetic to his antipodal surroundings, it is not surprising that Álvares was also — as we see by his participation in this legal matter — farther along the road of assimilation than any other member of the stalled expedition. But of course that didn't mean he wasn't just as homesick as the rest of the languishing Franks.

When the two men arrived at Court Álvares quickly discovered that the office held by Zaga's adversary made their chances of winning his land back look rather slim. Their opponent was the Court's Chief Page, one Abdenaguo, and "as all the messages went to the Prester through the pages [he and Zaga] had no means of putting in [their] word." Seeing how the ground lay, they immediately appealed to a high-ranking judge who, even though he was a personal friend of the Chief Page, "for the sake of justice ... made [it] known to the Prester how we had come and for what." This soon prompted an inquiry to Álvares from Lebna Dengel, inviting him to explain why he had ridden south. Our priest replied with what appears to have been a well-prepared brief on Zaga's behalf, and one which, tactfully, relied entirely on cool arguments involving diplomatic protocol rather than on the pleader's favored status in the eyes of the King:

> I gave an account of all, and said that the injury and unreasonable thing done to Zagabo, was done rather to the King of Portugal and to us Portuguese than to him, since he was absent from his land and lordship for the service of the King of Portugal and the company of us Portuguese, by the order of His Highness [i.e., the *Negus*], and that his land should be confirmed to him, and not usurped and forcibly taken from him: and that in our countries those who traveled in the service of kings, not only themselves, but moreover their servants, factors, majordomos, property, revenues, and lordships were greatly favored and protected. And so it was hoped that His Highness would favor his Ambassador and order justice to be done, and that he should be restored to his lordship.

In what remained of the interview they succeeded in getting Lebna Dengel to appoint a brace of pages who would relay all their subsequent messages concerning this matter to the King without interference from Abdenaguo, and to designate two of the country's highest-ranking judges, whom Zaga deemed sufficiently impartial, to preside over the case. The pair of appellants then went to see these jurists and the trial was scheduled to take place under one of the Tents of Justice (just outside the royal compound) upon a certain date and at a particular "hour of the sun," which they "point[ed] ... out to us in the sky."

Álvares noted that all Abyssinian law cases were purely verbal affairs, with nothing being written down, including the verdict, and though this seemed to leave the question of legal precedent at the mercy of fallible or partisan memories, that did not in itself prejudice the position of either man in this particular dispute. The question at issue revolved around *gult*— a word which could, depending on the context, refer either to a piece of land managed like a feudal fief, or to the income generated by the peasants laboring upon that fief, or to the rights of an upper-class Ethiopian to control and inherit that income. Land ownership in the Prester's realm was essentially a feudal affair, with landless peasant farmers surrendering a portion of their crops or the income derived from those crops to their land-owning overlords higher up the *gult* system, who in turn might hand off a portion of their feudal takings to the King or some other high official. What this meant was that in the eyes of Renaissance Europeans such as the members of the embassy, the social organization of Abyssinia would have appeared immediately recognizable, and indeed any modern-day social scientist would certainly find little to distinguish the economic system of sixteenth-century Ethiopia from that of Portugal. So who owned the *gult*-land in question, or who had a right to the *gult* produced from that land — Zaga or Abdenaguo? "The judges concluded with the sentence that the land and *gulto* which Zagabo claimed was very small, and that it was subject to another big estate and lordship of which Abdenaguo was lord, and that it was right that the great wind should go into all the land, and thus the revenue could not be denied to Abdenaguo, great lord as he was." All our priest's careful preparation and subtle triangulation of royal influence had thus been in vain, and he reports that he and his friend were thoroughly "benumbed by this sentence."

After licking their wounds for little while, though, they did not hesitate to make more direct use of their extra-legal influence and "complained to the King. He sent to tell us to go to our quarters, and not to be troubled, that all would turn out well, and that next day we should go and plead to the Chief Justice, and he would do us justice." This seemed to auger well, and they accordingly waylaid that supreme jurist on his way to work the following morning. He told them he had already heard something about the case from the *Negus* himself, to whose couch he had even now been summoned, and that he

Eleven. Sermons in Stone

felt sure he would soon have something reassuring to say to them. This appeared to auger even better, and the priest and the Ambassador waited in good spirits for the Chief Justice to re-emerge from the King's apartments. Unfortunately, he did so in the custody of two pages, who summarily dragged him into the presence of the Court "executioners," stripped his clothes from his body, and tied him to the ground face-down and spread-eagled. There he began to suffer one of those potentially deadly but only intermittently agonizing floggings mentioned before, in which perhaps one in three passes of the lash actually hit home. What on earth was going on, and did it involve the two of them as well? It took some discrete inquiries, but before long Álvares discovered that Zaga's case had been overtaken by the *Negus'* desire to conclude some festering family business.

Waiting in line to be flogged after the Chief Justice were two men, one the elderly head of a monastic house, and the other a monk from his establishment, this last aged about forty and appearing "respectable"—that is to say, cultured and aristocratic. This younger monk, writes Álvares with the breezy assurance of a Court insider, had been previously married to the sister of Lebna Dengel's uncle, the former *Negus* Eskender, who had ruled between 1478 and 1494, just previous to Lebna Dengel's own father. At some point, however, the man had separated from his wife and gotten re-married to one of the current King's sisters. This unnamed younger woman, however, "behaved scandalously and did what she pleased," though for a long time her husband "did not dare meddle with this from fear of the Prester, and also because in this country the faults of women are not looked at with much surprise." Still, he eventually got fed up with the serial cuckolding and tried to return to his first wife, which drew the anger of Lebna Dengel, who ordered him to return to his current monarch's sister and make the best of it. Instead of complying, however, the man had decided to flee from both politics and womankind simultaneously and forever by donning a monk's habit and entering a monastery. Thus, the Chief Justice was being flogged for a recent ruling of his declaring that the man had become a monk in the proper legal manner, the old monk for admitting the man into his order, and the younger man for disobeying Lebna Dengel and insulting his sister. Obviously, a mere land dispute among underlings would have to wait.

And there were other official events likely to monopolize the *Negus'* attention during that January of 1525. For one thing, it was the season in which the various provincial governors arrived bearing their yearly tithes to present to His Highness, and Álvares expends a good deal of ink detailing the massive parades of horses, fabrics, and gold bars that were paraded before the royal reviewing stand over the course of several days. Here too, however, a volatile mixture of familial and sexual matters soured the atmosphere. One of the *Bitwaddads* had been tasked with bringing in the annual loot from a province that had once been the special domain of the late Queen Eleni. (Though the farsighted dowager had died in 1522, her memory still drew lines of weeping mourners to her tent, which had been left standing within the royal compound as a memorial.) After duly marshalling the annual payment under the Prester's eyes, however, he was arrested. When, soon afterwards, the Court picked up stakes and began traveling to a new location, our priest caught sight of the prisoner riding past him on mule-back, hung with chains and surrounded by guards, at which moment the unfortunate man reached out to him.

> [T]he Prester's Ambassador and I were by a river feeding the mules, and there passed by this Betudete who brought the *gibre* [i.e., tribute payment], and he said to me *Abba baraqua,* which means "Father give me your blessing." I answered *Izi baraqua,* which means "God bless you." This Betudete was accompanied by fifteen gentlemen on mules and fifty on foot, and we mounted and went on in his company. As soon as I approached him he took my hand and kissed it, and again asked for my blessing, saying, "What do you think of this; do they thus make prisoners of great men in your country?" I replied that in my country, if great lords were arrested for small matters or for the displeasure of the King, they gave them their own houses for prisons and if it was for great things they were quartered in large castles and prisons. He, with tears which ran down the whole of his face, again said to me: "Father, pray to God for me, for I shall die of this."

"This" was not, as one might expect given his recent duty, a charge of peculation. Rather, says Álvares, it "began to be muttered about" that the Prester had it in for the *Bitwaddad* because "he had had to do with his [i.e., Lebna Dengel's] mother," and that while "such had been the report when she was alive," including a rumor that the couple had produced a son, "the Prester did not choose to kill him in the lifetime of his mother [so] that she might not be more disgraced than she was already." Before long the Court gossips were whispering that the *Bitwaddad* had been spirited away to a barren mountaintop somewhere, there to die a lingering death for loving so close to the throne. For Álvares, the saddest aspect of the whole affair was the sight of the man's five sons traveling mutely after the migrating Court, bare-chested except for the black sheep-skin draped over one shoulder connoting patient submission to the *Negus'* pleasure, silently imploring the vengeful King for some word of their father's fate.

There were other arrests, including that of the *Tegre-makuannen,* and the other of the two *Bitwaddads,* though it remained unclear as to whether either of these supposed infractions also had a Freudian coloring. Throughout this month of political purges Álvares speaks as a man who had become quite knowledgeable of the scramble for suddenly vacant positions among grasping courtiers, whose proper names now come easily to his tongue. "In those days when we were at the Court, the other Betudete, who had been arrested, was deposed from his office and Araz Anobiata, who was Barnaigais, was made Betudete," while "they made Balgada Robel Tigrimahom." He is also willing to display his command of the whispered complaining that ricocheted about beneath the careful public pronouncements of the *Negus'* officials: "There was a great rumor and talk at the Court about the death of Queen Elena. They said that since she had died all of them had died great and small, and that while she lived, all lived and were defended and protected; and she was the father and mother of all, and if the King took this road [much longer], his kingdoms would become deserts." Had things worked out differently than they did for Álvares, these gossipy snippets give hints as to a possible alternative future for him as a favored fixture of the Ethiopian establishment, his naturally social nature and foreign birth making him a favorite dinner guest among those climbing the greased pole of the Prester's favor. One can almost imagine him eating his way through several platters of injera and honey wine well into the night, speculating with would-be movers and shakers about who was up, who down, and who about to be entirely out. Fortunately, though, a different destiny awaited him.

The last event that kept Lebna Dengel from settling Zaga's suit was the arrival of the queen of a tributary Muslim kingdom complaining that her brother-in-law was in revolt against herself and the Prester's writ. This was apparently the sister of that princess whom Lebna Dengel had earlier refused to marry because of her large front teeth, though Álvares gives no indication whether this lady in distress was burdened by similar features. As there was an extra measure of soldiery around the Court during the month of tribute collection the *Negus* quickly dispatched a force of *chavas*, or mounted warriors, to suppress the rebels. However, when word later arrived that the pacification campaign was stalled, Lebna Dengel decided to gather yet more fighting men and lead them into battle against the Queen's enemies himself. This incident is worth mentioning chiefly because of who accompanied the King on this military venture — none other than Jorge D'Abreu, who had been basking in the *Negus'* admiration of his martial displays for some time. What is frustrating, however, is that his departure to battle the Moors alongside Prester John is the last we hear of this turbulent *fidalgo*, and Álvares provides us no clue as to his ultimate fate, or as to whether or not the monarch's "own Abyssinian" ever retuned to Portugal. It may be that D'Abreu found outlet enough for his violent inclinations in Ethiopia's constant skirmishing against her Muslim neighbors. As for our priest's silence on the matter — well, it may have been that his relief at not having to endure a passage home with D'Abreu and De Lima circling each other on the same crowded deck accorded him such deep relief as to require no further comment.

Amidst all the flurry of activity and intrigue, Álvares reports that *Timkat* came and went without he or Zaga "pressing our request further, because we did not dare on account of the great affairs which we saw going on." However, they had not been forgotten, and before he departed for the wars "the Prester sent to call us" and gave satisfaction at last. He "took away from Abdenaguo, our adversary, the lordship which he held, and he bestowed on his Ambassador both the land which we were claiming and that lordship which he had taken away, and so he dismissed us very pleased."³ It was apparently a pleasant enough parting between the ruler and the traveler, though one which, given the busyness of the day, seems to have passed without any special marks of either formality or intimacy. It may have been that after so many false departures on Álvares' part—this was, in fact, the forth time he would be leaving Court, and the third to supposedly board a Portuguese ship for home—that both men might just have assumed the odds were in favor of them seeing each other again a year or two hence. But it was not to be—the lawsuit's happy resolution would mark the last meeting between the Ethiopian monarch and the Portuguese priest whose unlikely mutual affection had set in motion events that would eventually preserve Abyssinia from destruction. From here on, though they would both continue to struggle for the same ends, they would do so continents apart.

Because the lands returned to Zaga by the lawsuit lay not far off the northward road to Debarwa and Massawa, Álvares accompanied the Prester's Ambassador when he officially re-took possession of his estates, after which the two men pressed on toward the Red Sea. As it turned out, though, the embassy's dreams of finally starting homeward in earnest were to be frustrated yet once more. Álvares' description of his and his comrades' emotions at the failure of a Portuguese fleet to appear again that spring communicates heartache despite its stoic terseness. "Half way through Lent we arrived where our people were, with a great longing that the Portuguese would come for us that Easter. When Easter passed, which was the monsoon, and nobody came, we were sad as before." By now the chronicle of their balked attempts at departure made for dismal recollection. No fleet had arrived in 1521 or 1522; when one had in fact showed up in 1523, they had been prevented from meeting it; and now no ships had appeared in either 1524 or 1525. What was going on in the *Estado da Índia* to account for such repeated failures? The short answer was that by this time Portugal's eastern empire had metastasized to a point where resources could simply not be found to send a fleet into the Red Sea every year. In finer grain, the man who had been Governor of India since 1521 was not only incompetent, but also preoccupied with mutinies both at Hormuz in the Persian Gulf (where the Portuguese had a sizable trading center) and along the west coast of India itself. In 1524 an exasperated King João had gone so far as to send out the venerable Vasco Da Gama as Viceroy in order that he might put a bit of his famously heavy stick about, but the old explorer had died at Cochin in December of that year, and so the embassy was looking with false hope toward an *Estado* that was still enveloped in turmoil.⁴ To the great Albuquerque the Ethiopian mission had been the central facet of a glittering millennial enterprise; to the men who now ran the Portuguese East, however, it was a half-forgotten sideshow amidst a bureaucratic nightmare.

This time the order from Court decreed that the Portuguese were all to remove to a region close by Zaga's estate for the coming year. They were at first reluctant to do so, since that land lay considerably south of their previous quarters at Axum. "We were in great doubt as to whether we should make this journey or not, because it removed us a long way from the sea, and by very hard traveling we should not be able to reach the sea from that country in less than one month, and this with long marches." In the end they acquiesced — they could hardly do otherwise, dependent as they still were upon the *Negus'* dole — but they resolved among themselves to remain there no longer than the following January and thence to make for the sea once again without waiting for official permission. Over the coming months, while the rest of the embassy hunkered down to enjoy (if that was the word) yet another season of idleness and official hospitality, Father Álvares again heeded the pull of his curiosity by venturing out into the surrounding countryside to visit sites of interest, especially those possessing a religious significance. By now his half-decade of rambling through God-intoxicated Ethiopia had brought him face-to-face with many striking monuments of piety and spiritual imagination, but even so he could not have been fully prepared for what awaited him as he began to investigate the country of mountains and ravines round about Zaga Za Ab's fiefdom. This is because a day or two's ride to the south lay Lalibela, a city transformed into a religious site during Abyssinia's medieval Zagwe Dynasty, and the setting for the most haunting — and subversive — Christian architecture on the planet.

The Zagwe line of kings ruled Ethiopia between the downfall of the Axumite Empire and the rise (or as some would have it, the "re-establishment") of the "Solomonic" dynasty of which Lebna Dengel himself was a self-consciously proud continuer — that is to say, roughly between the late ninth and late eleventh centuries. Though accounts of their flourishing — most written long after the fact by bards of various Solomonic regimes — generally portrayed the Zagwes as an unfortunate interruption in the otherwise unbroken chain that linked the current *Negus* to Old Testament Jerusalem, no such chronicler ever attempted to downplay the churches of Lalibela or dissociate them from the other glories of Ethiopian civilization. They are startling, even weird — but no Abyssinian would wish to claim that they do not embody something central, something vital to the spirit of a country whose isolation from Mediterranean Christianity both transfigured and intensified its commitment to its faith. And thus although the town, when it served as the religious center of the usurping dynasty, was called Roha, for centuries the Zagwes' Solomonic successors had been at peace in naming it Lalibela, after the Zagwe king deemed mainly responsible for fashioning its chiseled wonders.

Unlike sojourners approaching sixteenth-century Rome or Jerusalem, no pilgrim on the road to Lalibela was ever greeted by the sparkle of sunlight glinting off pillars or steeples afar-off. Because the roofs of Lalibela's stone cathedrals are more-or-less level with the surrounding landscape, and because the town itself resides upon the gentle convex of a wide mountain flank, one comes upon them unexpectedly, at that startling moment when what the eye has been hitherto perceiving as an oddly symmetrical rock formation suddenly redefines itself into the ceilings of a sprawling subterranean city. It is, to say the least, a challenge to describe the churches of Lalibela in a manner that does them even minimal justice. Álvares made a giddy hash of it, prompting his tireless Victorian translator to complain in a footnote that "the descriptions which follow are very difficult to interpret," since "Álvares appears to have had little understanding of architecture." The earnest man even conjectures that "the text appears to be corrupt in places," to the extent that "much of the translation can only be tentative." But that is alright — our priest's wonder comes through well enough, and therein lies the truest account of the place. It is necessary, however, to begin with a clear explanation of what Lalibela's rock-cut churches are, which is inseparable from some speculation about how they were built. But "built" is not even the right word, for they were not built at all, in the usual sense, but rather excavated and sculpted into being.

First of all, visualize several hundred feet of relatively soft, volcanic rock lying under the topsoil of the town. If one had wanted to build conventional churches with this material, the procedure would have involved quarrying it, shaping it into portable blocks, and then stacking these in such a way as to raise walls, pillars, and roofs above some suitable piece of real estate a reasonable distance away. At Lalibela, however, huge square or rectangular blocks of such tufa (to use the proper scientific term) were isolated in place from the surrounding geology by means of wide trenches dug down into the stone to a depth of up to 50 feet, and which turned four 90-degree angles. This operation resulted in an exposed monolith with only its base attached to the underlying rock, and which was now completely surrounded by an extensive sunken courtyard. First the outsides of this block were chiseled to either an exacting smoothness or into the iterations of an elaborate ornamental pattern. Then, at the place that would eventually become the completed church's main door, and through an opening that could never become any larger than that portal's intended proportions, the artisans began hollowing-out the interior of the structure. But the truly miraculous thing is that this hollowing-out was no mere lithographic melon-balling designed to form some rude inner cavern, but rather a meticulous process of sculpting designed to replicate from living rock the same features found inside a conventional cathedral: pillars, arches, aisles, altars, chapels, and even tracery widows — every architectural and ecclesiastical feature that would have been either required or desired in a church raised upon the highest ground of a Christian city. And one must understand that these resulting interior structures are no mere "cave-man" parodies of their sunlit counterparts, but rather faithful duplications in everything from their load-bearing capacities to their most delicate and understated decorative filigrees. It is this unexpected, almost unbelievable fidelity to the world above that Álvares stumbles over himself to communicate when describing the largest of the edifices, Bet Medhane Alem (i.e, the Church of the World's Savior):

> It has five aisles, in each one seven square columns.... The[se] columns are very well worked, and there are arches which descend some way and are a span in thickness below the vault. The vaults are very well worked, and of great height, especially the centre one, which is very high. The rest are in proportion.... In the highest part of these aisles there is much tracery, such as rose-windows, or keystones, or roses, which they put on the vaults, on which they make roses and other graceful carvings. On the sides it has very beautiful windows with much tracery, long and narrow in the middle.... The chancel is very high, and the canopy above the altar is very high, with a support at each corner. All this is made from the same rock.

It is that last sentence, standing apart as if after a catching of the breath, which best conveys our priest's understandable awe: "all this is made from the same rock."[5] Were these things to be found within a regular cathedral they might be impressive enough, but to see and understand them to have been hewn from one undifferentiated hulk of stone is to become dizzy at the very moment of comprehension. Thus Castanhoso, in the midst of his later description of the place, repeats this amazing central fact as if to convince himself of its mind-bending reality: "Each church was formed from one stone, excavated on the inside with a pick," and "all from a single rock, with no other piece of any kind" for "in the whole edifice of the church there was nothing brought from the outside, but all cut from the same living rock."[6] One cannot blame him: to stand within one of the stone-carved churches of Lalibela is akin to entering a dream-world in which the Laocoon and David were somehow sculpted from the inside out.

It is worth taking a few moments to contemplate the daunting practical difficulties attending such an enterprise. Consider, for instance, the problems of measurement, for surely one of the hardest feats accomplished by the artisans was knowing exactly where to *cease* excavating along particular tangents radiating from the original opening in order to preserve the rock that would soon become the pillars and other interior features. Consider too the accuracy required when delimiting the interior walls, for while it is one thing to make the outside of a monolith plumb, it is altogether a different matter to match that exterior verticality with an interior one a mere foot farther in, which must be achieved while digging ever upwards inside what is still at that point a darkened cave. And then there is the irrevocability of even the slightest miscalculation or errant blow of the hammer, for whereas in a conventional building one can simply cast aside the marred block and substitute another, within these sculpted edifices every mistake is forever. Fearful symmetry indeed. The patience and exactitude of the architects must have been impeccable, the coordination between the workmen of a military caliber, the anxiety among everyone incessant. It is thus unsurprising that most of the legends surrounding the construction of the churches speak of supernatural inspiration and aid. The Ethiopian Royal Chronicles recount how the young king-to-be Lalibela was transported by angles to heaven where God showed him ten cathedrals hewn from stone, saying "it is not for the passing glory of this world that I will make you King, but that you may construct churches like those which you have seen." These sources go on to relate that when the time came to begin construction, angels descended upon Lalibela's court and that it was they who "made the measurements, indicating the required dimensions for all the churches, large and small." And then, so they claim, as work began in earnest this heavenly host took up the shovels and pickaxes laid down each evening

BET MEDHANE ALEM (CHURCH OF THE SAVIOR OF THE WORLD) is the largest of the rock-cut churches of Lalibela. The entire edifice, including the exterior columns shown here, was cut and then hollowed from one continuous piece of volcanic rock.

by the mortal laborers, and for each cubit carved out by the former during the day these industrious spirits removed another three by night.[7]

As to why the King Lalibela of history dedicated so much of his treasure and time to the construction of these houses of worship (or at least the commencement of their excavation), no firm answer is yet at hand. One theory has it that the rise of Islam was the catalyst, in that when Saracen control of the Holy Land made the regular and popular pilgrimages to Jerusalem prohibitively perilous, the monarch decided to build a kind of domestic Jerusalem within the safe confines of his own country, to which his people could journey in order to fulfill their spiritual obligations without endangering their lives. It is for this reason, say some, that the small stream which divides one cluster of the rock-cut cathedrals from the other is named, rather grandly, the River Jordan.[8]

Certainly Álvares, as he wandered in stunned admiration from church to church through the narrow trenches that connect one sunken courtyard to another, remarked the great variety in the buildings' sizes and architectural styles, as if the layering of centuries visible in the jumbled holy places of the

BET MARIAM AT LALIBELA, WITH ITS DISTINCTIVE PORCHES. Many of the rock-cut churches now reside under the protection of UNESCO scaffolding to prevent their further deterioration from rainfall.

actual Jerusalem had also been duplicated there by diverse geniuses within the space of decades. For instance, the massive Bet Medhame Alem (8,500 square feet), whose interior he described above, is surrounded by a portico supported by thirty-six external columns (all cut from the same original block as the church proper), which bestow upon it a somewhat classical appearance. Meanwhile Bet Mariam, a much more intimate church close by it, features small porches over each of its three entrances under which one could easily imagine a rural vicar shaking hands with his departing congregation. Farther on, Bet Emmanuel, another giant of a place, is built in imitation of the grand palaces of the Axuminte period, its outside a layer-cake of alternately recessing and projecting bands, with the mimicry carried right down to the inclusion of the faux timber gable-ends whose actual counterparts were a signature of King Ezana's palaces — a sort of Ethiopian Gothic revival. One of its proximate sisters, the smallish Bet Abba Libanos, is unique even amidst Lalibela's competing oddities. This tabernacle seems to have been intended to mirror Emmanuel and the other monoliths, given that its four vertical sides were tunneled free from the surrounding rock, until at some point the striking choice was made to keep its roof attached to the overhanging ledge, making it appear as some sort of fantastic squat stalactite that has grown down from the roof of the entrance to a cavern. As if in mimicry of the original Jerusalem, King Lalibela's Holy City thus gives one the impression of multiple strains of Christian faith attempting to outdo one another in grandeur or in the expression of competing notions of spiritual fidelity.

The courtyards' vertiginous outer walls, when they do not contain the narrow tombs of pilgrims and martyrs (whose mummified feet can still be seen protruding today) are sometimes the home of cave churches, dug into the rock with no attempts to expose their opposite sides to the daylight. Some of these structures boast interiors every bit as highly finished as those of their freestanding brethren — Bet Golgotha, for instance, in which Lalibela himself is supposedly entombed, also features seven life-size relief sculptures of saints at various points around its walls, which Álvares described as "so well done that they seem alive." Others that are more roughly hollowed, however, are reminiscent of the chapels of Rome's Catacombs, viscerally communicating the early Christian atmosphere of a faith still practiced in secrecy and primitive purity.[9] Indeed, amidst all the towering rock, the narrow communicating trenches, and the nearly subterranean chambers, it is easy to come to a wrong conclusion about the whole Lalibela complex — that it must have been at one time defensive in nature, built to withstand the attack of some remorseless Muslim hoard from the deserts below. But this is a canard, for no one engaged in medieval warfare in Ethiopia or anywhere else ever built a defensive position at the bottom of a well. The Grañ, for instance, had no trouble capturing the place, though he apparently evidenced some frustration at the impossibility of

BET EMMANUEL AT LALIBELA. This church, though built long after the Axumite period, is executed in the Axumite style—note especially the stone "timbers" projecting from around the windows. This demonstrates the unbroken nature of cultural memory in the Ethiopia that Álvares encountered.

burning it down. Abyssinia possessed military strongholds enough in its towering *ambas*; the churches of Lalibela, for all their massive solidity and bunker-like appearance, faced down all worldly dangers only with a radical vulnerability, and could only have entrusted their safety to the power of prayer.

They do, however, project a powerful idea, for in their strange autochthonous radiance they stand as an unsettling critique of centuries of upward-aspiring Christian architecture. What they possess, powerfully and ineluctably, is a grandeur utterly devoid of vanity, such that after seeing them one cannot look upon a Chartes or a Hagia Sophia without newfound doubts that those grand piles, pushed toward the clouds in the name of reverence, may be compromised by an irreverent pride. Indeed, who is to say that there is not something truer to the core of Christ's message to be got by descending into the earth to worship than by craning one's neck within a structure that presumes to soar heavenward? Whatever the answer, there is without doubt one particular aspect of Christian doctrine that the churches of Lalibela express more powerfully than any place of worship bathed in sunlight, for they are living *momenti mori* that nevertheless

Bet Giorgis at Lalibela, breathtakingly beautiful in its symmetry and proportions. This view gives the lie to any notion that the churches were hewn from rock for defensive purposes, since an attacker would have a significant advantage of height.

bespeak a labor of love and devotion so audacious and outsized and unlikely that it overawes the terrors of the grave. They are enough to make even a doubtful Christian believe that most extravagant of promises, that his narrow coffin might also be his New Jerusalem.

Álvares, though he visited Lalibela relatively late in his long sojourn, placed his description of it — as he did with that of Axum — close to the beginning of his book, turning to the remarkable pair of cities as the embassy's first inward journey reached its respective closest approaches to each. He appears to have settled on this arrangement in order to convince his skeptical readers early on that the Ethiopians had something not just strange or unsound to offer their fellow Christians, but something usefully different, something that eloquently penned a chapter in the chronicles of material piety that a self-satisfied Europe did not even realize it had left blank. Before he assaulted his audience with disturbing facts about circumcision, divorce, unchaste priests, and all that leaping during mass — and before he began his silent omissions of

AN INTERIOR VIEW OF BET MICHAEL AT LALIBELA, showing the remarkable precision with which the monolith was worked. At every point of the interior excavation, the architects would have had to calculate exactly where to *stop* cutting in order to sculpt (or rather, leave in place) perfected columns such as this one.

things much more dire — he wanted to demonstrate to them that the Abyssinians practiced an orthodoxy of intensity that was every bit as admirable as any conformity of gesture or formula. And if one can feel in our priest's clumsy but enthusiastic iterations of this many *covados* of height and that many handspans of width the anxieties of a man nervously attempting to get ahead of and redirect his reader's negative judgments, one can also hear at the end of it all his realization that he had probably failed to accomplish this aim.

> I weary of writing more about these buildings, because it seems to me that I shall not be believed if I write more, and because regarding what I have already written they may blame me for untruth, therefore I swear by God, in Whose power I am, that all that I have written is the truth to which nothing has been added, and [that] there is much more than what I have written, [but] I have left it that they may not tax me with its being falsehood[,] so great was my desire to make known this splendour to the world.

Francisco Álvares was an honest man and a careful observer of the alien realm through which he traveled, but the rock-cut churches of Lalibela defeated him. That in itself is a fair testament to their wondrousness.

Had Álvares' Jesuit successors in Ethiopia been as susceptible to the stone-carved sermons of Lalibela as he, many tears and much blood would have remained unshed. Unfortunately, most emissaries of the Catholic Church who followed our priest had made up their minds long before they left Europe that all Abyssinians were carriers of a virulent disease called monophysitism, and that it served no purpose to coddle the patients by delaying the painful procedure needed to cure them. In their view, there would be plenty of time to tour rock-cut churches and other curiosities once the heretical priests who infested them were thrown out (or burned) and their altars had been re-sanctified in the True Faith. This state of affairs emerged because, while Father Álvares may have held his tongue about the country's doctrinal errors, others did or could not. As soon as the embassy arrived back in Portugal various Inquisitors began pressing Zaga Za Ab and the smattering of Ethiopian pilgrims in Rome about the specifics of practice and belief in the Prester's realm and confirmed their darkest suspicions quickly enough. But the truth of the matter was that even a decade before the first Jesuit debarked at Massawa the acrimony had already commenced, with both sides in no doubt about what the other believed or what was at stake in the differences between them. For instance, as early as 1543, when Bermudez, the self-styled Roman Patriarch, first met Lebna Dengel's son and successor Galawdewos on the eve of their final victory over the Grañ, the two men soon became engaged in the game of who's-the-real-heretic. Bermudez knew full well that the Ethiopians were monophysites (and if he knew, then Álvares certainly had known), and attempted to convince the young *Negus* that his father had (under Bermudez's own guidance, of course) actually converted to Catholicism before sending him back to Europe as an ambassador.

"Therefore, confirming yourself with the will and rule of God, and imitating the virtue and intelligence of your father, you should submit yourself to the Holy father the Roman Pontiff, as thus you will do what God orders, and will have for friends, brothers, and helpers in your necessities, the King of Portugal and all the other Kings, his brothers and friends." To which he, not considering what he was saying, like a young boy, replied as follows: "You are not our father, nor a prelate but Patriarch of the Franks, and you are an Arian, for you have four Gods [i.e., Father, Holy Spirit, and a two-personed Christ] and you are not in future to call yourself my father." I turned and told him he lied, for I was not an Arian, and had not four Gods; and that as he would not obey the Holy Father, I held him to be excommunicate, and accursed; and that I would no longer be with him, or speak to him; with that I got up to go. He replied that I was excommunicated, not he.[11]

Clearly, part of what made Álvares and Lebna Dengel's working relationship possible was the fact that the former was either too wise, or too aware of his own limitations, or too respectful of Ethiopian culture (or all these things together) to attempt to convert the latter. When later visitors to Ethiopia abandoned such reticence, disasters quickly followed.

In 1555 a priest named Rodrigues arrived at Massawa in order to sound out Galawdewos about the prospect of accepting Catholic missionaries, only to be told by an embittered and long-marginalized Bermudez (who was now eager to get home) that only armed intervention could force the *Negus* to give up his heresy. Rodrigues then proceeded to Court, looked about him, and promptly penned a treatise entitled "The Errors of Ethiopia and the Truth of Our Holy Faith," which the Emperor read even though his *Abuna* forbade him to do so. Far from buckling at the supposedly ironclad logic contained in this piece of presumption, Galawdewos wrote a "Confession of Faith" as a rejoinder, in which he defended the Ethiopian Church against the charge that it followed Jewish practices by, among other things, explaining that Abyssinians circumcised their sons not because of a religious belief, but rather simply as a social custom, in the same way that other African societies scarified their faces or slit their ears. As for the Saturday Sabbath, he declared,

> [w]e do not honor it like the Jews ... For the Jews do not draw water, or light a fire, or cook a dish of food, or break bread, or go from one house to another. But we celebrate the Sabbath as the day in which we offer up the [Sacrament], and we make feasts thereon, even as our Fathers the Apostles commanded us.... For on the Sabbath our Lord Jesus Christ rose from the dead, and on it the Holy Spirit descended upon the Apostles in the upper room in Zion, and on it the Incarnation took place in the womb of Saint Mary, the perpetual Virgin, and on it [Christ] will come again to reward the just and to punish sinners.

In the long run, though, it was not regular clergy like Rodrigues but the Jesuits who were going to manage the conversion of Ethiopia, and in 1557 Bishop Andre de Oviedo, S. J., a Spaniard, arrived at Arquiquo. Galawdewos came to enjoy aggressively debating religious matters with the Bishop, but he wasn't about to assist him or his fellow Jesuits in spreading Frankish heresy around his nation, a stance which eventually prompted Oviedo to write a circular advising Christovão da Gama's ageing veterans (who had never found passage home) and their families not to mix with their schismatic hosts, since they continued "refractory and obstinate against the Church." When Galawdewos was killed in battle while attempting to conquer the Muslim city of Harrar the Bishop entertained high hopes, but the succeeding *Negus*, Minas, hated where his older brother had merely disdained, and reportedly had on one occasion to be restrained by his queen from strangling Oviedo with his bare hands.[12] Minas forbade the Jesuits from preaching altogether and banned further marriages between the Portuguese veterans and Ethiopian women, banishing the Bishop and his fellow priests to a hardscrabble existence in a remote quarter of the country. Minas was himself killed in battle in 1563, but the resulting period of civil war was no more propitious for evangelization than the previous decades of relative peace, and Oviedo dragged out the rest of his life in a thatched hut so devoid of resources that he was reduced to writing to the Pope upon the torn-off margins of his breviary.[13] (The Pope wrote back advising him to relocate to either China or Japan, where the Order's prospects looked brighter.[14]) When he died in 1577 with only two other Jesuits left alive in-country, it looked as though the Society of Jesus' mission to Ethiopia had died with him.

Early in the next century, however, the Order's Abyssinian enterprise was revived by a most remarkable man, and one whose attitude toward the Prester's realm strongly partook of the curiosity, sympathy, and patience evidenced by Álvares. Pedro Paez, born in Spain and educated in Portugal at the venerable University of Coimbra, had meant to arrive in Ethiopia some years before his actual landfall there in 1603. On his first attempt to reach the Red Sea from India, however, his vessel had been seized by pirates and the young Jesuit spent seven years in various modes of captivity across a swath of southern Arabia, including a stint as a galley slave, until finally being ransomed back by officials of the *Estado*. Undaunted, Paez sailed again for Massawa as soon as his health and circumstances allowed, this time reaching his destination without incident. From all reports he was the sort of man whom almost everyone took an instant liking to, and one who made it clear that his first priority was to learn all he could about Abyssinia by listening intently to what its people told him. Ironically, though, his winning manner made all too quick a convert of the reigning *Negus*, Za Dengel, who announced soon after meeting the charming man that he wanted to become a Roman Catholic. Paez, alarmed at this precipitousness, counseled the King to take things slowly and thoroughly prepare the nation for such a change, but his advice was ignored. Za Dengel made his conversion public and then threw gasoline on the fire by publishing an edict banning observance of the Saturday Sabbath. As the priest had feared, powerful segments of the nation rose up against the *Negus* and he was soon deposed, forcing Paez to lay low until the political situation again sorted itself out.

When the Jesuit was again invited to Court in 1610, this time by the *Negus* Susenyos, he found the new King to be keenly interested in theological matters and open to weighing the merits of the Catholic faith against the Ethiopian, but also considerably more prudent than the impulsive Za Dengel. For his part, Susenyos took an instant liking to Paez, remarking that "Whenever I set eyes on him, I look upon an angel." Paez soon became a fixture about the roving capital and instituted a regular discussion group on theological topics, prompting several nobles to move their tents closer to his in order to facilitate the frequent meetings of this fashionable klatch. Defenders of the Ethiopian Church became increasingly disturbed as first the *Negus'* brother and then other prominent men publicly went over to Rome, and they could not help but notice that Susenyos impulsively cheered every time one of the Jesuits scored a debating point off one of their own. Chief among these monophysite partisans was, understandably, the current *Abuna*, a man named Simon whose reputation at Court had been tarnished by stories that he kept a harem and exposed his unwanted bastards to be eaten by hyenas. He reacted against the *Negus'* growing affection for the Frankish priests first by excommunicating all those who held that Christ possessed two natures and then by extending his anathema to anyone who aided or even greeted a Jesuit, which by definition included Susenyos himself in the circle of the reprobate.

For his part, the Emperor was already well down the road to conversion, though he was determined to act incrementally. He wrote secretly to Rome (though the *Abuna* discovered the ploy) and then, in 1614, called the nation's scholars and abbots together for a grand council that he hoped would nudge the Abyssinian Church away from monophysitism. This meeting, however, bore all too great a likeness to the ecumenical councils of the early Christian era, in that monks and other clergy showed up armed and ready to gain their point by force rather than argument. It quickly degenerated into a shouting match, Simon publicly denounced the Emperor, and the departing clerics returned home and began inciting armed rebellion against the crown. These uprisings the *Negus* succeeded in putting down, but from here on in the price he would pay for his religious convictions was an incessant state of civil conflict, sometimes cold and brooding, often hot and bloody.

Susenyos did not ask Alexandria for another *Abuna* when Simon died in 1617, and by 1620 he had renewed and strengthened a previous condemnation of monophysitism and gone on to make it a punishable offense to observe the Saturday Sabbath. Still, it was another two years before the committed gradualist openly took communion and was himself officially received into the Catholic Church at the hands of Paez. When the latter died soon after, the *Negus* wrote to the Jesuits in India, crediting the growing adherence to the

Roman religion in Court and country to the example of Paez's kind and respectful behavior toward the Ethiopian people, which was far more effective than any theological argument in winning converts: "his humility and modesty were as great as his learning, and his cheerfulness and address were such that even those who hated his opinions loved the man." Citing the fifth-century heresiarch of monophysitism, he called Paez the "bright sun of the faith that cleared Ethiopia of the darkness of Eutyches."[15] In this last, however, he spoke too soon: not because his own cautious Catholicization of the country wasn't working — it was, just — but because the person chosen to replace Paez would prove as different from his beloved predecessor as night from day.

Bishop Afonso Mendes was a man who enjoyed the regalia and ceremony due his office. When leaving for the East he asked to be fitted out with special vestments from the Papal Wardrobe so that he might overawe "an uncultivated people" (the request was denied) and, though cautioned by the Jesuit Provincial at Goa to keep a low profile, he entered that city with such solemn pomp that the Turks were immediately tipped off as to his destination and mission. When he arrived at Susenyos' court early in 1626, accompanied by five musicians and two valets, he introduced himself to the assembled crowd with a 30,000 word speech crammed with classical quotations, which detailed the history of the wicked monophysite heresy and explained that he was there to stamp it out once and for all. The next day he issued a proclamation ordering that all Ethiopian priests were to desist saying mass until they had been presented to himself for re-ordination, that all churches would be closed until such time as they could be re-consecrated, and that no layman could be sure of heaven until he was re-baptized in the Catholic faith. Even the Abyssinian ban on spitting in church — so obviously the prejudice of "an uncultivated people"— was to be revoked.[16] Susenyos, who had hitherto done everything one step at a time, apparently felt obligated to obey the prelatic authority of the Church to which he now belonged, and therefore promulgated an order making Catholic observance compulsory on pain of death, surely with deep misgivings. No doubt many of his subjects thought it more than a coincidence that the year of Mendes' arrival was marked by drought, starvation, and serial plagues of mice, monkeys, and ravenous hyenas.[17]

Predictably, the various brush-fires of opposition against the *Negus* now swelled into conflagrations. By 1628 the country was in a state of full-blown civil war, and Susenyos was crisscrossing the highlands putting down one revolt after another that took as their rallying cries the ancient faith and customs of Ethiopia. And while the King was successful in routing each rebel army that came against him, he became increasingly fretful about the divided country that he would leave to his son, Fasilidas, and increasingly heartsick at the necessity of killing his own subjects on battlefield after battlefield. Things came to a head in June of 1632, when Susenyos toured the aftermath of an engagement in which 8,000 Abyssinians had been slain. Fasilidas, walking at his side, exclaimed, "How long shall we thrust our swords into our own bowels?" Mendes, who thought any amount of bloodshed to be justified by the cause of Catholic conversion, recounts how the rest of the *Negus'* advisors now seconded the son's anguish:

> "Look," they said, "not one of these men whose bones cover the earth is a foreigner; there is not one of us but has lost a brother or a son or someone bound to us by ties of blood. Whether we are vanquished or whether we vanquish, it is the same, we are the losers. It is five years since we did not have arms in our hands .... The cause of this plight is the name of the Roman faith.... If you do not permit these peasants and ignorant people their ancient customs, the kingdom is lost to you."

Mendes obviously thought the Emperor should have disdained such sentimental defeatism, but Susenyos was sick of fratricidal slaughter. Taking counsel with his son and lieutenants, he reluctantly issued a decree restoring the Ethiopian Church before the month was out, declaring that "We first gave you this faith [i.e., Catholicism] believing it to be good. But innumerable people have been slain.... For which reason we restore to you the faith of your forefathers. Let the former clergy return to their churches, let them restore their *tabots*, let them say their own liturgy. And do you rejoice." We are told that in response to this news the capital "rang with shouts and acclamations" as if the populace had secured "some great deliverance from the enemy." Before long a spontaneous ditty was being sung by all and sundry that lauded the early-Christian promulgators of the monophysite faith:

> At length the Sheep of Ethiopia freed
>   From the bold lions of the West,
> Securely in their pastures feed.
>   St. Mark and Cyril's doctrine have overcome
> The follies of the Church of Rome.
>   Rejoice, rejoice, sing Hallelujahs all,
> No more the western wolves
>   Our Ethiopia shall enthrall.

After a few days of such delirious celebration, collective re-baptisms into the old faith were held as well as "a general circumcision," the latter of which must have been quite a remarkable sight.

Taking no part in these festivities was Susenyos, who immediately abdicated in favor of Fasilidas and went into a steep physical decline. By September the broken man was on his deathbed, from which his last words declared his unwavering faith in the Catholic religion that he had failed to convince his countrymen to adopt either by reason or the sword, and in whose cause he had hardened his own heart until it finally shattered from self-reproach. Once

Fasilidas succeeded to his father's throne, he lost no time in expelling the Jesuits and closing all Abyssinian ports to any European whatsoever. When Mendes wrote to him refusing to leave, he replied, "What does you Lordship mean by saying, 'I have vowed not to leave Ethiopia?' Your Lordship is not leaving Ethiopia — it is she who has left Your Lordship! Your Lordship does not fly from her, she has fled from you!" Mendes wrote to Goa asking for Portuguese troops to reinstate Catholicism by force, but the *Estado* had no intention of opening a new front in a country that had been an ally until the Bishop himself set foot upon it. This fanatical Jesuit tasted the dregs of humiliation when, having fallen into the hands of the Turks after his ejection from the Prester's realm, he watched from a cell in Suakin as the next *Abuna*, freshly requested by Fasilidas from Alexandria, passed through town on his way to the *Negus'* court.

The expulsion of the Jesuits by Fasilidas (and his hunting down and hanging of those who attempted to secretly remain) marked the beginning of an era of self-imposed Ethiopian isolation from the West that lasted until the nineteenth century. And though a Portuguese influence persisted, most visibly in the impressive European-inspired castles that Fasilidas and his descendents constructed at the new fixed capital of Gonder, Edward Gibbon's wry remark that from this point on "the gates of that solitary realm were for ever shut against the arts, the science and the fanaticism of Europe" was true enough.[18] The reason why the Jesuit mission to Abyssinia ended in blood-soaked folly and failure is easily stated: of the Society's three principle spiritual emissaries to that land — Oviedo, Paez, and Mendes — only the middle one possessed a temperament at all comparable to that first displayed to the Ethiopians by Francisco Álvares. Only Paez was anxious to understand the culture before he attempted to change it; only he possessed the empathy to feel how deeply centuries-old customs take root in a people's sense of themselves; only he cared not a straw whether the work of conversion was accomplished during his own lifetime. And perhaps after so many years amidst an alien but zealously Christian culture, Paez also came to occasionally suspect, as Álvares seemingly had, that the God he worshipped was large-hearted and patient enough not to reject a prayer murmured at a Saturday mass or directed toward a single-natured Savior. After seasons on end of witnessing Ethiopians worshiping in joy and suffering in patience, who knows what self-questionings occasionally disturbed this or that certainty embraced in his youth? Granting such seditious moments their say may have been the secret of his success, for if both Father Álvares and Padre Paez are still remembered with fondness by Ethiopians to this day, it is not merely because they arrived brimming with Christian love — no doubt Oviedo and Mendes were lousy with that dangerously volatile stuff as well — but because they had the courage to open their hearts to the quieter, complicating, redeeming tincture of doubt, both of their own purposes, and those of the God they labored to serve.

Twelve

Duty's Prisoner

The Portuguese had vowed that come what may the spring of 1526 would find them properly positioned to step aboard a rescue fleet, whether such an undertaking actually materialized over the horizon or not. In consequence, before January of that new year was half out they had decamped from the territory around Zaga's estates, where they had been boarded for over six months, and headed directly for Debarwa in the province of the *Bahr-nagas*. This determination to take in hand whatever portion of their own destiny they could grasp can be heard in Álvares' assertion that they left the precincts of Lalibela without official permission from the *Negus*, and that "neither did [they] wait for the Ambassador [i.e., Zaga Za Ab], nor inform him, so that he should not encumber [them], but [rather they] went on [their] own." But could this have been literally the case? True, they were a long way from Court, but Zaga at least was close at hand and it is difficult to believe that even their preparations for such an unsanctioned departure could have been effectively concealed from him. And then too, it seems unlikely that our priest would have actively colluded in deceiving a man he had obviously become close to. A better explanation is that Álvares' statement reflects a resolute decision by the Portuguese that Zaga both knew about ahead of time and understood the reasons for, but which he needed some plausible deniability concerning, just in case the fickle Lebna Dengel came up with some last-minute notion that might again imperil the foreigners' departure from Ethiopia. As it turned out, the Portuguese were wise to have acted as they did.

Zaga's reaction to the removal supports the notion that he had prior warning of it, since it was entirely practical and not in the slightest apoplectic: "the said Ambassador, as soon as he knew of our departure, sent two men after us begging us to take them with us, and to send one back with any news there might be of the Portuguese." The whole thing has a choreographed air about it. Indeed, if anything, Zaga's manufactured surprise shows how far he was willing to go to aid the wishes of Álvares and his countrymen, since it was clear that when it came to the movement of his officials around his country, Lebna Dengel didn't countenance any surprises. One need only recall that the officers who arrested the imploding embassy back in 1521 had suffered a despairing indecision about where to proceed with their prisoners in the absence of orders from the *Negus* covering such a circumstance (and that although their decisions seemed blameless they were both eventually sent back to Court to "receive punishment") to understand the consequences of unauthorized rambling. Some scholars have used various comparisons between Lebna Dengel's reign and those of his predecessors to postulate that the early sixteenth-century was a period when the central authority of the *Negus* was in decline and the feudal lords he claimed to rule were establishing independent and dangerously centrifugal power-bases around the nation. However, everything we can gather from our priest's account paints the picture of a polity in which the regional grandees were well-advised to ask royal permission before so much as saddling a mule.¹

Arriving in Debarwa the embassy found themselves on familiar ground, for over the course of their Ethiopian sojourn they had spent what cumulatively amounted to two years in that anteroom of escape. Despite their iron resolve not to miss any European ships, however, it still made more sense for them to wait there instead of pushing on to the torrid littoral at the escarpment's foot. Therefore, says Álvares, in phrases that strain to conjure up the luck they were aching to encounter, "we sent two men to the sea to bring us the good news that our Portuguese were coming for us." On the last day of March, the eve of that year's Easter Sunday, these scouts reappeared in Debarwa, but their countenances prefaced a ghastly tale:

> [T]hey came desperate and senseless, and they began to say, "There are no Portuguese there to come for us, nor are there in India, for all are routed and India is lost"; and they said that they learnt this news from the Moors of three ships which had arrived at the island of [Massawa] with much sounding of music and festivity, and very rich merchandise, and that with much festivity they had disembarked at the said island. These Moors gave this news because such was their wish, and in asserting it they relied on the capture of a Portuguese galley close to [Diu], a port of the King of [Gujerat, in India]. These Portuguese who brought this news came senseless and fainting, and we were the same at this news, so bad for us.

It was a vividly appalling picture these messengers presented, what with Muslim sailors capering into the *Negus'* port to the tune of cymbals and pipes, so free were they from the need for caution now that once mighty Portuguese India was no more than a smoldering ruin. These dire tidings appeared all too plausible to the members of the embassy, since in the years preceding their own disappearance into the Abyssinian interior the *Estado* had been repeatedly threatened both by hostile Muslim fleets emerging from the Red Sea and by restive and conspiring Hindu principalities all up and down the Malabar coast.

Their countrymen had always managed in the end to beat back such attacks, but several engagements had teetered on the edge of disaster, and now it appeared that the fortunes of war and the favor of the Almighty had shifted away from the Portuguese East. It did not take long for it to become apparent to all of them that they were now stranded beyond all hope of return. Among the hardest hit by this latest and heaviest blow was Father Álvares, beacon of optimism and forbearance though he had hitherto been. Indeed, he was so miserably downcast that when Dom Rodrigo said to him, "Father, let us say mass to-morrow very early, and commend ourselves to God," he gave a most uncharacteristic reply: "I answered him that my heart was not quiet nor in such tranquility that I could say mass, but that we would go very early to the chief church and hear mass with the Barnagais." For the last seven years our priest had consistently put the spiritual welfare of others before his own, but at this moment his vision seems to have been wrenched sharply inward by disappointment, forcing him to admit that he could be no fit vessel of grace for his companions since his own heart was newly hardened with resentment toward the inexplicable purposes of God. Thus it was a bleak and solitary vigil they each kept that night, and the dawn of Easter day seemed to bring only a lifeless round of rote gestures, for "when the morning became light and the mass of the Resurrection was finished, the Barnagais invited us to come and dine with him, [but] we excused ourselves on account of the feast day, and because each of us wished to honour his own quarters: and we did this because we felt so little joy." Given the new and seemingly hopeless circumstances that now hung over the Portuguese, not even the most joyous day of the Christian calendar could produce much Christian fellowship, either between the Europeans and their Ethiopian hosts or even among the envoys themselves.

Father Álvares, however, had previously invited "eight Portuguese and Genoese" (the latter from among the Prester's resident Franks) to dine with him later that afternoon, and this gathering he did not cancel, though it was clear that he was not up to it. Our priest had never concealed his enjoyment of a hearty supper spiced with company, and perhaps he thought that this shared meal would snap him out of his gloom. It did not—in fact, he had to leave his guests abruptly in order not to burden them with a display of sorrow and bitterness he could no longer conceal. "When we had done eating I left them in the house with my nephew who always accompanied me, and I went alone up a steam as far as a great rock which made shade on the sand of the river, and I wept all the way, and with tears and sighs I laid myself down in that shade for more than an hour." His grief is not difficult to fathom, for didn't he actually have more to mourn for than the rest of his fellows? After all, they had largely stumbled through the last half-decade at the mercy of outward events and their own ungoverned passions. If the tale of their destinies was now fated to peter out in the inglorious obscurity of an unending exile, well, that was shame enough for the toughest man, but just one more blow of fate, really. But Father Álvares must have had some inkling that he had been instrumental in altering the *Negus'* determination to detain the embassy, and thus in preventing — or *seeming* to prevent — just such a slow debacle years before. And while it is one thing to be just another traveler on a doomed quest, it is quite another to have quietly slain it's nemesis, and yet still live to see it fail.

Just at that moment, however, our priest discovered, or rather, rediscovered, something within himself— some reservoir of resilient energy and calming humility that had served himself and his heedless compatriots so well over the last six years of reiterated balkings. Listening to the murmur of those deep waters, his blank paralysis melted away, to be replaced by a vision, like that attributed to the biblical Ruth, of endurable tomorrows lived out far distant from the land of one's birth.

> [S]topping my tears, I recovered myself, and talking to myself I said: "Now this comes from God, and he is served by me in this land: the Lord be praised for ever since it is so. I know this country better than any native of it does, because I go in pursuit of game, and know its mountains and waters, and the land which is good for cultivation and which will give all that is planted or sown in it. I have got good slaves and fourteen cows, and I have got rams which I will exchange for ewes. I shall go off near to some water, and have a strong bush fence made to keep off the wild beasts, and I shall pitch my tent in which I can shelter with my attendants, and I will make a hermitage within, and each day I will say mass, and commend myself to God, since the Lord is pleased that I should be here. I will order the bushes to be cut so I can make gardens, and I will sow grain of all sorts: and with my crops and game I will support myself and attendants and servants." With this I was comforted, as though good news had come to me, and I arose and returned down stream to my house.

This was a remarkable re-imagining of his future, for the life he foresaw for himself was markedly different from that he had so far lived, excepting the vital continuity of his faith. In this vision the world traveler becomes sedentary, the social companion almost solitary, and the rescuer of others now attends to his own salvation. Here the order and simplicity of his day-dreamed retreat seems at once both a modest reward for a duty fulfilled and a tonic of spareness for some deep psychic wound or acknowledgment of sin. In Álvares' intriguing mélange of hermit's cave and pleasure dome, he becomes a simple Abyssinian farmer and herder, though he lives not under thatch as they do, but in a tent, as if he were a humbler version of the *Negus* himself. There is no thought of accumulating riches or extending his demesne, and yet the slaves and other attendants never disappear either. In this Half-Way Covenant with the religious virtue of *contemptus mundi,* pride in his sagacity about soils and crops and climes makes comfortable a life now circumscribed within a simple, well-chosen shelter from the haunts of vanity. And of course there would be some hunting.

Reentering his own house, he discovered that the time of his absence had worked some good in the mood of his companions, for there sat "the Ambassador Dom Rodrigo and the Portuguese and Genoese, and all our company, playing and enjoying themselves." Perhaps after so many cancelled embarkations, even this new and irrevocable one was robbed of some of its sting. At any rate, De Lima was already thinking about the most comfortable way to live out his days as a resident Frank, and asked of our priest, "Father, what shall we do?" Answering his own question before Álvares could respond, he said: "My opinion is that we should write to the Court to our friends to say to the Prester John that he should order us to return to the Court." This was sensible enough, as there were few places in Abyssinia better fitted to the tastes of a European than the environs of the royal compound, provided one could inure oneself to its migratory nature. Álvares' reply, however, was interestingly self-revelatory. "I answered him: 'Do not do it, [for] I may never come back if I go there.'" He must have realized that the one kind life in Ethiopia that might tempt him away from his newly conceived rural hermitage would be that of a sought-after social insider amid the King's jostling courtiers and yes-men. It was a statement that displayed clear-eyed understanding of his own weaknesses, but Dom Rodrigo was quick to point out that the decision of where they pitched their tents might not be left in their own hands. "And when he said to me, 'What shall we do if the Prester orders us to go?' I answered, 'If His Highness sends to say that the Portuguese should come, and does not say let Father Francisco come, as he always says, I shall not go: and if he names me I will go, even though I should regret it.'" In the moment he pronounced that phrase — "let Father Francisco come, as he always says" — it must have occurred to our priest that his very closeness to the *Negus* might doom his spiritual aspirations, for Lebna Dengel was not the man to deprive himself of the company of someone whose presence he consistently enjoyed.

Naturally enough, Álvares' dinner guests now wanted to know, if he didn't wish to return to Court, where exactly he *did* desire to go. Amusingly, their enthusiastic reaction to his explanation threatened to overrun his solitary cloister with a passel of gentleman-farmers.

> And when he asked me what I would do if I did not go, I gave him an account of how I had gone after dinner up stream as far as the shade and had lain down; and of the thoughts I had had, and the decision I had taken, and that I had come away comforted. All that were there arose and embraced me except the Ambassador, who did not agree to this; and all of them said, and each one separately: "This is a thing which comes from God, and we will all go with you, and we will bring our wives and sons and slaves; we have got very good mules, and we know the sea very well and the markets of the country, and some will remain with you, and others will go and trade, and we will grow rich, and we will make a town of our own in which we will breed cattle, and we will make big tilled fields."

Their sights set on riches and the kind of sprawling estates that Da Covilhã and the other longtime captives now enjoyed, they remained oblivious to Álvares' desire for a spiritual sanctuary. We are told that "when the Ambassador heard this he answered nothing," but for once Dom Rodrigo didn't instantly pull rank — even he might have realized that in the changed circumstances his authority as head of the Portuguese embassy was quickly attenuating into vapor. At any rate, far from arguing further with Álvares, he made the friendly suggestion that they all go hunting the next day and then eat the catch as their dinner at his own house. Unsurprisingly, our priest reports that this idea "pleased [him] very much."

This next day's outing came off well, for Álvares says the company "rode out to hunt, and killed many hares and three or four bustards, and went to have supper at the house of the Ambassador." It was after this native game had been festively consumed and night had fallen, and when "all of us [were] going home to our quarters, and all with me to conduct me to mine," that once again breathless tidings reached the embassy. "There came up to us on the road a servant of mine named Abetay, a married man of the country. And he came running so fast that he could not speak from fatigue: and he began to say: 'Sir, sir, the Portuguese on the sea.' I asked him: 'Abetay, who told you this?' He replied, 'A man said it who has now arrived from the sea and is with the Barnagais.'" To the credit of his honesty, Álvares includes the stuttering prolixity of his own reply to this news: "Abetay. If this is true, of nine mules that I have got, five of mine and four of my nephew's, excepting the one the Prester John gave me, on which you cannot ride, I will give you the best, and I will not sleep until I see this man." He accordingly made a bee-line for the Ruler of the Seaboard's compound and shouted for admittance at the gates. He does not say whether the current *Bahr-nagas* was the same passive-aggressive lordling whose disdain had cost the Portuguese so much pain and delay back in 1520 — almost certainly it was not — but the attitude that Frankish business could wait was apparently a prerequisite for the office, and thus our priest got no satisfaction until breakfast.

When he finally obtained an interview with the man who had come from the coast, it turned out that the fellow's information was at best equivocal. No, he had not seen any Portuguese ships himself, but everyone in Massawa and Arquiquo had heard bombards being fired out among the Dahlak Islands on Easter morning, and had drawn the conclusion that there must be Christian ships in the area, which intelligence he had been tasked by the Sultan of Arquiquo to bring to the attention of the *Bahr-nagas*. Álvares, who knew that Muslim ships sometimes fired salutes to mark the new moon's arrival, did some quick calculations to see whether Easter morning had coincided with such an advent. It hadn't, but this was hardly the certainty they were looking for. Huddling with the rest of the embassy, it was decided that, per their agreement with the Prester's ambassador, one of Zaga's men should be sent south to tell him that their countrymen might be in the offing, though some pessimists among the group (or were they merely realists) insisted that "this firing of bombards was [only] the Moors rejoicing on being assured of the loss of India." After so many disappointments, they all knew well the embittering dangers of dashed hopes, and yet most could not help but harbor them anew.

Mercifully, they had not long to wait in so agonizing a limbo, for that very night "while we were thus neither believing nor disbelieving either the good or the bad news, there came to us a letter from Eitor da Silveira, Captain Major of the Indian sea, who had come for us, and [who] was stopping in [Massawa]." Their long ordeal of deferred hopes and suspended destinies was at an end — they were going home. The story told by the Muslim sailors about the fall of Portuguese India had been nothing but a cruel hoax. Says Álvares concerning this moment, "here I do not know how to say how pleased we all were, except that we went out of our senses, so great was the joy." This was no doubt true for some matter of minutes, but our priest soon took it upon himself to insure that there was no unseemly race to the beach. Messengers with an answer to Da Silveira were sent immediately toward Massawa, but when Dom Rodrigo declared that they would all follow suit the next morning, Father Álvares objected. "I said that it did not seem to me a good thing; because, up to this time we had been held to be Christians, and if we travelled on such a great feast, they would say that we were not, and that [consequently] we should keep the Octave [of Easter] until [next] Monday." It can only be a tribute to our priest's undiminished authority — spiritual rather than temporal — that the embassy, though giddy with a desire to depart homeward at last, complied with his wishes.

When the exiles finally reached Arquiquo on Saturday, April 14th, they came accompanied by a sizable host, for the *Bahr-nagas* had decided that the Portuguese fleet must be welcomed with all official pomp, and thus personally escorted Álvares and his companions to the sea at the head of a retinue of 1000 on mule-back and 600 on foot. In addition, their party merged en route with the regular Massawa-bound caravan, which further swelled their numbers. It must therefore have looked to Da Silveira's sailors as if the Portuguese standards descending the escarpment were swaying at the head of a sizable native army. Although by noon of that day the embassy had completed erecting their camp outside Arquiquo, there was no rush toward the ships, for the *Bahr-nagas* insisted that he must formally present the envoys to their newly-arrived compatriots, a ceremony which could not properly come off until the following day. Still, admits Álvares, "at night, when we were at liberty, we went to see our people, and they us." There must have been much to talk about, though one can also imagine that members of the embassy spent some time pinching their countrymen and tapping the timbers of their vessels, just to prove to themselves that they were not merely dreaming their deliverance. Next morning, reports Álvares, under a blazing sun and amidst oppressive heat "the Barnagais and his Captains, we going with him, led us to where Eitor da Silveira was, and delivered us up to him with much pleasure and joy." The Ruler of the Seaboard presented the Admiral with cows, sheep, fowls and fish to replenish his ships' stores, and the latter reciprocated with bales of Indian cloth and pepper. The next day saw the arrival of Zaga, who had ridden hard from the interior as soon as he had been informed that the rescue fleet might be nigh. With the *Negus'* ambassador to King João now also formally transferred to Da Silveira by the *Bahr-nagas,* all seemed in readiness for the lot of them to depart.

It was at this moment, however, that runners arrived from Court, bringing a message from Lebna Dengel that, given past experience, the embassy must have been anticipating with a good deal of dread. They first announced that the *Negus* had received "news by Zeila that the Portuguese fleet had entered the Red Sea, and that they thought they were coming for us." If there had thus remained any doubt that back in 1523 the King had known that a previous convoy had been approaching when he summoned the Portuguese out of its reach, this hasty and perhaps inadvertent admission clinched it. The rest of the message seemed to threaten a repeat of that earlier foiling: "Since it was a long time since we had left his Court, and we might be displeased, that we should at once return to him, and he would give us much gold and clothes, and would send us joyful and contented to the King of Portugal his brother." But was Lebna Dengel actually attempting to prevent them from leaving once again? This seems very unlikely, given that ever since the incident of the map he had consistently appeared to facilitate their return. Rather it is the mention of the gifts that points toward the King's actual motivation. It was the old defensiveness and gnawing anxiety about how Ethiopia would appear to its distant Christian sisters that probably yanked this last and utterly impractical idea from Lebna Dengel's brain. Now that the Portuguese were actually leaving, his fear of national inadequacy had been re-ignited and he wanted one more chance to load down the returning Franks with sufficient splendor to widen the eyes of his European counterparts.

We need not speculate about the embassy's feelings concerning this summons, and in rejecting it they encountered no second-guessing from the Admiral, whose eyes were fixed upon the narrow seasonal window for escaping through the Gate of Tears. "Eitor da Silveira answered, and we with him, to the said *calacems* [i.e., messengers], that by no means could we turn back, nor could he wait, nor did the monsoon allow it, and that if we did not go away now at once, other ships would never come for us, [but] that his Ambassador [i.e., Zaga] might return if he liked." Because the *Negus'* letter was couched in the form of a request to the embassy and Da Silveira, but *ordered* Zaga to comply, the Prester's Ambassador now found himself in a true subordinate's

TWELVE. *Duty's Prisoner* 267

conundrum, with conflicting orders to, on the one hand, return to Court and, on the other, to stick with the embassy which was definitely about to depart for Europe. Performing some rough out-year calculations about the probable royal mood given each alternative, he eventually "replied that by no means would he return without us because [Lebna Dengel] would order him to be thrown to the lions." This last detaining hand having failed to grasp its prey, Álvares says that "we were all very pleased," except of course the messengers, whose "labor had been in vain." At this point, however, the *Bahr-nagas* piped up with quite reasonable concerns about one of the King's orders being defied on his territory and indeed under his very eyes — he apparently had visions of waving good-bye to the Portuguese and then finding himself recalled to Court in order to stretch a lion's belly. The only solution to hand was for the Europeans to write an elaborate and flowery letter of apology and exculpation to Lebna Dengel, which was signed by both Dom Rodrigo and Da Silveira but which was almost certainly written by Álvares, for his knowledge of both Amharic and of the missive's recipient was far better than anyone else's. To this the *Bahr-nagas* added his own no doubt fawning account of his heroic bodily attempts to prevent the stubborn Franks from leaving, whereupon both were sent south accompanied by a sweetener from the Admiral in the form of additional bales of pepper, fine linen, and velvet, as well as large quantities of sandal-wood and other aromatics.[2] These final farewells to Prester John having been duly dispatched, the members of the embassy waded out to the fleet's longboats and pushed off forever from the country that had been their abode for the past six years.

Father Álvares did not pause to record his emotions at that specific moment of leave-taking. That he had come to appreciate, respect, and love the Ethiopian people is clear enough, but at the same time it must have been difficult or impossible for him to have experienced the unimpeded force of such affinities while the very people (and the land itself) they encompassed continued to be implicated — either by commission or association — in his own imprisonment. He had been the author of the embassy's liberation and he had wept bitter tears at the thought of never being able to go home, and yet at the same time he had immersed himself in the country far more deeply than any of his fellows and had quickly made his peace with the prospect of remaining there forever. And so as the Abyssinian shore retreated, perhaps he found himself the victim of a sudden and painful ambivalence. What we know for certain is that once the realm of Prester John was far enough over the horizon for Francisco Álvares to accept how strongly he would always miss it, he decided to honor those feelings by honoring the charge given him by that nation's monarch, despite the mountain of misunderstanding, bigotry, and indifference his much-altered homeland would heap up in his path. In the years to come, whatever the obstacle confronting him, he persisted in his efforts to reach the Pope and deliver to His Holiness the letters addressed to him from Lebna Dengel, letters which urged the Pontiff to strive for a united and peaceful Europe toward which the Lion of Judah might finally reach out a hand in fellowship and confidence of victory. If he made himself a pest in the process, if he gained the reputation of a crank upon the subject, that was no matter, for he possessed the courage that all those who genuinely love possess when their dearest cause is at issue: he wasn't the least afraid of looking foolish.

Before he could prove his fidelity amid the courts of Europe, though, he first had to reach them, and that spring the Red Sea was practicing its usual torpid malignancy. For three days out from Massawa the monsoon blew steady and favorably, but on the fourth day it failed, bringing the fleet up short in sight of that long-established Portuguese graveyard, the Kamaran Islands. However, as if intent upon proving that his own brand of Christian faith made him immune from any fear of spirits, Álvares used the enforced delay to go ashore and visit one particular grave. Remembering that back in 1517 he had marked the final resting place of Duarte Galvão — the patriarch of the millenarian faction who had originally been chosen as the first Portuguese ambassador to the *Negus*— our priest determined to recover his remains. Taking only a single slave with him, and revealing his purpose to no one else except "one Gaspar de Saa, factor of the said fleet, who had been brought up in [Galvão's] household," he searched either at dawn or at dusk, or perhaps even by the light of the moon, for the modest marker he had planted nearly a decade before. This secrecy was necessary because if Father Álvares was not superstitious, the same could not be said of the Portuguese sailors, who would have mutinied at the knowledge that a human skeleton was being taken aboard their ship. "I ordered him to be dug up, and all his bones to be collected and put in order ... in a little box, [after which] we brought his remains to the galleon." More than just a posthumous act of friendship, our priest's gathering of Galvão's dust was akin to a soldier's care for the remains of a fallen comrade once the battle has been won, for as we have seen it was Father Álvares, not Dom Rodrigo, who had managed to keep the skeptical and wary Lebna Dengel open to Galvão's dream of an ambitious anti-Islamic alliance with Portugal. Duarte Galvão had likely died believing that both his and his son's life, ended by the incompetence of Lopo Soares, had been thrown away upon a doomed enterprise, but could he have only read the letters that Father Álvares was now carrying away from Ethiopia's *Negus*, he might have held out hope that his grand strategies for Christian conquest were still alive. At any rate, our priest's clandestine activities seemed to please at least one quadrant of the heavens, for "as soon as we had got the said remains on board the galleon, the wind changed to a fore wind, and that hour we set sail, and [the] factor said to me: 'Certainly, as Duarte Galvã[o] was a good man and ended his days in the service of God, so God gives us a good wind for his sake.'" Before the week was out they had safely cleared the Gate of Tears.

During the remainder of his journey home to Portugal, Father Álvares experienced many of the near-disasters that were regular fare in the world of sixteenth-century sea journeys. These included seeing a man washed overboard, going for days with only a few drops of fresh water, sailing in a dangerously heeling vessel, and rescuing emaciated castaways from a small boat. Between such routine encounters with death, our priest spent some time ashore in Ormuz, where he attended the ceremony at which Dom Rodrigo delivered to the current Governor the letters Lebna Dengel had written to that man's predecessor six years previously. Later while in India, he himself sought out Duarte Galvão's son Antonio and handed over to him his father's bones, after which our priest accepted that grateful captain's invitation to travel back to Lisbon on his ship rather than that to which Dom Rodrigo and Zaga had been assigned. Álvares' galleon, which because of its heeling could not keep up with its fellows in the convoy, wound up rounding the Cape of Good Hope on its own. Such was a common occurrence, but once they reached the Azores they were required to wait until a proper squadron could be reconstituted from ships homeward bound from Guinea, Brazil, and other far-flung Portuguese possessions. The reason for this precaution was one which would have spread a deep frown across the *Negus'* countenance: it was done, reveals Álvares, in "fear of the French," who were then plundering the shipping of King João and several other Christian sovereigns. In this aspect at least, some things in Europe hadn't changed much at all since his departure twelve years before. The French gauntlet was, however, successfully run, and our priest's ship entered Lisbon harbor on July 24, 1527. The city he could now see spread before him, though not his native place, must surely have done duty as the shorthand for homecoming on many a restless night in Abyssinia, but close as he was at that moment, he was not to enter it anytime soon on account of another common hazard of the sixteenth century. Soon after they dropped anchor "a caravel came out with a message from the King our lord, saying that His Highness ordered that those who came with the embassy of the Prester John were not to land in Lisbon, because it was prevented by the plague." Instead, they were to board smaller boats that would take them fifty miles upriver to Santarém, from which town they would then proceed by land to His Highness' summer Court at Coimbra, all expenses paid. Forgoing the long-anticipated feeling of Lisbon's cobblestones beneath their feet was frustrating, but at least they could console themselves with the fact that King João appeared anxious to meet them.

Before their transports for the journey up the River Tagus arrived, however, their ship was also visited by a bevy of craft assigned to transfer its cargo of spices and other commodities to the *Casa da Índia,* Lisbon's entrepôt for the fruits of eastern trade and the spoils of imperial conquest. At that waterside complex of warehouses and bureaucratic offices His Majesty's absolute monopoly on the resale of cinnamon, pepper, and cloves was overseen and his thirty percent tax on all other commodities imposed. Álvares reasonably enough believed that his personal items of bedding, clothing, and various souvenirs lay outside the purview of the *Casa*, and thus arranged for such items to be carried into the safekeeping of another one of his nephews, who was the agent of a nearby monastery. However, he later learned that an order of sequestration had been levied by the *Casa's* officials against his linens, and that their minions had raided the holy sanctuary and made off with "all that was good and choice, and left [only] the old and worn." In the eyes of the taxmen, the embassy to the great Preter John of the Indies was apparently just another money-making outfit required to fork over the King's share of whatever it had managed to haul back from the ends of the earth.

Long before our priest discovered this theft of his traveling clothes, however, he had donned a new set, for once landed at Santarém he reports that the envoys dressed themselves "in the Portuguese fashion." (Does this mean that Álvares had adopted the robes of an Ethiopian priest at some point during his long stay in Abyssinia? It would fit with much else we know of him if he had.) Unfortunately, Dom Rodrigo went overboard in this regard. He had been given two captured Moorish pilots by the embassy's rescuer, Eitor da Silveira, and he now insisted on dressing them "in *pelotes*, waistcoats, jackets, shirts, trousers, shoes and caps, to present to the King." This might have caused no harm were it not for the fact that their first day of road travel onward from Santarém took place, according to our priest, "in the greatest heat I ever felt." The envoys were tramping along in three separate groups, so Álvares had neither De Lima nor Zaga in sight as all of them began to quickly succumb to the torrid atmosphere:

> The King's servant took me out of the town, and we went to stop at the Almonda bridge, where I thought I should die of the heat. Our Lord was pleased that I should find a lodging with much cold water, and a very good host, who when he saw me thus began to encourage me and give me cucumbers and cool wine, with which he cooled me and drew out the heat. Upon this Dom Rodrigo arrived galloping on a horse, shouting and saying, "For the love of God bring me up some animals, for the Moorish pilots of the King and my slaves are half dead from the heat." There were some muleteers there, who at once ran up with four beasts and Dom Rodrigo with them, and they brought the said Moors and slaves, and they came in such a state that one of these Moors never recovered his senses. It did no good anointing him with verjuice, nor [with] many other remedies which they applied to him; he died at midnight and the fevers never left the other Moorish pilot until he died. We said about this that they had suffocated with the clothes which they were not used to. We who were used to them had a pretty bad time.

After living for six years at an elevation of between eight and fourteen thousand feet, these prodigals had lost their tolerance for the scorching summers of home. And of course Dom Rodrigo's attempt to spruce up his human present to King João had rather backfired. In consequence, De Lima was sentenced to thirty days in quarantine, not on a charge of negligent manslaughter, but because the sudden death of the two Moors made some royal officials suspicious that the entire party had visited plague-stricken Lisbon after all, and nobody was taking any chances with the King's safety.

This enforced month of idleness, spent at a small town five miles from the royal seat of Coimbra, ended with the arrival of a familiar face. Sent to escort the envoys on the last leg of their approach to João's throne was the Victualler Royal, Diogo Lopez de Sequeira, the same man who, when Governor of the *Estado* in 1520, had transported the Portuguese mission to Ethiopia, and who (says Álvares, exaggerating somewhat) "looked upon this embassy as a thing of his own, and his own handiwork." The reunion was a happy one, during which Sequeira embraced "the Ambassador, and the Prester John's Ambassador, and all of us separately, saying that the King had sent him, and that we were to eat heartily, and set out and go with him by the field road, because all the Court was coming to receive us." If this long-serving courtier could somehow have gleaned the details of the embassy's experiences in Ethiopia, he might have justifiably flattered himself on the wise (though unheeded) parting words he had bestowed upon its leader: "Dom Rodrigo, I do not send the father Francisco Álvares with you, but I send you with him, and do not do anything without his advice." The former Governor was something of a political relic, for all the true-believers in the millenarian mold had by now passed from the scene, leaving only a cadre of practical cynics who inhabited a moral spectrum that stretched from pencil-pushing to piracy. Sequeira, who had at least carried out the orders of the dreamers and cared enough about their pet expedition to recognize and promote its most reasonable member, was the closest the envoys could find to someone who understood the excitement that had once launched them into *terra incognita* with such high hopes. Still, on this day at least, the rest of the royal establishment turned out in force, if mostly from curiosity, and thus as the travelers approached the gates of Coimbra they "found the roads full of all the Bishops, priests, and Counts, and lords that were at the Court," a throng in finery "who [had come] there to look for or receive" their long-absent countrymen.

Entering into the reception hall of the King's palace after a progress though the city's major avenues, Álvares and his fellows were met with a blizzard of diplomatic courtesy. "The Marquiss of Vilareal led the Ambassador of the Prester John by the hand until he kissed the hands of the King and Queen our Lords, and of the Cardinal and the Infantes, and we all kissed them in the same way." Then followed the required questions from João to Zaga Za Ab about the *Negus*' health and that of his Queen, to which the Ambassador answered reassuringly and stated that his master was anxious to hear the same about them. After the King told Zaga that he could inform the Prester that his great

Christian ally was hale and happy, he asked whether the Ambassador had been properly treated by all His Highness' subjects in India, on board various ships, and subsequently in Portugal (there was, after all, the unfortunate precedent of Matthew's seaborne abuse). No one could have received or desired more comfort or courtesy than himself both ashore and afloat, replied Zaga. These hoops of conventional politeness having been successfully negotiated, "the King said to him that he must be tired and [that] he should go to his lodging, and all of us in company with him, and rest ourselves." Once all the travelers were sufficiently refreshed, "His Highness would send to call us in order that we might give a full account of the Prester John" a few days hence. Álvares, as he was escorted from the audience chamber, might have been forgiven for feeling a bit discombobulated, for while the royal interview had possessed all the outward trappings of their long-awaited goal — crowds, trumpets, a smiling King — it had been practically empty of substance, for João had said nothing about Portugal and Ethiopia's glorious future together. Still, this had been merely a scripted ceremony of welcome; the real business would surely commence next time around.

Two days later Álvares, De Lima, and Zaga Za Ab were summoned from their quarters in a nearby monastery for a second and longer meeting with His Highness. It was at this ceremony that the Ethiopian Ambassador was allowed to present King João with the official letters from Lebna Dengel, both the one addressed specifically to the current monarch and the superceded one originally penned to his father, King Manoel. Each of these missives, recall, had been painstakingly rendered into Portuguese, Arabic, and Ge'ez, though among those witnessing this transfer only Father Álvares and Zaga understood how many scriptorium candles had been sacrificed in ridding them of anything that might cause a European to snicker over an Abyssinian blunder. But, as no one on the Portuguese side seemed interested in reading them aloud then and there, our priest's scholarship was not put to an immediate test. Zaga also bestowed upon João the crown of silver and gold that Lebna Dengel had originally sent to the late king his father as a sign of symbolic "submission" to a monarch the *Negus* had then believed to be more powerful than himself. However, as this gift had been made before the Prester had beheld the puniness of Portugal upon a world map and experienced the buffoonery of her subjects upon his hillsides, Zaga accompanied the gift with an oration that subtly put João on notice that any earlier offer of submission on the part of Lebna Dengel had been replaced by one proposing an alliance between equals.

> [Zaga Za Ab], the Ambassador of the Prester John, then said to the King: "[Lebna Dengel], my lord, sent this crown with these letters to the King your father, may he be in holy glory. And he sent to tell him that ... by this sign of the crown he, [Lebna Dengel], was known, loved, feared, and obeyed in his Kingdoms and lordships; and being a son he sent to the King his father this crown,

that [Manoel] might be assured that [Lebna Dengel's] Kingdoms, lordships, and peoples were at His Highness' command; and when he knew of the King his father's death, may he be in holy glory, he had said: 'The crown and letters which I was sending to my father Dom Manoel, are to go to my brother the King Dom Joam.'"

Zaga's address stopped there, without giving out any opinion as to which nation's history might qualify its sovereign as the elder brother in this orphaned Christian family.

It was now time to inform João about the special mission to the Vatican with which Father Álvares had been charged. Accordingly, the priest stepped forward and handed up to the King the brocaded bag containing the *Negus'* communications addressed to the Pope and the gift of a small golden cross which was to accompany them, explaining "how the Prester had ordered that these letters and the cross should be delivered to His Highness, and should be given by the hand of His Highness [back] to me, Francisco Álvares, to take to His Holiness." The King accepted the letters and the present into his hands and kissed them both, saying that he was very pleased to be concerned in such a holy errand. Rather than return them to Álvares, however, he passed them into the keeping of his secretary, while reassuring all present that "he trusted in the Lord it would be completed very soon." If our priest felt any stab of misgiving as the articles entrusted specifically to him by the distant King were borne away into the hidden recesses of João's palace, he did not betray them in his account, saying only that His Highness thereupon "sent [them] away to [their] quarters very cheerful." In the months and years ahead, however, he would often rue surrendering Lebna Dengel's parchment and gold into the hands of those for whom Ethiopia remained only a vague and distant abstraction.

In the short term, the one traveler from the Prester's realm who possessed the best reason to be in fact "very cheerful" was Zaga, who found himself the recipient of an extraordinary outpouring of royal largess:

> [T]he King ordered a regular allowance and riding animals to be given to the Ambassador, namely, three mules, one for him, and two for two monks who came with him; and two *cruzados* each day for his table, that is, sixty *cruzados* a month, and one *tostam* a day for fodder for the mules; and a rich bed and bedding for him to sleep on, silver plate for his table, table-cloths, and all he needed, and a butler by name Francisco Piriz, to take charge of the silver, bed, and hangings, for he ordered everything to be given him. He also gave him one Francisco de Lemos, a knight of His Highness' guard, as Arabic interpreter to speak for him, and to collect his allowance and anything he might need.[3]

In hindsight, one can legitimately wonder whether this shower of gifts was meant as a marker of King's João's respect for the *Negus'* representative and their two nation's presumptive mutual interests, or as a kind of pre-emptive bribe to forestall the protests of a loyal emissary who was about to be put on ice.

At any rate, it appears that such luxury, even if genuinely well meant, did Zaga a good deal of moral harm when combined with another more dubious gift that João also ladled out to the Ambassador, and to Álvares as well: that of copious boredom. For it fell out that after the brief week of pomp and courtesy and official thanks, came ... precisely nothing: no consultations on strategy against the Moors, no inquiries as to the details of the Prester's military might, no commencement of a letter to him in return — and no talk of sending Father Álvares on to Rome either. The fundamental reason for this deafening silence was the fact that the Europe the embassy had returned to in 1526 was a far different place from the one they had left more than a decade before. For instance, in late 1517, while Álvares and Matthew had been recovering in India from Lopo Soares' disastrously abortive foray into the Red Sea, a German monk named Martin Luther had nailed his list of ninety-five theses attacking the sale of spiritual indulgences to a church door in Wittenburg. By the time the embassy first laid eyes on the Prester's silken capital in October of 1520 Luther's books were being burned by the authorities at the University of Louvain, and before they experienced their first *Timkat* celebration Luther himself had publicly torched the Papal bull that demanded his recantation. While the Portuguese envoys languished atop the Roof of Africa, sometimes as guests and sometimes as prisoners, back home the Protestant Reformation was undergoing its prodigious birth, and they had remained ignorant of several crucial conclaves convened in reaction to the religious revolution convulsing those Christian nations north of the Alps. The Diet of Worms, designed to halt the spread of Luther's doctrines, had been in full swing at the time of their arrest, while the Diet of Speyer, which recognized that some states had already become essentially "Lutheran," was concluding just as they bent their knees before João in Coimbra. In other words, as far as the staunchly Catholic Iberian kings were now concerned, there was a new and closer enemy to worry about than the Moslems. Not that the Islamic threat, in the form of the Ottoman Empire, had ceased to threaten Europe. Indeed, Under Suleiman the Magnificent the Turks had expanded explosively across the Balkans, were now the masters of Hungary, and would soon lay siege to Vienna. And these were the same Ottoman Turks who controlled the Red Sea, and who presumably could have been at least distracted from their rampages on the Danube by a joint Portuguese-Ethiopian thrust against their southern phalanx. But of course there is no war quite so bitter as a civil war, and Christendom's growing division made Lutherans, Moravians and Anabaptists a more potent focus of Catholic hatred and fear than the followers of Mohammad. The Turks might be outside the gates of Vienna, but the Protestants were running city hall in Strassburg.

And yet matters were worse still, for the half of Europe that had so far remained immune from the Protestant fever was distracted from combating it by internecine warfare. As Álvares explains:

[S]ometimes I reminded His Highness about sending me to complete the journey which I had promised and sworn to the Prester John to make, namely, to carry his letters and a cross of gold and his obedience to the Holy Father in Rome. His Highness told me that he was fully mindful of this, but that the roads did not give an opportunity for this, on account of the wars with France.

This was true enough, since for most of the 1520s France and Spain had been at war over claims to Lombardy and other lands. And, since King Charles of Spain had also reigned as the Holy Roman Emperor since 1520, these hostilities had prevented that Catholic ruler from struggling more effectively against the growing Reformation in his German territories. Still, João's excuse for holding up Álvares was somewhat disingenuous, since he could always have put him aboard a ship bound for the Holy See at any time — it wasn't as if the Mediterranean was closed for business, since there was always a war on somewhere. Once winter arrived and the King moved his court back to Lisbon, the insistent Álvares tells us that he again "reminded His Highness of [his] dispatch to Rome," only to receive once more "the answer mentioned above." In truth, this serial rebuffing of our priest was merely an indication of how different João's priorities were from those of his father, Manoel. Far from subscribing to any millenarian enthusiasms about Portugal's place in world history, he was distinctly put out by the growing realization that his country's burgeoning eastern empire was starting to cost more to run than it paid in spices and other goods. Where Manoel, like his great predecessor Henry the Navigator, had always kept his eyes fixed on the horizon, João looked for opportunities closer to home. It so happened that at the time of the embassy's return he thought he was on to a particularly ripe one, and this too served to hinder Álvares' progress toward Rome.

Since soon after his ascension to the throne, João had been casting envious eyes on the Spanish Inquisition, which since 1480 had been prosecuting Jewish converts to Christianity (or "New Christians," as they were called) for secretly practicing Judaic rites and harboring Judaic beliefs. He was attracted not by the Inquisition's supposed purification of Spanish Christianity, but by the fact that those convicted by its tribunals forfeited their property, much of it to the crown. Now that the Empire no longer paid, here was a reliable revenue stream. Because over 90,000 Jews had already fled Spain for Portugal, and because back in 1497 King Manoel had ordered all resident Jews to be forcibly baptized and forbidden to leave the country, João knew that Portugal would be a hunting ground rich in secret Judaizers if he could get a similar operation up and running in his own realm. Unfortunately for him, his father had also issued a decree guaranteeing Portuguese Jews (or rather, the now forcibly baptized New Christians) freedom from inquiry into their religions practices until 1534, meaning that João would have to petition the Pope if he wanted to start prosecutions anytime soon. When Álvares got wind sometime during 1529 that the

King was sending Bras Neto, his Ambassador to the Holy See, to Rome in order to approach the Pope about setting up a Portuguese Inquisition without delay, he attempted to hitch a ride, apparently with the Ambassador's own approval.

> He, Bras Neto, begged me to ask the King to send me with him. I begged of the King the favour to send me with Bras Neto, since he was going to Rome. His Highness told me that Bras Neto was going to the Emperor and not to Rome [i.e, to Charles V, the Holy Roman Emperor, who was frequently in Italy], and that he well remembered about sending me, but that I could not go.

The King was now simply lying to Álvares, as our priest must have realized from talking with the Ambassador himself, but he was helpless to do anything about the situation. The King simply didn't want his request for an Inquisition watered down by Ethiopian distractions. As it turned out, though, João's attempt to focus the Vatican's attention failed, for the Roman Curia refused his pious petition, saying that they knew he was just trying to shake down Jews.

In point of fact, the cultural tensions (and intermittent mob violence) surrounding New Christians across the Iberian peninsula helps explain why Ethiopia's stock was in free-fall by the time Álvares and his fellows returned to Portugal. Our priest may have suppressed his knowledge about the Abyssinians' monophysite heresy, but he made no effort to conceal from anyone their Judaizing practices, and of course such clearly visible ceremonies must have been one of the first bits of news off the tongues of the embassy's returned laymen as well. But if the authorities of both Spain and Portugal were now keen to see all domestic Judaizers given over to the strappados and thumbscrews of the Inquisition, then it was hard to justify spending treasure on an alliance with a whole nation of foreign crypto-Hebrews.[4] And the nascent Reformation also played its part in cooling the enthusiasms of Portuguese elites toward the great Prester John, no matter how long these same men had been seeking him. From a Catholic perspective, one of the most noxious aspects of Luther and his allies was their questioning of the Pope's authority to rule on spiritual matters, and this automatically cast the Ethiopian Church's allegiance to the Coptic Patriarch of Alexandria in a darker light than it had appeared before. It was just a bad time to be associated with a country of circumcised blackamoors who let Egyptians tell their married priests when to celebrate Easter.

It was at this moment that Álvares suddenly found himself appointed by the King to a benefice in the Archbishopric of Braga, but whether this preferment was intended as a reward for service, a handsome bribe, or just an attempt to get the nagging cleric out of his hair (Braga being a long way from Lisbon) we can't be certain. Meanwhile, Zaga Za Ab found himself equally encumbered with worldly advantages and equally unhappy. He had arrived in Portugal expecting to be the busy conduit for information about and communication with his distant homeland, and the resulting lack of any calls upon his knowledge and office apparently sent his morale plunging. He was ignored and neglected by everyone at Court, with one unwelcome exception, for if the King's secular advisors had no questions for him, various ecclesiastical detectives did, and these priests were quick to sniff out heresy. Thus the man who had hoped to act as a bridge between the Christians of Portugal and Ethiopia found himself an isolated and disdained figure, with whom none of the local churchmen would so much as share holy communion. We know from his campaign of head-cracking back in Abyssinia that Zaga was not the type of man to meekly swallow an affront, but since he could not very well cudgel his European interrogators as he had the embassy's recalcitrant porters, he seems to have transferred his anger into a course of licentious living upon the King's purse — which of course just served to harden attitudes toward him in the palace's antechambers. Still, when he was finally asked by a Portuguese humanist to put his understanding of Ethiopian Christianity on paper, he produced a document that strongly suggested that he had imbibed Álvares' ecumenical vision of a Christendom in which specific doctrinal differences would be rendered invisible by the bright light of a commitment to shared modes, emphases, and intensities of spiritual striving: "It would be much wiser to welcome in charity and Christian love all Christians, be they Greeks, Armenians, Ethiopians, or those belonging to any other of the seven Christian churches. They all should be allowed to live with and move among other Christian brothers, because we are all sons of baptism and share the true faith." Indeed, when attempting to square the earlier bully of 1520 with the peacemaker of the next decade, the many years Zaga spent riding by the side of Francisco Álvares emerges as the most likely cause of the change. If our priest had opened his heart to anyone about why he had ceased to care about what his superiors called heresy, it would surely have been to this monk who had been his close companion across so many mountains and seas. Still, things did not go well for this kinder and gentler Zaga. In this same treatise he complains that he "was not sent by [his] most powerful master, the Emperor of Ethiopia, to the Roman Pope and to his Highness King John of Portugal to quarrel at debates and contentions, but to contract friendship and fellowship." But alas, no one in Portugal would allow him to do any such thing. His writings were eventually suppressed as dangerous by the Catholic Church and after years of frustration we find him an embittered man reduced to begging King João simply for permission to go home: "I entreat you for the sake of Our Lord Jesus Christ's death and Passion, and by the great mercy of Our Lady, His blessed mother, that you will not let me die in your realm."[5] Perhaps, then, he actually did react with relief when Bermudez showed up in 1537 claiming to be his replacement, despite the fact that he couldn't have fully believed the imposter's self-serving stories. By that time any proffered end to his useless exile must have seemed a welcome prospect.

As the years dragged on, Álvares continued to badger his sovereign into letting him complete his mission, but did not receive a favorable answer until, in 1532, he was finally allowed to travel to Italy in the company of Dom Martinho de Portugal, the Papal Nuncio at Lisbon. It was arranged that he would finally deliver Lebna Dengel's letters to Pope Clement VII at a consistory (i.e., an assembly of cardinals) to be held in Bologna's main cathedral in January of 1533 — *Timkat* season, our priest might have reminded himself. It is worth noting, though, just how unsuitable a Pontiff Clement was to be the recipient of the *Negus'* call to world-wide Christian unity. Giulio de'Medici, as he had been known before his elevation to the See of Peter, was described by a friend as "rather morose and disagreeable, reputed to be avaricious, by no means trustworthy and naturally disinclined to do a kindness." But this was hardly the worst of it, for his signal failing was a thoroughgoing inability to make up his mind, which earned him the nickname of "I will and I won't." And this vacillating nature was yoked to a strategic short-sightedness that focused all his attentions on the shifting politics of the Italian peninsula, not that he was ever the gainer from such myopic scrutiny of his own backyard. For years Clement had shuttled the allegiance of the Vatican and the outlying Papal States back and forth between the dour Holy Roman Emperor Charles V and that permanent adolescent, Francis I of France, the two rival claimants for large chunks of northern Italy. His manic dithering had, five years before, directly contributed to the brutal sacking of Rome by Imperial troops, from which disaster he had been forced to ignominiously flee in disguise. The salient fact is that the Pope had spent so much energy playing off the two monarchs against each other for the supposed advantages to his small collection of Church duchies that he had managed to do nothing effective himself about the metastasizing Reformation while simultaneously distracting both Catholic kings from doing anything either.[6] And thus even though Álvares beheld upon entering Bologna's cathedral a newly cowed Pontiff enthroned uncomfortably next to the now-triumphant Emperor he had more than once betrayed, he was facing a man whose dire reverses had spurred him to no wider vision of the Church he fecklessly led. Christians in Ethiopia? — as far as Clement was concerned, you might as well talk to him about men on the moon.

Standing amidst all the splendor of golden robes and crimson hats, Francisco Álvares must by this late date have comprehended the unpromising fate of all his own quietly ambitious projects. He must now have realized that his suppression of the Ethiopians' heresy was not likely to beguile his fellow Catholic churchmen into understanding and appreciating that nation's prodigious spirituality before they condemned its alien doctrines. He must also have seen that a Portuguese-Abyssinian alliance against Islam had now been rendered moot thanks to Christendom's raging internecine struggle. And so if he had stubbornly persisted to this very hour in his efforts to stand before the Pope and render unto him the letters from Lebna Dengel, it must have been largely from a sense of personal obligation. His friend the *Negus* had asked something important of him, and he meant to fulfill his promise: finally, after so much travel and so much delay, he had arrived at his destination.

When the Portuguese delegation was called before the twin thrones, Dom Martinho first read out a self-congratulatory letter from João to the Pontiff bragging about Portuguese victories over the forces of Mohammad, including various exploits of glory upon the Red Sea, which was a bit rich considering that João had by then practically ceded that body of water to the Turks. In the course of this missive the King also waxed enthusiastic about a future reunification of the Ethiopian and Roman Churches, without offering any explanation as to why he had stymied Álvares for so many years and allowed Zaga Za Ab to languish in disuse. He then ended by giving thanks that Portugal had been chosen by God as the vessel through which Christian solidarity might soon be furthered. Satisfaction at all this having been returned from the pontifical dais, it was now our priest's turn to step forward.

He first handed up the letters from Lebna Dengel to the Pope, followed by the small and simple golden cross that the *Negus* had sent along as an accompanying gift to a Pontiff he had imagined would be an un-worldly and saintlike figure. The letters were then read aloud in Latin by the Papal secretary. These documents, in addition to their plea for harmony among Europe's Christians so that Ethiopia's alliance with them might not be in vain, contained Lebna Dengel's "recognition" of the Pope's spiritual sovereignty and his "submission" to him. These statements, of course, were not by any means a pledge on the *Negus'* part to alter the religion of Ethiopia to fit Catholic notions of doctrinal correctness. They were at best generic offerings of respect emanating from within an imperfect understanding of the actual issues that divided the two churches. Some of the cardinals and other ecclesiastics who heard these words might have sighed with relief at the erroneous thought that the Ethiopians were obviously now, and had always been, orthodox Catholics. Others, having heard the disturbing rumors out of Portugal, might have been encouraged by the belief that the Prester was announcing his own conversion, which his nation would surely emulate soon enough. Álvares knew that both of these assumptions were wrong, but what was he going to say about them when the time came for him to speak? An observer wrote down his words, and one way to interpret them would be to say that he simply papered over the issues.

> Most Holy and Blessed Father, the most serene and powerful lord [Lebna Dengel], king of the great and high Ethiopia, by the masses called Prester John, no less eminent in his practice of the true religion than in power, wealth, and kingdoms, sent this ambassador of his to Your Holiness with these letters which he delivered to you, together with the command that he render to Your Holiness, as true vicar of Christ, successor of Peter, and supreme pontiff of the universal

Church, true obedience and submission in the name of His Majesty and of all his kingdoms and in all humility, as he has in fact done, and that he offer to Your Holiness this little gift of a gold cross, which should be esteemed not so much for its value, which is slight, as for the veneration due that cross on which Our Lord Jesus Christ deigned to suffer for us, at the same time beseeching you humbly, in the name of that prince of his, to deign to accept all these things with the pious affection of a father from his most devoted son.[7]

It is of course possible that, awed by the presence of the Pope and the Holy Roman Emperor, Father Álvares prudently decided not to antagonize them with a tedious list of disappointing caveats. But given what we know of our priest's character and of the bold acts of disguise he had already committed, a more plausible explanation is that he was merely being true to his course of principled silence before an audience that he knew could never accept the ideas and experiences that had motivated him to undertake it. According to this reading, when he declared that the *Negus* was "eminent in his practice of the true religion," he spoke neither from ignorance nor from fear of making a scene, but rather from his acquired conviction that a spiritually *true* definition of "the true religion" was one large and robust and humane enough to encompass both Lebna Dengel and Clement VII's differing visions of their Savior. In other words, he could honestly report that Prester John was submitting himself to the Pope because in his own wider conception of Christianity, a monophysite monarch could do so to a Catholic Pope without contradiction. Under the high and glittering dome at Bologna, our priest remained steadfast to the hard-won largeness of his own mind and heart.

Having carried out his duty at last and in full, Álvares — and along with him all discussion of matters Abyssinian — was quickly dismissed from the consistory, for Clement had other urgent business to attend to. King Henry the VIII of England was attempting to divorce the aunt of the glowering Emperor seated next to him and marry some chit named Anne Boleyn (in fact the two had been secretly married since November), and thus there were many lawyers to be consulted. But in all fairness one can't really blame His Holiness for not quite knowing what to do with the ornate letters that had come to him from a king who claimed to rule the distant Roof of Africa. For in the final analysis Ethiopia in the sixteenth century was simply a bit too far from either Rome or Lisbon — geographically, historically, culturally — to sustain any practical European endeavor concerning her for long. The Franks she had made happiest had, ever since the arrival of the Prester's original Letter, been the romantic dreamers, but when it came to workaday matters like military alliances, commerce, and conversion, her *ambas* always proved too high, their ramparts too steep. This pattern of rewarding only the restless, the reckless and the poetic would continue down the centuries, as various men set out from Europe, in flesh or in thought, searching for the source of the Nile, or the Happy Valley of Rasselas, or King Solomon's mines. The actual Abyssinia, with its resilient people and remarkable history, would always be a place well worth knowing, but for centuries to come it was to remain such a thing as only dreams were made on.

Following our priest out of the cathedral and into the cool of that Italian January, we soon begin to lose track of him. We know that his book recounting the Ethiopian embassy, though completed and circulated long before, was first printed in Lisbon in 1540, and that it was soon translated into Spanish, French, German, and English. There is some evidence that the tome which has come down to us was constructed from a much larger hoard of material about Abyssinia that Álvares had managed to collect, and some scholars speculate that he eventually planned to write a five-volume encyclopedia on the country, though no such work has survived in any library or attic that we know of. We do not even know for sure where, after his promise to the *Negus* had been fulfilled, he spent the rest of his days. Given his birth and his benefice, one might naturally assume that he simply returned to Portugal, but there are hints that place him in Rome during the subsequent and final decade of his life. If he did remain in the Eternal City, its sights must have afforded him a daily reminder of just how many miles he had traveled in his endeavors to serve God and his fellow men, for the priest who had once known the mountains and gorges of Christendom's remotest outpost like no other Frank now trod the avenues of that religion's ornate capital city. Every couple of years a handful of Ethiopian pilgrims arrived in Rome, and it seems inconceivable that Álvares did not seek them out for news of their homeland, and to hear some word concerning this or that acquaintance made during his own days of journeying. He must then have learned about Lebna Dengel's desperate struggles against the Grañ, and worried long into many a night about the fate of the youthful king he had befriended in a faraway nation. Talking with such men, one wonders if he did not come to understand that his own years in Ethiopia, as riddled with hardship, danger, and frustration as they had certainly been, yet constituted the happiest time of his life. And if, as some fragmentary sources suggest, our priest might have survived until as late as 1542,[8] another intriguing meeting can be imagined on the streets of Rome, for in late 1536 he might well have been amazed to see Joam Bermudez arrive at the Vatican clamoring for an audience with the Pope in the midst of his fantastical and egomaniacal charade. Neither man wrote about such a meeting in their respective books, but then again they wouldn't have, Álvares because the story he wanted to tell had closed years before and Bermudez because in all probability the modest man whom everyone liked simply made him uncomfortable. Certainly this silence is about the only thing their two volumes have in common. Even their tombs are a study in contrasts. That of Bermudez is showy and self-aggrandizing, heralding to passers-by his false honors and invented titles; that of Francisco Álvares, though searched for on several occasions, has never been discovered.

Chapter Notes

Chapter One

1. From Charles Mierow's translation of Bishop Otto of Freising's account, quoted in Vsevolod Slessarev, *Prester John: The Letter and the Legend* (Minneapolis: University of Minnesota Press, 1959), p. 27
2. Quoted in Slessarev, *Letter and the Legend*, p. 27.
3. Robert Silverberg, *The Realm of Prester John* (Garden City: Doubleday, 1972), pp. 8–9, suggests this motive.
4. Quoted in Slessarev, *Letter and the Legend*, p. 27.
5. Richard C. Trexler, *The Journey of the Magi: Meanings in History of a Christian Story* (Princeton: Princeton University Press, 1997), pp. 9–14.
6. Quotations of Prester John's original letter are from Silverberg, *Realm of Prester John*, pp. 41–45, who reprints the translated version of Friedrich Zarncke.
7. Silverberg, *Realm of Prester John*, pp. 48–52, and Slessarev, *Letter and the Legend*, p. 47.
8. Silverberg, *Realm of Prester John*, pp. 41–45.
9. *Ibid.*, pp. 63–4.
10. *Ibid.*, pp. 65, 142–5.
11. *Ibid.*, pp. 143 6.
12. Quoted in Slessarev, *Letter and the Legend*, p. 68.
13. Slessarev, *Letter and the Legend*, pp. 47, 52–3.
14. Slessarev mentions this possibility without enthusiasm, *Letter and the Legend*, p. 55.
15. The opinion of the Italian scholar Leonardo Olschki, quoted in Silverberg, *Realm of Prester John*, p. 55.
16. David Morgan, "Prester John and the Mongols," in *Prester John, the Mongols, and the Ten Lost Tribes*, eds. Charles F. Beckingham and Bernard Hamilton (Aldershot: Variorum), pp. 159–60; Bernard Hamilton, "Continental Drift: Prester John's Progress Through the Indies," in Beckingham and Hamilton, *Ten Lost Tribes*, pp. 244–5; Silverberg, *Realm of Prester John*, p. 71.
17. Morgan, "Prester John and the Mongols," in *Ten Lost Tribes*, pp. 162–6; Hamilton, "Continental Drift," in *Ten Lost Tribes*, pp. 248–9.
18. C. F. Beckingham, "The Achievements of Prester John," in *Ten Lost Tribes*, p. 15; Hamilton, "Continental Drift," in *Ten Lost Tribes*, p. 239.
19. Bernard Hamilton, "Prester John and the Three Kings of Cologne," in *Ten Lost Tribes*, pp. 173–4; Hamilton, "Continental Drift," in *Ten Lost Tribes*, p. 249.
20. All the preceding excerpts are quoted by Hamilton, "Continental Drift," in *Ten Lost Tribes*, pp. 240, 244, 247, 252, and 254.
21. C. F. Beckingham, *Between Islam and Christendom: Travelers, Facts and Legends in the Middle Ages and the Renaissance* (London: Variorum Reprints, 1983), Reprint X, pp. 1–2.
22. Beckingham, *Between Islam and Christendom*, Reprint II, p. 299.
23. Eric Axelson, *Congo to Cape: Early Portuguese Explorers* (New York: Barnes & Noble), 1973, p. 29.

24. Jack Turner, in *Spice: The History of a Temptation* (New York: Vintage, 2004), p. 5, asserts that the markup for such spices could be more than 1000 percent by the time they reached Europe.
25. Richard Pankhurst, *The Ethiopians* (Oxford: Blackwell, 1998), p. 77, and Beckingham, *Between Islam and Christendom*, Reprint II, pp. 293–4.
26. Beckingham, *Between Islam and Christendom*, Reprint IX, p. 10.
27. Silverberg, *Realm of Prester John*, 164–5.
28. *Ibid.*, p. 178; Richard Pankhurst, *The Ethiopians*, p. 78
29. Edward Ullendorff, *The Ethiopians: An Introduction to Country and People* (London: Oxford University Press, 1962), p. 3.
30. Axelson, *Congo to Cape*, p. 34; Silverberg, *Realm of Prester John*, pp. 179–80.
31. Richard Pankhurst, *The Ethiopians*, p. 78.
32. O. G. S. Crawford, ed., *Ethiopian Itineraries Circa 1400–1524, Including Those Collected by Allesandro Zorzi at Venice in the Years 1519–24* (Cambridge: Cambridge University Press for The Hakluyt Society, 1958), p. 10; Silverberg, *Realm of Prester John*, p. 189.

Chapter Two

1. A. J. R. Russell-Wood, *The Portuguese Empire 1415–1808: A World on the Move* (Baltimore: Johns Hopkins University Press, 1998), p. 9.
2. Peter Russell, *Prince Henry "The Navigator": A Life* (New Haven: Yale University Press, 2000), pp. 123–5.
3. Axelson, *Congo to Cape*, pp. 33–4; Russell, *Prince Henry*, pp. 306–8.
4. Axelson, *Congo to Cape*, pp. 54–5, 67–80.
5. Beckingham, *Between Islam and Christendom*, Reprint II, pp. 304–5.
6. Axelson, *Congo to Cape*, pp. 99–100, 107–11, 113.
7. *Ibid.*, p. 189; Beckingham, *Between Islam and Christendom*, Reprint I, pp. 22–3, Reprint IX, pp. 12–13, 15–6.
8. Axelson, *Congo to Cape*, pp. 181–9.
9. *Ibid.*, pp. 177–81. The quotations are from an Italian translation of Rui de Pina's report of the Congo embassy, the original of which is lost.
10. *A Journal of the First Voyage of Vasco Da Gama, 1497–1499*, trans. E. G. Ravenstein (New York: Burt Franklin, 1963), pp. 13, 23–5, 28, 30–1; Sanjay Subrahmanyam, *The Career and Legend of Vasco Da Gama* (Cambridge: Cambridge University Press, 1997), pp. 93–4, 112–5.
11. *Voyage of Vasco Da Gama*, pp. 36–37, 40–46, 48–55; Subrahmanyam, *Legend of Vasco Da Gama*, pp. 115–20, 131–3; Turner, *Spice*, p. 18.
12. *Voyage of Vasco Da Gama*, pp. 76–87.
13. Subrahmanyam, *Legend of Vasco Da Gama*, pp. 175, 179–81, 205–7, 215; Gaspar Correa, *The Three Voyages of Vasco Da Gama and His Viceroyalty*, trans. Henry E. J. Stanley (New York: Burt Franklin), pp. 312–18, 326–332.
14. Subrahmanyam, *Legend of Vasco Da Gama*, pp. 187, 195, 160; John Keay, *The Spice Route: A History* (Berkeley: University of California Press, 2006), pp. 171, 181.
15. Both letters quoted in Silverberg, *Realm of Prester John*, pp. 211, 214.

Chapter Three

1. H. Morse Stephens, *Rulers of India: Albuquerque* (Oxford: Clarendon Press, 1912), pp. 126–7; Edgar Prestage, *Afonso De Albuquerque, Governor of India: His Life, Conquests and Administration* (Watford, 1929), p. 53; K. G. Jayne, *Vasco Da Gama And His Successors, 1460–1580* (New York: Barnes & Noble, 1970), pp. 91–93.
2. Bailey W. Diffie and George D. Winius, *Foundations of the Portuguese Empire, 1415–1580* (Minneapolis: University of Minnesota Press, 1977), p. 265; Jayne, *Da Gama and His Successors*, p. 93. The passage is quoted in F. E. Peters, *Mecca: A Literary History of the Muslim Holy Land* (Princeton: Princeton University Press, 1994), p. 187.
3. Diffie and Winius, *Foundations of the Portuguese Empire*, p. 266; quoted in Prestage, *Governor of India*, p. 54.

4. Letters quoted in Stephens, *Rulers of India*, p. 123, and in Diffie and Winius, *Foundations of the Portuguese Empire*, p. 278.
5. Silverberg, *Realm of Prester John*, pp. 232–3.
6. Quoted in Stephens, *Rulers of India*, p. 139; Diffie and Winius, *Foundations of the Portuguese Empire*, p. 270.
7. Silverberg, *Realm of Prester John*, p. 232.
8. Diffie and Winius, *Foundations of the Portuguese Empire*, pp. 272–76; Peters, *Mecca: A Literary History*, pp. 210–15; Silverberg, *Realm of Prester John*, pp. 232–35.
9. Diffie and Winius, *Foundations of the Portuguese Empire*, p. 277; Silverberg, *Realm of Prester John*, p. 235.
10. Francisco Álvares, *The Prester John of the Indies: A True Relation of the Lands of the Prester John, being the Narrative of the Portuguese Embassy to Ethiopia in 1520 Written by Father Francisco Alvares*, trans. Lord Stanley of Alderley, revised and edited by C. F. Beckingham and G. W. B. Huntingford (Cambridge: The Hakluyt Society, 1961; reprinted Millwood, NY: Kraus, 1975), p. 53.
11. *Ibid.*, pp. 52, 54, 57.
12. *Ibid.*, pp. 60–4.

Chapter Four

1. Álvares did, toward the end of his book, include a catalog of strange creatures and people, but was careful to point out that he had only heard others speak of such beings and had seen none of them first hand; throughout these chapters his skepticism is apparent.
2. Álvares, pp. 65–6.
3. *Ibid.*, pp. 68–74.
4. Although round churches were much more common in the southern half of sixteenth-century Ethiopia than in the northern region around Bizam, extant sketches of that monastery, admittedly dating from the nineteenth century, appear to show a round church there. See J. T. Bent, *The Sacred City of the Ethiopians* (London, 1896).
5. Álvares, pp. 75–83.
6. *Ibid.*, pp. 84–86, 91–92, 85, 85 n. 2.
7. *Ibid.*, p. 87.
8. *Ibid.*, pp. 95–96.
9. Robert E. Hood, *Begrimed and Black: Christian Traditions on Blacks and Blackness* (Minneapolis: Fortress Press, 1994), pp. 115, 96. For an overview of how black Ethiopians were perceived by Europeans prior to the early-modern period, see Matteo Salvadore, "The Ethiopian Age of Exploration: Prester John's Discovery of Europe, 1306–1458," *Journal of World History*, Vol. 21, No. 4 (2011), pp. 593–627.
10. Álvares, pp. 96–101.
11. *Ibid.*, pp. 119–20, 107, 108, 105.
12. *Ibid.*, pp. 109–10.
13. *Ibid.*, pp. 104, 113, 112, 131.
14. *Ibid.*, pp. 122–3, 130, 138–9.

Chapter Five

1. Álvares, pp. 140, 169.
2. *Ibid.*, pp. 143, 144, 171, 167, 169.
3. *Ibid.*, p. 141.
4. Philip Briggs, *Ethiopia: The Bradt Travel Guide* (Guilford, CT: Globe Pequot, 2005), pp. 263–4.
5. Richard Pankhurst, *The Ethiopians*, pp. 13–15; Harold G. Marcus, *A History of Ethiopia: Updated Version* (Berkeley: University of California Press, 2002), p. 3
6. Álvares, p. 141; Pankhurst, *The Ethiopians*, pp. 23–27, 33–4; Marcus, *History of Ethiopia*, pp. 8–9.
7. Álvares, p. 158; Pankhurst, *The Ethiopians*, pp. 28–30.

8. *Ibid.*, pp. 172–4.
9. *Ibid.*, pp. 179–82.
10. Mordechai Abir, *Ethiopia and the Red Sea: The Rise and Decline of the Solomonic Dynasty and Muslim-European Rivalry in the Region* (London: Frank Cass, 1980), pp. 69–72, 77–88.
11. Álvares, pp. 186–9.
12. *Ibid.*, pp. 193, 195, 180, 200.
13. *Ibid.*, pp. 195–6.
14. Donald Crummey, *Land and Society in the Christian Kingdom of Ethiopia: From the Thirteenth to the Twentieth Century* (Urbana: University of Illinois Press, 2000), pp. 37–9.
15. Álvares, pp. 228–35, 250–1, 257–9.
16. Taddesse Tamrat, *Church and State in Ethiopia, 1270–1527* (Oxford: Clarendon Press, 1972), pp. 107–8, 112–14, 206–30.
17. Álvares, pp. 249, 251–2, 258–9, 265.
18. Tamrat, *Church and State in Ethiopia*, pp. 269–75.
19. Ronald J. Horvath, "The Wandering Capitals of Ethiopia," *Journal of African History* X, 2 (1969), pp. 210–11, 215, 214.

Chapter Six

1. Richard Pankhurst, *The Ethiopians* (Oxford: Blackwell, 1998), pp. 53–7.
2. Álvares, pp. 266–72.
3. *Ibid.*, pp. 272–81.
4. J. Spencer Trimingham, *Islam in Ethiopia* (London: Frank Cass, 1965), pp. 82–3.
5. Álvares, pp. 281–88.
6. *Ibid.*, pp. 288–303.
7. *Ibid.*, pp. 303–307. Some material is summarized from Gaspar Correa's *Lendas da Índia* by Álvares' editors in a note to page 306.

Chapter Seven

1. Álvares, pp. 308–20.
2. *Ibid.*, pp. 336–7.
3. *Ibid.*, pp. 320, 323–4, 335.
4. Tamrat, *Church and State in Ethiopia* (Oxford: Clarendon Press, 1972), p. 221; David Buxton, *The Abyssinians* (New York: Praeger, 1970), pp. 48–9; Abir, *Ethiopia and the Red Sea*, pp. 44, 70; Richard Pankhurst, *The Ethiopians*, pp. 64–5.
5. Sylvia Pankhurst, *Ethiopia: A Cultural History* (Woodford Green, Essex: Lalibela House, 1955), pp. 238–9.
6. Álvares, pp. 325–30.
7. This mode of depicting the Trinity was outlawed in the West by the Council of Trent. See Buxton, *The Abyssinians*, p. 145.
8. Quoted in Sylvia Pankhurst, *Cultural History*, p. 329.
9. Álvares, pp. 331–41.

Chapter Eight

1. For overviews of the monophysite controversy, monophysite doctrines, and the early history of monophysite churches, see W.H.C. Frend, *The Rise of the Monophysite Movement: Chapters in the History of The Church in the Fifth and Sixth Centuries* (Cambridge: Cambridge University Press, 1972), pp. 1–50; David Christie-Murray, *A History of Heresy* (London: New English Library, 1976), pp. 69–83; and J. W. C. Wand, *The Four Great Heresies* (London: A. R. Mowbray & Co., 1967), pp. 110–30.
2. Álvares, pp. 341–8.
3. Abir, *Ethiopia and the Red Sea*, p. 60.
4. Álvares, pp. 348–59.

5. *Ibid.*, pp. 360–81.
6. *Ibid.*, pp. 381–9

Chapter Nine

1. Álvares, pp. 389, 88, 91.
2. *Ibid.*, pp. 389–397.
3. Abir, *Ethiopia and the Red Sea*, p. 88.
4. Álvares, pp. 449–51.
5. Sihab as-Din Ahmad bin Abd al-Qader bin Salem bin Utman, *The Conquest of Abyssinia*, trans. Paul Lester Stenhouse (Hollywood: Tsehai, 2003); also quoted in Trimingham, *Islam In Ethiopia*, pp. 84–6.
6. Álvares, p. 397. Beckingham, in *Between Islam and Christendom*, Reprint XII, p. 6, says of this Lenten journey that "we do not know why or precisely when they went," but given the surrounding circumstances, I think the *Negus'* motives for insisting upon it are clear enough.
7. *Ibid.*, pp. 397–407.
8. As this incident occurs after "we had then been three years in the country" (Álvares, p. 132) and "in the town of Barua" [i.e., Debarwa], the only time which seems to fit is the late summer of 1523. See Beckingham, *Between Islam and Christendom*, Reprint XII, pp. 6–7.
9. Álvares, pp. 132–37.
10. Álvares says only that it occurred when "we were going from the sea to the Court." However, the only times when members of the embassy traveled the entirety of the distance from Massawa to the Prester's capital in one continuous journey occurred upon their arrival in 1520 (which cannot be meant) and in late 1523, when returning from their investigation of what De Meneses had left for them.
11. Álvares, pp. 237–48; 424.
12. *Ibid.*, pp. 409, 415–18.
13. Quoted in Sylvia Pankhurst, *Ethiopia: A Cultural History*, p. 323.
14. Álvares, pp. 418–20.

Chapter Ten

1. Richard Pankhurst, *The Ethiopians*, pp. 84–5.
2. Mordechai Abir, *Ethiopia and the Red Sea*, p. 89.
3. Sihab as-Din Ahmad, *Conquest of Abyssinia*, pp. 153–4.
4. *Ibid.*, p. 192.
5. Richard Pankhurst, *The Ethiopians*, pp. 86–7.
6. Sihab as-Din Ahmad, *Conquest of Abyssinia*, pp. 238–9, 241, 345, 331.
7. R. S. Whiteway, trans., ed., *The Portuguese Expedition to Abyssinia in 1541–1543 as Narrated by Castanhoso, with some Contemporary Letters, the Short Account of Bermudez, and certain Extracts from Correa* (London: The Hakluyt Society, 1902), p. 108.
8. *Ibid.*, *Portuguese Expedition*, pp. 129–32.
9. Beckingham, *Between Islam and Christendom*, Reprint XI, p. 164.
10. Whiteway, *Portuguese Expedition*, p. lxxxiv.
11. *Ibid.*, pp. 107–8.
12. Abir, *Ethiopia and the Red Sea*, p. 97.
13. Quoted in Elaine Sanceau, *The Land of Prester John: A Chronicle of Portuguese Exploration* (New York: Knopf, 1944), p. 110.
14. Whiteway, *Portuguese Expedition*, pp. xl–xli, 265; Sanceau, *Land of Prester John*, pp. 109–116.
15. Whiteway, *Portuguese Expedition*, pp. xlii–xliii, 272–4.
16. *Ibid.*, p. 277; Sanceau, *Land of Prester John*, pp. 117–20.
17. Whiteway, *Portuguese Expedition*, pp. 5–20.
18. *Ibid.*, *Portuguese Expedition*, pp. 23–47.
19. *Ibid.*, pp. lv–lviii, 47–55.
20. Graham Hancock, *The Sign and the Seal* (New York: Touchstone, 1992), pp. 132–49, 455–8.

21. Whiteway, *Portuguese Expedition*, pp. 56–60.
22. *Ibid.*, pp. 60–68.
23. Sanceau, *Land of Prester John*, p. 149.
24. Whiteway, *Portuguese Expedition*, pp. 72–80.
25. Quoted in Sanceau, *Land of Prester John*, p. 158.
26. Whiteway, *Portuguese Expedition*, pp. 147, 152, 155, 162–4, 167–8, 172, 178–92, 249.

Chapter Eleven

1. Frend, *Rise of the Monophysite Movement*, p. 56.
2. Álvares, pp. 421, 145–64.
3. *Ibid.*, pp. 421–35.
4. Subrahmanyam, *Legend of Vasco Da Gama*, pp. 287–97, 334–5.
5. Álvares, pp. 464–5, 207 n. 2, 222.
6. Whiteway, *Portuguese Expedition*, pp. 95.
7. Richard K. P. Pankhurst, ed., *The Ethiopian Royal Chronicles* (London: Oxford University Press, 1967), pp. 8–12.
8. Richard Pankhurst, *The Ethiopians*, pp. 48–53.
9. Briggs, *Travel Guide*, pp. 347–51; Álvares, p. 221.
10. Álvares, p. 226.
11. Whiteway, *Portuguese Expedition*, p. 181.
12. Sanceau, *Land of Prester John*, p. 179.
13. Philip Caraman, *The Lost Empire: The Story of the Jesuits in Ethiopia 1555–1634* (South Bend: University of Notre Dame Press, 1985), pp. 10–15. Galawdewos' *Confession* is quoted there and in Richard Pankhurst, *The Ethiopians*, pp. 93–5.
14. Girma Beshah and Merid Wolde Aregay, *The Question of the Union of Churches in Luso-Ethiopian Relations 1500–1632* (Lisbon: Junta de Investigacões do Ultramar and Centro de Estudos Históricos Ultramarinos, 1964), p. 67.
15. Caraman, *Lost Empire*, pp. 18, 51–55, 73–4, 88, 117–9, 132.
16. Sylvia Pankhurst, *Ethiopia: A Cultural History*, p. 355.
17. Caraman, *Lost Empire*, pp. 138–9, 141–4.
18. Caraman, *Lost Empire*, pp. 151–6; Richard Pankhurst, *The Ethiopians*, pp. 104–8.

Chapter Twelve

1. See Mordechai Abir, *Ethiopia and the Red Sea*, pp. 43, 70, 81, 82–3, 97, and Trimingham, *Islam in Ethiopia*, pp. 75, 82–5.
2. Álvares, pp. 465–471, 471 n. 1.
3. *Ibid.*, pp. 472–5, 481–494.
4. Álvares, pp. 507–8; Charles E. Nowell, *A History of Portugal* (Princeton: D. Van Nostrand, 1962), pp. 102–3; Michael Alpert, *Crypto-Judaism and the Spanish Inquisition* (New York: Palgrave, 2001), pp. 31–3; Diarmaid MacCulloch, *The Reformation: A History* (New York: Viking, 2003), p. 426.
5. Elizabeth Feist Hirsch, *Damião De Gois: The Life and Thought of a Portuguese Humanist, 1502–1574* (The Hague: Martinus Nijhoff, 1967), pp. 147–55; Sanceau, *Land of Prester John*, p. 165.
6. E. R. Chamberlin, *The Bad Popes* (News York: The Dial Press, 1969), pp. 258, 260, 263, 265, 273, 278, 280, 282; Wim Blockmans, *Emperor Charles V, 1500–1558* (New York: Oxford University Press, 2002), pp. 57–64.
7. Francis M. Rogers, *The Quest for Eastern Christians: Travels and Rumor in the Age of Discovery* (Minneapolis: University of Minnesota Press, 1962), pp. 148–51; Álvares, pp. 507–8.
8. Beckingham, *Between Islam and Christendom*, Reprint XII, pp. 8–11, Reprint XIII, pp. 139–44.

Bibliography

Abir, Mordechai. *Ethiopia and the Red Sea: The Rise and Decline of the Solomonic Dynasty and Muslim-European Rivalry in the Region.* London: Frank Cass, 1980.
Adrea, Taddesse, and Ali Jimale Ahmed, eds. *Silence Is Not Golden: A Critical Anthology of Ethiopian Literature.* Lawrenceville: RSP, 1999.
Albuquerque, Afonso de. *The Commentaries of the Great Afonso D'Alboquerque, Second Viceroy of India.* Edited by Walter De Gray Birch. London: The Hakluyt Society, 1875.
Alpert, Michael. *Crypto-Judaism and the Spanish Inquisition.* New York: Palgrave, 2001.
Álvares, Francisco. *The Prester John of the Indies: A True Relation of the Lands of the Prester John, Being the Narrative of the Portuguese Embassy to Ethiopia in 1520 Written by Father Franciso Alvares.* Translated by Lord Stanley of Alderley. Revised and edited by C. F. Beckingham and G. W. B. Huntingford. Millwood, NY: Kraus Reprint, for The Hakluyt Society, 1975.
Axelson, Eric. *Congo to Cape: Early Portuguese Explorers.* New York: Barnes & Noble, 1973.
Azurara, Gomes Eannes de. *The Discovery and Conquest of Guinea.* Translated by C. R. Beazley and Edgar Prestage. London: The Hakluyt Society, 1896.
Barbosa, Duarte. *The Book of Duarte Barbosa. An Account of the Countries Bordering on the Indian Ocean and their Inhabitants... Completed about the Year 1518 A. D.* Translated by M. L. Dames. Two volumes. London: The Hakluyt Society, 1918.
Beazley, C. Raymond. *The Dawn of Modern Geography.* Three volumes. London: John Murray, 1906.
Beckingham, C. F. "The Achievements of Prester John." In *Prester John, the Mongols, and the Ten Lost Tribes,* edited by C. F. Beckingham and Bernard Hamilton. Aldershot: Variorum, 1996.
_____. *Between Islam and Christendom: Travellers, Facts and Legends in the Middle Ages and the Renaissance.* London: Variorum Reprints, 1983.
Bent, J. T. *The Sacred City of the Ethiopians.* London, 1896.
Beshah, Girma, and Merid Wolde Aregay. *The Question of the Union of Churches in Luso-Ethiopian Relations 1500–1632.* Lisbon: Junta de Investigacões do Ultramar and Centro de Estudos Históricos Ultramarinos, 1964.
Blockmans, Wim. *Emperor Charles V, 1500–1558.* London: Arnold, 2002.
Briggs, Philip. *Ethiopia: The Bradt Travel Guide.* Guilford, CT: Globe Pequot, 2005.
Bruce, James. *Travels to Discover the Source of the Nile.* Selected and edited by C. F. Beckingham. Edinburgh: Edinburgh University Press, 1964.
Burstein, Stanley, ed. *Ancient African Civilizations: Kush and Axum.* Princeton: Marcus Wiener, 2009.
Buxton, David. *The Abyssinians.* New York: Praeger, 1970.

Caraman, Philip. *The Lost Empire: The Story of the Jesuits in Ethiopia 1555–1634.* South Bend: University of Notre Dame Press, 1985.

Chamberline, E. R. *The Bad Popes.* New York: Dial Press, 1969.

Chapman, Walker. *The Golden Dream: Seekers of El Dorado.* New York: Bobbs-Merrill, 1967.

Christie-Murray, David. *A History of Heresy.* London: New English Library, 1976.

Correa, Gaspar. *The Three Voyages of Vasco Da Gama and His Viceroyalty.* Translated by Henry E. J. Stanley. New York: Burt Franklin, 1963.

Crawford, O. G. S., ed. *Ethiopian Itineraries, ca. 1400–1524, Including those Collected by Allesandro Zorzi at Venice in the Years 1519–24.* Cambridge: Cambridge University Press for The Hakluyt Society, 1958.

Crummy, Donald E. *African Zion: The Sacred Art of Ethiopia.* New Haven: Yale University Press, 1993.

_____. *Land and Society in the Christian Kingdom of Ethiopia: From the Thirteenth to the Twentieth Century.* Chicago: University of Illinois Press, 2000.

Diffie, Bailey W., and George D. Winius. *Foundations of the Portuguese Empire, 1415–1580.* Minneapolis: University of Minnesota Press, 1977.

Disney, Anthony, and Emily Booth, eds. *Vasco da Gama and the Linking of Europe and Asia.* Oxford: Oxford University Press, 2000.

Duffy, Eamon. *Saints and Sinners: A History of the Popes, Second Edition.* New Haven: Yale University Press, 2001.

Frend, W. H. C. *The Rise of the Monophysite Movement: Chapters in the History of the Church in the Fifth and Sixth Centuries.* Cambridge: Cambridge University Press, 1972.

George, Leonard. *Crimes of Perception: An Encyclopedia of Heresies and Heretics.* New York: Paragon House, 1995.

Hamilton, Bernard. "Continental Drift: Prester John's Progress Through the Indies." In *Prester John, The Mongols, and the Ten Lost Tribes,* edited by C. F. Beckingham and Bernard Hamilton. Aldershot: Variorum, 1966.

_____. "Prester John and the Three Kings of Cologne." In *Prester John, The Mongols, and the Ten Lost Tribes,* edited by C. F. Beckingham and Bernard Hamilton. Aldershot: Variorum, 1996.

Hancock, Graham. *The Sign and the Seal: The Quest for the Lost Ark of the Covenant.* New York: Touchstone, 1993.

Hass, Christopher. *Alexandria in Late Antiquity: Topography and Social Conflict.* Baltimore: Johns Hopkins University Press, 1997.

Hinson, E. Glenn. *The Early Church: Origins to the Dawn of the Middle Ages.* Nashville: Abingdon Press, 1996.

Hirsch, Elisabet Feist. *Damião De Gois: The Life and Thought of a Portuguese Humanist, 1502–1547.* The Hague: Martinus Nijhoff, 1967.

Hood, Robert E. *Begrimed and Black: Christian Traditions on Blacks and Blackness.* Minneapolis: Fortress Press, 1994.

Horowitz, Deborah E., Ed. *Ethiopian Art.* Lingfield, Surrey: Third Millennium, 2001.

Horvath, Ronald J. "The Wandering Capitals of Ethiopia." *Journal of African History* 10, No. 2 (1969), pp. 205–19.

Huntingford, G. W. B., and Richard Pankhurst. *The Historical Geography of Ethiopia from the 1st Century AD to 1704.* Oxford: Oxford University Press, 1989.

Jayne, K. G. *Vasco Da Gama and His Successors, 1460–1580.* New York: Barnes & Noble, 1970.

Jones, A. H. M., and Elizabeth Monroe. *A History of Ethiopia.* Oxford: Oxford University Press, 1955.

A Journal of the First Voyage of Vasco Da Gama, 1497–1499. Translated by E. G. Ravenstein. New York: Burt Franklin, 1963.

Keay, John. *The Spice Route: A History.* Berkeley: University of California Press, 2006.
Lord, Edith. *Queen of Sheba's Heirs: Cultural Patterns of Ethiopia.* Washington: Acropolis Books, 1970.
MacCulloch, Diarmaid. *The Reformation: A History.* New York: Viking, 2003.
Major, R. H., ed. *India in the Fifteenth Century: Being a Collection of Narratives of Voyages to India, in the Century preceding the Portuguese Discovery of the Cape of Good Hope; from Latin, Persian, Russian and Italian Sources.* London: The Hakluyt Society, 1857.
Mann, C. Griffith, *Art of Ethiopia.* London: Sam Fogg, 2005.
Marcus, Harold G. *A History of Ethiopia: Updated Edition.* Berkeley: University of California Press, 2002.
Morgan, David. "Prester John and the Mongols." In *Prester John, the Mongols, and the Ten Lost Tribes,* edited by Charles F. Beckingham and Bernard Hamilton. Aldershot: Variorum, 1996.
Munro-Hay, Stuart. *Aksum: An African Civilization of Late Antiquity.* Edinburgh: Edinburgh University Press, 1991.
———. *Ethiopia: The Unknown Land; A Cultural and Historical Guide.* London: I. B. Tauris, 2002.
Munro-Hay, Stuart, and Richard Pankhurst. *Ethiopia: World Bibliographical Series, Volume 179.* Oxford: Clio Press, 1995.
Nowell, Charles. "The Historical Prester John." *Speculum* 28 (1953), pp. 435–45.
———. *A History of Portugal.* Princeton: D. Van Nostrand, 1962.
Olschki, Leonardo. *Marco Polo's Asia.* Berkeley: University of California Press, 1960.
Pankhurst, Richard. *The Ethiopians.* Oxford: Blackwell, 1998.
———. *A Social History of Ethiopia: The Northern and Central Highlands from Early Medieval Times to the Rise of Emperor Téwodros II.* Addis Ababa: Institute of Ethiopian Studies, 1990.
———, ed. *The Ethiopian Royal Chronicles.* Addis Ababa: Oxford University Press, 1967.
———, ed. *Travellers in Ethiopia.* Oxford: Oxford University Press, 1965.
Pankhurst, Sylvia. *Ethiopia, A Cultural History.* Woodford Green, Essex: Lalibela House, 1955.
Parry, J. H. *The Age of Reconnaissance.* London: Weidenfeld & Nicholson, 1963.
Penrose, Boies. *Travel and Discovery in the Renaissance.* Cambridge: Harvard University Press, 1955.
Peters, F. E. *Mecca: A Literary History of the Muslim Holy Land.* Princeton: Princeton University Press, 1994.
Prakash, Om. *The New Cambridge History of India, II, 5: European Commercial Enterprise in Pre-Colonial India.* Cambridge: Cambridge University Press, 1998.
Prestage, Edgar. *Afonso De Albuquerque, Governor of India: His Life, Conquests and Administration.* Watford: Voss & Michael 1929.
Phillipson, David W. *Ancient Ethiopia: Aksum, Its Antecedents and Successors.* London: British Museum Press, 1998.
Rogers, Francis M. *The Quest for Eastern Christians: Travels and Rumor in the Age of Discovery.* Minneapolis: University of Minnesota Press, 1962.
Russell, Peter. *Prince Henry The Navigator: A Life.* New Haven: Yale University Press, 2000.
Russell-Wood, A. J. R. *The Portuguese Empire 1415–1808: A World on the Move.* Baltimore: Johns Hopkins University Press, 1992.
Salvadore, Matteo. "The Ethiopian Age of Exploration: Prester John's Discovery of Europe, 1306–1458." *Journal of World History* Vol. 21, No. 4 (2011), pp. 593–627.
Sanceau, Elaine. *The Land of Prester John: A Chronicle of Portuguese Exploration.* New York: Knopf, 1944.
Schwartz, Stuart B., ed. *Implicit Understandings: Observing, Reporting, and Reflecting on the Encounters Between Europeans and Other Peoples in the Early Modern Era.* Cambridge: Cambridge University Press, 1994.

Shinn, David H., and Thomas P. Ofcansky. *Historical Dictionary of Ethiopia*. Toronto: Scarecrow Press, 2004.

Shihab al-Din Ahmad bin Abd al-Qader bin Salem bin Utman. *The Conquest of Abyssinia*. Translated by Paul Lester Stenhouse. Hollywood: Tsehai, 2003.

Silverberg, Robert. *The Realm of Prester John*. Athens: Ohio University Press, 1972.

Slessarev, Vsevolod. *Prester John: The Letter and the Legend*. Minneapolis: University of Minnesota Press, 1959.

Smith, Robert C. *The Art of Portugal, 1500–1800*. London: Weidenfield & Nicholson, 1968.

Strandes, Justus. *The Portuguese Period in East Africa*. Translated by Jean F. Wallwork. Edited by J. S. Kirkman. Nairobi: Kenya Literature Bureau, 1989.

Stephens, H. Morse. *Rulers of India: Albuquerque*. Oxford: Clarendon Press, 1912.

Subrahmanyam, Sanjay. *The Career and Legend of Vasco Da Gama*. Cambridge: Cambridge University Press, 1997.

Tamrat, Taddesse. *Church and State in Ethiopia, 1270–1527*. Oxford: Clarendon Press, 1972.

Trexler, Richard C. *The Journey of the Magi: Meanings in History of a Christian Story*. Princeton: Princeton University Press, 1997.

Trimingham, J. Spenser. *Islam in Ethiopia*. London: Frank Cass, 1965.

Turner, Jack. *Spice: The History of a Temptation*. New York: Vintage, 2004.

Ullendorff, Edward. *The Ethiopians: An Introduction to Country and People*. London: Oxford University Press, 1962.

Wand, J. W. C. *The Four Great Heresies*. London: A. R. Mowbray, 1967.

Whiteway, R. S., trans. and ed. *The Portuguese Expedition to Abyssinia in 1541–1543, as Narrated by Castanhoso, with some Contemporary Letters, the Short Account of Bermudez, and Certain Extracts from Correa*. London: The Hakluyt Society, 1902.

Index

Abuna (Ethiopian Pope) 104, 126, 146, 160–168, 170, 204–205, 208, 229–230, 235, 253, 255, 258
Adal, Kingdom of 121, 128
Aden 47–50, 57, 58–59, 182
Alexander the Great 8, 14
Alexander III, Pope 13
Álvares, Francisco: audience with Pope 275–276, 278–280; as Catholic apologist 125–129, 134–138, 142–143, 146–151, 161–162; discovery of heresy 2, 94, 134, 152–158, 179; early life 55–56; ecumenical outlook 251–252, 258, 277, 278, 280; final years 281; friendship with Lebna Dengel 3, 124–132, 134, 149, 152, 154–155, 171, 179, 184, 189, 200, 237, 242, 263, 279; as peacemaker 34–5, 88, 140; racial attitudes 69–70; reconcilement to exile 232, 237, 240–241, 261–264, 267; silence concerning heresy 2, 155, 158, 163, 179–181, 231, 252, 276, 278, 280; writing method 69–70
Amba Geshen (mountaintop prison) 89–91, 146, 191–195, 203, 207
Amba Sanyat 214
Amda Seyon, *Negus* of Ethiopia 111
Angoteraz (office, Governor of Angote) 101–102
Aqabe sa'at (office, Guardian of the Hours) 114–115, 130, 146, 149, 152, 161
Arianism 235–236
Ark of the Covenant 77, 111, 220
Arquiquo see Massawa
asceticism, in Ethiopian Church 180–181
Ashege, Lake 220
Axum, stelae at 94–5, 232–236
Axumite Kingdom 92–3, 98, 111, **233**–236, 243, 248

Ba'ala mashaf (office, Master of Books) 139–140

Bahr-nagas (office, Governor of the Seaboard) 61–63, 65–67, 74, 80, 82–84; 86–7, 176–179, 211, 212, 229, 261, 264–267
baptism, in Ethiopian Church 84–85, 159–163
Barnagais see *Bahr-nagas*
Bartoli, Antonio 22
Benin, Kingdom of 28
Bermudez, Joam 64, 73, 101, 170, 204–210, 219, 223, 228–231, 252–253, 277, 281
Betudete see *Bitwaddad*
Bible, Ethiopian 129
Bitwaddad (office, Military Leader) 114, 117–118, 141, 144, 146, 239–240
Bizam, Monastery of 66, 70–80, 179–180
Brancaleone, Nicolo 137–8, 152
Byzantine Empire 10, 19, 93, 235–236

Cabeata see *Aqube sa'at*
Cabral, Pedro 41, 43
Calicut 32, 37–42
Calixtus II, Pope 18
Candice, Queen of Ethiopia 19, 94, 112, 135, 236
Cão, Diogo 27–29, 31
capital, wandering, Ethiopian 107–110, 112–113, 117–119, 139–140, 143–145, 151–2, 263
Casa da India 269–270
Catalani, Jordan 20
Chalcedon, Council of 93, 126–7, 137, 157
Charles V, Holy Roman Emperor 275, 278
Christianity, arrival in Ethiopia 93, 104, 112, 135, 157, 235–236
churches, Ethiopian 153–154, 168, 202, 204, 236; circular 75–76, 136, 152, 204; rock-cut 95, 181, 243–252
circumcision, female 85
Clement VII, Pope 199, 278–280
clergy, in Ethiopian Church 84, 103, 124, 136, 166

293

communion, infant 85, 166
Congo River 26, 27–29, 33–34
Coptic Church 94, 103–4, 126, 163–164, 167, 205, 235, 258, 276
Crusades 7–8, 15, 16, 19–20

Da Carignano, Giovanni 22
Da Covilhã, Pêro 32–34, 37, 104–105, 117–118, 169, 170, 173, 186, 188, 264
Da Gama, Christovão 209–226, 228–229
Da Gama, Estevão 207–211, 215–217
Da Gama, Manuel 208–209
Da Gama, Vasco 31, 32, 34–43, 242
Dahlak Islands 57, 58, 121, 171, 264
Damot (ancient East-African kingdom) 92
Da Silveira, Eitor 265–267, 270
De Albergaria, Lopo Soares 54–59, 120, 268
De Albuquerque, Afonso 44–55, 182
Debarwa 174–175, 177–179, 183–184, 191, 211, 260
De Castanhoso, Miguel 210, 214, 228, 231, 245
De Cosmo, Lourenço 56, 58
degredados 38
De Lima, Rodrigo: appointed Ambassador to Prester John 63–65; undiplomatic bearing 82–83, 86–7, 95, 101, 117, 158, 175, 196–197
De Meneses, Luis 187–188, 199
De Oviedo, Bishop Andre 253–254, 258
De Pavia, Afonso 32
De Sequeira, Diogo 59–65, 187, 271
De Vilalobos, Lopo 56, 59
Dias, Bartolomeo 25, 29–31

Easter 185–186
Eleni (Helena), Dowager Queen of Ethiopia 44–46, 54, 121–122, 146, 149, 168, 182, 240, 241
Embassy, Portuguese to Prester John: arrest of 176–178; detention of 178, 183–185, 187–189; disillusionment of 99–100, 105, 109, 158; gifts carried by 65, 115–121, 158; internal dissentions 72, 95–6, 105, 123, 130, 133, 139–142, 169, 171–178, 189, 241; inward journey of 67–109; members of 63–4; reception at Ethiopian Court 112–133; release of 196–200; rescue of 265–268; return to Portugal 269–273; return, wider implications of 200–201; strandings of 174, 184, 187, 201, 232, 242, 260–261
Ephesus, Council of 17
Eskender (Alexander), *Negus* of Ethiopia 33, 146, 239
Estado da India 43–46, 52–55, 122, 206, 207, 242–243, 258, 260–261, 275
Ethiopia: climate 73, 87, 100–101, 212; currency 100–101; feudalism (*gult* system)

238; flora and fauna 82, 85–6, 88, 91–2; foodways 91, 102, 116; foreign trade 98, 108, 184; geography 61, 68, 88–89, 98, 103, 105–106, 151–2, 211, 214, 220, 226; taxation 101, 239–241
Eugene III, Pope 7
Eugene IV, Pope 81
Eutyches 256
Ewostatewos (founder of monastic order) 135
Ezana, King of Axum 93–94, 104, 235–236, 248; *see also* Axumite Kingdom

Falashas see Jews, Ethiopian
Fasilidas, *Negus* of Ethiopia 256–258
Florence, Council of 23, 81
Francis I, King of France 278

Gabra Maskel, King of Axum 147; *see also* Axumite Kingdom
Galawdewos, *Negus* of Ethiopia 207–208, 209, 211, 212, 214, 220, 221, 225–228, 230, 252–254
Galvão, Duarte 54, 57–58, 268
Gambia River 27
Geography (discipline), Classical 26–29, 31
Gibbon, Edward 93, 258
Gonder 258
Grañ, Ahmed (Ahmed ibn Ibrahim al-Ghazi) 153, 183, 201–204, 207–208, 211–212, 217–220, 224–228, 230, 236, 248

Harrar 201, 254
Henry the Navigator 25–26, 31, 275
Herodotus 26
Hugh, Bishop of Jabala 7–9

inquisitors 137, 155, 252, 275–277
Investiture Crisis 9
Islam, conflict with 61, 98–99, 108–9, 112, 121–122, 128, 132–4, 167, 182–183, 198–199, 201–230, 241, 247

Jerusalem 20, 23, 31, 182, 247
Jesuit order 252–258
Jews, Ethiopian 220–221
João II, King of Portugal 28–29, 31–34
João III, King of Portugal 187–188, 206, 230, 242, 269, 271–273, 275–276
Judaizing practices (of Ethiopians) 66, 79, 84, 103–4, 128, 136, 164, 179, 253
judicial practices, Ethiopian 194, 237–242
Justinian the Great 80

Kamaran Islands 51–52, 58–59, 171, 268
Knights Hospitalers 14

Lalibela *see* churches, Ethiopian, rock-cut

Lebna Dengel, *Negus* of Ethiopia 44, 63, 110–112, 121–122, 124, 127, 131–3, 207, 259–260, 266–267; anxiety over European perceptions 140, 149, 169, 174, 184, 197, 266; disaffection with De Lima 140–142, 155, 158, 171–172, 179; letters to Europe 138–139, 170–172, 188, 197–199, 204–205, 267–268, 272–273, 279–280; as "Solomonic" dynast 111, 243
Leo the Great, Pope 126–127, 137, 157
locusts 190–191

Mafouz, Emir of Harrar 98, 121, 128, 147, 182–183, 201–202
Magi 9
Mamluck Sultanate (of Egypt) 21, 43, 45, 56–57, 122, 167, 183
Manoel I, King of Portugal 34, 43, 52–54, 187, 275
marital customs, Ethiopian 84, 91
mass, Ethiopian conduct of 75–78
Massawa 60–61, 96, 118, 121, 123, 132–3, 138–9, 145, 171, 174, 182, 183–184, 188, 207, 208, 211, 260, 264
Matthew (Ethiopian ambassador to Portugal) 44–46, 53–55, 57–8, 60–63, 66–67, 70–74, 121–122, 133, 149, 158
Mendes, Bishop Afonso 256–258
Milton, John 195
Minas, *Negus* of Ethiopia 254
monasteries, Ethiopian 103, 134–5, 179, 207, 212, 239; *see also* Bizam; Ewostatewos; Tekla Haymanot
Mongol Empire 17
monophysitism 2, 93–4, 126–7, 152–158, 235–236, 252–257

Na'od, *Negus* of Ethiopia 121, 168
Nestorianism 17, 18, 38–9, 157, 158
Nicaea, Council of 126, 137, 161
Nile River 26, 68, 106, 167, 182
nuns, Ethiopian 99

Odoric of Pordenone 17–18
ordination, in Ethiopian Church 163–168
Ottoman Empire 122, 167, 182–183, 202–203, 220, 225, 274

Paez, Pedro 254–256, 258
Paul III, Pope 205–206, 231
pepper 83, 102, 115, 118–119, 188–189, 267
Polo, Marco 17, 19

Portugal, factions at Court 52–55, 59, 271; rescue of Ethiopia 207–230
Prester John: legend of 7–15, 39, 54–5, 62–63, 69, 99–100, 109, 112, 133, 206, 208, 231, 280; search for, general European 15–23; search for, Portuguese 24–35, 44–60
Protestant Reformation 274, 276, 278
Ptolemy 28, 31, 34
Punt (ancient East-African kingdom) 92

Red Sea 46–48, 50–60, 93, 171, 182, 207–208, 220, 268, 274, 279
Rombulo, Pietro 22–3

St. Phillip 94, 112, 135, 236
Sebla Wangél (widow of Lebna Dengel) 207, 212–219, 221, 223, 225
Sheba, Queen of 111, 236
slavery 27–8, 69, 80–82
spice trade 14, 21, 29, 31, 32, 35–38, 40–41, 43, 47, 55, 182
succession, royal, Ethiopian 145–146
Susenyos, *Negus* of Ethiopia 255–257

tabots (Ethiopian altar stones) 75, 125, 136, 144–5, 159, 190, 257
Takla Haymanot, (founder of monastic order) 135
T'ana, Lake 226
Tegre-makuannen (office, Governor of Tigré) 95
Timkat (Epiphany celebrations) 158–163, 228
Trent, Council of 156

Venice 43–4
villages, Ethiopian 85
Vivaldi Brothers 21, 27

William of Rubruck 17

Yared the Deacon 147–148
Yeha 92, 93–94

Za Dengel, *Negus* of Ethiopia 254–255
Zaga Za Ab (Ethiopian ambassador to Portugal) 96–99, 101–104, 108–109, 116–118, 170, 172, 173, 199, 205–206, 237, 242, 252, 259, 266–267, 271–273, 276–277
Zagwe dynasty 111, 243
Zara Yaqob, *Negus* of Ethiopia 104, 121, 146
Zeila 98, 123, 128, 132–3, 171, 184, 196, 201, 220

www.ingramcontent.com/pod-product-compliance
Lightning Source LLC
Chambersburg PA
CBHW051210300426
44116CB00006B/502